Understanding SGML and XML Tools

Practical programs for handling structured text

RELATED PUBLICATIONS

THE SGML FAQ BOOK: Understanding the Foundation of HTML and XML
Steven J. DeRose
ISBN: 0-7923-9943-9

INFORMATION RETRIEVAL AND HYPERTEXT, Maristella Agosti, Alan Smeaton, editors
ISBN: 0-7923-9710-X

HTML AND THE ART OF AUTHORING FOR WORLD WIDE WEB, Bebo White
ISBN: 0-7923-9691-X

RETHINKING HYPERMEDIA: The Microcosm Approach, Wendy Hall, Hugh Davis, Gerard Hutchings
ISBN: 0-7923-9679-0

MAKING HYPERMEDIA WORK: A User's Guide to HyTime, Steven J. DeRose, David G. Durand
ISBN: 0-7923-9432-1

PRACTICAL SGML, Second Edition, Eric van Herwijnen
ISBN: 0-7923-9434-8

PRACTICAL SGML, Eric van Herwijnen
ISBN: 0-7923-0635-X

Understanding SGML and XML Tools

Practical programs for handling structured text

by

Peter Flynn

KLUWER ACADEMIC PUBLISHERS
Boston/Dordrecht/London

Distributors for North America:
Kluwer Academic Publishers
101 Philip Drive
Assinippi Park
Norwell Massachusetts 02061 USA

Distributors for all other countries:
Kluwer Academic Publishers Group
Distribution Centre
Post Office Box 322
3300 AH Dordrecht, THE NETHERLANDS

Library of Congress Cataloging-in-Publication Data

A C.I.P. Catalogue record for this book is available
from the Library of Congress.

ISBN-13: 978-1-4684-6713-0 e-ISBN-13: 978-1-4684-6711-6
DOI: 10.1007/978-1-4684-6711-6

Printed on acid-free paper.

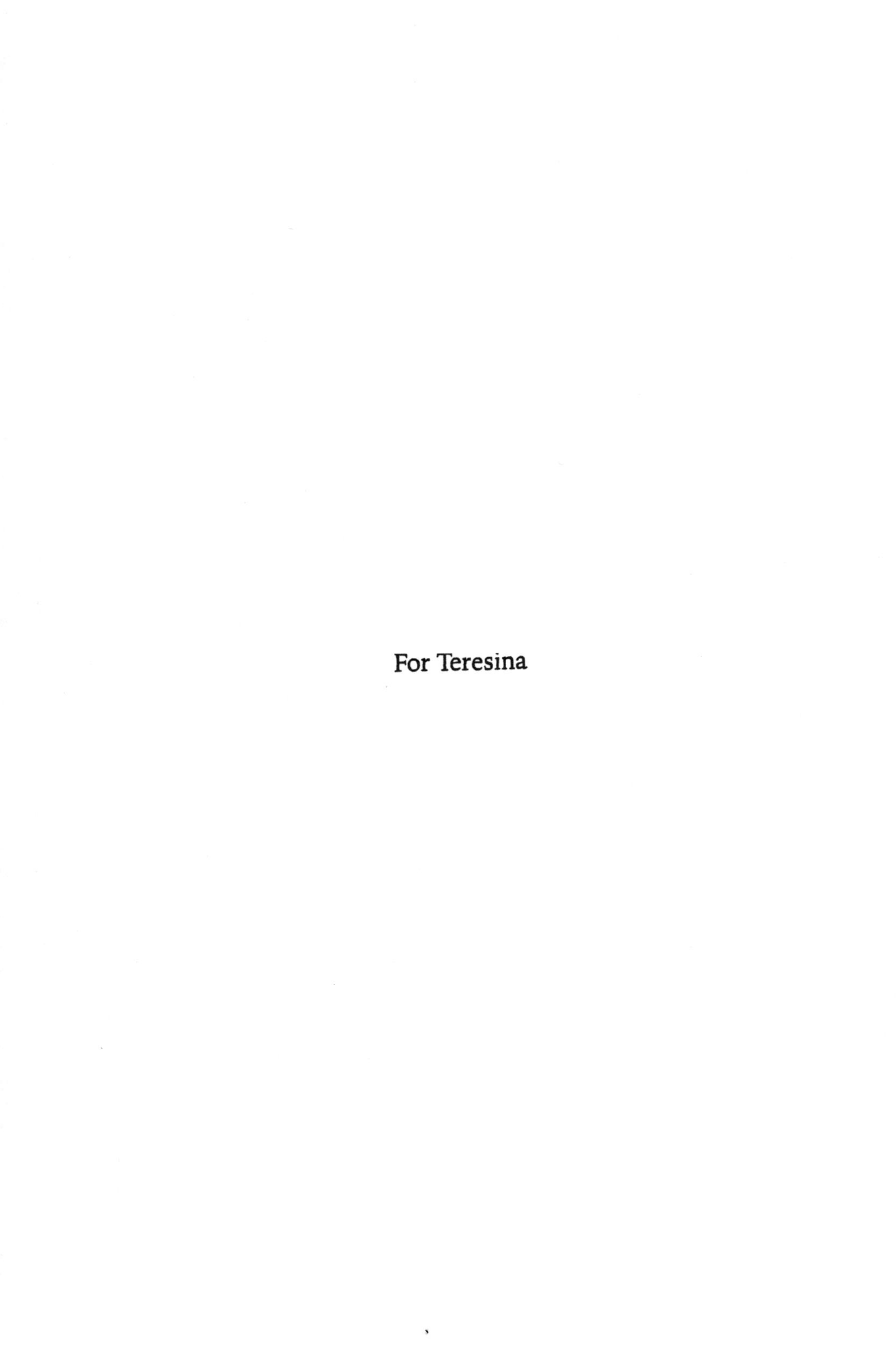

For Teresina

Table of Contents

How to use this book

If you've used SGML before, or if you haven't but you're in a hurry:

- Section 1.4 has a short list and explanation of the chapters.
- Each chapter has a mini table of contents at the start, so you can see what it covers.

Otherwise if you're just starting with SGML, read chapter 1 first, and use the software on the CD-ROM to get a feel for how it works and what you can do.

I use a few standard typographical and indexing conventions:

- markup and other examples of computer text are in `fixed-width type`: element names, attribute names, and other SGML parameters are indexed separately starting on page 425;
- I use ***bold italics*** the first time a new term is introduced: it is summarized in the Glossary starting on page 401 and it gets a page number in bold in the Index so you can find it again;
- company and program author names are indexed separately starting on page 423.

Foreword

Peter Flynn has been an enthusiastic and skillful contributor in the world of SGML and XML for many years, and it is a pleasure to see him set some of his expertise down in writing as well. The range and power of SGML tools have taken a sharp upward turn: the first step leading to this was that the Web came along with HTML, and showed the whole world that pointy brackets and (at least somewhat) descriptive markup could make a difference. Soon afterward, 'HTML claustrophobia' began to grow and XML came to the rescue. Since XML is fundamentally an elegant subset of SGML that reduces complexity without reducing functionality, the movement to XML is great for SGML too.

The massive interest in XML is bringing forth a huge variety of new, faster, more powerful, and cheaper software tools. Peter has caught the cusp of this change and shows in detail how SGML and XML tools fit together into integrated solutions that return value for your investment in structured information.

SGML long ago became the normative way of doing serious documents in mission-critical and large-scale publishing; my own work has largely been in developing SGML delivery systems used in the aerospace, power, telecommunications, hardware and software industries, where technical manuals often outweigh the aircraft or other devices they document. SGML was the only practical choice for such information, and software that could handle huge SGML documents safely, reliably, and rapidly improved productivity and costs often by many millions of dollars per company per year.

SGML also caught on in a second arena under quite different circumstances: scholarly texts. Although no one is likely to die if an SGML system fails on complicated markup for manuscripts variation or multilingual synchronization, such texts often stress tools even further in terms of features and performance than most high-end publishing applications. As Michael Sperberg-McQueen noted in the closing keynote of SGML/XML '97, scholars are the 'canaries in the mineshaft' of the SGML community. They are far more sensitive to problems (such as poor DTD design, unscalable software, *etc*) and therefore tend to keel over sooner, signaling those in the industry of problems. And just as in the depths of a coal mine, those less sensitive are well advised to notice and fix the problem, lest it get to them soon after.

SGML moved beyond these two areas only slowly, however, until the Web. Now everyone is experiencing different markup systems first-hand. They go to beautiful pages with carefully adjusted layouts, then come back with a different browser version or a different window size, and fail. Or they go to sites that adjust automatically, using their built-in knowledge of structure in their information resources to customize display for exactly the user's circumstances and preferences. Web managers with the first sort of site are watching their costs skyrocket, and are (sometimes desperately) seeking tools to manage rapidly growing complexity. In short, the power of descriptive markup is now a perceived need.

This new popularity also makes for a large and diverse tool environment, and it is there that Peter's book is perhaps most valuable. He provides a guide to the labyrinth of SGML and XML tools, organized carefully in the way many users need it: in terms of the life-cycle of their documents. Rather than going into every detail of each system, or providing a user's guide that would be wholly outdated almost before reaching the shelves, he presents various systems' distinctives: what is it that stands out in product X, and why might I use it? These distinctives often reflect the fundamental approach of each system, which is much more stable than the feature details of a given release. The focus here is on seeing the SGML and XML tool landscape, rather than individual trees (or as in a few books, the veins in the leaves!). This approach promises great practical advantages in helping the reader actually evaluate tools and make wise choices in the face of ever-growing diversity.

Such a book could easily be dry, but the reader will quickly realize that this book comes out of real experience with the tools. The many anecdotes and witty summaries make it much more accessible. The survey of DTDs reflects this as well: few authors could speak competently about the enormous range of DTDs covered here, or do so with a sense of history. Anyone considering work with SGML or XML will find this book very useful indeed.

Steve DeRose
March 1988

Preface

In Charles Manby Smith's *A Working Man's Way in the World*[37] there is an example quoted of a 19th century printer's proofreader at work, with his reading-boy sitting beside him reading the copy aloud while the proofreader checks it:

> 'This *ruling passion* **two ital par** the most enduring of all the passions which obtains a mastery over the mind **close** is described in Pope's **eps** thus **turns** odious in woollen 'twould a saint provoke **close** were the last words that poor narcissa spoke **turns** no let a charming chintz and Brussels lace wrap my cold limbs and shade my lifeless face one need not sure be frightful though one's dead and Betty.' [...] 'Give my cheek a little red **close turns again** I give and devise **close** old Euclid said and sighed **turns** my lands and tenements to Ned **close turns again** your money sir **close turns again** my money sir what all why if I must **close** then wept **turns again** I give it Paul **close** he cried **turns again** not that I cannot part with that **close** and he died **pop ep one oct ed p two five three.**'

Smith clearly picked this particular example because it was popular in 1846 (he notes that 'everybody knows the above passage', although I have been unable to trace it), but the point he was making was that to achieve correct printing, the text had to be interlarded with technical terms (distinguished in the quotation) when it was spoken to a proofreader. Any errors would be marked up on the printed proof, and returned for correction to the compositor who set the type. Although proof-correction markup is not quite the same thing as SGML markup, the intention is similar: to indicate the meaning behind the text. Emphasis, quotation, and poetic linebreaks can all be seen in the example above.

In this sense electronic texts are no different from paper ones: they also need markup, and the conventional way of applying this in a word processor or desktop publishing system is to press the buttons or use the mouse until the text 'looks right'. The difference between paper and electronic texts, however, is that computers cannot generally detect the significance of a word just by its position and appearance, as humans can. Putting these words *into italics*, for example, has no actual meaning unless you know what the italics signify, and this often depends on the context. Italics could mean *emphasis*, a *product name*, a *scientific name*, a *foreign word*, a *program variable*, a *list sub-heading*, or just *sloping letters because they look nice*.

Just making things *look* right is fine if the sole destination is print, and the text is guaranteed never, ever to be wanted for any other purpose. For text which is to be handled by a computer for any other reason, and especially for reprocessing for a variety of other outputs, it needs clear and unambiguous markup that can be read by different programs on different computers, but following the same series of well-defined steps. SGML provides a language for defining exactly this kind of markup, and this book is all about how to make it work and some of the programs you can use with it.

If you are actually doing the writing yourself — whether you are using SGML for business reports, space station manuals, legal records, a thesis, or your latest novel — you are probably more interested in *what* you are writing (the words, the meanings, the thoughts) than in its final appearance. This is normally at least true while you are occupied in the process of writing, because you may in fact not yet know what the final formatting is going to look like, and you may not have any control over it, either.

There certainly have been authors who spent their lives looking over the compositor's shoulder to make sure the typesetting was done exactly to their specification, but with a few exceptions their works have sunk below the horizon now. Everyone wants their work to 'look right', of course, but an author who spends more time fiddling with fonts and layouts than in doing the writing is unlikely to be very productive as a writer.

And nowadays, especially, that we have more media than just print to handle, we need a new paradigm, and a new set of tools to help us cope with them. This book is designed to guide you through the different types of tool you can expect to see.

Acknowledgments

Dozens of people have helped in the making of this book, from the users whose comments on a mailing list or at a meeting made me ask questions, to the regular denizens of the `comp.text.sgml` newsgroup who have put up with my own questions for so long. Many of them distinguished themselves by answering my queries in great detail, unfortunately far too many to list them individually here, so I thank them now as a group for taking so much of their time to ensure I represented the facts correctly: if I have got it wrong anywhere, the blame is mine alone.

A special thank-you goes to all the software vendors who lent me review copies, sometimes including unpublished manuals and beta releases at short notice; and to the authors of public domain software and shareware for their unstinting generosity, both to me and to the SGML community at large. I would also like to express my gratitude to those who lent me equipment, time on their machines, software, manuals, and training material, as without them a substantial chunk of the book would have remained unwritten.

I want to thank my reviewers, Elaine Brennan, Martin Bryan, Steve DeRose, Betty Harvey, Eve Maler, James Mason, Liam Quin, and Wayne Wohler. Their suggestions were invaluable, and kept me from publicly putting my foot in my mouth quite spectacularly on at least five occasions (perhaps I should release the out-takes like film studios do!).

Some smaller sections of the text were also reviewed by an assortment of students, colleagues, and friends, and them I thank also.

Two people, however, deserve not just my own thanks but that of almost every SGML user who has ventured onto the Internet in search of answers: Robin Cover for maintaining the SGML Web pages, and Steve Pepper, whose invaluable *Whirlwind Guide to SGML Tools*[34] remains the canonical online listing.

Most importantly to my wife Teresina goes my love and thanks for having put up with precarious stacks of software and manuals, and with my virtual absence while I blunted my fingers on the keyboard each evening. And to my children Rachael, Thomas, and Olivia I say thank you too for being so patient, and I promise we'll go places again now.

A final word of thanks must go posthumously to Yuri Rubinsky, for his encouraging words about the idea for this book while it was still only an idea, and only a couple of weeks before his untimely death. Along with many others I posted my own tribute to his memory, but I reproduce here his words that I quoted then, because as I write, what he said is on the verge of becoming reality. I had spoken with him at the end of 1992 about the Web and HTML: he was full of enthusiasm and said, 'Just think of it, in a few years the whole world could be using SGML.' It has taken a little over five years for the use of HTML-as-RTF to turn into SGML-as-XML, but it is possible that we are now passing a critical point of inflection on the adoption curve of SGML, and that the whole world will indeed be taking a much keener interest in how it works and what it can do for everyone. If this book helps you to move up that curve, then it has all been worthwhile.

Cork, April 1998

Technical notes

When I was finishing *The World Wide Web Handbook*[19], I was asked to include a note on what I had used to write it. At the time, HTML3 was still under discussion, and I said that I thought it unlikely that HTML in any form could be meaningfully used for a book. I still hold to this, although given enough semantic loading of attributes, it would probably just about be possible.

This book, like the previous one, was done using the Davenport Group's *DocBook* DTD, which is markup designed for computer manuals, the closest there is to computer books. I made a few very small changes to enable the use of tables and to add a few attributes to make life easier: these are documented in section 2.6.1.2. I used a variety of editors to do the actual writing, because it was all in SGML, which meant I could copy the text from platform to platform and back again according to where I was working and the kind of software I was looking at, allowing me to have the text open beside me all the time. The principal systems I used for the bulk of the writing were SoftQuad's *Author/Editor* and GNU *Emacs*.

Screenshots were mostly taken using JASC, Inc's *Paint Shop Pro* (PSP) v4.12 and Bruce Schuchardt's *xgrabsc*, saved as TIFF or XWD files and converted to PostScript with Jef Poskanzer's *PBM* or John Bradley's *xv* for printing. Despite its ubiquity, TIFF can be a pain in the neck, as every manufacturer has invented their own little proprietary extensions for it, which are often stored in the file in weird ways. *PSP* is a great utility, but conversion to PostScript is not quite as good as in *PBM*, which in turn is not quite as robust as in *xv*.

For printed proofs, I used *Panorama Publisher* and *MultiDoc Pro*, both of which performed well. For the final output I experimented with several systems but fell back upon LaTeX partly because I know it better than anything else, and because it is very stable and reliable, dimensionally accurate, exhaustively documented, heavily supported, highly extensible and programmable, and runs on almost anything. The conversion of the *DocBook* SGML to LaTeX was done with *Omnimark LE*.

1. Introduction

Never explain. Your friends do not need it and your enemies will not believe you anyway.

Elbert Hubbard, *The Note Book*

- The purpose of this book
- Selection of tools: what's here and why
- How much you need to know about computing
- How the book is arranged
- A short guide to markup and SGML

1.1. What it's all about

This is a book about computer techniques and computer programs that can be used with the Standard Generalized Markup Language (SGML: ISO 8879) and the Extensible Markup Language (XML) to make your life with text easier and help you produce better-quality work. It doesn't claim to cover everything — no single book ever could — but it does contain the experience of many years working with SGML and with the people who make and use the programs.

All too often the information about which program to use, how to get hold of it, how to install it, and how to make it work, is either hidden in obscure README documents, or written solely for the wizard or guru, or simply doesn't exist at all. While I'm all in favor of the serendipity of discovery — it's part of the fun of working at the sharp end, and one of the reasons for the success of the World Wide Web — it can be a real timewaster if you just need to get a job done fast. There are still program manuals being produced which hide the installation instructions in an appendix tucked away at the end, and not even mentioned in the Table of Contents!

I've also tried to bear in mind always the pleas of those who write to magazines and journals, or post messages to electronic forums like `comp.text.sgml` looking for help. Having frequent occasion to do this myself I feel the greatest sympathy for requests like:

- 'I can't seem to get it to work'
- 'I've done all it says in the manual but it still won't do what it's supposed to'
- 'Has anyone ever found a program to do *X*?'
- 'What's the trick in getting *Y* to do *Z*?'
- 'Why isn't there a program to do this?'
- 'There aren't any instructions with it, how do you make it work?'

It's by no means restricted to SGML or XML, of course, and certainly it's not restricted to newcomers. In another field, I recently had to install some new software I'd never used before, and I got just as badly stuck as any beginner, despite 25 years in the business, until an expert spotted my question in a Usenet newsgroup and solved the problem in a single sentence. I had taken all the documentation on trust, without recognizing that it was written by and for people to whom that program was already an open book, rather than for the novice: one crucial item of information had been omitted.

What I have tried to do in this book is avoid making that mistake. Perhaps when you have read it, you'll tell me if I have succeeded. Tell me too if you think I have been too harsh or too lenient with the authors of the software: I know there have been occasions when I have found features that turned out to be bugs, as well as the bugs that turned out to be features.

The success of technical documentation rests on knowing at what level to pitch the information: too much detail and it confuses the beginners and annoys the experts; not enough detail leaves the beginners stranded and the experts frustrated. I have therefore adopted a few assumptions, and I hope the experts will bear with me on occasion if I seem to be laboring points which to them are obvious. These assumptions are listed at the end of section 1.3.

If you haven't yet had any experience with SGML or XML, read the remainder of this chapter first, before dipping into anything else. It contains a lot of information about the way they work, the way people use them, and the things they want to do with them, and is designed to get you started (as well as to resolve some of the popular misunderstandings about the languages).

XML and SGML

With a few exceptions, most of the points I make about SGML apply equally to XML. They share a common syntax, and XML is basically a subset of SGML with all the optional bits removed. I'm therefore not going to say 'SGML and XML' and 'SGML or XML' every single time I refer to one or other of them: you should treat the acronym SGML as properly including XML (and, indeed, HTML) except where I explicitly make a distinction, for example when you can do something with one that you cannot with the other, or when certain programs or facilities only work with one of them.

XML was under development all the time I was writing this book, so I kept having to edit bits each time the language specification was changed. Version 1.0 was approved in February 1998, but many aspects were still awaiting refinement — linking, for example — so I'm going to refer those of you who are interested to the online documentation for the latest news:

`http://www.w3.org/TR/WD-xml` for the specification;

`http://www.sil.org/sgml/xml.html` for the Web pages;

`http://www.ucc.ie/xml/` for the FAQ.

1.2. Selection of tools

The selection of programs I describe is eclectic, and is based on several criteria:

- some of the programs I use myself in daily production because they match the requirements of the tasks I have;
- some are included because I know they work well anyway, having installed and evaluated them, or used them in the past;
- others have proved themselves publicly over the years in many areas, so they stand on their own reputation;
- yet others are in because they are indispensable, handy, or just plain clever;
- and some are new, or even experimental, but show promise or indicate future trends.

It is important to understand that this book is a sampling, a selection designed to show you the different kinds of program that exist, sufficient for you to then be able to classify programs by yourself, and start evaluating them for your own uses. It is not a catalog, so I haven't attempted to include every known SGML or XML program on the planet — for that there is Steve Pepper's excellent online summary, *The Whirlwind Guide to SGML Tools*[34], and the hefty and comprehensive volume of the *SGML Buyers' Guide*[22] which partly derived from it.

What You Read Is What You Get: all the screens are from live products in actual use, not marketing pack shots or advertising dummies, but you need to bear in mind that the manufacturers are constantly updating their products. Even using the latest technology, there is a finite delay between writing a book and getting it on the shelves in your bookstore, so by the time you read this and go to buy some software, What You Get will probably end up being even better than What You Read.

Unavoidably there are some well-known packages which are not in this book. Some of them were not available because they run on specialized equipment, or they are designed as software libraries to be built into much larger systems rather than run as standalone programs, or because they are restricted for military, political, or economic reasons. But in some cases, the makers didn't want to let me try them out, or surrounded them with so much bureaucracy that it became impossible to pursue the matter. One vendor of a £40 program demanded that I agree to return their single floppy disk 'at my own expense' after evaluation (and presumably they would have sued me if hadn't). And one large company refused to send me an evaluation copy: they don't do them because 'a propper evaluation requires the implementation of a DTD[...]further more[...]knowledge is required to see the strenghs of this product[...]not a simple SGML Editor but an SGML publishing system': the clear implication being that all this SGML stuff was too difficult for me to understand. And undoubtedly there are some which aren't here because I simply haven't come across them yet. One of life's Higher Mysteries is why some companies with excellent products sometimes never seem to publicize them.

1.3. How much do I need to know about computers?

Most of the tools and techniques I describe assume that you know something about computing, textual information, and SGML. I don't think this is unreasonable: if I was discussing how to use a carpenter's lathe I would assume you already knew something about woodworking.

But if you're completely new to SGML, don't worry: most of the remainder of this chapter is for you, to bring you up to speed.

1.3.1. Essential: basic computing

In terms of simply knowing your computer system, I am assuming:

- you have a computer (or access to one) and are completely familiar with using it;
- you know how to create, save, delete, rename, move, and copy files and folders (directories), either by using the menus or mouse, or by typing commands;
- you know how to run a program (either by clicking on an icon or by typing the name) and how to stop running a program;
- you know how to install software from floppy disk or CD-ROM;
- you know how to use a plaintext editor (*not* a word processor) for creating and modifying files of unmarked, unformatted text.

If you haven't done some of these things before, you may want to look them up in your manuals, or get someone who knows your kind of computer and software to show you how.

In particular, if you haven't come across the concept of plaintext before, it can seem a little strange: raw text with no fonts, using just the characters `A-Z`, `a-z`, `0-9`, and punctuation, like an old typewriter. To get familiar with the idea, use the plaintext editor provided on your computer to look at any of the `.txt` or `.sgml` files on the CD-ROM.

Platform	Editor	Program	How to get out of it
Unix	*vi*	`/usr/ucb/vi`	**Esc :q! Enter**
	Emacs	`/usr/local/bin/emacs`	**Files|*Exit*** or **Ctrl-X Ctrl-C**
Mac	*SimpleText*	Apple menu	**File|*Exit***
	TeachText	Apple menu	**File|*Exit***
DOS	*edit*	`c:\dos\edit.com`	**Alt** then **F X**
	dosedit	`c:\dos\dosedit.com`	**Alt** then **F X**
Windows	*edit* (DOS)	`c:\windows\command\edit.com`	**Alt** then **F X**
	NotePad	`c:\windows\notepad.exe`	**File|*Exit***
VMS	*EDT*	`edit/edt`	**Ctrl-Z** `exit` **Enter**
	TPU	`edit/tpu`	**Ctrl-Z**

The advantage of plaintext is precisely that it is *not* tied to any particular make or model of hardware or software: it can be used with any program on any computer, with no special facilities required.

1.3.2. Important: textual skills

Separate from your computing skills but equally important for working with SGML is some understanding of text: the simple text structures and what they contain. I am assuming that you are familiar with:

- the idea of paragraphs, headings, lists of various kinds, chapters, sections, subsections, appendixes, glossaries, and indexes;
- the way in which they are put together, sometimes in a hierarchy, to form documents;
- some simple terms from printing, word processing, and desktop publishing, such as fonts, typefaces, bold and italic, point sizes, and white-space.

An understanding of some of the basic concepts of hypertext and navigation is useful but not essential. This deals with the linking together of one or more pieces of text in a usable manner, and how you refer from one to the other. If you've used *Hypercard*, Windows Help, or the World Wide Web, then you've already seen hypertext and navigation in action.

1.3.3. Nice-to-have: basic networking

A very large amount of SGML information and software is available via the Internet, so in some places I have also made the following assumptions (but see the note below):

- you have a connection to the Internet, or access to one. This can be either via a phone and a modem or through a permanent link, and could be at home, at your place of work, or perhaps in a Public Library or Internet Café;
- you have (or can get hold of) the main programs needed for accessing information: an email program, a newsreader, copies of Telnet and FTP, and a World Wide Web browser;
- you know how to access information when given a network address; for example an email address, a Usenet newsgroup, a hostname, FTP sitename, or a World Wide Web URL (Uniform Resource Locator); and that you know how to use a username and password for Telnet and FTP, as well as how to use Anonymous FTP;

- you know how to download and install software (how to unwrap compressed or archived files like `.zip`, `.tar`, or `.sit/.hqx` files).

If you are unfamiliar with any of this, you may want to get someone who knows the Internet to show you how to use it, or read one of the many books on the subject. Chapters 3 and 4 of the *World Wide Web Handbook*[19] briefly describe the Internet, and you can find more detail in other books such as Ed Krol's *The Whole Internet User's Guide and Catalog*[27] or Dan Dern's *The Internet Guide for New Users*[15].

The Internet

A huge amount of information about SGML and XML can be found on the Internet, and the SGML Web pages at `http://www.sil.org/sgml/` are a fundamental resource.

However, despite the hype, not everyone has access to the Internet, so although it's useful if you need to provide or get hold of information fast, it's not essential to the reading of this book, although obviously many of the programs themselves require access to the Internet to operate, especially for XML, which is designed for use on a network.

If you have got electronic mail, but no *direct* connection to the Internet, it's worth remembering you can request Web files by email: send a 1-line message to `webmail@www.ucc.ie` containing the command `get` followed by the URL (Web address) you want, for example

```
get  http://www.sil.org/sgml/
```

The HTML file will be sent back to you by email, and you can then open it using a browser.

1.4. Organization of the book

I'd hate to write a book like this without saying 'hello' to newcomers. The SGML community is still relatively small and close-knit, even after 12 years, and new friends are always welcome. If you've been involved with SGML before, you'll recognize this; if you're a first-time user, then join the gang — you may want to go through the next section with special care, as it lays the foundations for the rest of the book.

The chapters of this book take a 'life-cycle' approach to the concept of the document. SGML isn't only about text and printing, as we'll see, but 'the document' — however you define it — is still very much at the heart of it. These closely match the categories used by Steve Pepper in his network document *The Whirlwind Guide to SGML Tools*[34] (which in turn are used in the *SGML Buyers Guide*[22]), with some small exceptions: I treat display separately from printing, and I also separate out software development tools.

1. **Introduction** — for those new to SGML: what all the fuss is about, how it works, and how to set up an environment for using SGML successfully;
2. **What type of document** — how DTDs work, how to choose and use them, and software for viewing and designing them;
3. **Editing** — how you get your text into SGML: editors, filters, composition, and data capture systems;
4. **Parsing and validating** — making sure it works: checking conformance and testing validity;
5. **Conversion and manipulation** — one half of SGML output: software for interchange and conversion to other formats;
6. **Finding, viewing and printing** — the other half of SGML output: search systems, browsers, display formatters and printing or publishing systems, with a note about databases, archiving and storage;
7. **Rolling your own** — For those who want to write their own programs: a summary of some SGML software development tools.

I have not played favorites with the sequence of software: the tools and techniques in each chapter are in not in any specific order. You don't have to begin at the beginning: if you're not going to be inputting or editing text, for example, just displaying or printing someone else's, you can just as easily start with chapter 6. If someone has already set up DTDs for you, then you can go straight to chapter 3.

1.5. The quick-start guide to SGML

This is a short introduction to the background and principles which make markup and SGML work. It explains the basics for people new to the field, defines what you need to get started, does away with some of the mythology that has grown up over the years, and provides a checklist of things to watch for if you or your organization are new to SGML (or are still considering it).

There is a list of other useful guides to SGML and related subjects in Appendix B. For beginners I recommend in particular reading the *Gentle Guide to SGML*, which is published as part of the Text Encoding Initiative's *Guidelines for Electronic Text Encoding and Interchange*[39] (we'll come across more about the TEI later, in section 2.3.6). It is included on the CD-ROM by kind permission of the authors (in the `doc` directory of the `sgml` folder as `gentle.sgml`).

1.5.1. So what is markup and what is SGML?

'Markup' is a term you're going to be seeing more often, so you need to have a good understanding of what it is and what it implies. Many of the difficulties people experience in making use of text-handling systems stem from not fully realizing what markup is and how it can affect what you can do with your information.

A discussion of markup is also a good place to introduce some of the SGML terminology that we'll need throughout the rest of the book, and the best way to get acquainted with it is to see it used in practice, so there are illustrations or examples at frequent intervals.

1.5.1.1. Background to markup

In the days of manuscripts, the scribes and authors had methods of indicating to their readers the importance of special words and phrases. They would write them or their explanations around the edge of the text, or squeezed into the margins, because goat-hides and sheep-hides for the vellum on which they wrote were expensive, and not to be wasted. Important explanations and comments, and sometimes initial letters, were often written using an ink made with *terra rubrica*, the Latin name for a kind of red earth (where we get the word 'rubric' for the instructions on a form or at a ceremony), so that they stood out from the rest of the text.

When printing started to take over from handwritten copying in the late 15th century, the printer-editors of the day at first followed the examples of their calligraphic forerunners, mimicking the vellum with paper, and copying the style of lettering with their types. Rather than trying to fool the reader into thinking it was a manuscript, they were simply bowing to conservative public feeling about what people felt a book should look like[40]. All the conventions that a 15th century reader knew and expected therefore came to be transferred into the

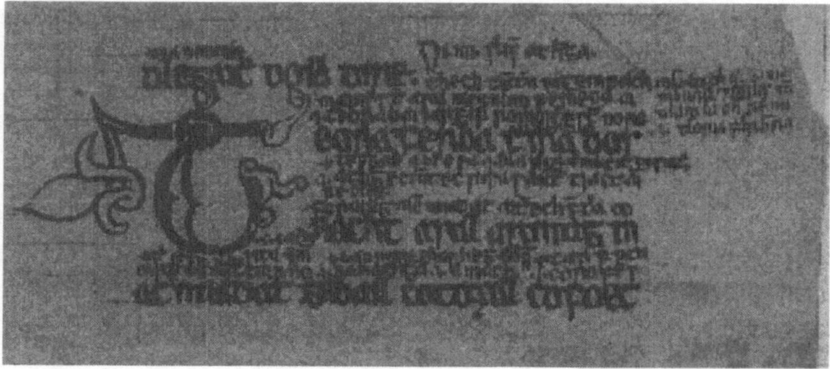

Figure 1. Early markup: the text (in large lettering) has explanations and comments between the lines and in the margins

new technology. Figure 1 shows some of the complexity they had to deal with

In the centuries that followed, typography slowly moved away from resembling manuscripts, and in western Europe the conventions of page layout and design eventually became formalized in the use of italic and bold type, spacing, and different typefaces (fonts) and sizes. Punctuation and spelling became regularized, and books settled into the familiar pattern of chapters, sections, and paragraphs, with tables of contents, cross-references, and indexes — so the book of 1840 was quite unrecognizable to the reader of 1480, and *vice versa*.

The conventions we follow in the westernized world are so common that almost everyone who reads knows what they mean: they are so common that they are almost invisible (these are just a few of the more popular English-language ones):

- italics for the titles of books, newspapers, and other documents;
- italics also for emphasis, and for product names;
- bold or large type for headings;
- bold also for extra emphasis, and for names in the gossip columns;
- small capitals for subtitles or running heads;
- centering for some, but not all, classes of heading and titling;
- italics for foreign and scientific words, and mathematical letters;
- small type sizes for subscripts and superscripts, also for footnotes;
- semicolons between items in a list;
- commas between lines in an address;
- spaces between words, commas between phrases, periods at the end of sentences, semicolons between phrases;
- indentation at the start of paragraphs, narrower text for quotations.

We learn many of these in childhood without realizing it, and we use the same techniques today, both on paper and electronically, that evolved hundreds of years ago, some of them before the dawn of printing. Despite the many advances in computer handling of text, What You See Is Not Always What You Meant — the text on the paper or the screen still needs a human to interpret it, because the visual appearance could be ambiguous to a computer.

As printing and publishing eventually became two separate industries, the people who edited the writer's text needed to explain to the people who printed it which letters, words, or phrases needed all this special typesetting. They would 'mark up' the author's handwritten (and later, typewritten) text with words and symbols for the printer to follow, and use the same practise when making corrections. Because the conventions had become so established, the proofreader would not bother explaining that *Alice in Wonderland* was the title of a book, but only say 'put this in italics', and leave it to the good sense of the reader to work out why it was italicized.

Markup therefore showed the layout, capitals, italics, centering, and spacing so that the compositor would know what to typeset, and the reader would understand that there was something significant being shown (the example in the Preface indicates the complexity needed even for simple material). Anyone who has ever had to prepare their own or someone else's text for the printer will be familiar with this method. It works perfectly so long as the text is being processed (read) by a human being.

But what happens when it has to be processed by a computer? How can a computer resolve the ambiguities which we barely even have to think about? There's no typographic distinction between many of the items in the list above, and even when there is, many word processors only use the font changes for printing, and are incapable of using them for another purpose.

What got lost in the midst of all the technology of printing was any means of recording the *reasons why* certain letters, words, or phrases were printed the way they were: the need for this only became apparent when people started to use computers to read and work on the text, because computers can do lots of useful things when they know about the *nature* of the data. But at the moment they cannot easily and accurately disambiguate the use of typefaces or spacing into the separate human reasons for their existence, so they need to be told. This is what markup is for.

When this work of dealing with text started to move from metal type and paper onto computer, the concept of markup moved with it. Compositors were no longer dealing with pencil and paper but with markup on the screen. The word 'markup' changed its meaning slightly, from the written symbols used by printers to the embedded instructions used by text-handling programs: it is an agreed collection of symbols used to show that certain pieces of information need a particular action or mean something special in relation to the document they form part of.

1.5.1.2. Different kinds of markup

Markup varies enormously from one system to another. Many word processing and desktop publishing authors invented their own, because there was no standard way of doing it. The results are well-known to every user who has had to exchange files with a user of a different system, or had the misfortune to have to change word processing system themselves, even sometimes only to a different version of the same program.

To see how word processor markup works, I'm going to use a small example. I'm approaching it from the word processing and printing point of view, because this is the commonest business/office application of text. Markup, especially with SGML, can be used in thousands of other ways, but the methods described below should be immediately familiar. Look at this extract from a business report:

> **Soft cheeses**
>
> The market for soft cheeses is estimated at $3.5M *per annum*. There has been considerable activity by domestic manufacturers in the last two years, and they now control approximately 35% of the market, the remainder being supplied from the European continent, notably from France[1].
>
> There has been public concern over health-related matters, particularly after an outbreak in 1997 of food poisoning attributed to *Listeria spp*. due to labeling errors. Given the size of the market, I believe it is vital for the company to make its presence felt *as soon as possible*. We cannot risk a repeat of the problem outlined in the recent DHA report Marketing Cheese Abroad.
>
> [1]45% of imported cheese is French.

Whoever wrote or edited this added some information along the lines of the conventions we saw earlier, which our brains can interpret straight away, but which could be ambiguous to a machine:

- The heading is in bold type, on a line by itself, with some white space below it;
- The Latin phrase *per annum* is in italics (a bit pedantic, but still very common);
- The scientific name of the bacterium *L. spp.* is in italics (standard scientific practice)
- The word 'France' has a raised numeral, because there is a footnote;
- The phrase 'as soon as possible' is in bold type because it is being emphasized as something very important;
- The title of a report is in italics (it could have been in quotes instead).

This is all so easy to do in a word processor that we don't notice doing it, mostly because we're so used to it (remember the comment about the conservatism of the reading public). It works well in print because everyone immediately recognizes the meaning attached to the formatting. But a word processor can understand only what it looks like, not what it means: it doesn't have any idea about the reason *why* a particular word is in italics or bold or superscript, so it cannot distinguish between similar appearances unaided. Similarly, a linebreak may or may not have a meaning: at the end of a normal line of type, it's purely accidental. It's only there because the edge of the sheet is getting close and the next word won't fit. This kind of linebreak has no meaning: it doesn't stop your flow of reading or call for special action. But in a list, or in poetry, linebreaks are critical: if you get them wrong you may destroy the meaning. But a machine cannot know this: it has to be told.

In a so-called WYSIWYG (What You See Is What You Get) word processor, you format the text manually on the screen as you type it, or as you revise it for printing. If you have a lot of repetitive formatting, you'll probably use a stylesheet, which lets you attach standardized appearances to frequently-recurring objects like headings or lists or special names or references. What you *don't* see is the markup itself, unless you have one of those word processors which specifically allow you to examine the markup by revealing it on the screen.

Let's look at the extract again, this time marked up for printing using a word processor which does exactly that: *PC-Write*, which was a popular system for DOS PCs. Here we've revealed the underlying markup, which is normally hidden while you type your report:

The markup is all the instructional material that you *don't* see when it's printed (see Figure 2). In this case it includes a group of global settings at the top to define the font, paper size, and margins. Then there's a ruler with tab stops, just like a typewriter, but with a J at

```
^G.r:q         (Times Roman 12pt)
^G.W : 21.0 c  (Width)
^G.L : 29.7 c  (Length)
^G.XT:  1.0 i  (Top margin)
^G.XI:  1.0 i  (Left margin)
^G.XJ:  1.0 i  (Right margin)
^G.XB:  2.0 i  (Bottom margin)
^GL---+---T2----+-T--3----T----4--T-+----5T---+---T6----+-T--7-YJ|@10/i
^OSoft cheeses

The market for soft cheeses is estimated at $3.5M ^Iper annum^I. There
has been considerable activity by domestic manufacturers in the last
two years, and they now control approximately 35% of the market, the
remainder being supplied from the European continent, notably from
France^H2^H.
^G.DD          (Begin footnote)
^E^H2^H 45% of imported cheese is French.
^G.DQ          (End of note)

There has been public concern over health-related matters, particularly
after an outbreak in 1997 of food poisoning attributed to ^IListeria
spp.^I due to labeling errors. Given the size of the market, I believe
it is vital for the company to make its presence felt ^Bas soon as^B
^Bpossible^B. We cannot risk a repeat of the problem outlined in the
recent DHA report ^IMarketing Cheese Abroad^I.
```

Figure 2. Report marked up in PC-Write

the end to specify a justified right-hand margin. The footnote is clearly visible at the end of the first paragraph. So far the markup is explicit because *PC-Write* inserts comments with it to explain what it's for. Less clear are the font-control characters used in the body of the text, which the user inserts with the **Alt** key. In order of occurrence these are:

Symbol	Meaning
`^G`	signals the start of a markup line
`^O`	large bold
`^H`	Highline (superscript)
`^I`	italics
`^E`	'Elite' type used for 10pt Times
`^B`	bold

The resulting text when printed, however, will look largely the same as in many other word processors (Figure 3).

Soft cheeses

The market for soft cheeses is estimated at $3.5M *per annum*. There has been considerable activity by domestic manufacturers in the last two years, and they now control approximately 35% of the market, the remainder being supplied from the European continent, notably from France[2].

There has been public concern over health-related matters, particularly after an outbreak in 1996 of food poisoning attributed to *Listeria spp.* due to labeling errors. Given the size of the market, I believe it is vital for the company to make its presence felt as soon as possible. We cannot risk a repeat of the problem outlined in the recent DHA report *Marketing Cheese Abroad.*

[2] 45% of imported cheese is French.

Figure 3. Report printed using a word processor

Let's look at another example before we turn to SGML. This time it's done using the LaTeX document preparation macros developed for the TeX typesetting system. You can see immediately a significant difference between this and a word processor in the first few lines because the instructions are in something approximating to a human language. TeX systems use the backslash character to signal the markup, and curly braces to group together relevant words or characters (Figure 4).

The word processor principle of hidden control codes and cryptic symbols has been replaced by explicit information on what role each piece of text plays in the document. Most of the formatting and appearance is kept separately in a stylesheet: the implications of this are described below. This shift of paradigm means several things are now different about the text:

1. The document has been classed as a report (which is exactly what it is, but many word processors can't do this — this can have major implications for ease of identification if you use a document database);
2. The font selection is automated with a package (here, one which sets up the Charter font family);
3. I'm assuming in the third line that Acme Cheeses has developed a corporate style package called `acme.sty` (even small companies have their own styles for documents);
4. The beginning and the end of the document text are clearly marked;

```
\documentclass{report}
\usepackage{charter}
\usepackage{acme}
\begin{document}
\section{Soft cheeses}

The market for soft cheeses is estimated at \$3.5M \frn{per annum}.
There has been considerable activity by domestic manufacturers in the
last two years, and they now control approximately 35\% of the
market, the remainder being supplied from the European continent,
notably from France\footnote{45\% of imported cheese is French.}.

There has been public concern over health-related matters,
particularly after an outbreak in 1996 of food poisoning attributed
to \sci{Listeria spp.} due to labeling errors. Given the size of the
market, I believe it is vital for the company to make its presence
felt \emph{as soon as possible}. We cannot risk a repeat of the
problem outlined in the recent DHA report \xref{Marketing Cheese
Abroad}.

\end{document}
```

Figure 4. Report marked up in LaTeX

5. The section heading is automated: the style file will correctly allocate the font and perform the spacing;
6. Foreign-language phrases and scientific terms are identified, as is emphasis and the cross-reference;
7. The positioning, numbering, and typography of the footnote is automatic;
8. TeX has a few special symbols, like many other systems: the dollar sign and the percent sign characters have a special meaning on their own (math and comment), so to get printed dollar signs and percents, you have to 'escape' from the special meaning by preceding the character with a backslash;
9. There is no need to format the text on the screen — indeed there is no point in formatting it, as TeX's typesetting engine does it for you.

The printed output from this again resembles that produced by most other systems (see Figure 5), but you can already see that the markup needed to produce it is much simpler and more related to the logic of what it describes.

The principles can be applied to any system where style files can be used:

2.1 Soft cheeses

The market for soft cheeses is estimated at $3.5M *per annum*. There has been considerable activity by domestic manufacturers in the last two years, and they now control approximately 35% of the market, the remainder being supplied from the European continent, notably from France[2].

There has been public concern over health-related matters, particularly after an outbreak in 1996 of food poisoning attributed to a bacterial infection of *Clostridium botulinium* due to labeling errors. Given the size of the market, I believe it is vital for the company to make its presence felt **as soon as possible.** We cannot risk a repeat of the problem outlined in the recent DHA report *Marketing Cheese Abroad*.

[2]45% of imported cheese is French.

Figure 5. Report being typeset using LaTeX

- you can change appearance more easily, by making the adjustment once in the style file, and all occurrences of that style then follow suit, rather than by doing tedious and error-prone bulk repeat-replace editing;
- styles can be named, so it becomes easier to locate occurrences of them with a simple text search;
- if the style information itself is kept in a standard form, it can be used by many different programs.

It's not easy to show you the insides of most word processor systems' files, because they are usually ***binary***: a non-printable symbolic format, used partly for speed (not so important as processors get faster), partly for efficiency (still important), and partly to make it harder for you to move to a competitor's product (a strong disincentive). But as an example, Figure 6 shows a portion of the same text from the insides of a Microsoft *Word* file. You can see the text surrounded by the encoded markup information. The file is in fact twelve times the size of the other two examples because it carries an overhead of formatting and printing information.

The printed output from all these systems is broadly comparable (assuming a competent operator). The reasons for the different ways of working are partly commercial, partly historical, and partly technical; but they all fulfil their primary role: getting text printed on paper. The problem is, that's not the only thing you might want to do with it.

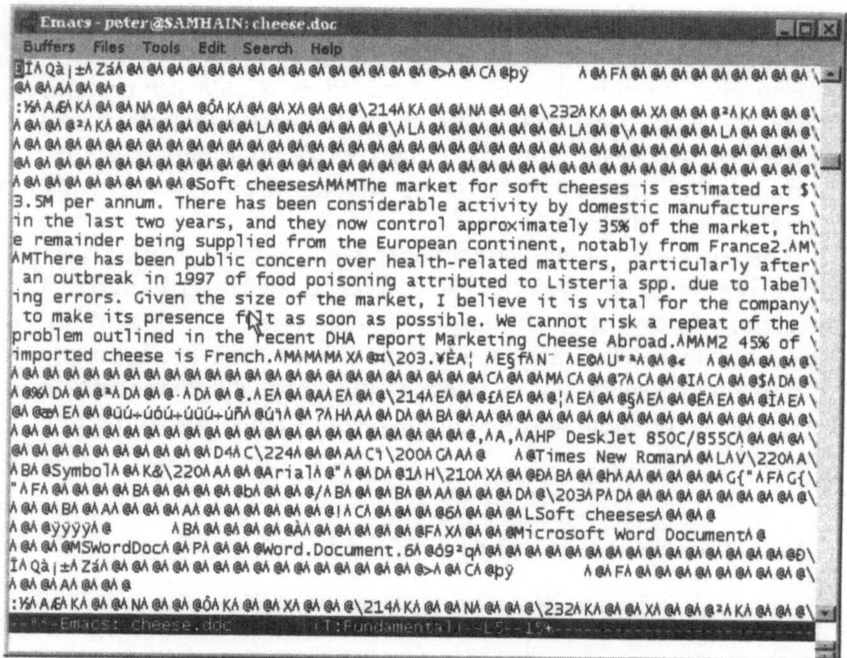

Figure 6. What you never see: the internal storage format of a word processor file, revealed by using a standard plaintext editor

1.5.1.3. Different uses for markup

By now it is becoming clear that if you wanted to search all your word processor documents for the chapter or section headings, or all references to scientific names, or mentions of other documents by title, or all phrases that were emphasized, or personal names, or product names (the list can go on and on) you couldn't just search for italics or bold, because your computer would have no way to distinguish the different uses: you'd just get all the other italics and bold coming out as well, and you'd have a huge manual task to disambiguate them.

The reason for this is that italics, bold, *etc* in themselves have no actual meaning: as we've seen, it's the conventions we associate with them that we are really looking for. Scholars call this 'semantics', the association of meaning with a symbol. All the typeface on its own says is, in effect, 'hello, I'm a different-looking style of type'; it then leaves it up to the reader to know already what that means.

While this is just fine for printing, it is not adequate if you want the computer to be able to use the meaning attached to a phrase, rather than simply the appearance. After all, the use of bold type and spacing for headings varies widely between users, designers, publishers, and applications, and doesn't have any 'meaning' on its own anyway. What is important about the phrase 'Soft cheeses' above is that it is a *heading*, quite distinct from any other use of the same words in the sentence that follows it. While its appearance is critically important for presentation to a human reader, it is usually quite unimportant in terms of storage and recognition by computer.

So in addition to identifying behavior (like changes in appearance), markup can let you describe certain parts of the text according to their function or meaning. In the examples above, we used mostly ***visual markup***, because this is commonly used when printing is the only objective. However, there are lots of other things that people may want to do with your text apart from print it:

- display it on a screen (a bit like printing, but with printing you control the paper: you may not be able to control what kind of screen your reader has);
- archive it: preserve it over the passage of time, regardless of the system used to write it with;
- send it to someone else: transfer it to some other computer system;
- transfer it to a million other systems by putting it onto the World Wide Web;
- put it into a database or searching system so that people can refer to it and extract topics from it;
- repurpose it: a report can become a chapter of a manual; an article in the in-house magazine can become a story for the press; a research note can become part of a training system;
- print it again, but in a different style, perhaps in large type, or in Braille;
- turn it into a spoken recording, or a script for video use;
- analyze it for content, for research purposes.

To do all this kind of thing we need to use the markup to indicate the meanings, reasoning, or purpose behind the text, rather than just its appearance, and let the appearance be specified separately. This use of markup is called ***logical markup***, because it can be processed by computer logic (the terms 'visual' and 'logical' markup are from an article by Leslie Lamport[28]). Using logical markup you can call a heading a heading, a list a list, a paragraph a paragraph, and leave it to a style sheet to specify how each of those elements appears. By separating form from function, you can immediately make your text more usable, because the very uses to which it can be put are no longer cast in concrete.

In some applications, it is extremely important to impose a structure, to prescribe what can and cannot go where. Office reports, letters, and memos; job applications; technical descriptions and specifications or manuals; books, periodicals, articles, and essays; all of them tend to use a structure where some pieces of information are essential (compulsory) and others are optional. ***Prescriptive markup*** defines what is *needed* and what is *permitted* (software is available which can help enforce compliance with prescriptive markup):

- my sister-in-law is a journalist: her articles *must* have a title, date, and byline (her name) on them, otherwise she won't get paid;
- letters or email messages *must* have the recipient's name and address, or they won't get delivered; they *ought* to have the date, usually a subject and at least one piece of textual content; they *may* have many more pieces of text of various kinds; and they *must* have the name and address of the sender;
- when you apply for a job, you *have to* give your name, address, your work experience, and a variety of other information, but some things are *optional*, like your hobbies.

There are also times when you want to indicate the existence of some special class of information, but it may or may not have a specific visual appearance. A good example is index keywords, place names, personal names, and other items readers want to be able to look up, but which just print as regular text. This is ***descriptive markup***: if you look up 'email' in the index, you'll find an entry referring to this page, but there's nothing special about the word: it has no special appearance, I just marked it for indexing.

Frequently you get descriptive and prescriptive markup, as well as visual and logical markup, working together: some pieces of information are essential for the immediate needs, others are there for future use.

1.5.1.4. Markup using SGML

SGML is a language which lets you define systems of markup to describe things in a way that a computer can use and reuse. It works on the principle that documents are typically made up of repeated occurrences of basic elements, like a house is built of many individual bricks, doors, windows, pieces of wood, fixtures, and fittings. For a house, the architect's plan describes what goes where; for an SGML document, the Document Type Definition (DTD) performs this task.

The basic elements for a building can be combined in different ways on different occasions to produce different kinds of structure called 'a house': for instance a bungalow, a town-house, a country mansion, or an inner-city tenement. A different combination, excluding some elements and including some new ones, is needed to produce instances

Picturing SGML

P. Ó Floinn

It's usually far easier to learn about something by looking at it than by reading about it. This short note tries to make plain the anatomy of an SGML file. It shows some of the major features:

1. a Document Type Declaration with a Formal Public Identifier referring to an external DTD[1] locatable using a System Identifier ;
2. nested element markup enclosing text between a start-tag and an end-tag;
3. an attribute inside a start-tag with its attribute value;
4. an element identified by an ID being referred to from elsewhere;
5. accented characters done with entity references.

The ID/IDREF mechanism is referred to in item 4. (Comments never end up in the output.)

[1]Document Type Definition

```
<!DOCTYPE note PUBLIC "+//Silmaril//DTD Technical Note//EN"
   "http://www.ucc.ie/dtds/tecnote.dtd">
<note><title>Picturing SGML</title><by>P. &Oacute; Floinn</by>
<para>It's usually far easier to learn about something by
looking at it than by reading about it. This short note tries
to make plain the anatomy of an SGML file. It shows some of the
major features:</para><list type="enumerate"><item>a Document
Type Declaration with a Formal Public Identifier referring to
an external DTD<fn>Document Type Definition</fn> locatable
using a System Identifier;</item><item>nested element markup
enclosing text between a start-tag and an end-tag;</item>
<item>an attribute with a value inside a start-tag;</item>
<item id="here">an element identified by an ID being referred
to from elsewhere;</item><item>accented characters done with
entity references.</item></list><para>The ID/IDREF mechanism
is referred to in <xref to="here">.</para></note>
<!--Here's a comment to finish with-->
```

Figure 7. The anatomy of an SGML file

of 'an office'; yet another different set of elements is needed to produce instances of 'a bridge', or 'a spaceship'.

For a building, you can use standard, pre-existing sizes of bricks, windows, doors, and lumber. In SGML you need to define the elements yourself, or use someone else's (an existing DTD). Neither SGML nor XML themselves come with a 'starter set' of elements (you have to define them), whereas HTML *is* one of those predefined sets (defined by the DTD or the browser makers, which ever set of markup you wish to follow).

For a document, one set of elements can be used to describe 'a letter'; another set to describe a report; yet another set to describe a newspaper. Documents tend to fall naturally into different classes called ***document types***, so SGML lets you describe what goes to make up each type of document you deal with. It lets you define different types of document, as many as you want, appropriate for the job in hand. The idea is that you very rarely create a single type of document on a once-off basis never to be used again, although with DTD-less XML (see section 2.4.1.3) that is indeed possible: the assumption is that most documents fall into some kind of classification. For this reason, just as you can buy pre-formed architectural assemblies like roof trusses, it is also possible to define 'architectural' forms of common markup concepts so that they can be used and reused in many DTDs (see section 2.7.2.3).

DTDs let you specify things as tightly or as loosely as you need. When you build a house, the design specifies that you don't fill a doorway opening with bricks, you fill it with a doorframe and a door, which is made of some wood, a handle, and possibly some glass. With document design, SGML lets you specify what each element can sensibly contain: for example a list might have a heading followed by one or more items, each of which may be one or more paragraphs long, and may contain just continuous text or possibly other objects like footnotes.

With this in mind, let's look again at the cheese market report, but this time with some different markup, so you can see how this might be indicated:

```
<!doctype sec public "+//Acme Cheeses Inc//DTD Report//EN">
<sec><title>Soft cheeses</title><par>The market for soft cheeses
is estimated at $3.5M <for>per annum</for>. There has been
considerable activity by domestic manufacturers in the last two
years, and they now control approximately 35% of the market, the
remainder being supplied from the European continent, notably
from France<fn>45% of imported cheese is French.</fn>.<par>There
has been public concern over health-related matters,
particularly after an outbreak in 1996 of food poisoning
attributed to <sci>Listeria spp.</sci> due to labeling errors.
Given the size of the market, I believe it is vital for the
```

```
company to make its presence felt <emph>as soon as
possible</emph>. We cannot risk a repeat of the problem outlined
in the recent DHA report <ref id="dha-mca-97">Marketing Cheese
Abroad</ref>.</par></sec>
```

There's nothing in there now about bold or italics or spacing at all: the point is that there doesn't need to be. As we saw, all that can be carried in a stylesheet, ready for application to any piece of text of this type, and there can be many different stylesheets for different purposes. The document already contains all the information necessary to identify what needs to be recognized, so that formatting can be carried out automatically by an editing system or a browser or print program or a database.

The markup used in the instance above is typical of many SGML documents and shows some of the main features of regular SGML (an XML version of the document would be almost identical: we'll look at the differences later). You can also see these illustrated in Figure 7:

- the ***document type*** is declared at the beginning (here `<sec>`, as it's only a section of the whole report), and identified as being part of a particular definition (Acme Cheese, Inc's report definitions);
- each ***element*** of text is contained within pairs of ***tags*** made up of the name of the element enclosed in angle brackets (like mathematical 'less-than' and 'greater-than' signs);
- a ***start-tag*** at the beginning of each element is matched by an ***end-tag*** at the end, containing the same name but prefixed with a slash;
- some elements carry additional information within the angle brackets of the start-tag, called ***attributes***: these are made up of an ***attribute name*** and an ***attribute value*** separated by an equals sign, with the value in quotes, and a space between each name/value pair (see the cross-reference ID in the last line but one);
- all text appears inside at least one set of tags: some of it is 'nested' inside several levels of them.

(There's one exception to the rule of matching start- and end-tags in this example, which is explained in section 1.5.1.6: see if you can find it.) Because an external stylesheet is used for formatting, the file itself can be unformatted, as above, or it could be visually formatted to aid editing or proofing before the stylesheet is applied. The following file is identical as far as all practical purposes are concerned, but is a lot easier to read unaided:

```
<!doctype sec public "+//Acme Cheeses Inc//DTD Report//EN">
<sec>
  <title>Soft cheeses</title>
  <par>The market for soft cheeses is estimated at $3.5M
```

```
<for>per annum</for>. There has been considerable activity by
domestic manufacturers in the last two years, and they now
control approximately 35% of the market, the remainder being
supplied from the European continent, notably from
France<fn>45% of imported cheese is French.</fn>.
  <par>There has been public concern over health-related
matters, particularly after an outbreak in 1996 of food
poisoning attributed to <sci>Listeria spp.</sci> due to
labeling errors. Given the size of the market, I believe it
is vital for the company to make its presence felt <emph>as
soon as possible</emph>. We cannot risk a repeat of the
problem outlined in the recent DHA report <ref
id="dha-mca-97">Marketing Cheese Abroad</ref>.</par></sec>
```

See Figure 7 for another example (it also shows the major components of SGML). For this kind of structure to work, the computer needs to know something about the type of document being used, before it can start processing the document itself. Two other things may precede the document itself, which are not shown above:

1. the ***SGML Declaration***, if there is one. This is a file of settings to specify the parameters for this document type: among other things, what character set will be used, and whether any special features of SGML are to be switched on or off. There is a default declaration which is assumed by SGML software, and this can be used if a DTD does not require any special facilities, which is the case with this example.
   In XML there is a predefined declaration, constant for all XML files, and it cannot be varied, so it is never supplied with an XML file, but is instead built into processing software.
2. the formal definition of this type of document, one or more files making up the ***Document Type Definition*** (DTD). This is what is being referred to in the ***Document Type Declaration*** in the first line of the document, where it says '`+//Acme Cheeses Inc//DTD Report//EN`'. A DTD is compulsory for full SGML.
   XML documents don't have to have a formal DTD: their structure may be deduced from their markup. If they do have a DTD, it must be referred to by a URL or filename: the longer, more formal naming used in this example is only optional in XML.

As with so much other computer software, all this (declaration, DTD, and markup itself) is usually hidden from view by SGML editors: Figure 8 shows how the report might look on your screen. On the left it shows the markup revealed, and on the right the markup is hidden (the reason for wanting it revealed is explained in chapter 3). Note that the footnote is kept next to its point of reference, and only moved to the

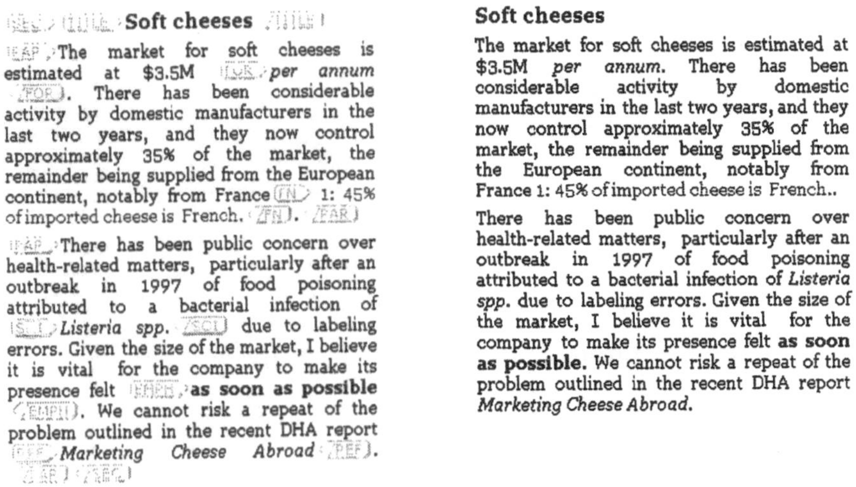

Soft cheeses

The market for soft cheeses is estimated at $3.5M *per annum*. There has been considerable activity by domestic manufacturers in the last two years, and they now control approximately 35% of the market, the remainder being supplied from the European continent, notably from France 1: 45% of imported cheese is French.

There has been public concern over health-related matters, particularly after an outbreak in 1997 of food poisoning attributed to a bacterial infection of *Listeria spp.* due to labeling errors. Given the size of the market, I believe it is vital for the company to make its presence felt **as soon as possible**. We cannot risk a repeat of the problem outlined in the recent DHA report *Marketing Cheese Abroad*.

Soft cheeses

The market for soft cheeses is estimated at $3.5M *per annum*. There has been considerable activity by domestic manufacturers in the last two years, and they now control approximately 35% of the market, the remainder being supplied from the European continent, notably from France 1: 45% of imported cheese is French..

There has been public concern over health-related matters, particularly after an outbreak in 1997 of food poisoning attributed to a bacterial infection of *Listeria spp.* due to labeling errors. Given the size of the market, I believe it is vital for the company to make its presence felt **as soon as possible**. We cannot risk a repeat of the problem outlined in the recent DHA report *Marketing Cheese Abroad*.

Figure 8. An SGML editor at work

foot of the page when printed, or when formatted on-screen. This is partly for ease of editing, and partly because an editing environment is often pageless: unless you have a fullpage screen, it's not meaningful to display the footnote in the 'right' place while you're still making changes to the text.

1.5.1.5. Structure and hierarchy

The key to making all this work is the ***Document Type Definition*** (DTD). Whether you want to enforce compliance with a particular structure or appearance, or whether you want to enable users to describe freely what they write, you need to define in a machine-readable manner how it can be done. In either case, the definition of a document type in SGML acts as a road map through the file. It says which elements of text are compulsory or to be expected in which places, and which make sense to be allowed in others.

The cheese report above is defined as a section of a report, so this design of document could be described in graphical terms as a kind of family tree (see Figure 9).

This tree structure is very useful in SGML because it shows the 'belonging' nature of one element within another. In our example, we have `<title>` and `<par>` being 'children' of `<sec>`, and `<for>`, `<fn>`, `<sci>`, `<emph>`, and `<ref>` being 'children' of `<par>`. You can see that the full definition of a report contains other elements as well, some of which can contain other elements and some of which contain just text (the 'A' and ruled-lines symbols).

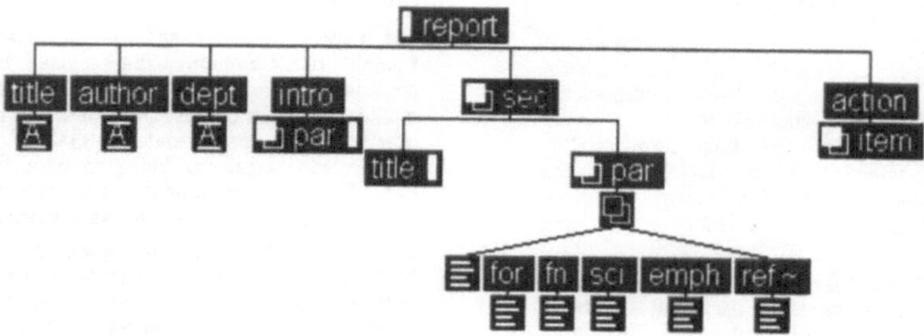

Figure 9. Graphical diagram of a document type structure

> ## Diagram notation for DTDs
>
> The graphical notation used here comes from the *Near&Far* DTD display and edit program, which is explained in more detail in section 2.6.2. I shall be using these diagrams extensively in the next chapter, but because of the shape of the printed page, and the length of the names which need fitting in, most of them are displayed with the tree-structure issuing out from the left side rather than down from the top.

A hierarchical structure like this is not compulsory: you could define a DTD which allowed almost any element of text almost anywhere in the file (some versions of HTML do exactly this, as used in many Web pages: see section 2.3.9.1), but this kind of design is usually less meaningful for reuse of the information, as there is little structure.

1.5.1.6. How DTDs work

To make a definition like this machine-readable, computers need the information in textual, rather than graphical, form. SGML is the language for doing exactly this. Here is the DTD for the part of the document called <sec> — it declares the names of the elements and what can go inside them. In practice, of course, there is much more: the document title, author, and department; the introduction and list of actions; and the illustrations, diagrams, tables, lists, and all the other elements that go to make up a report.

```
<!element sec   - - (title,par+)>
<!element title - - CDATA>
<!element par   - O ((#PCDATA)|for|sci|fn|emph|ref)*>
<!element (for|fn|sci|emph|ref) - - (#PCDATA)>
```

A DTD is a specification of what fits where, and it follows that a file which fits into this structure can be read analytically ('parsed') by a program, using the DTD as the set of rules to adhere to. This is fundamentally why an SGML file structure can be 'understood' easily by a computer and other text file formats cannot.

If you examine the DTD example above, you can see how it describes the structure. The syntax of these declarations is fairly straightforward:

- the open angle bracket followed by the exclamation mark means this is a ***markup declaration*** rather than a tag belonging to the text markup itself;
- the keyword `ELEMENT` means that this is an ***element declaration*** (there are other kinds of declaration possible);
- this is followed either by the name of a single element being declared, or a group of them being declared all at the same time (in parentheses, separated by commas);
- the hyphens and the letter 'O' (not a zero) specify that the start- and end-tags respectively are either *required* (a hyphen) or *omissible* under certain circumstances (an 'O'). This is a technique used to allow encoders to avoid clutter, and is called ***minimization*** (see below) — it is not used at all in XML, where all start-tags and end-tags are compulsory, so the hyphens and 'O's are omitted in XML DTDs;
- finally there is a ***content model***, usually in parentheses, which defines what other elements can be used within this element. This uses a notation of parentheses, vertical bars, asterisks, and other punctuation to indicate ***occurrence***: qualities like 'in this order' (separated by commas), 'one or many' (the plus sign), and 'compulsory' (otherwise unmarked).

From the example you can see:

1. there is an element called `<sec>`, which must contain one `<title>` element followed by (note the comma) one or more (note the plus sign) `<par>` elements;
2. the `<title>` element may contain only simple text ('character data' or `CDATA`): no further markup;
3. there are elements called `<for>`, `<fn>`, `<sci>`, `<emph>`, and `<ref>`, which can contain text only;
4. the `<par>` element may contain any mixture of text ('parsed character data' or `PCDATA`) and markup (foreign words, scientific terms, emphasis, footnotes, and references).

In this example, all start- and end-tags must be present on all elements, *except* for paragraphs, which may omit the end-tag `</par>`. This is an example of minimization, and the answer to the question asked in section 1.5.1.4 about what had been left out of the cheese report example. The reason for it is simple: in this DTD, a section can contain *only* paragraphs, once the `<title>` has been given: therefore starting a new paragraph *must* logically mean the previous `<par>` has finished, because only another `<par>` can occur at that point; and this can be deduced automatically and unambiguously by SGML programs from the DTD, and the DTD allows this, so the end-tag can be omitted.

This omission of the end-tag occurs in the cheese report example after the footnote. Minimization was introduced in SGML in the days when markup was typed by hand, as a way of saving effort as well as storage space. With the aid of an SGML editor to insert matching start- and end-tags for you, the effort argument has become less relevant, but in large documents, minimization can save very significant amounts of space or transmission time. There are other forms of minimization which you can read about in more detailed books on the design of DTDs such as the one by Maler and el Andaloussi[30].

1.5.1.7. The SGML Declaration

Every DTD must have an SGML Declaration, either implicit or explicit. It provides SGML software with advance notice of a number of facilities or limitations the document type designer wants or needs to use: what ranges of character codes are going to be used; how much storage space (memory) will be needed to handle SGML names, attribute values, literal strings, and other symbols and variables involved in processing; which features of SGML are turned on and which ones are turned off; whether or not case-sensitivity is in force; and many more aspects of processing.

Many DTDs come with an SGML Declaration in a file provided by the designer or author, and all you need to do is tell your SGML software the name of this file before processing starts. This can be done either in an OASIS catalog (see section 2.5.4) or in a configuration file or setup dialog, depending on the nature of your software.

The special case has already been referred to earlier: in XML the declaration is fixed in the specification, and is built into browsers, so there is no need for it to be supplied.

DTDs which do not have a separate SGML Declaration of their own (usually the smaller ones, but not always) are assumed to use the default specified in the SGML standard. In this case there is usually nothing to specify, as most software comes with this default built in (see the box).

SGML and XML default syntax

SGML defines just the *concepts* of markup and how they work: it does not specify how they should be implemented. ISO 8879 hardly mentions pointy brackets, slashes, ampersands, semicolons, and percent signs but instead uses names for them. For example a start-tag is said to begin with a Start-Tag Open character (STAGO) and end with a Tag Close character (TAGC), and you can define the actual character to be used in an SGML Declaration for each document type. However, there is a basic set of delimiters for reference purposes, known as the RDS (Reference Delimiter Set) which is used for the defaults in most DTDs, such as STAGO being the '<' sign (Goldfarb[20] p.360).

Because SGML does not enforce the use of any specific characters, it is said to use an **abstract syntax** to explain things. However, to make it possible to refer to concrete examples, the standard provides a **concrete syntax** for reference purposes, known as the RCS (Reference Concrete Syntax). This declares the base character set and some specific characters such as Record-End (RE), Record-Start (RS), Space and TAB, and defines the characters to be used in NAME tokens (see the box). It also sets case-sensitivity off for everything except entity names, and sets the remaining delimiters, names, capacities and quantities to their Reference values.

XML has a single SGML Declaration which is fixed by the Specification (part of the effort to keep things simple). It uses the RDS and the RCS modified to allow large character sets; to remove some of SGML's numeric limitations; to enable the NETSC delimiter to replace the Null End Tag trick (which makes the EMPTY syntax <foo/> possible), and to change the Processing Instruction Close to '?>'. XML uses the features of the WebSGML Adaptations (see section 2.7.1.3), so it is only usable by SGML software which recognizes them.

The only time you should need to change anything in the SGML Declaration is when a parser or validator complains that one or more of the capacities, quantities, or other parameters is too small or out of range (bear in mind that you can't change the SGML Declaration for XML: it's fixed, but the values are all set to their maximum anyway). These settings are usually set correctly by the document type designer, but different pieces of software occasionally take slightly idiosyncratic views on how the values are to be used, and different versions of a DTD may need different values:

Names, capacities, and quantities

Names are the tokens used in SGML to label things: elements, entities, attributes, and identifiers. The default length of a name is eight characters, and the default characters are the 26 letters of the Latin alphabet, 10 digits, period and hyphen. A name must start with a letter, and all lowercase letters are folded to uppercase when matching is needed.

XML, however, has no name length limit, and names can be made from any letters or digits plus the hyphen, period, underscore, and colon (the colon is experimental). Names cannot begin with a digit, and a 'letter' is defined as 'an alphabetic or syllabic base character possibly followed by one or more combining characters, or [...] an ideographic character' from ISO 10646 (Unicode). Because of this, XML is case-sensitive throughout.

Capacities are measures of storage requirements, mostly in units of characters or tokens, designed to allow programs to set up their internal storage to cope with the document type being processed. For example, an IDCAP of 2,000 would mean that no document could use more than 2,000 ID attributes: the actual maximum storage space occupied by each ID attribute is specified separately by a 'quantity' (see below). The standard sets the default for all capacities to 35,000 (even the total, which is a way of saying that a program should not care how the storage is distributed between them: see Goldfarb, p.367). XML currently sets all capacities to the maximum (99999999), meaning in effect no limits.

Quantities are mostly measures of length, in characters, of the items used in calculating capacities (Goldfarb, p.470). For example, each ID attribute value is limited to the maximum length specified by the NAMELEN quantity, which defaults to eight characters. Some quantities measure in other units, for example GRPLVL measures the maximum depth of nesting of content model groups (the parenthesized subselections of elements making up a content model). XML does not restrict quantities (as for capacities).

Put somewhat simply, names are labels, restricted to certain characters; quantities are the size limits on individual objects; and capacities are limits on how many of them there can be, or how much space they can take up in total.

- As an example of the how values are used, Open Text's *sgmlregion* markup indexer for the now defunct PAT search system complained about one SGML Declaration I used, and said that `TAGLVL` had to be 1,000 and `NAMELEN` had to be 'over 80', and that `GRPCAP` was too small at 100,000 (reasons are not available for these rather curious values: they were unrelated to the nature of the files, and were different from values used by other parsers). At the other extreme, *WordPerfect Suite* (the SGML version on the CD-ROM) reset `ATTCNT`, `LITLEN`, and `TAGLVL` to its own (lower) values during compilation of the *DocBook* DTD (see Figure 80).
- As an example of the use of different DTD versions, when I tried to compile the TEI DTD (see section 2.3.6) for use with SoftQuad's *Author/Editor* (see section 3.3.2), using Formal Public Identifiers (FPIs, the long descriptive labels for DTD and other files, see section 2.5) the *RulesBuilder* compiler complained that `The length of a name must not exceed NAMELEN (32) characters.` A quick inspection of the file mentioned in the error message showed that many of the FPIs were much longer than the 32 characters specified in the SGML Declaration I was working from, so I edited this to say `NAMELEN 64` instead of `NAMELEN 32`, and at an early opportunity I downloaded an updated version with this and other changes from the TEI Web site.

The use of a different coded character set may also mean changes to the specification of what character codes are valid for what purposes. This is usually a task for an expert in character sets, but with the approaching availability of systems using ISO 10646 or Unicode character encodings, you need to be aware that facilities for making these changes exist. The Reference Concrete Syntax limits the expression of coded character values to eight digits in any SGML Declaration, which gives a maximum of 99,999,999 — nowhere near big enough to handle the vastness of ISO 10646. The WebSGML Adaptations for ISO 8879 (see section 2.7.1.3) raise this, and other, limits for XML with the value `NOLIMITS`, but the value of 99999999 is still used while older software remains in use.

Writing SGML Declarations is normally a job for a document type designer, but there is an excellent paper on how to use and understand the internals of the Declaration, published by Omnimark on their Web site, and included by permission on the CD-ROM, in `sgml/doc/sgmldecl.html`.

1.5.2. Why you should consider SGML or XML

SGML and XML systems provide a valuable alternative to regular word processor or DTP formats for managing and storing your textual data. Although HTML was defined using SGML, the way it has been implemented in browsers makes it difficult to rely on them to handle HTML files in a predictable or controllable manner, even though the more advanced versions of HTML provide many useful facilities. SGML properly applied (and thus XML) is much more rigorous and offers far greater stability.

Most of the reasons below are just plain business common-sense. But they involve a change in the way we think about text: it's not just for print any more. We need to start regarding it as a source of information about what we are doing, a business resource which can be used and reused, and which has quantifiable value for the organization.

Remove some of the risk of mistakes Although it is familiar, the visual markup of italics-and-bold is limited and confusing when you start to apply it to anything non-trivial, because two or three font variations can be used for dozens of different or conflicting meanings. Punctuation can help the markup, but it has to be picked with care to avoid ambiguity. Mistakes caused by omissions or additions, but particularly in meanings, can be costly: *by using some type of formal control over how your text is handled you can remove a part of the risk.*

Cut out unnecessary duplication Keeping multiple parallel versions of documents is a waste of time, space, and effort, especially when the only differences are in the formatting or the layout. *Keeping a single master source from which you can generate different versions is much more cost-effective.*

Cut out unnecessary conversion Maintaining multiple sequential versions is just as bad, especially when the changes are only to the file format, not the content, and are dictated by someone else. If you have to convert all 200,000 corporate documents in your database every time your word processor manufacturer brings out a new version, it's worth considering *keeping your master version in a single format which does not need to change over time* (that is, the contents can change as much as you like, but the type of file never needs to).

Work your text harder Instead of using visual representations alone for all the different types of information, you can use computer logic to identify each type separately within the document — but still have them printed or displayed the way you want them for the reader. In effect, you can separate the visual form of the text from its logical function, so that it prints and displays the same as before, but *your documents can be put to work in other ways that were impossible before*. Think of the number of times you've searched a database for a word or phrase you thought would be close to unique, only to find it used in hundreds of ways you never imagined. Now imagine being able to disambiguate them all, and zero in on the one you want, just by using markup. (If only searching the Web could use this method!)

Make better use of your technology base Having to convert files from one format to another repeatedly can be an error-prone and unproductive task, and is only 100% effective on very simple material (test: convert a report, then convert it straight back again. Now print it and compare with the original). Using a robust and reliable means of document interchange means that *information is available with zero loss regardless of the make or model of computer or software*.

Protect your operation from the future Software and hardware comes and goes. The dominant suppliers today could be the lame ducks of tomorrow, and new inventions can sweep away years of work overnight. *An independent, external format for your information is not at the mercy of arbitrary changes in technology or its suppliers and frees you from dependence on someone else's decisions*.

For more information on the business case for SGML, see Liora Alschuler's book *ABCD...SGML*[3] and Chet Ensign's *The Billion-Dollar Secret*[18].

1.5.3. Dispelling some of the myths about SGML

Computer systems seem to attract anecdotes about their abilities and shortcomings and about the people who use them. Most myths are based on misunderstandings, particularly when people only see the product from the outside and never actually explore what it can do. This is especially true of programming or specification languages: even though they can be applied to all kinds of tasks, they are open to misinterpretation because the end user may be exposed only to a part of the system.

A metalanguage like SGML or XML is in this category: it is capable of application in many different fields, but there is more chance of misunderstandings creeping in when only a little of the technology

Some thoughts on proprietary markup

This answer was posted to the Usenet newsgroup `comp.text.sgml` in June 1993 by Eliot Kimber.

```
>>I have received a request from another individual that I work
>>with about SGML. Although I support the use of SGML (they want
>>to compare its use with MML from Framemaker) I by no means can
>>explain its benefits over a proprietary markup language...

Ask this person if they would mind if when they bought a car:

  * they could only get gasoline and service from the car maker;
  * if they could only drive it on roads provided by the car
    maker;
  * and it could only be driven by people who had been trained
    to drive that particular make and model of car.

That's what you sign up for when you tie yourself to a
proprietary data format.

The mistake people make is that they think what they are
creating when they create documents with computers is *printed
pages*, when in fact they are creating *databases of information*.
You can test this by comparing the cost of losing the printed
pages with the cost of losing the source files from which they
were generated.

As Tim Bray pointed out at SGML'92, no MIS manager would in his
right mind consider using a proprietary data format for
relational information.  So it should be for textual
information.
```

is exposed to view. Business users whose sole application is for text databases think of SGML as a database language; scholars who only use it for maintaining the structure of linguistic corpora think of it as a concordance tool; clerical staff who use SGML editors to produce letters and reports think of it as a word processor; Internet users whose sole exposure is to HTML think that all SGML is HTML.

It's a bit like the user who called me once to complain about her *WordPerfect*, and it took me a while to realize that *this was what she called her computer*: she was actually using *Word* but didn't know that, and had always referred to 'switching on the *WordPerfect*' and 'my *WordPerfect* is broken', unaware that it could be used for anything else. While this is an extreme case, the problem is largely due to poor training or bad documentation. I am aware that many organizations work on the fashionable basis that you should only give people exactly the information they need to do the job and no more, especially in training courses: I also believe this approach to be entirely wrong.

The myths I list here are commonplace in articles and messages posted to Usenet newsgroups and mailing lists, and as questions raised at seminars and conferences. While they don't exactly constitute Frequently Asked Questions in their own right, there is no denying that they crop up with considerable regularity. They are also frighteningly common in newspaper and magazine articles, sometimes from very reputable journalists who have obviously been badly misled. For almost any FAQ (Frequently Asked Question) about the use and operation of SGML you will find an answer in Steve DeRose's *SGML FAQ Book*[16]: the ones here are Urban Myths *par excellence*.

Despite the very significant role played by HTML — however unevenly — in bringing SGML awareness to the front of people's minds, there is still a long way to go. I hope the following explanations will prove useful in nailing down rumor when it threatens to become destructive.

SGML is a 'word processor or DTP system from . . . There is a popular view that SGML is program: a product, a binary executable which can be bought.

SGML is an international standard, ISO 8879 — a large printed document. There are lots of software products which use SGML, but SGML itself is not a program: it's a syntax for writing descriptions of document types which can be used by programs.

SGML's rapid development in publishing and printing has perhaps to some extent accidentally led to this confusion of standard and product.

XML 'is a Microsoft product' Several articles make this claim, which only serve to demonstrate (if it were needed) that writers cannot afford to rely on hearsay or the 'expertise' of people who are no experts at all. Microsoft, as a member of the World Wide Web Consortium, is an active participant in the development of XML, but has never claimed to own it.

SGML can be 'downloaded from the Internet' This raises a vexed question concerning how the average user can obtain a copy of the

SGML standards document itself. This is copyright of the ISO (International Organization for Standardization), and ISO standards have to be bought from your national standards body or ordered through a bookstore or a library.

This approach is understandable in the case of rare and exotic standards sought only by a handful of gurus and funded by large organizations, but is more difficult to justify in the case of something now so widespread as SGML, and there is a case to be made for the document to be made even more accessible than the standard text which contains a full copy of ISO 8879, Charles Goldfarb's *SGML Handbook*[20].

The ISO is, however, constrained by the rules of the international agreement between governments which founded the organization, so changing these rules is a matter for your Public Representatives. Ask them next time you have an election.

SGML is 'too difficult' It's a language, and like any other language, human or computer, it needs to be learned. In general it's not the level of difficulty that puts people off, it's the effort of having to think differently. When you have spent your life looking at the arrangement of words and types simply in order to read them, it's hard to start thinking about *why* they're set out as they are.

It's then another step beyond that to think about how you could use the information more efficiently and effectively if the ambiguities left behind by the appearance could be cleared up. SGML is another way of looking at the same tasks you've always done, but it's a *different* way.

As an International Standard, SGML is written in a very formal, precise language, designed specifically to describe exactly what is meant and nothing else. Trying to learn it from the standards document alone is not recommended: see the Bibliography for details of books *about* SGML.

SGML is 'a programming language' If you show someone a raw plain-text SGML file, and they've never seen anything like it before, this is going to be a common conclusion. In many DTDs, element names are the same as (or close to) the name for their assumed or desired effect in some kind of output, so it is understandable to assume cause and effect even where none may exist. For example, everyone knows what a 'list' and an 'item' are, and have assumptions about what they look like.

It's also inescapable that a lot of SGML work *is* based — for good reasons — on naming elements after this kind of cause and effect (such as calling the element which holds the name of a section of text a <HEAD> instead of a <TITLE>: the former presupposes a type of visualization which the latter does not).

But SGML still isn't a programming language, and this sometimes needs to be explained carefully to people who want to know how to add 2+2 in SGML, or want to know what SGML's GOTO statement is (having said which, it would even be possible to use SGML syntax for a programming language, rather like XSL [see section 2.4.3]). One of the reasons computer scientists are not taught anything about SGML is precisely because it is *not* a programming language: it's a markup language, and computer science students are not taught about markup.

SGML is 'inflexible' This is a common misunderstanding by users who have been exposed to only one SGML application and don't know that others exist. In fact SGML is mind-bendingly flexible, as anyone who follows `comp.text.sgml` can testify: it's being used for an enormous range of tasks.

But it does have its limitations: it isn't a word processor, or a DTP system, or a database program; and there are some data storage constructs which are difficult or impossible to describe in SGML. Like any carefully-designed system, it needs to be used for what was intended.

SGML is 'too expensive' It doesn't have to be. A large number of the tools presented in this book are completely free, and some are available at very low prices. Many of them are even more reliable and better-supported than some commercial programs.

If you want the latest and glossiest system with all the smartest bells and whistles, however, it will probably not be free: it is undeniable that some SGML software costs an arm and a leg. In defense of this it must be said that formal programming for SGML systems is very complex, and costs large amounts of time and money, and that there are companies (and government departments and agencies, including armies, navies, and air forces) out there with enough money to pay for it. On the other hand, there is less justification for high prices as XML starts to move SGML out of niche markets, and competition and economies of scale bring costs and prices down.

As more and more software authors build SGML capabilities into their products, it may cease to be a case of buying 'an SGML editor' or 'an SGML database'. Instead, you'll buy whatever editor or database you want, and SGML will be one of the possible ways (perhaps the only way) of working.

'There aren't any WYSIWYG interfaces' to SGML There are in fact many of them, some of which are discussed in this book. Some people who are shown the plaintext internals of an SGML file leap to an entirely wrong conclusion that that is the only way of viewing it. 'What You See Is What You Get' is in any event a very misleading phrase, as almost no word processors or DTP systems provide it, unless you have a paper-white monitor with the same resolution as your printer: 'What You See Is A Rough Approximation To What You'll Get If You're Lucky' is nearer the mark. And as we saw in section 1.5.1.3, doing things just for appearances' sake, without a reason, is rarely meaningful.

SGML (or XML) 'predefines the tag names' (Also known as 'HTML is a subset of SGML'.) This is a very common misunderstanding, particularly for people who have only ever seen one type of SGML document (HTML for example). It is also a popular misnomer to refer to elements as tags.

SGML and XML are in fact exactly the opposite of this myth: they don't define any names of any elements at all. They are languages to let you define your *own* names for elements. SGML was used to predefine everything in HTML, so HTML is an SGML application, not a subset.

The aspect most open to misunderstanding is the Document Type Definition (DTD): you *do* have to use one with regular SGML (the WebSGML Adaptations to ISO 8879 make it optional with XML). With regular SGML you cannot just invent element names and put them in a file with some text and call the result 'SGML'. With XML, however, you can do almost exactly that, without a DTD, provided you stick to the simple rules about the structure.

SGML is 'a US military word processor' This is a surprisingly common misapprehension, both inside and outside the USA, even by quite reputable writers. SGML grew out of earlier work within IBM on markup languages, and was eventually put together as an International Standard under the editorship of Charles Goldfarb. SGML is not a word processor and has no military leanings, inherent or otherwise: if anyone is in doubt they have only to buy a copy of the standard or read Goldfarb's book[20].

What *is* true is that the USA's defense forces (and those of various other countries) decided it was a useful technology they could use to standardize documentation formats and speed training (one application cut training time on an engine by three weeks). Once CALS (see section 2.3.5) became a reality, suppliers of equipment and services to the US and other armed forces were prepared to spend money to have software written to enable them to use it, so some of today's regular commercial SGML software did get its first outing on military applications.

1.5.4. Where to get more information

There are many places you can go for help and advice on SGML:

- Books and technical documentation
- Computer networks
- Conferences and meetings
- Training organizations and consultancies
- Existing users (word of mouth)
- SGML advocacy groups
- SGML User Groups

With the exception of existing users, some of whom may be known to you, these all tend to cost money. The cheapest is probably the Internet, even in countries with high call charges or access rates, but you need to be able to sort the information into a form that is immediately applicable to you.

Books and technical documentation The Bibliography at the end of this book lists those books and documents that I have referred to, and it is followed by a short list of other SGML books I have found useful in several areas.
There is a very extensive SGML Bibliography maintained at `http://www.sil.org/sgml/biblio.html` by Robin Cover as part of the SGML Web pages (see below). While no bibliography can ever be 100% complete, this does seem to cover all the articles, books, and reports of any significance. If you come across an item that isn't listed, you should consider submitting it for inclusion.

Computer networks As mentioned elsewhere, the principal forum for online discussions is the Usenet newsgroup `comp.text.sgml`. Ask your Internet Service Provider (ISP) to tell you how to access it. Usenet newsgroups work over many networks, not just the Internet.
There are also many mailing lists on specific SGML topics: see the list in Appendix B and the Web pages mentioned below.

There are many sites on the Web with SGML information, but the most comprehensive by far is run by Robin Cover at the Summer Institute for Linguistics. This should be your first stop for anything you are searching for in the SGML field (`http://www.sil.org/sgml/sgml.html`). Many organizations involved with SGML also carry information about SGML on their Web sites: one of the major players is OASIS (Organization for the Advancement of Structured Information) (`http://www.oasis-open.org/`).

Both SGML and XML have their 'FAQ' documents: lists of Frequently-Asked Questions, which are intended to avoid the overuse of time and space occasioned by every newcomer having to ask the same questions in newsgroups and mailing lists. The SGML FAQ is posted at regular intervals to `comp.text.sgml` and is indexed at `http://www.sil.org/sgml/general.html#faq`. The XML FAQ is at `http://www.ucc.ie/xml/`.

Conferences and meetings The Graphics Communications Association (GCA) currently runs the annual SGML/XML conferences for Europe, Asia/Pacific, and the USA, in that order each year. These are commercial conferences and are priced accordingly. Details are on the GCA's Web site (`http://www.gca.org/`).

Many other SGML-related projects and organizations around the world also hold annual or more frequent meetings, such as the HyTime Conference, for users of ISO 10744; the Seybold publishing conferences and seminars; Documation, for those in the technical documentation field; CALS Expo, for military applications; the XML Developers' Days; HL7 for SGML in the Healthcare field; and many more. Details of these are often posted to `comp.text.sgml` and are available on the SGML Web pages already mentioned (`http://www.sil.org/sgml/conf.html`).

Training organizations and consultancies Organizations running training courses, either publicly or in-house on your premises, often announce their schedules in `comp.text.sgml`, and many of them have Web sites where more detail can be found.

Consultancies range from the individual operating alone to the largest management consultancy companies. These are *not* listed in the SGML Web pages, but are more frequently found at SGML conferences.

Existing users Existing users are best located via the user groups or through software suppliers. Many users have strong feelings about furthering the use of SGML, and are happy to offer help and advice.

SGML advocacy groups The best known are OASIS ('Organization for the Advancement of Structured Information Standards', formerly SGML Open) and the GCA (Graphic Communications Association): there is a list of many others in the SGML Web pages at `http://www.sil.org/sgml/groups.html`.

OASIS (`http://www.oasis-open.org/`) was started in 1993 as the SGML Open organization, a 'non-profit, international consortium of product and service providers dedicated to the application and implementation of SGML'. As the principal trade association, OASIS has been particularly active in producing technical recommendations and white papers on many aspects of SGML.

The Graphic Communications Association (`http://www.gca.org`) was formed in 1966 to 'apply computer technology to printing, publishing, and related industries'. They currently run the annual SGML/XML conferences.

SGML User Groups The International SGML Users Group (ISUG) was founded in 1984 and exists 'to promote the use of the Standard Generalized Markup Language and to provide a forum for exchange of information about SGML' (see section B.4).

2. What type of document?

> Up early and...to the Privy Seale and got my bill perfected there, and at the Signet: and then...to Mr Beale to get my patent engrossed,...but I could find none that could write the [Chancery] hand...To Mr Spong, whom I found in his night-gown writing of my patent...Mr Kipps got me the Chancellor's recepi to my bill; and so carried it to Mr Beale for a dockett; but he was very angry, and unwilling to do it, because he said it was ill-writ (because I had got it writ by another hand, and not by him); but by much importunity I got [him to] make an end of my patent; and in the mean time Mr Beale to be preparing my dockett, which being done, I did give him two pieces, after which it was strange how civil...he was to me.
>
> Samuel Pepys, *Diary*, 12–13 July 1660

- **How to describe the different types of documents**
- **Understanding Document Type Definitions**
- **What DTDs are available in public**
- **XML: the Extensible Markup Language**
- **Identifying the DTD**
- **Writing and modifying DTDs**
- **An update on the status of SGML**

Bureaucracy in the 17th century was not dissimilar to that of our own time, as anyone who has stood in line for official documents can attest. Everywhere we turn we find text of all descriptions, and yet we pay scant attention to how we pigeonhole our documents unless we have a passion for filing: the average desk or hard disk has letters jumbled in with reports, expense claims with the minutes of the weekly project meetings, sports club membership lists with memos from management.

The life of a document is usually assumed to start with its creation — in an editor or word processor, from a database, as scribbles on an envelope. But before we put pen to paper or finger to keyboard, we usually have an idea in our head of what type of document it will be. No novelist sits down to write a novel by typing text in the form of a business report (unless it's about murder in the company, perhaps). I certainly don't start writing a technical manual by deciding on a plot, a cast list, and some character development plans (maybe I should try it one day).

We almost always know in advance that we are going to write a letter, a memo, a report, a manual, a novel, a poem, a play, a sermon, an article, a manifesto, a shopping list, or whatever. Each of these types of document has a different structure, and requires different facilities (although there is obviously a lot of overlap).

SGML follows the same path: before you can start writing you need to decide what type of document you are going to write. The same holds true if you are generating an SGML file from another source, or piecing one together from the contributions of others, or preparing an existing file for another use, such as printing.

SGML itself does not force any particular structure on you, but restrictions may be imposed on you by those who control a particular type of document, such as your company, your publisher, your professor, or your political leader. A document type, as we saw in the previous chapter, can be either ***prescriptive***, ensuring that you put the right items in the right places; or it can be ***descriptive***, allowing you to describe how a document is currently structured or how it appears; or it can be somewhere between the two: they are not mutually exclusive, and they are not absolutes. And if you can't find an existing SGML document type to suit your purpose, you can always create your own.

This chapter is about the most important SGML tool of all: the Document Type Definition.

2.1. Describing the type of document

A complete SGML document is made up of three components: the ***SGML Declaration***, the ***Document Type Definition*** (DTD), and the ***Document Instance*** (the formal term for your SGML file). These are usually three separate files, but they could be combined in one or two. The SGML Declaration and DTD together make up the ***prolog***.

In most cases your SGML instance is a separate file, so processing programs need to be able to identify the following pieces of information one after another in order to handle it:

1. what type of document it is (the name of the outermost element);

Declaration vs Definition

There is a clear distinction between these terms in SGML, although they can be a little confusing to start with as they appear so similar:

- The Document Type *Declaration* is a line or few at the beginning of an SGML instance (your SGML file), *declaring* what type of document it is: it looks something like this:

```
<!DOCTYPE HTML PUBLIC "-//IETF//DTD HTML 2.0//EN">
```

- The Document Type *Definition* (DTD) is usually in one or more external files, and *defines* what elements belong in this document type.

The waters are muddied by the fact that the Document Type *Definition* (DTD) is made up of 'declarations' — the individual statements declaring what elements may exist and how they fit together to make a definition.

The crucial difference in terminology is that only the Document Type *Definition* is represented by the acronym 'DTD'. For the Document Type *Declaration* I have used the abbreviation 'DocType Declaration' throughout.

2. what Document Type Definition (DTD) it adheres to;
3. where to find the files containing the SGML Declaration, the DTD and any ancillary files.

To do all this, SGML uses a ***Document Type Declaration***. This is compulsory, and goes at the top of your instance, before the first element begins. It states the name of this first element, and the title or name of the Document Type Definition that it belongs to. There can be other things in there as well, but we'll come to them later. The rules for XML files differ slightly (see section 2.4): you can omit the Document Type Declaration and thus dispense with a DTD altogether if you wish.

If you have examined an SGML file with a plaintext editor (or by printing it out), you will probably have seen a line or two at the top looking something like this:

```
<!DOCTYPE article PUBLIC "+//Silmaril//DTD Article v3//EN"
 "article.dtd">
```

This is a DocType Declaration (see the box), and this example shows the formal way of telling the user or their program what type of document to expect. You can see the following features, each separated by a space:

- the Markup Declaration Open symbol ('<!') with the keyword 'DOCTYPE';
- the name of the Document Type ('article'), which will also be the name of the first (outermost) markup element of the document: <article>;
- the keyword 'PUBLIC', meaning 'here follows a Formal Public Identifier for this Document Type';
- the Formal Public Identifier (FPI) itself, in quotes (more in section 2.5 about FPIs);
- an optional System Identifier (SI), also in quotes (more about them later, too);
- the Markup Declaration Close symbol ('>').

If you don't have, don't know, or can't find a Formal Public Identifier for the DTD you plan to use, you can make up one of your own, following the rules in section 2.5, or (easier but less portable) you can just use a System Identifier:

```
<!DOCTYPE article SYSTEM "article.dtd">
```

In this case, you need to make sure you give people a copy of the file `article.dtd` along with a copy of your document, if you want them to be able to use it. The danger of using an SI (System Identifier) which is a simple filename is that many other authors or publishers will have similarly-named files for similar types of document which are not actually the same (many publishers or printers may have access to a dozen or more files called `article.dtd`, each one different from the rest).

The danger of using local pathnames in addition to the filename (*eg* `Hard Disk:Documents:SGML:DTDs:article`) is that they are not portable between different systems. You can avoid both these problems by using an FPI (Formal Public Identifier), or if your audience can be assumed to have an Internet connection, by using a URL (Universal Resource Locator), which is a World Wide Web address (in XML this is compulsory: see the box):

```
<!DOCTYPE article SYSTEM "http://www.foo.org/dtds/article.dtd">
```

It is conventional to store the DTD for each application in a separate file from your actual text document files, because this makes it easier to manage the DTD for editing and maintenance. Such DTDs are said to be 'external' because they are kept outside the text files that use them.

XML and the DocType Declaration

In an XML DocType Declaration it is compulsory to provide a URL as the System Identifier, either alone or following an optional FPI. I strongly recommend using both, to maximize the chances of your readers being able to locate the right DTD.

(Strictly speaking, it's a URI, not a URL, but for the moment URL will do. If you know the difference, you'll understand why: if not, you probably don't need to right now, but you can read all about it in RFC 1738 and RFC 1808 on the CD-ROM.)

XML requires the keywords `DOCTYPE`, `PUBLIC`, and `SYSTEM` to be in CAPITALS. In regular SGML it varies: you can specify in the SGML Declaration for each DTD whether uppercase or mixed case is allowed for an application, but traditionally most regular SGML DTDs allow any mix of capitals and lowercase.

Large DTDs may be split into many files so that they can be maintained more easily, and so that you don't have to use all of them all the time.

But it is also possible to store all or part of a DTD inside a file that uses it, in the DocType Declaration, and this is often done for temporary modifications, so that one subset of the DTD is stored externally in a separate file, and another subset is stored internally in the document. These locations are referred to as the ***External Subset*** and ***Internal Subset*** respectively.

2.1.1. The DocType Declaration Internal Subset

The DocType Declaration can therefore contain an Internal Subset, which is usually additional markup affecting the DTD but it could be the whole DTD. It is enclosed in square brackets, after the document type name and identifiers, but before the closing '>' of the declaration. This is the conventional way to make local modifications to a DTD on a per-document basis, for example:

```
<?xml version="1.0"?>
<!DOCTYPE pressrel SYSTEM "http://www.megabuck.shop/dtds/press.dtd" [
<!ENTITY icbm "Intercontinental Brotherhood of Manipulators">
]>
```

Here, an in-house DTD for a Press release has had a ***General Entity*** added to it, so that the author can type `&icbm;` as an abbreviation (or pick it from a menu) and have it expand to the full meaning when journalists display the file in their browsers. Entities are discussed in more detail in section 2.2.1.1, and have many uses, but this is an example of one used as a simple method of avoiding misspellings in long names or phrases (it also saves a little on storage or transmission if the phrase is used frequently in a document). The advantage of using the internal subset is that you can add this kind of declaration any time you want, without having to modify or even have access to the master copy of the DTD.

Another common use for the Internal Subset employs a different kind of entity to allow different parts of DTD to be changed to suit circumstances without affecting other parts. DTDs have to be designed in 'modules' to be used this way: you can't do it with all of them. Inside such DTDs the modules are controlled by the use of ***parameters***, which are like 'activate' and 'deactivate' switches, used to let you include some things and exclude others. This style of DTD design lets you customize within certain limits, by inserting or omitting files, and by setting parameters to ignore or include parts of the DTD to suit your needs. Here, a general-purpose 'letter' document type is declared, used in an English-language version (the EN at the end of the Formal Public Identifier):

```
<!DOCTYPE letter PUBLIC "+//Acme//DTD General Letter//EN" [
<!ENTITY % english.names "IGNORE">
<!ENTITY % techlet PUBLIC "-//Acme Research France//ELEMENTS
  Conseiller Technique//FR">
%techlet;
]>
<lettre><sal>Cher M. Dupr&eacute;</sal><sujet>Le M&eacute;tro ...
```

However, as this letter is being written by the company's Paris office, they use a ***Parameter Entity*** as a switch, set to ignore the English-language element names, and then immediately include an external ***File Entity*** containing changes or additions relevant for their work as technical consultants, and renaming the elements into French. The file entity declaration gives it a name and a Formal Public Identifier, and it is then referenced (`%techlet;`) which causes its contents to be read and acted on. There are some worked examples of more detailed modifications like this in section 2.6.1.

A parameter entity is identified by the percent sign in its declaration, and is used here because it has to be activated and used *right there and then, in the DTD*. The earlier example of a general entity (no percent sign) applies when you are declaring the entity for use *in the instance*.

```
<?xml version="1.0"?>
<!DOCTYPE shoppinglist [
  <!ELEMENT shoppinglist (item)+>
  <!ELEMENT item (#pcdata)>
]>
<shoppinglist>
  <item>Butter</item>
  <item>Sugar</item>
  <item>Chocolate<items>
  <item>Evaporated milk</item>
</shoppinglist>
```

Figure 10. DTD defined in the internal subset

It's also possible to declare an entire (but usually small) DTD in the internal subset. Figure 10 shows a simple XML DTD for a shopping list and an instance immediately following it. An FPI could be used, purely for identification, but a System Identifier would not meaningful, as there is no file name to point at: the DTD is defined right there.

DocType Declarations in a graphical editor

If you are using a graphical system (Windows 95, Mac, X Windows), what appears on the screen is just a typographic *interpretation* of the document for the convenience of editing: the DocType Declaration along with all the markup is usually held in an internal format which you never get to see, just as with a word processor (although you may be able to reveal it for inspection).

Most editing systems insert or maintain the DocType Declaration at the top of the file for you automatically when you export or save a document in the conventional plaintext format used for storage, transmission, or use in other systems.

2.2. Understanding Document Type Definitions

In the next section, and elsewhere in the book, I am going to be using a diagrammatic method of representing a Document Type Definition.

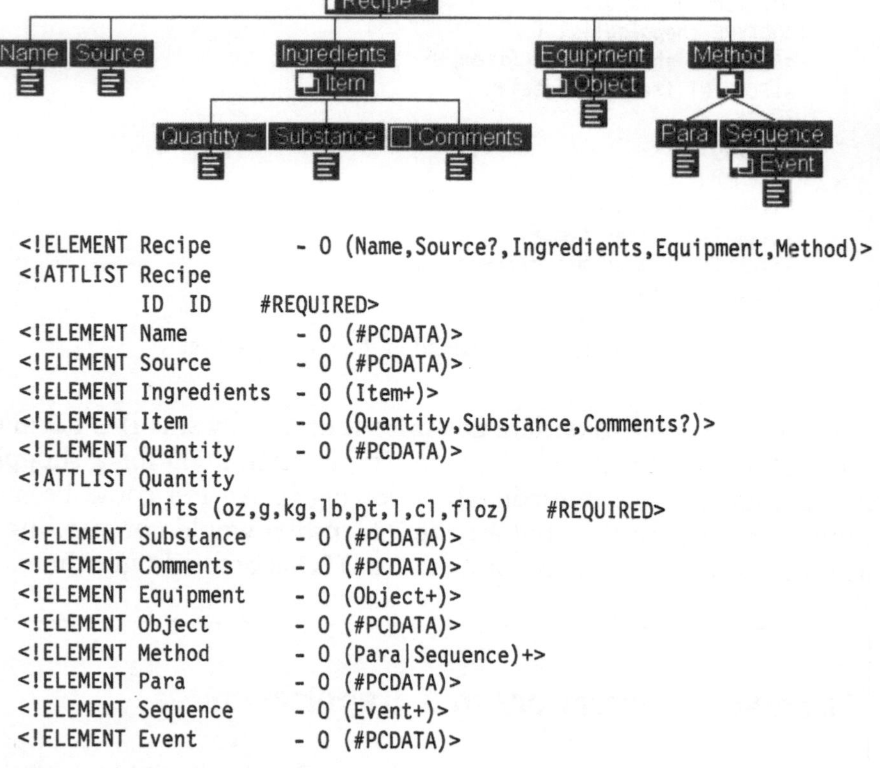


```
<!ELEMENT Recipe       - O (Name,Source?,Ingredients,Equipment,Method)>
<!ATTLIST Recipe
          ID  ID    #REQUIRED>
<!ELEMENT Name         - O (#PCDATA)>
<!ELEMENT Source       - O (#PCDATA)>
<!ELEMENT Ingredients  - O (Item+)>
<!ELEMENT Item         - O (Quantity,Substance,Comments?)>
<!ELEMENT Quantity     - O (#PCDATA)>
<!ATTLIST Quantity
          Units (oz,g,kg,lb,pt,l,cl,floz)   #REQUIRED>
<!ELEMENT Substance    - O (#PCDATA)>
<!ELEMENT Comments     - O (#PCDATA)>
<!ELEMENT Equipment    - O (Object+)>
<!ELEMENT Object       - O (#PCDATA)>
<!ELEMENT Method       - O (Para|Sequence)+>
<!ELEMENT Para         - O (#PCDATA)>
<!ELEMENT Sequence     - O (Event+)>
<!ELEMENT Event        - O (#PCDATA)>
```

Figure 11. Example DTD structure: a recipe in graphical and DTD code form

It's a lot easier to grasp the structure of a DTD from a diagram, but the drawback is that due to the limitations of the size of the page, it cannot show all the features at once (except for very small examples), so sometimes two or three diagrams are needed.

The diagram structure is called CADE (Computer Aided Document Engineering), implemented in Microstar's *Near&Far Designer*, a DTD design tool whose technology also powers Corel's *DTD Viewer*. In these diagrams there are a few symbols used in icon form (see Figure 12), which you should familiarize yourself with before going any deeper into this section.

As an example, let's look at a small Document Type Definition for a recipe, such as you might find in a cookery book. Figure 11 gives a diagrammatic view of the structure of a recipe. We're going to follow the structure from the diagram to the actual DTD code through to a real-life recipe by looking at it in non-graphical form so you can see what's happening. Although it's perfectly possible to use SGML without knowing how it works, it will make you far more productive if

Symbol	Meaning
[illegible]	An element declaration
[illegible]	An entity declaration
[illegible]	The expansion of this element is already shown elsewhere in the diagram
[illegible]	There are attributes declared for this element
[illegible]	One and only one occurrence (the element is compulsory)
[illegible]	Optional: zero or one occurrences
[illegible]	At least one occurrence, maybe more
[illegible]	Optional: zero or more occurrences
[illegible]	Bracketed elements must occur in the order given
[illegible]	Bracketed elements may occur in any order
[illegible]	Only one of the elements shown may be used
[illegible]	Inclusion exception (allow these elements in this content model)
[illegible]	Exclusion exception (forbid these elements in this content model)
[illegible]	Parsed Character Data (PCDATA): text which may potentially contain markup and entity references
[illegible]	Replaceable Character Data (RCDATA): text with no markup, but entity references allowed
[illegible]	Character Data (CDATA): just plain text, no markup or entity references
[illegible]	Any text or markup
[illegible]	Empty: no data allowed

Figure 12. Symbols used in CADE notation for DTD diagrams in this book

you understand a little of what's going on. In particular, although it is easy to use XML with no DTD, any document type which is going to be used on more than a few occasions is rapidly going to get out of hand if there is no DTD to guide the author.

Follow the 'family tree' structure in Figure 11. Each subelement must occur in order from left to right (that's the meaning of the horizontal and vertical lines) except when you get to the method, where angled lines mean a choice. The items of information are thus:

- a name for the recipe;

- a source, the place that the author got the recipe from (*optional*: that's the open square in the diagram);
- a list of ingredients composed of items (*at least one*: that's the meaning of the overlapping filled and empty squares symbol), where each item must contain the quantity and the substance, plus an optional comment;
- a list of equipment composed of at least one object;
- a cooking method composed of a mix of descriptive paragraphs and sequences of at least one event each.

Ultimately, each of the elements at the bottom of each 'line of descent' of the diagram ends up containing text data (the square symbol containing horizontal lines). Note that in some later diagrams, the tree structure is shown horizontally, with the 'root' element on the left-hand side, because of the limitations of the shape of a page when there are many long names to fit in.

Two of the elements have compulsory ***attributes*** (their presence, but not their exact nature, is shown in the diagram by the swung dash [~] symbol): in fact each `<recipe>` must have an `id` attribute (used by processing systems for cross-referencing) and each `<quantity>` must specify `units`. The whole structure is represented in the actual Document Type Definition file by the declarations shown in Figure 11.

The visual alignment of these declarations is only for ease of human reading and has no effect on the DTD itself. Each element is declared in the same manner:

- the element is named;
- the name is followed by two 'minimization' parameters: symbols which represent the start-tag and the end-tag. A hyphen means the tag must be present and a letter O means the tag can be omitted in certain circumstances (see section 2.2.1.2). These would not be used in an XML version, as minimization is not allowed in XML, so the `<Comments>` element would be declared just as `<!ELEMENT Comments (#PCDATA)>`.
- the possible content of the element is given by a 'content model' in parentheses, a list of the other elements which are required or permitted, or the type of textual content (or both: see the box);

The capitalization in this example is for neatness and convenience, as most regular SGML systems are caseless where element and attribute names are concerned. XML, however, is case-sensitive, so not only must the declaration keywords be in upper-case letters, but the capitalization of element and attribute names predefines how they must be used in the document instance, so if you say `<!ELEMENT Event (#PCDATA)>` , you must then use `<Event>...</Event>` and not suddenly switch to

<event>...</event> unless you have also declared a lowercase element by that name.

A suitable SGML Declaration would be needed for this example, because some of the element names exceed the default eight characters. As this is the only change, it simply means taking a copy of the default declaration and changing NAMELEN to (say) 12. Armed with these files, an SGML editor can handle all the markup needed to encode recipes. Figure 13 shows how one specific recipe would look when encoded in this DTD.

Notice how in this recipe, the elements have been indented for human visual clarity while editing: this is done automatically by the editor I used (*Emacs* with *psgml*), but it is not a requirement, and white-space inserted in ***element content*** (between elements) like this is *not* significant and is ignored by processors. White-space in ***mixed content*** (character data and markup intermingled inside paragraphs, *etc*) *is* significant and is always retained. See sections page 63 and page 139 for an explanation in more detail.

Most graphical editors in windowing systems therefore omit any extra white-space between elements because it's not relevant for displaying the file in a typographical manner, where all the spacing and positioning is controlled by a stylesheet. Figure 14 shows how the file might look in one such editor.

A stylesheet can also control the addition of extra text or symbols generated by an editor or other processor based on the position of the elements or the values of attributes. See if you can work out from Figures page 54 and page 55 what is being added here (hint: think of HTML lists and how they work).

If the recipe(s) are to be typeset for display on the screen or printing in a book, the formatting system therefore needs to be given a stylesheet, specifying typesetting instructions for each element to show the style and size of type, the position relative to adjacent elements, and so on (see Figure 15). In some cases the stylesheet used by an SGML editor can also be used by a typesetter, but this is an area of poor standardization, so it is common for editing stylesheets to provide a general guide to appearance, and a more sophisticated stylesheet to be used for printing.

One of the advantages of SGML is that it can separate the appearance of the document from the actual content of the file, so the style used for editing does not in fact even have to be the style used for printing or display. This means a style can be set up to make the editing very easy and ergonomic, and typeset the document quite differently. Anyone who has had to use a WYSIWYG system to edit a document which is

```
<!DOCTYPE recipe PUBLIC "+//Silmaril//DTD Recipes//EN"
  "http://www.cook.book/dtds/recipe.dtd">
<recipe id="a1">
  <name>Chocolate Fudge</name>
  <source>A very easy recipe of my mother's</source>
  <ingredients>
    <item><quantity units="lb">1</quantity>
      <substance>Sugar</substance></item>
    <item><quantity units="oz">4</quantity>
      <substance>Butter</substance></item>
    <item><quantity units="oz">4</quantity>
      <substance>Chocolate</substance>
      <comments>Only use plain chocolate with a high cocoa
content, never milk or white chocolate or chocolate
substitutes</comments></item>
    <item><quantity units="floz">4</quantity>
      <substance>Evaporated milk</substance></item>
  </ingredients>
  <equipment>
    <object>Large, heavy-bottomed pan</object>
    <object>Wooden spoon</object>
    <object>Sugar (candy) thermometer</object>
  </equipment>
  <method>
    <para>This is very fast to make, so keep a close eye on the
temperature</para>
    <sequence>
      <event>Mix all the ingredients in the pan with the
spoon</event>
      <event>Heat gently until the sugar is dissolved, stirring
all the time</event>
      <event>Raise the heat and keep stirring gently</event>
      <event>Bring to the boil and keep stirring until it gets
to 240 degrees on the thermometer</event>
      <event>Remove from heat and stir briskly until it
crystallizes</event>
      <event>Turn into greased pan and leave to cool if you
can keep your fingers off it</event>
    </sequence>
  </method>
</recipe>
```

Figure 13. A recipe encoded using the example DTD

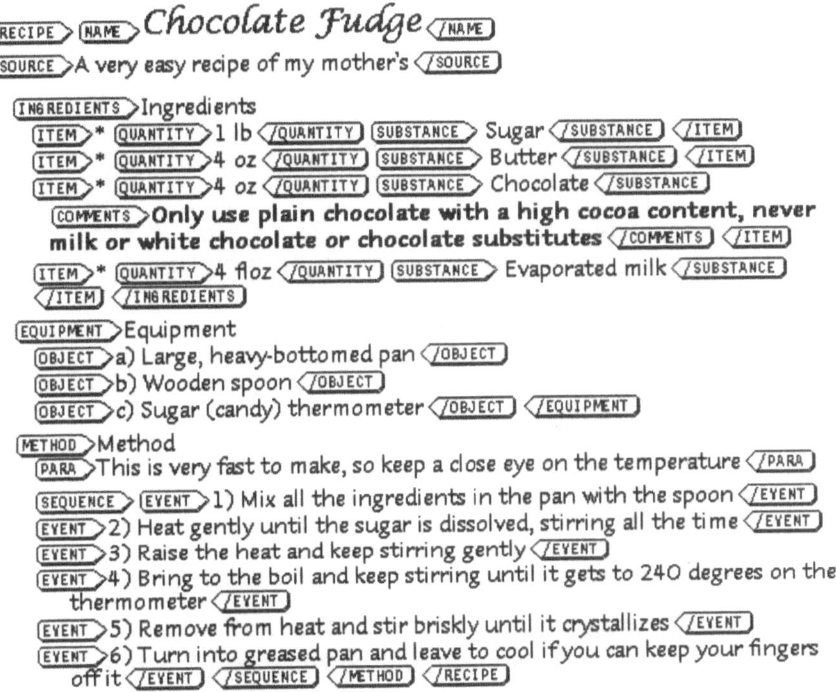

RECIPE NAME Chocolate Fudge /NAME
SOURCE A very easy recipe of my mother's /SOURCE
INGREDIENTS Ingredients
ITEM * QUANTITY 1 lb /QUANTITY SUBSTANCE Sugar /SUBSTANCE /ITEM
ITEM * QUANTITY 4 oz /QUANTITY SUBSTANCE Butter /SUBSTANCE /ITEM
ITEM * QUANTITY 4 oz /QUANTITY SUBSTANCE Chocolate /SUBSTANCE
COMMENTS Only use plain chocolate with a high cocoa content, never milk or white chocolate or chocolate substitutes /COMMENTS /ITEM
ITEM * QUANTITY 4 floz /QUANTITY SUBSTANCE Evaporated milk /SUBSTANCE
/ITEM /INGREDIENTS
EQUIPMENT Equipment
OBJECT a) Large, heavy-bottomed pan /OBJECT
OBJECT b) Wooden spoon /OBJECT
OBJECT c) Sugar (candy) thermometer /OBJECT /EQUIPMENT
METHOD Method
PARA This is very fast to make, so keep a close eye on the temperature /PARA
SEQUENCE EVENT 1) Mix all the ingredients in the pan with the spoon /EVENT
EVENT 2) Heat gently until the sugar is dissolved, stirring all the time /EVENT
EVENT 3) Raise the heat and keep stirring gently /EVENT
EVENT 4) Bring to the boil and keep stirring until it gets to 240 degrees on the thermometer /EVENT
EVENT 5) Remove from heat and stir briskly until it crystallizes /EVENT
EVENT 6) Turn into greased pan and leave to cool if you can keep your fingers off it /EVENT /SEQUENCE /METHOD /RECIPE

Figure 14. A recipe being edited in a graphical editor.

to be typeset in a very small size will appreciate the benefits of this approach.

Having created, edited, printed, and published your collection of recipes, the 'lifecycle' approach can perhaps be extended to place the recipe in a database on the Web or CD-ROM. In many cases, trying to maintain the appearance the same as in a printed edition may now become almost irrelevant: the lighting conditions in a kitchen or cookery school classroom, the age or reading ability of the users, and a dozen other factors, can mean that you need big type, or stronger colors, or no color at all. In fact it may be far more important for the user to be able to extract all fudge recipes, for example, or all those *not* using nuts, or all those recipes using chocolate *and* butter *but not* vanilla. The power of the markup can be seen if you consider the ability of a search system to distinguish between the different implications of 'a nut of butter', 'peanut butter', and 'the nuts' all occurring within the same recipe. There is actually a project under way to create an XML DTD for recipes, called DESSERT (Document Encoding and Structuring Standard for Electronic Recipe Transfer) which may help regularize this: details are at `http://dessert.home.mindspring.com`.

Chocolate Fudge

A very easy recipe of my mother's

Ingredients

1 LB Sugar

4 OZ Butter

4 OZ Chocolate *(Only use plain chocolate with a high cocoa content, never milk or white chocolate or chocolate substitutes)*

4 FLOZ Evaporated milk

Equipment

▷Large, heavy-bottomed pan

▷Wooden spoon

▷Sugar (candy) thermometer

Method

This is very fast to make, so keep a close eye on the temperature

1. Mix all the ingredients in the pan with the spoon
2. Heat gently until the sugar is dissolved, stirring all the time
3. Raise the heat and keep stirring gently
4. Bring to the boil and keep stirring until it gets to 240 degrees on the thermometer
5. Remove from heat and stir briskly until it crystallizes
6. Turn into greased pan and leave to cool if you can keep your fingers off it

Figure 15. The fudge recipe previewed in a browser

2.2.1. Terms and techniques in DTD construction

A full analysis and discussion of writing DTDs is beyond the scope of this book, although some of the tools which can be used are shown in section 2.6. However, if you investigate the innards of DTDs you use, or read about them in `comp.text.sgml`, you may come across some of the following aspects of SGML which are not always apparent to the user accustomed to dealing simply with elements and attributes.

If you want to get into writing your own DTDs, or making major changes to other people's, you should read the book by Maler and el Andaloussi[30] referred to in section 2.6.

2.2.1.1. Entity references

If you have used SGML before, you may well have encountered Entities. These are named references which are replaced during parsing or display by their declared expansion. Character and some general entities (as we saw in section 2.1.1) are similar in concept to the technique of 'macros' used in conventional programming and in some word processors (although different in behavior), and in some senses similar to the 'abbrevs' or 'AutoText' shortcut features of editors. Parameter entities (and general entities referring to whole files) are more like `#include` features of programming languages. These are three types of entity in SGML:

Character entities are used to give names to characters or symbols (such as accented letters and other symbols not found in the default base character set), so that they can be referred to in a machine-independent way. For example, to get the 'æ' ligature, you insert the Character Entity Reference `æ` in your document. This particular one is declared in the standard ISO 8859–1 (Latin–1) character entity file, which the DTD has to refer to to enable the character entities to be used. There are many hundreds of other such entities, most of which are supplied and installed with SGML software so that DTDs can refer to them.

You can also declare your own in a DTD or in the DocType Declaration Subset (see section 2.1):

```
<!ENTITY ptilde SDATA "p̃">
```

SDATA (Specific Character Data) is used for these because the replacement text (in quotes) is often a symbol whose encoding is specific to a particular make or model of hardware or software (I've got a 'p' with a tilde over it in my system: you may not have).

General entities can be simple replacement strings: for example

```
<!entity MIT "Massachusetts Institute of Technology">
```

declares one which you can type as `&MIT;` in the text of a document and a parser will replace it by the fully-expanded text. A general entity could also be a whole file, such as:

```
<!ENTITY chap1 SYSTEM "http://my.books.co/novels/chapter1.sgm">
```

This can be included in your document by entering `&chap1;`.

Parameter entities are similar but have a specialist function: the concept of substitution remains the same, but the expansion itself may then get interpreted and acted upon. They are used within a DTD (only, not within your document) to control and implement substitution in markup declarations and to provide a method of file inclusion in DTDs.

This way you can specify a reusable list of element names, for example:

```
<!entity % struct "para|list|table|pic">
```

(note the percent sign (%) which marks it as a Parameter Entity Declaration). This can then be referenced in subsequent declarations where it will be expanded:

```
<!element sect - - ((#PCDATA) | %struct;)*>
```

'File entities' are files which are referenced in parameter entities so that they can be included in the DTD, or in general entities so that they can be included in the document instance:

```
<!entity % tables system
"http://www.markup.store/odds/table-markup.dtd">
%tables;
...
<!entity chap1 system "/books/recipes/chap1.sgml">
<!entity chap2 system "/books/recipes/chap2.sgml">
...end of DTD, start of document...
&chap1;
&chap2;
...
```

See sections page 47 and page 60 for more examples of file inclusion in DTDs using parameter entities.

SGML provides additional keywords to declare specific types of entity, such as Notation Data (NDATA), for identifying non-SGML files such as TIFF images or WAV sound files whose file type has been declared as a NOTATION:

```
<!NOTATION GIF87a PUBLIC "-//CompuServe//NOTATION Graphics
  Interchange Format 87a//EN">
<!ENTITY CorpLogo system
 "http://www.corp.corp/public/logos/logo.gif"
  NDATA GIF87a>
...
<LEGALSTUFF>Copyright 1999 by The Corporation
<GRAPHIC ent="CorpLogo" style="inline"
height="2pc"></LEGALSTUFF>
```

This is a fairly standard way of doing images. It is especially convenient for logos because the location only has to be declared once and can then be referred to many times.

Less common is the subordinate document — SUBDOC, one traditionally sharing the same SGML Declaration and even part of the DTD.

This is still not widely supported but is used in the TEI DTD (see section 2.3.6) to declare some parts of the definition of writing systems (see also the short example on the Web at http://imbolc.ucc.ie/~pflynn/wsd/).

2.2.1.2. Minimization

In an SGML DTD, all elements can be set so that their start-tag or end-tag (or both) can be omitted if its presence can be inferred automatically from the context. This is specified with the two characters 'hyphen' and 'O', one or other for the start-tag and the end-tag, separated by a space (note this is a capital 'oh', not digit 'zero'; lower-case 'oh' is possible if the SGML Declaration permits it with NAMECASE GENERAL NO as XML does). The hyphen means the tag is compulsory if the element gets used; the O means it can potentially be omitted (the exact circumstances depend on the element's position in relation to its 'parents', the presence or absence of its 'children', and on settings in the SGML Declaration).

This allows SGML files, especially hand-written ones, to be much smaller than would otherwise be the case, because end-tags in particular can often be omitted if it is unambiguous to do so. In these circumstances, the end of an element can be worked out by a program automatically when the next element begins:

```
<!element list - - (item+)>
<!element item - O (#pcdata)>
...
  <list>
    <item>Fix air tickets for next week
    <item>Circulate agenda for safety meeting
    <item>Check on new stocktaking procedures
  </list>
...
```

For example, when a program sees a list containing a second or subsequent <item> which has been declared in this way, without having encountered a </item>, it can tell from the DTD that the only possible thing that can have occurred is that the previous item must be finished, so the 'missing' </item> is inferred from the context.

In an XML DTD the minimization parameters are omitted entirely because all elements must have start- and end-tags (except when using the special form of markup for EMPTY elements, in which case the end-tag can actually be said to be present in an abbreviated form; see section 2.4.1.5). The two declarations above would thus read:

```
<!element list (item+)>
<!element item (#pcdata)>
```

Gavin Nicol, one of the W3C's XML Special Interest Group members, reports (199705211641.MAA19198@www19.w3.org) that he experimented with a 1024×1024 table, with (longish) markup (<row> and <column>). This took 27.6Mb whereas with minimization it took 21.3Mb (about 29% greater because of the presence of end-tags), although it should be noted that when the file was compressed with *gzip*, the presence of end-tags added only 2% to the compressed file size.

2.2.1.3. Marked sections

SGML provides for a way to label sections of a DTD or a document in such a way that they can be shielded from normal SGML processing. This means that sections marked in this way will not be analyzed by a parser (a program that identifies and recognizes syntax) but will instead be treated as plain text, even if they do actually contain markup. The syntax of the construct is best shown by an example of an IGNORE Marked Section:

```
<![IGNORE[All this text, including <emph>markup</emph>, is ignored]]>
```

Note this is a Markup *Declaration* (it's got an exclamation mark after the opening angle bracket). It can be used in SGML documents to allow you to remove a portion of text from use, without deleting it from the file. It is strongly recommended that you use this whenever you want to prevent a piece of text from being processed, rather than use a comment declaration, simply because it is *not* a comment: it's a piece of text being ignored, and should be marked as such. Comment markup `<!-- like this -->` should be kept for comments.

It's easy to have it included again later, without the need to locate the closing]]> characters, by making it an INCLUDE Marked Section. Simply change the word IGNORE to INCLUDE, leaving the markup intact. Of course, if your text included further markup, that would now get parsed, so it has to be valid for the context.

To make it easier to handle many occurrences of ignoring and inclusion, the keyword IGNORE or INCLUDE can be replaced by an entity reference:

```
<![%peter-text;[
  <!--Stuff Peter wants included when his files are processed.-->
  <!entity PF "Peter Flynn">
]]>
```

If this construction occurs many times throughout a DTD, it's then easy to set the entity at the start of the file:

```
<!entity % peter-text "INCLUDE">
```

Setting it this way includes all my text; setting it to `IGNORE` would ignore it all. In large DTDs you will find this method used extensively to enable or defeat the inclusion of elements, entities, and external files.

Another use of Marked Sections is to allow the inclusion of text (character data) which may contain markup which you do not want recognized as such. The `CDATA` Marked Section is very common in documentation about SGML itself, or anywhere you want to include text which may contain markup characters you want preserved, not acted on:

```
<![CDATA[<!entity % peter-text "INCLUDE">]]>
```

This means that the actual literal characters

```
<!entity % peter-text "INCLUDE">
```

will get sent to the output by a parser, without the markup being interpreted at all: as far as SGML is concerned, it's just character data.

2.2.1.4. EMPTY elements in SGML and XML

At first sight, the concept of an empty element may seem to defeat the objective of SGML's 'elements-contain-things' model. In practice, an element defined as `EMPTY` consists of a start-tag only, usually (but not always) in order to carry additional information in attributes. A well-known example of an empty element is the image element in HTML, which is declared something like this:

```
<!ELEMENT IMG - O EMPTY>
<!ATTLIST IMG ALIGN (top|middle|bottom|left|right) #IMPLIED
              ALT   CDATA      #REQUIRED
              SRC   %URL;      #REQUIRED >
```

(I have abbreviated the attribute list for the purposes of illustration.) This element is used in mixed content as well as in element content, with the `SRC` attribute holding the URL of the illustration, the `ALT` attribute holding explanatory text for users with no graphics, and the `ALIGN` attribute set to one of the permitted values for positioning:

```
<img src="http://www.foo.com/bar.tif"
 alt="My favorite pub" align="top">
```

HTML also has `<BR>`, the line-break, which is an example of an element most often used without attributes. Both `<BR>` and `<IMG>` are examples of 'point markup': markup which exists simply at a single location, between words, letters, or other markup, with no content of its own. Such elements are declared `EMPTY` in the DTD, which not only means they cannot have an end-tag, but they cannot have any content either.

XML introduces the possibility of a file *without a DTD*, using just the constraint of being 'well-formed' (see section 2.4 for details) or 'tag-valid' (see section 2.7.1.3). In the absence of a DTD to declare EMPTYness, there therefore had to be some other way of letting a parser know that no end-tag should be expected for EMPTY elements (so that the parser wouldn't keep reading to the end of the file, looking for one). This can be done either by using a trick involving one of regular SGML's minimization features, the Null End Tag (NET), or (with the WebSGML Adaptations, as in XML) by enabling the NETSC delimiter. In any case, XML also interprets an element with a start-tag and end-tag but no content as if it were an element declared EMPTY.

The technique with the Null End Tag in regular SGML is to allow one slash to terminate a start-tag and another to act as an end-tag by itself, thus delimiting the content with a minimum number of keystrokes: so <emph/this/ can be a shorthand for <emph>this</emph>, a valuable saving in the days when SGML was typed by hand and storage was at a premium. When a representation for a tag with no content was needed in the development stage of XML, the trick was invented of using the format <img/>, which is regular SGML syntax, representing an EMPTY element.

The WebSGML Adaptations, however, provide the NETSC delimiter (NET-enabling Start-Tag Close), which when set to '/', enables all EMPTY elements terminate with '/>' anyway, so the <IMG> link above would look like this in an XML version of HTML:

```
<img src="http://www.foo.com/bar.tif"
 alt="My favorite pub" align="right"/>
```

and a line-break would look like <BR/>. The alternative is just to use both start-tag and end-tag (<IMG SRC="mypic.gif"></IMG>) but never put any content in the element. The XML specification makes it clear (3.1) that for interoperability between XML and regular SGML, the special form of the EMPTY element (ending with />) must be used for elements which are declared EMPTY in a DTD.

2.2.1.5. Inclusions and exclusions

The content model of an element usually consists of the names of the other elements which are permitted or required within it, or of parameter entities which expand to the desired list of such elements:

```
<!entity % para.content "emphasis|acronym|link|date|name">
<!element numberedlist - - (listheading,(item)+)>
<!element item - - (#PCDATA | %para.content; )>
```

Here a <NUMBEREDLIST> is defined as containing a <LISTHEADING> followed by at least one <ITEM>, and an <ITEM> is defined as containing mixed content (see section 2.2.1.6): any mixture of #PCDATA and any of the paragraph-level elements named in the `%para.content;` parameter entity.

However, there are occasions when a long list of elements in a frequently-used parameter entity contains one or two elements which you do *not* want included, or omits some that you do want on special occasions.

SGML provides an additional meaning for the plus and minus (hyphen) signs, to let you handle these exceptions: the plus for ***inclusions*** and the minus for ***exclusions***. For example if we have a `<math>` element which can occur along with many others in the content model for a paragraph and other text-bearing elements, we may want the same set of elements to be allowed inside `<math>`, with the sole exception of `<math>` itself (math inside math doesn't make sense). An ***exclusion exception*** for this might look like this (the structure has been simplified for illustration):

```
<!entity % para.content "emph|foreign|quote|math|index|gloss|xref">
<!entity % math.content "sqrt|frac|root|subformula|sum|prod">
<!element p    - - ((#PCDATA)|%para.content;)*>
<!element math - - ((#PCDATA)|%math.content;|%para.content;)* -(math)>
```

Here, `<math>` is specified in terms of the desired content in the last line, minus the math element itself.

An ***inclusion exception*** using the plus sign can be made in a similar way to add in an individual element on specific occasions when it is needed but not already included in the parameter entities being used.

2.2.1.6. Mixed content and element content

The term ***mixed content*** describes the common position of an element content model which can have regular character data arbitrarily mixed with markup. This is normally the case for paragraphs, for example:

```
<!element para - o (#PCDATA|emph|sci|for)*)>
```

Here, the paragraph may contain any quantity of character data intermixed in any order with any combination of elements for emphasis, scientific names, and foreign words.

The opposite of mixed content is ***element content***: the position held by content models which permit only further element markup and never any character data (text) at that level. For example a `<CHAPTER>` element would be expected to contain only other (structural) elements, and not text, because text would normally go inside further markup, for example:

```
<!ELEMENT chapter - o (head,(para|list|table)*,section+)>
```

In this case, a <CHAPTER> cannot contain any character data at all, only other elements: first a <HEAD>, then any mix of <PARAGRAPH>s, <LIST>s, or <TABLE>s, and then possibly some <SECTION>s. Note the comma specifying 'followed by', the vertical bar for 'your choice of', the asterisk for 'zero or more of', and the plus sign for 'one or more of'. This particular example is quite restrictive: it means a chapter *must* contain at least one section: a chapter full of paragraphs and no sections would be in error.

It is an axiom of regular SGML that white-space *in mixed content* is regarded as 'significant' (it has to be: it's usually the spaces between words), whereas white-space between the end of one element and the start of the next *in element content* is regarded as 'insignificant'. A parser is normally *required to omit* all insignificant white-space when passing parsed data to an application, which is why you can leave arbitrary amounts of white-space between elements in element content and it has no effect on the document. The HTML specification additionally requires an application to squeeze all multiple white-space characters to a single space in mixed content as well, and to omit any white-space immediately following a start-tag and immediately preceding an end-tag. SGML will ignore record ends (RE characters, usually equivalent to linebreaks) immediately after start-tags and immediately before end-tags, but not other forms of white-space. XML parsers are required to pass *all* white-space to their application (browser, formatter), butt o identify whether or not it was found in element content or mixed content.

The problems which have led to the term 'mixed content' being used as invective arise when a content model in a DTD specifies both character data and markup in such a way as to make it possible for an otherwise innocuous space, tab, or linebreak to be treated as significant character data instead of irrelevant white-space. For example, here is an element intended to allow surnames to be marked separately in a naming element, a device used by some publishers to enable surname-based sorting in bibliographies:

```
<!element name - - (#PCDATA,surname?)>
<!element surname - o (#PCDATA)>
```

It specifies that a name contains any amount of character data, possibly followed by a <SURNAME> element. This is fine with tag omission enabled, so long as every occurrence looks like this (with or without the space after 'Clinton'):

```
<name>Bill <surname>Clinton </name>
```

The DTD specified that the end-tag could be omitted from the surname, so the trailing space after the surname *is assumed by a parser to be a part of the surname*. Until the parser gets to the </NAME> it cannot know whether the surname has ended or not. Now suppose instead that the data has been produced in the following form:

```
<name>
Bill
<surname>
Clinton
</surname>
</name>
```

The user (or perhaps a database programmer) has thought to be helpful by separating markup from content on a line-by-line basis, misled by having seen *element content* done this way. Unfortunately a parser will now say something like

```
C:\SP\BIN\NSGMLS.EXE:nametest.sgm:12:10:E:
character data is not allowed here
```

with the line and character reference pointing at the > in </SURNAME>. The linebreak between the end of the </SURNAME> end-tag and the start of the </NAME> end-tag has been treated as character data because the <SURNAME> element has finished, and the DTD specifically says that nothing further is allowed at that point except the end-tag for </name>.

The guideline is that *spaces, tabs, and linebreaks are only significant when they occur in mixed content*. When a DTD fails to (or perhaps cannot) allow for cases where unwanted space may occur after the need for character data has passed, as in the above example, the situation is referred to as 'pernicious' mixed content, and needs to be treated with care to avoid the error described above.

The answer is usually to use only the vertical bar when writing mixed content models in a DTD, never the comma, but this has the side-effect of making #PCDATA permissible *anywhere* in the element, which may be something the document type designer wants to avoid. Pernicious mixed content is often caused by attempts to make the DTD too prescriptive, in a perfectly genuine need to try and guarantee that users can only put specific data items in carefully-defined places. It's less of a problem when the data is being exported or generated from a database or similar source under program control; as the documentation for *RainbowMaker* (see section 5.3.1) says: 'Mixed content is dangerous only when humans are editing SGML documents'. Some document type designers seem to make a feature of pernicious mixed content, to the extent that one harassed user has referred to a particular industry DTD as containing 'vindictive mixed content'! The *nsgmls* parser (see section 4.3.5) has a warning flag (-wmixed) which can be used to warn of mixed content which does not permit #PCDATA anywhere.

2.3. What's available in public?

Almost every SGML application program comes with sample DTDs which demonstrate the capabilities of the software. Some even come with copies of popular DTDs to save you the trouble of obtaining them yourself, although as these go out of date, it's sometimes less than useful.

In this section I have gathered together both classes: the samples and the freely-available public DTDs. They are all on the CD-ROM, so you have plenty of choice if you're just getting started with SGML.

These are the most up-to-date copies available as we went to press, but if you decide that you want to use one of the public DTDs, it is worth checking with the canonical source on the Internet to see if there is a more recent version or an update.

2.3.1. DTDs for office documents

There must be thousands of DTDs created for private use within companies, but there are far fewer available publicly. The widespread use of Web technology now means that corporate text can be distributed within the organization using intranets and extranets, and in the case of marketing and technical support material, by using the public Web itself. HTML and XML are therefore distinct possibilities for these applications, and are discussed separately in section 2.3.9.

Other office DTDs are hard to come by, partly because there are still relatively few companies using SGML for the daily bread-and-butter of letters, minutes, and memos (although perhaps slightly more for reports), and partly because they are corporate property, and thus not available outside the company. In particular, the use of SGML has been something of a 'secret weapon' for many years, giving its users a commercial advantage in their use and reuse of information, and such companies are understandably reluctant to give away valuable work to the competition.

However, general-purpose report, letter, and memo DTDs are often supplied with SGML software, and although these are relatively low-level (they are often intended for demonstration purposes), many are nevertheless usable, and make a good starting-point for organizations just starting down the SGML training road.

Once their limitations are identified, the more adventurous readers can try extending them with some of the DTD creation and management tools discussed at the end of this chapter, although for industrial-strength use, it's better to have a document engineer create the DTD to your specification. I would not recommend the sample DTDs for production use because they are not intended for that environment.

The DTDs covered here, therefore, are those supplied with some of the other software discussed elsewhere in the book. They are copyright of the companies who wrote them, and are intended for use in learning SGML, rather than for general office use. In particular, some of them exhibit features designed specifically to show off aspects of the software they accompany, rather than to enhance their usability in a production environment.

I have included them on the CD-ROM separately from (and in addition to) their existence within any of the demonstration installation software. They thus appear in the catalog file supplied, and can be referenced by their FPIs in the normal way. For those that had no FPI or an invalid FPI, I have invented one; these are indicated in the subsections that follow by the use of the imaginary unregistered Public Owner '`Rincewind`'. Details of the catalog entry format are covered in section 2.5.4.

2.3.1.1. Report DTDs

2.3.1.1.1. Near&Far Designer Test Document DTD

```
-//Microstar//DTD Test//EN
```

This DTD is documented as being designed specifically to test some of the capabilities of Microstar's software, so it is not suitable for production use. It does, however, illustrate a number of important points about DTD design, particularly that frequently-needed objects like paragraphs can be defined once and can then re-occur at various places in the DTD. You can see from Figure 16 that `<para>` appears within `<frontmatter>`, where it is expanded so you can see what it contains. It also occurs in `<body>`, `<list>`, and `<rearmatter>` where it is shown with the white bar indicating that its expansion is already displayed elsewhere on the screen.

Structurally, this DTD provides for introductory and final material (front matter and rear matter, albeit in only paragraph form), and has no divisional structure, but its most striking features for a small DTD are that it includes some of the more complex objects such as tables and mathematics. The math element is shown expanded once in the separate diagram at Figure 17 because the complex nesting of math term inside math term inside math term significantly clutters a graphical display.

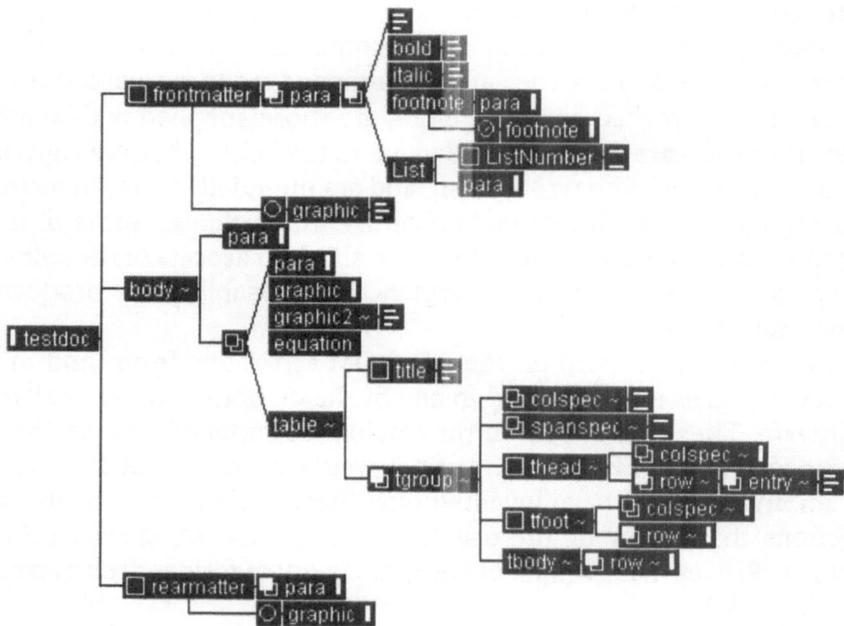

Figure 16. Microstar's Test Document DTD

```
<!DOCTYPE testdoc PUBLIC "-//Microstar//DTD Test//EN">
<testdoc>
  <frontmatter>
    <para><bold>TEST REPORT</bold></para>
  </frontmatter>
  <body>
    <para>Paragraph of text</para>
    <table>
      <tgroup cols="2">
<tbody>
  <row>
    <entry>first row, first col</entry>
    <entry>first row, second col</entry>
  </row>
  <row>
    <entry>second row, first col</entry>
    <entry>second row, second col</entry>
  </row>
</tbody>
      </tgroup>
    </table>
    <equation>b<sub>4</sub>i<sqrt>u</sqrt><frac>
<numer>ru</numer>
<over>16</over>
      </frac>qt&pi;</equation></body></testdoc>
```

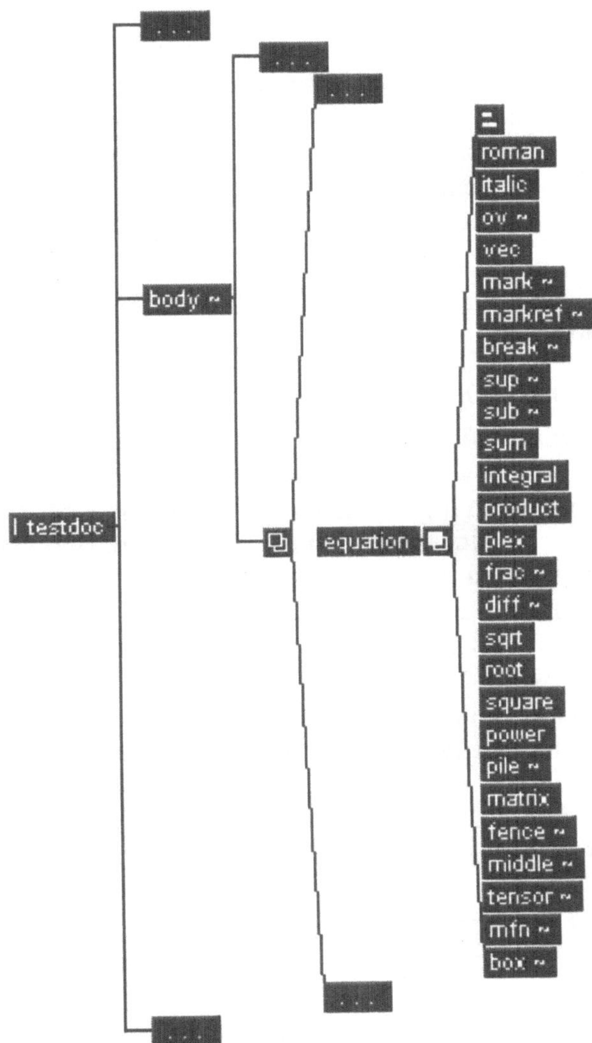

Figure 17. The math content of Microstar's Test Document DTD expanded

If you want to see it, it's best to use something like Microstar's *Near&Far Designer* (or the copy of their demonstration viewer on the CD-ROM) and expand the math element yourself, so you can scroll through it in more detail. All that can be shown within the bounds of a book page is that each element within `<equation>` can itself be expanded, some of them recursively to cater for the needs of mathematicians (roots inside fractions within fractions inside expressions within fractions...and so on). Alternatives are discussed in section 2.3.8.

2.3.1.2. Letter DTDs

Business letters are one of the most obvious applications for SGML. The structure of the business letter is relatively simple, and virtually identical across many national and linguistic boundaries, and even the visual format varies only slightly. However, letters tend to be short-lived and not to be reused, so the cost of managing them in a formal SGML database may not be justified unless they contain mission-critical information.

2.3.1.2.1. SoftQuad

```
-//Rincewind//DTD SQ Letter//EN
```

One of the hardest things to get across to the new user is the concept that the sequence in which information is recorded is not necessarily the sequence in which it gets used. This DTD illustrates that by placing the date before the address, which is a perfectly possible order to print them in — depending on your letter designer — but by no means the only order (many corporate letters put the date after the address). It shouldn't matter: software can be programmed to read the date when it occurs but print it elsewhere, although it is astonishing how few programs allow the user to do this.

The `<pre>` element holds date, address, and salutation (Figure 18; nothing whatever to do with the `<pre>` element in HTML, it's used here in the original sense of 'before'). The address is broken up into the conventional lines, with the name and street address elements repeatable.

The body of the letter consists just of paragraphs, within which you can use three degrees of emphasis (usable for font changes), and lists with items.

The `<after>` element holds the closing peroration, author's name, and a list of people to copy, one per item. There must be millions of letters written daily which follow this pattern.

2.3.1.2.2. The SGML Tagger Letter DTD

```
-//Rincewind//DTD OUP Tagger Letter//EN
```

This DTD takes the opposite approach to the SoftQuad one and places the date after the address. It also adds a `<ref>` element which is a key factor in most business correspondence. The address, however, distinguishes only lines and the postal code, a viable option where the code is fine enough to pinpoint separate buildings, or where there is no need to have detailed management of address detail.

Address markup

If you're designing a DTD with addressing markup, you need to consider how it's going to be used. The temptation is either to oversimplify, like the TEI, and just call each part of the address an 'address line'; or to try and emulate a database, with carefully optionalized 'fields' with every possible fragment of an address separately named.

In many countries the 'street' part of the address is simply inadequate, as both buildings and houses can have names instead of numbers. Even the need for a street address can occur more than once, if you live in a laneway off a small street off a major street. It's also interesting to see people in remote hamlets, Pop. 47, uncomplainingly filling in their location as a `<city>` — if you're creating a DTD which will be used outside North America, it's worth considering a more generic element name like `<locale>`, qualified with an attribute like `type="town"`, because 'city' can have very specific legal and civic connotations elsewhere.

Zip codes are an American name: everywhere else calls them postal codes, if they have one at all, so `<postcode>` must be optional, never compulsory. The same goes for `<state>`, which can be synonymous with 'country' in geographically smaller jurisdictions.

The text body again includes paragraphs and lists with items, although here lists can occur separately as well as embedded in paragraphs. There is also a `<note>` element with the same content as paragraphs. Four qualities of phrase-level distinction are available. The final salutation distinguishes the name of the sender from the text of the salutation.

2.3.1.3. Memo DTDs

2.3.1.3.1. Near&Far

`-//Rincewind//DTD Microstar Memo//EN`

The *Near&Far Designer* graphical DTD tool comes with a good example of a small memo DTD suitable for interoffice use, faxes, or email. Figure 20 shows the structure, with the conventional header and body.

The header elements reflect the usual nature of memos and email:

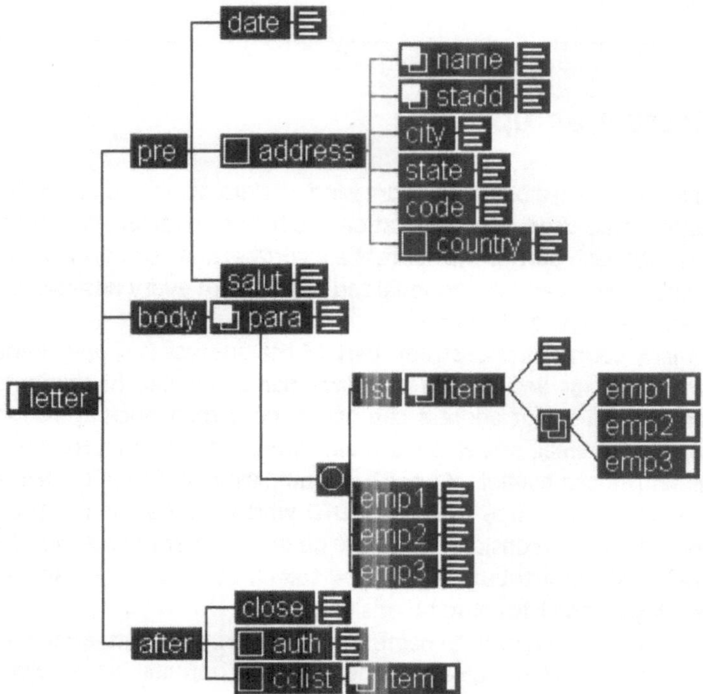

Figure 18. The SoftQuad Letter DTD

- <to> is compulsory, but may occur more than once (multiple recipients);
- <from> is also compulsory, but may occur only once;
- <cc> (carbon-copy) and <bcc> (blind-carbon-copy) are an unordered choice, neither is required, but both may have multiple occurrences;
- <date> is compulsory (once), whereas <sysdate> is optional, and is declared EMPTY (so the system date has to go in an attribute);
- the <subject> can hold any text, with optional bold, italics, and even an image;
- the body can just have paragraphs and footnotes, but <footnote> has been added in an inclusion exception, in order to allow it to be modeled with an exclusion exception of itself (meaning footnotes cannot themselves have footnotes: this is just a safety net to prevent it happening);
- paragraphs and footnotes may contain the same model of text as the subject (shown unexpanded in the diagram because the %text; parameter entity is already expanded for display in the <subject> element.

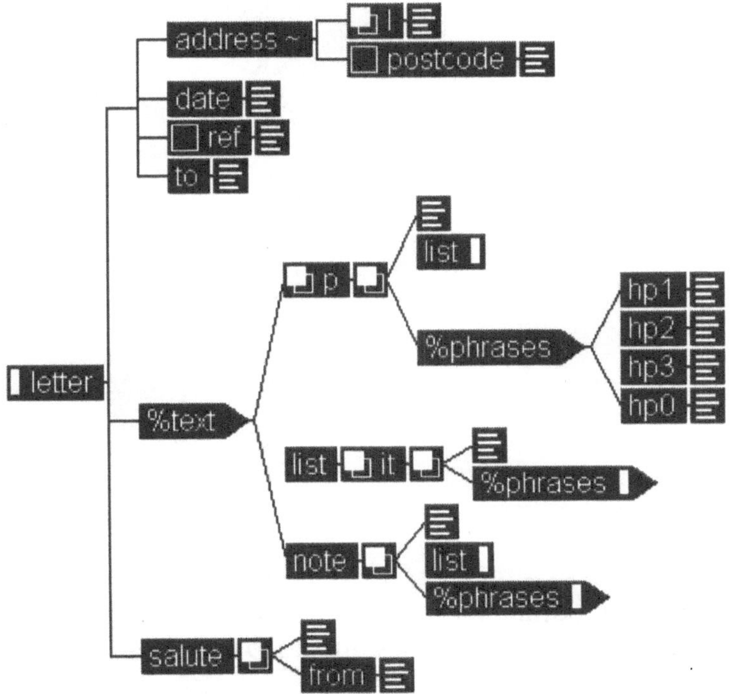

Figure 19. The SGML Tagger Letter DTD

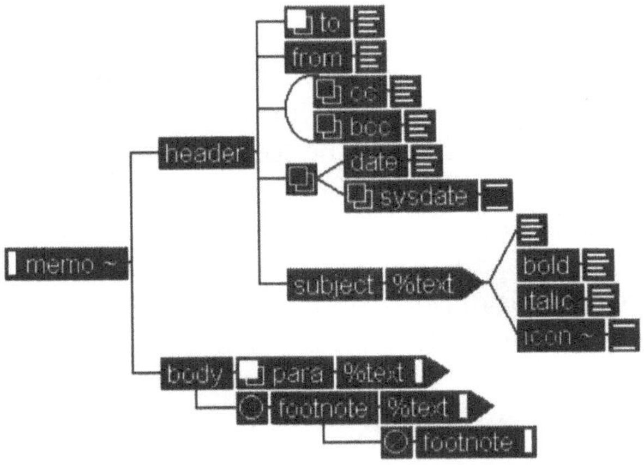

Figure 20. The sample Memo DTD from *Near&Far Designer*

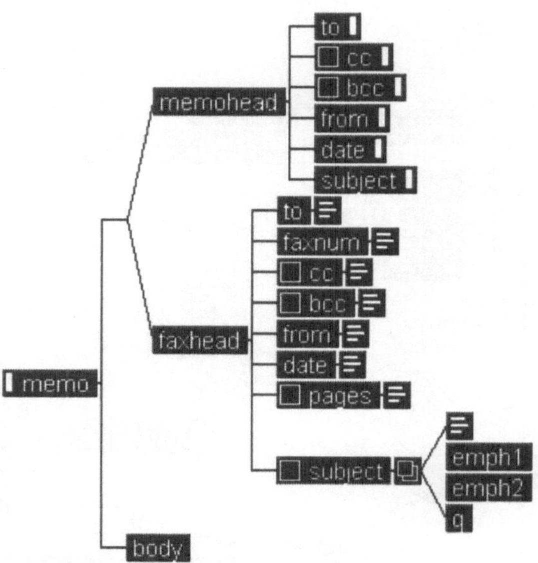

Figure 21. Headers of the *Author/Editor* memo DTD

The inclusion of footnotes is perhaps a little unusual in a memo, but it is a good example of how the design of a DTD can affect the behavior of an editor in permitting an element in one place and forbidding it in another.

2.3.1.3.2. Author/Editor

```
-//Rincewind//DTD SQ Faxmemo//EN
```

This DTD is relatively extensive for what is normally a small application. Figure 21 shows the header, which comes in two flavors, one for memos and one for faxes. The additions for faxes are one element for the fax number and another for the total number of pages.

As with the N&F memo, the conventional header elements appear in a similar order, although in this case they follow strictly in sequence with no optionality apart from <cc> and <bcc>. In the fax header, however, the page count is optional and so is the subject. This is an example of the kind of conditional structural design you can build into an SGML DTD.

For content markup, two kinds of emphasis are provided, and an element for quotes. These are evident in the subject element of the fax header, and reappear in all the textual elements of the body. Figure 22 shows the body, with a considerably more complex content model than other memo DTDs.

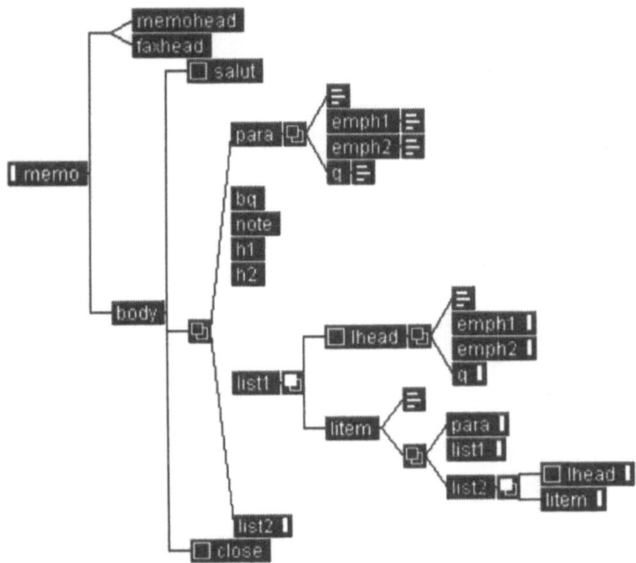

Figure 22. Body of the *Author/Editor* memo DTD

There is provision for a separate salutation and close ('Dear...' and 'Yours...' respectively), and the body can contain paragraphs, block quotations, notes, two sorts of header and two sorts of list. Each of them can have the same content (text, emphases, and quotes). The two kinds of list are presumably intended for bulleted and numbered use: each can have a list heading and must then contain one or more list items, each of which in turn can hold paragraphs or further lists.

This is a relatively powerful model for a memo, and can cope with most of what anyone in an office would want to pass around in memo form. Anything more complex than this kind of structure, and you probably want to start looking at a report structure rather than a memo.

2.3.1.3.3. SGML Systems Engineering

```
-//SGMLSYSENG//DTD Simple Memo//EN
```

By contrast the Memo DTD which comes with one of the *SGMLC* sample applications (see section 5.2.2) is for test purposes only. It contains no header or body separation, and just two elements, for headings and paragraphs (Figure 23).

It is of course nevertheless quite possible to write a memo to someone using this DTD:

Figure 23. The *SGMLC* Memo DTD

```
<!DOCTYPE memo PUBLIC "-//SGMLSYSENG//DTD Simple Memo//EN">
<memo>
  <h>To:      Jack</h>
  <h>From:    Jill</h>
  <h>Date:    29 Feb 1998</h>
  <h>Subject: Water supplies</h>
  <p>I have reminded you frequently of the need to keep the pail
     filled, and I noticed again this morning that it was empty.</p>
  <p>I would be grateful if you would call to my office this morning
     so that we can discuss the matter.</p>
  <p>Jill.</p>
</memo>
```

The sample application is shown rendering this to HTML and RTF in section 5.2.2.

2.3.2. Industrial DTDs

The pattern of development is quite different when you look at separate industries. A large number of sector-specific DTDs have been created, often by trade associations or technical consortiums wanting a method of improving data exchange. The transportation industries, especially air and rail, have been leading this field, but almost every industry from music to medicine now has some organization working on one or more DTDs, and some of these are now being rewritten in XML (see section 2.4).

A few examples are mentioned briefly here: the Air Industry (ATA and AECMA), the Rail Industry (RIF EPCES), and Telecoms (EFTI CTD and TCIF/IPI TIM)[3], but the DTDs are usually available only by paying a fee to the relevant company or industry standards body.

Many industries and government departments in countries around the world are also developing DTDs, sometimes on a shared basis, and the same pattern is developing among international organizations and in the NGO (Non-Governmental Organization) field. Military DTDs can be seen as a special case of industrial DTD development, although

[3]I make no apology for the prevalence of acronyms here and in other sections: they are endemic both to computing and to industrial and governmental bureaucracies everywhere.

with a longer history, but because of their significance in SGML development, they are dealt with separately in section 2.3.5.

2.3.2.1. ATA and AECMA SPECs

`http://www.spec2000.com/`

AECMA: Gulledelle 94, B-1200 Bruxelles, Belgium

SPEC 2000 replaces the earlier (paper-based) ATA Spec 200 with a more up-to-date specification of standard formats to exchange information electronically between airlines and their suppliers. It covers the industry requirements for documenting procurement and repair transactions for aircraft maintenance. It has been adopted by the international airline community under the auspices of the ATA (Air Transport Association of America) and it is recognized as the industry standard.

The DTDs themselves are available on an ATA CD-ROM from the URL given at the start of this section.

Within Europe, AECMA (Association Européenne de Constructeurs de Matériel Aérospatial) [European Association of Aerospace Industries] have devised the 1000D standard for similar purposes, and the DTDs are available from AECMA at the address given at the start of this section.

Adobe are reported to be releasing a *Frame+SGML* 'starter kit' for AECMA (see section 6.5.2.1).

2.3.2.2. RIF EPCES

`http://www.eccnet.com/rif/`

The RIF (Railroad Industry Forum) was created by the North American railroad industry working with the National Association of Purchasing Managers to develop a standard for the exchange of electronic parts catalog data. The RIF members are major railroads and railroad manufacturers.

EPCES (Electronic Parts Catalog Exchange Standard) was developed for the interchange and presentation of illustrated parts catalogs. Some of the structure draws on work done on the automated interchange of technical information in MIL-STD-1840B (now C).

Figure 24 shows the structure of the DTD. A crucial part of this (and many other data-based DTDs: here, in CALS, and in many places in the technical field) are the 'effectivities', classifications which determine which components fit or apply to which models or makes of product. In SGML, this data is usually held in attributes.

The rest of the `<epc-info>` element and the `<front>` element hold descriptive material about the document The chapter/section/subsection

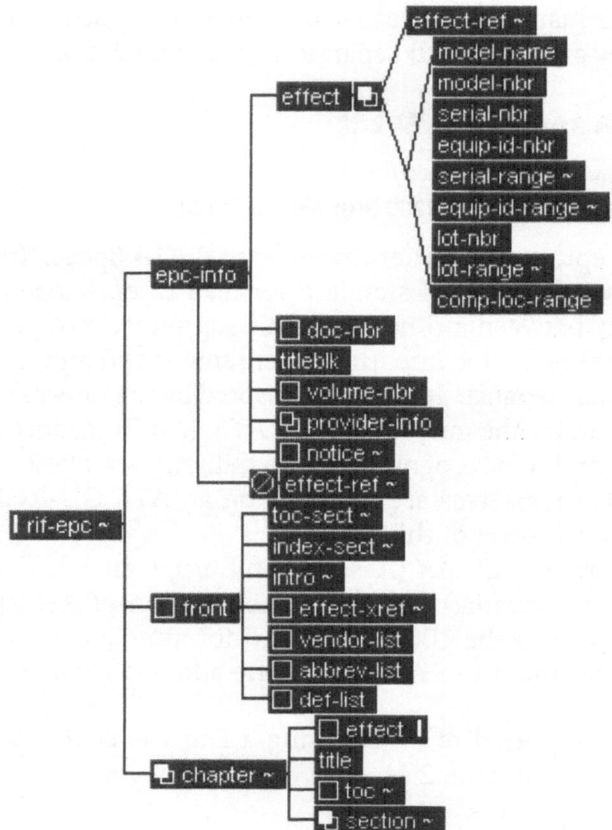

Figure 24. The RIF EPCES DTD for Railroad parts catalog data

structure (see Figure 25) carries no paragraph-style data in the upper levels, but instead has a fairly fine-grained content model for describing exactly the parts list, with illustrations and effectivities, and provides space for annotation in the `<assoc-text>` element.

2.3.2.3. CTD and TIM

`http://www.atis.org/atis/tcif/ipi`

The TIM (Telecommunications Interchange Markup) DTD comes from the TCIF (Telecommunications Industry Forum), and was designed for the interchange of (existing) technical documents within the Telecom industry. A comment in the DTD notes that it is 'not necessarily appropriate for authoring applications, archival storage of information, or direct input to browsers'.

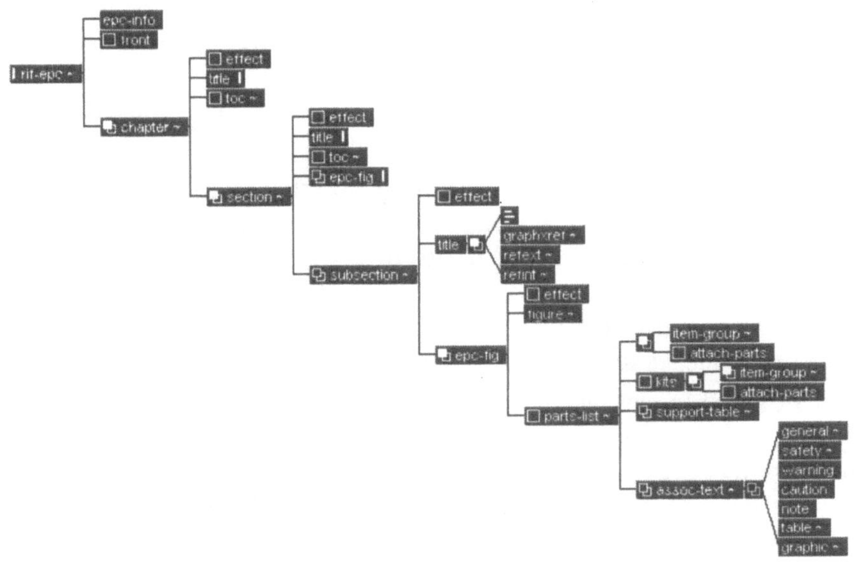

Figure 25. The RIF EPCES DTD data structure

The CTD (Common Telecom DTD) is the European equivalent from EFTI (European Forum for Telecom Industry Information Interchange) on the other hand 'offers both specific content-based structures for operation and maintenance documentation [as well as] generic text structures'. The groundwork for the CTD was defined within an EU-funded project and is being supported by most of the large European (formerly state-run) telcos. The intention in providing a wider range of granularity is to offer the possibility of gradually expanding its usage from telecom-specific structures to more formal text structures. 'A design principle for the contents-based ('semantic') structures and the telecom-specific set of elements within the CTD was to build the intersection of structures and elements within different vendors' and operators' documents (as far as possible).' [Quotations are from articles in `comp.text.sgml` in May 1997 by two of the participants, Henning Moeller and Klaus Meusel.]

2.3.3. DTDs for technical writing and documentation

Technical writers, particularly those documenting computer systems, were among the earliest users of SGML. As experienced computer users, some authors had no problems using editors, running parsers, or writing formatters. However, there were low levels of acceptance from publishers, who had barely gotten used to the idea of authors sending them text on diskette instead of paper, and the lack of affordable commercial SGML writing tools for desktop systems meant a low level of takeup.

With some word processors now cheap enough almost to be given away, and DTP systems capable of a close approximation to professional typesetting, there is a strong incentive to stick to the visual model described in section 1.5.1.3, and leave aside considerations like platform portability, reusability, or structured design. However, as even some word processors now implement internal stylesheet models which are beginning to follow the SGML pattern of nested markup, the underlying markup concepts are becoming more familiar.

A noticeable catalyst in the use of SGML has been the demand for Web-based documentation for all kinds of products. After the initial impetus to do everything in HTML, some of the advantages of using a more descriptive and robust format for the master copies are becoming apparent. From formats like *DocBook* you can generate HTML or XML versions of varying sophistication according to need, but also produce printed versions or CD-ROM versions, various proprietary formats like Windows Help, and compare and collate the data with other product-related resources like parts lists or safety checks. As described in section 2.3.5, it is possible to create interactive electronic technical manuals from a database of very small sections or subdivisions of text, each describing a single activity or an even smaller event or object.

2.3.3.1. QWERTZ (LinuxDoc; SGML-Tools)

The *QWERTZ* DTD has been around for a long time in SGML terms. It was devised in the late 1980s as part of the toolbox developed for the QWERTZ artificial intelligence action planning project run by the Institute for Applied Information Technology (FIT) at the German National Research Centre for Computer Science (GMD), and it was used in the *DAPHNE* documentation project conversion software from the German Research Network (DFN). (The name comes from the six top right-hand letter-keys on a standard German keyboard, in (I think accidental) mimicry of the sentient typesetter in Fredric Brown's science fiction short story *ETAOIN SHRDLU*[12], which was called after rows on the Linotype keyboard.)

QWERTZ was designed to be easy to convert to LaTeX document types: article, book, letter, slides, and report, with the addition of fax, notes and manpage (the Unix manual pages). The objective was purely pragmatic, and little attempt was made to 'improve' on Lamport's basic structure.

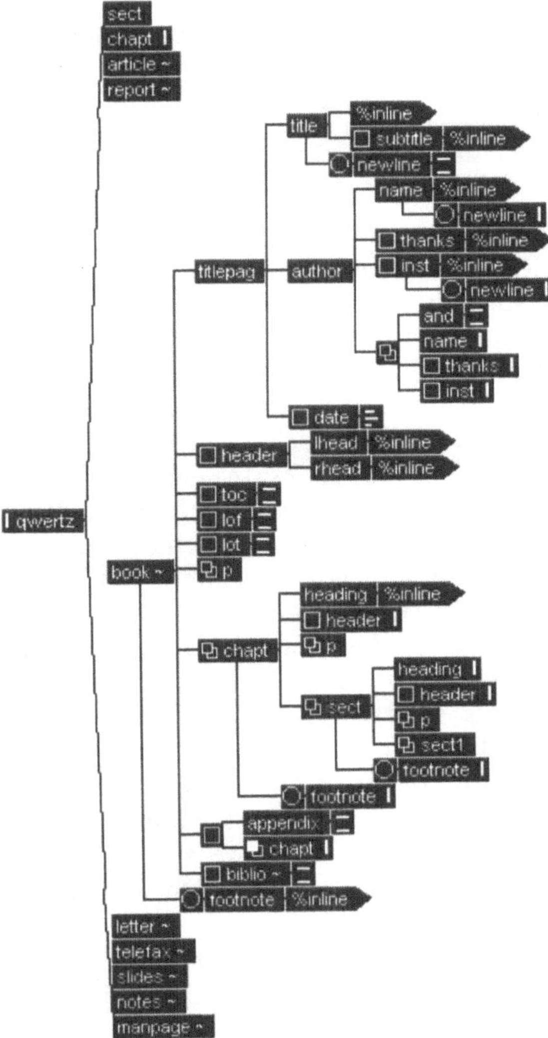

Figure 26. The QWERTZ DTD

The result was that conversion was relatively simple and robust, and formatting for printing could be done with LaTeX, which is available both commercially and free for almost any computing environment. This combination provided a significant advantage for users, as a major problem at the time was the lack of SGML output formatting at a reasonable cost.

LaTeX had been originally selected as the documentation format for the *Linux* operating system. SGML using QWERTZ was chosen later as the base document format for the LinuxDoc-SGML project (now called

SGML-Tools; see section 5.3.7). The project is now moving documentation into *DocBook* (see below), which provides more facilities.

2.3.3.2. DocBook (Davenport)

```
-//Davenport//DTD DocBook V3.0//EN
http://www.ora.com/davenport/
```

The *DocBook* DTD is the largest and most adaptable of the general-purpose technical DTDs. It is a product of the Davenport Group, a discussion forum sponsored by individuals representing large-scale producers and consumers of software documentation.

The design allows for books and book-like structures, including sets of books (sets of manuals, for example, or books in a series) down to the level of the individual article or section. The document header information is carried in the `<bookinfo>` element immediately after the title and subtitle (see Figure 27) and there is provision for a glossary and bibliography at the start of a document as well as at the end.

The chapter-level or article-level content model is very extensive, and has a wide range of structures commonly encountered in computer documentation. Many of these can also recur within paragraph-level elements, where the content model is mixed with an even wider range of descriptive elements. The result is a powerful tool for technical authors, although you need to read the online documentation very closely to understand the nature of each element, as many of them have several slightly different variants. The online documentation assumes a sound understanding of SGML, but there are a number of publications in preparation about the use of *DocBook* which should help new users get used to it.

Early versions required some deep surgery to implement modifications, which meant that it has been cannibalized extensively by many software vendors, either to fit software limitations, or to add or remove specific components according to application requirements. In support of this, a major re-engineering was carried out in 1995–96, which resulted in almost everything being parameterized, much as the TEI DTD was. The result is a very flexible DTD, and one which is now heavily used in its intended fields. Because of this, I'm going to use it later in the section on how to customize a DTD (section 2.6.1), although you need to bear in mind that the techniques I describe only work with a DTD which has been designed with this level of parameterization — many DTD authors specifically do not want people to change their DTDs.

DocBook itself is in several files. The first is a 'driver', the file actually called `docbook.dtd`, which is the one you open when compiling for an

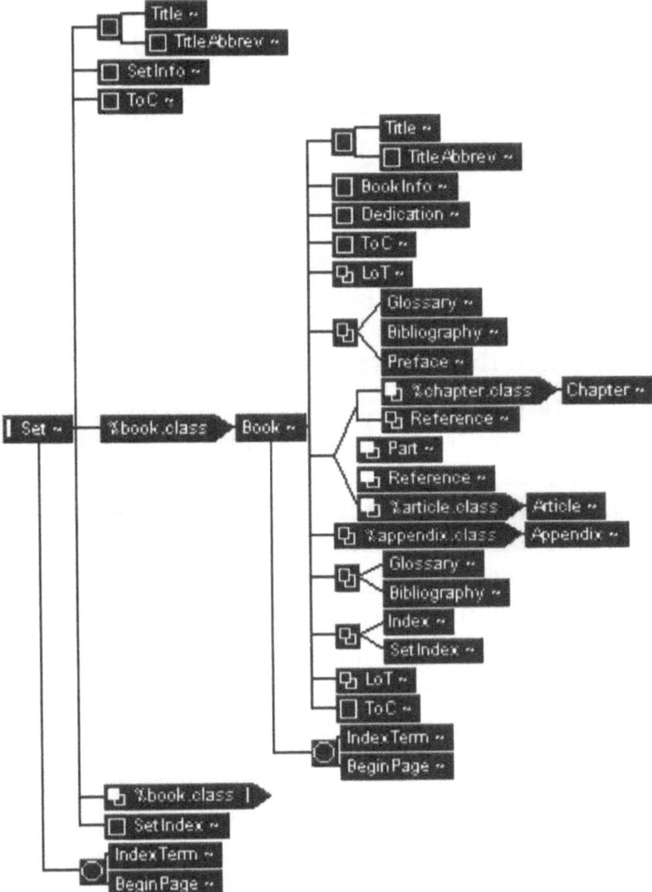

Figure 27. The *DocBook* DTD

SGML system, or when referencing the DTD in a DocType Declaration (the file that the FPI points to). This file contains the references to notations and character entity files, and to the two other major modules, the 'hierarchy specification' and the 'content model pool'.

These two files, `dbhier.mod` and `dbpool.mod`, contain the bulk of the DTD code. The first defines the markup that makes up the document type (the unique characteristics of Sets, Books, and others), and the second defines markup that makes up the 'information type' (markup specific to computer publishing information). The distinction is a bit fuzzy, but it was chosen to maximize the possibility that you might want to replace the book structure with something similar but not identical (such as an online help module structure or a training lesson structure) while retaining the content markup. They both use parameter entities to enable modifications without the need to edit the files themselves.

An example of modifying the *DocBook* DTD (adding HTML math and forms ability) is given in section 2.6.1. Some aspects of *DocBook* are harder to modify, though, as things you may want to change may lie deeper in the parameterized structure: to respecify the order of elements in a `<figure>`, for example, allowing the caption (`<TITLE>`) to come after the `<GRAPHIC>` instead of before, you need to alter the entire segment which defines figures (by setting the Parameter Entity which controls it to `IGNORE`, and adding a whole new set of modified declarations afresh in the DocType subset.

In this case it is arguable that the order in which you type or store the data need not be connected with the order in which it's printed. This is quite true, and it is relatively trivial in TeX and other programmable formatters to use a variable to store the value of the caption, and emit it after the graphic has been positioned. But the argument ignores the needs of simpler processors such as those used for conversion to HTML, or those which display in a non-programmable browser.

Despite the ease with which it can be modified, *DocBook*'s strength lies in its general acceptance by the documentation community as a useful common-format tool which works well with all the software in popular use.

2.3.4. DTDs for general publishing

One of the early ventures into SGML for publishers was by the AAP (Association of American Publishers), who produced several DTDs which are still in use. They cover the structure well, but the element names are abbreviated to the point of being cryptic, and documentation is not easily available.

The AAP DTDs were the foundation for a more recent suite of DTDs which have become an international standard, ISO 12083. Despite this, they have not yet been implemented very widely, perhaps because their design — for the publisher and printer — is not always suitable for non-paper reuse.

Elsevier also have a long history in SGML, and their DTDs were developed for use by people doing text entry for them, particularly where there was a need to ensure that all volumes or articles in a series shared an identical markup pattern.

2.3.4.1. The AAP Article DTD

```
-//USA/AAP//DTD ART-1//EN
```

The AAP DTDs follow closely a single pattern, of which the Article DTD is a fair representative. It has short element names and simple high-level structure, but at the text (data) level it has a considerable descriptive power for representing the appearance of an article in print — the publisher's primary concern.

Figure 28 shows the front matter, body, appendix matter, and back matter with figures and other floating elements. At the section level and below, the model gets more complex, with lists, block quotations, tables, and figures both within and peer to the paragraph-level elements.

The very short element names make for a less cluttered screen when tags are displayed, but there are many of them, and as the DTD was designed for use by publishers, not their authors, the abbreviations often stand for terms not immediately apparent to the casual user.

2.3.4.2. The ISO 12083 DTDs

ISO 12083 (officially titled *Electronic Manuscript Preparation and Markup*) was formalized in 1993 to provide a standard for books, articles, serials (journals), and some mathematics. It was based on a number of previous standards, notably the AAP DTDs (see previous section) and ANSI Z39.58-1988. The Book and Article DTDs contain a large amount in common: only the Book DTD is covered here.

The structure again follows the conventional front — body — back structure, with the addition of a separate structure for Appendices (see Figure 29). The body provides for a structure with Parts separately from one with only Chapters, rather than simply make Parts an optional enclosure for Chapters.

Apart from its status as a standard, this is one of the few Book DTDs which directly caters for mathematics, by inclusion of the ISO 12083 Math DTD. The paragraph content has elements fora wide range of cross-references, and sufficient descriptive markup for general use — there is no attempt to provide the kind of specialist markup contained in technical DTDs like *DocBook*.

One significant feature is that it does include the SDA (SGML Disabled Access) `FIXED` attributes for enabling conversion to braille, large print, or voice-generators (see section 6.3), something few DTDs have incorporated.

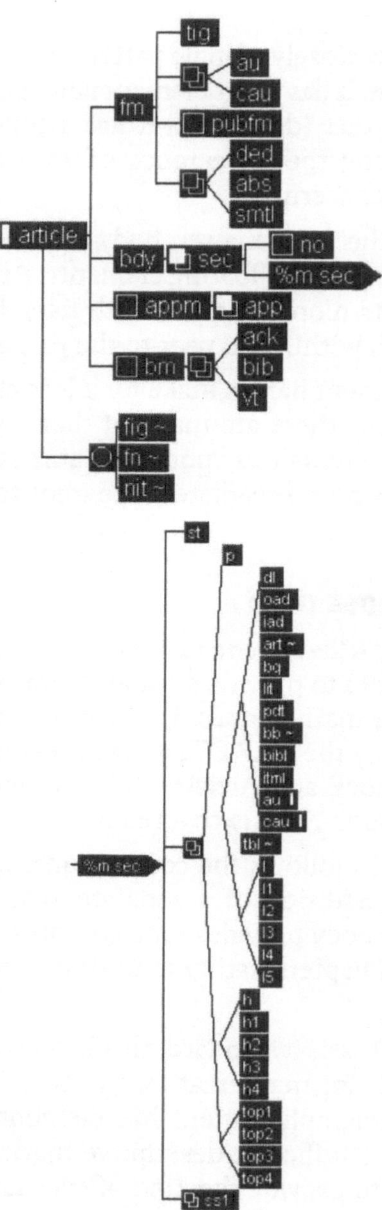

Figure 28. The AAP Article DTD

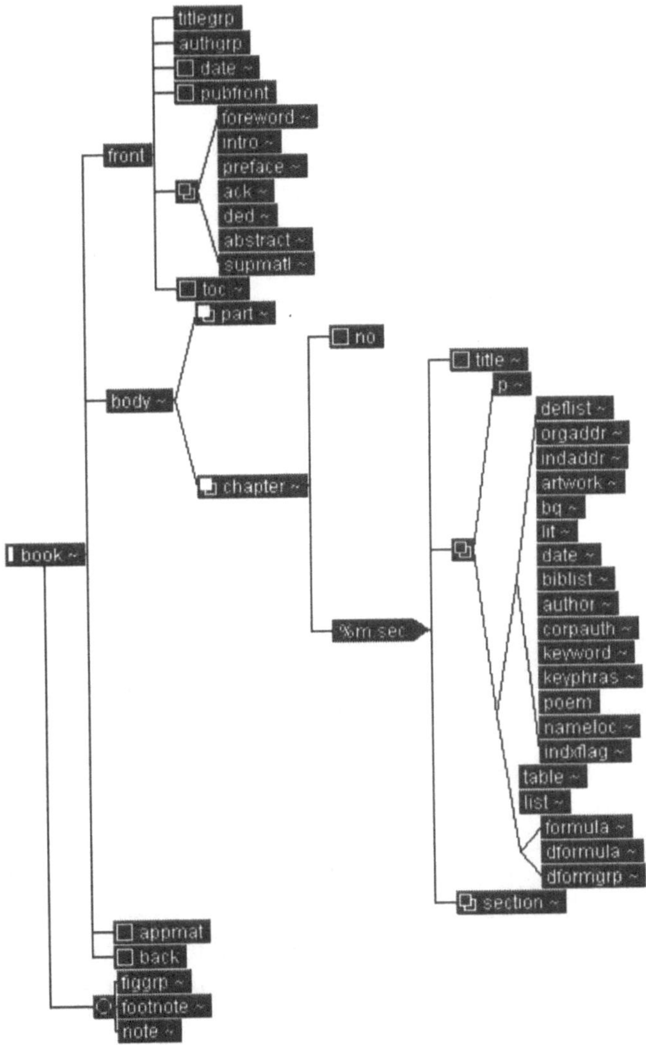

Figure 29. The ISO 12083 Book DTD

2.3.4.3. The Elsevier Article DTD

```
-//ES//DTD full length article DTD version 4.1.0//EN
```

Elsevier's well-known 'article' DTD (the ART300 series) became something of a standard among the many people who work on encoding articles for their scientific journals. As of March 1998, this was replaced by the ART400 series, currently at version 4.1, which makes a large number of small and sometimes subtle changes. As in the AAP DTDs, the element names are highly abbreviated, making it suitable for use

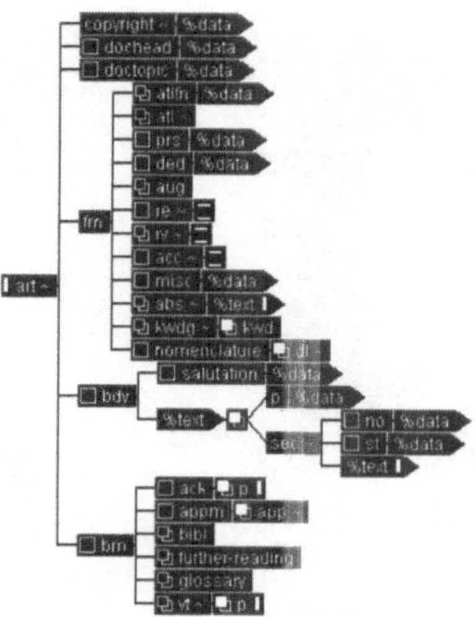

Figure 30. The Elsevier ART410 DTD

in plaintext editing environments where the number of keystrokes has to be minimized. It does mean that frequent use is needed to learn the element names, as they cannot always be deduced by casual inspection.

The structure is simple and pragmatic: heading information followed by front, body, and back matter, with the body infinitely subdividable into sections (note the use in Figure 30 of a parameter entity `%text;` which expands to a definition containing a `<sec>` element which in turn uses `%text;`). This provides the only real depth of nesting needed for publishing an article on paper. At paragraph level, however, there is extensive provision for mathematical markup, as well as cross-referencing and font changes.

Elsevier previously provided software for data entry, in particular the *Pandora* program, a specialized, modified data entry system based on DOS *WordPerfect*, but this is not being updated to handle ART400. A conversion program to move files from ART300 markup to ART400 is functional, but is not being updated to handle v4.1 and later, as suppliers are expected to provide their own editing and conversion software.

If you use the Elsevier DTDs, take care to check the Formal Public Identifier, as there are invalid versions in some files which have only a single slash before the 'DTD' Public Text Class: it should be a double slash, as at the start of this section.

2.3.5. DTDs for military use

One of the earliest moves towards large-scale use of SGML came from a US DoD (Department of Defense) program called (originally) CALS (Computer Aided Logistic Support). Among the targets was the implementation of a vendor-neutral format for electronic documentation, especially for technical manuals for weaponry and support systems. The objective was compatibility between documentation formats so that the manuals could be used in the same way regardless of who supplied them.

Over the years, the acronym has changed several times, and the current meaning of CALS (Continuous Acquisition and Lifecycle Support) is already under pressure from a number of less useful expansions from the marketing community, such as 'Commerce At Light Speed'. CALS is thus now a joint DoD and industry strategy 'to enable more effective generation, exchange, management, and use of digital data supporting defense systems'. The primary goal is still to migrate from manual, paper-intensive operations to integrated, highly automated acquisition and support processes, as a paper-based system would now be unusable simply because of the weight and volume of documentation.

Similar projects and principles have been adopted by the armed forces of several other nations, notably Canada, Australia, the United Kingdom, Sweden, and Japan, in some cases (such as Canada) using the same acronym and similar DTDs, adapted for local conditions. A guide to the implementation of the US program was published in the handbook *Computer-Aided Acquisition and Logistic Support (CALS) Program Implementation Guide*[5].

In the USA, the baseline markup requirements were outlined in MIL-M-28001 (1988) *Markup Requirements and Generic Style Specification for Electronic Printed Output and Exchange of Text*[6], which specified SGML for the markup and an SGML-based language, FOSI (Formatting Output Specification Instance), for defining appearance. A more general standard for document interchange and storage is defined in *Automated Interchange of Technical Information*[4]. There are separate standards for graphics and CAD technical drawings.

One of the principal document types involved is MIL-M-38784B (see Figure 31), written for documents conforming to *Technical Manuals: General Style and Format Requirements*[7], and many versions of this DTD are distributed as examples with SGML software. The structure of a 38784 manual is necessarily different to that used in office documents, and there is a separate layer of quality control involved in the generation of these documents. The front–body–back structure is conventional, but

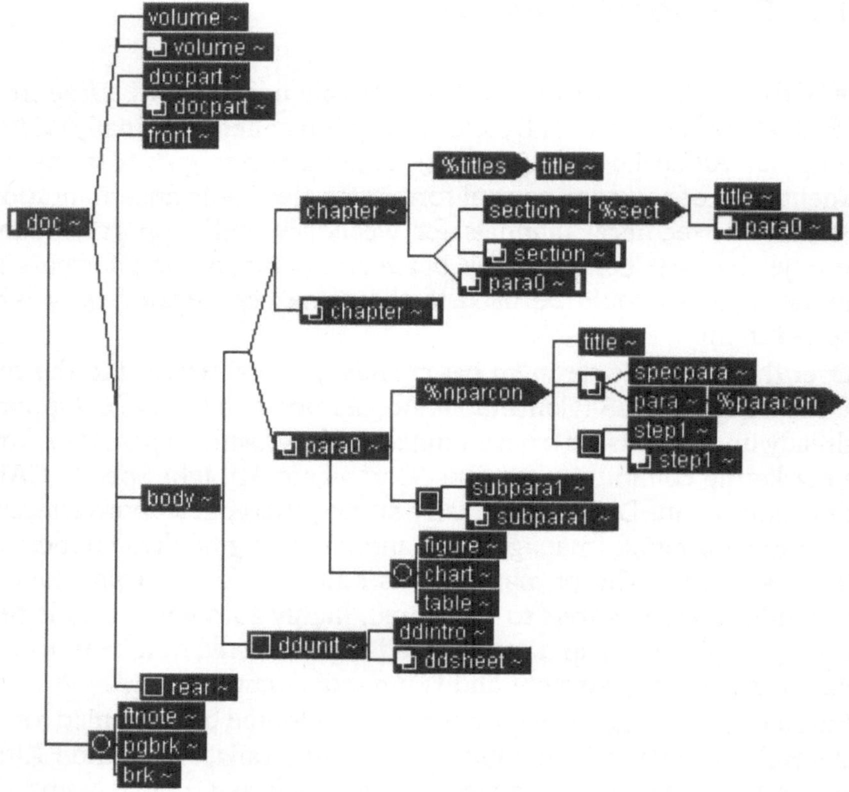

Figure 31. The MIL-M-38784 DTD for technical manuals

the body structure allows documents to be constructed of just sectional and difference data, as well as in chapter format.

The stage beyond printed or static documentation is the interactive manual, a large and fast-growing field. The US military standard for an IETM (Interactive Electronic Technical Manual) is now set down in the performance specification MIL-PRF-87268A, originally the GCSFUI (General Content, Style, Format, and User Interaction) of the *Requirements for Interactive Electronic Technical Manuals*[9]. This is a 'package of information required for the diagnosis and maintenance of a weapons system, optimally arranged and formatted for interactive screen presentation to the end-user'.

There are five classes of IETM:

1. the 'Page Turner' with some navigational ability. Systems are mostly non-SGML at the point of delivery, and may use commonly-available commercial software (*eg* PDF);

2. the Electronically Scrolling Document: more sophisticated navigation (often but not necessarily SGML);
3. Linearly Structured IETM Documents: these are all SGML;
4. Hierarchical Structured IETM: this class is conformant to MIL-D-87269 and is thus database-driven;
5. Integrated Electronic Information System (expert Systems and AI).

Class 3 onwards takes advantage of more of the facilities of SGML: single-master authoring (no reauthoring for paper or electronic versions), faster deployment to the field and schoolhouse, multiple-media distribution, and multimedia in the content. Class 4 uses the IETMDB (IETM Data Base) approach (see below) and brings other benefits like authoring for optimum productivity, the ability completely to disaggregate the information at the point of delivery so the information is more finely targeted, and the use of 'fault trees', where users can provide feedback information tightly bound to a specific route through the document. But it's expensive, and once committed to the structured format, cannot easily be converted back to a single paper manual.

The standard for IETMDBs is MIL-PRF-87269A *Revisable Data Base for the Support of Interactive Electronic Technical Manuals*[10]. In this format, the contents of the information base are held at a high level of disaggregation, using two layers of DTD, 'generic' and 'content'. The text and images are only formed into a recognizable 'document' at the point of delivery, using facilities now based on HyTime (section 2.7.2.1) for the complex cross-referencing needed.

Ideally, all IETMs should be platform-independent and interoperable, so that applications and databases from any manufacturer can work together with all the rest. There are formidable theoretical and practical problems, though, and a number of proposed solutions such as MID, the Metafile for Interactive Documents, have encountered significant controversy. A sample of the level of work is shown by the IBMIDDOC DTD inFigure 33.

While adherence to the CALS standards is essential for military work, there have been a number of spin-offs for civil use of SGML. The first has been the funding, which led to the development of many of the SGML tools we use today; and the second is the CALS Table DTD (see section 2.3.7.1). This contains a model for SGML tables which has been adopted almost universally by creators of DTDs, partly because it's already in existence, and partly because it seems to handle most of what people want.

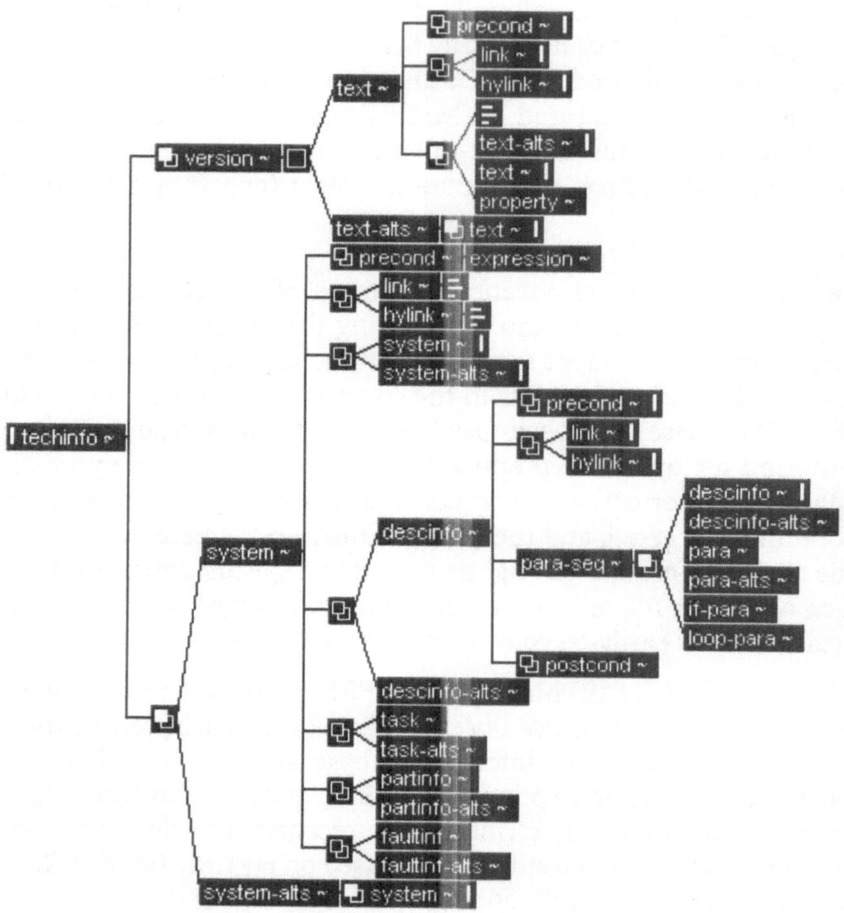

Figure 32. The MIL-M-87269 DTD for IETMs

2.3.6. DTDs for research and academic use

Although academic and research interest dates from an early stage in SGML, DTDs specifically for these areas are few in number and have tended to be designed for very highly specific applications, so they are not intended for use outside their own field.

One in particular, however, stands out because it was designed explicitly to be applied in a wide range of academic and research uses, especially in the Humanities: the DTD of the TEI (Text Encoding Initiative). A number of interesting and useful developments have stemmed from this, especially the EAD (Electronic Archival Description) and the Ebind DTD.

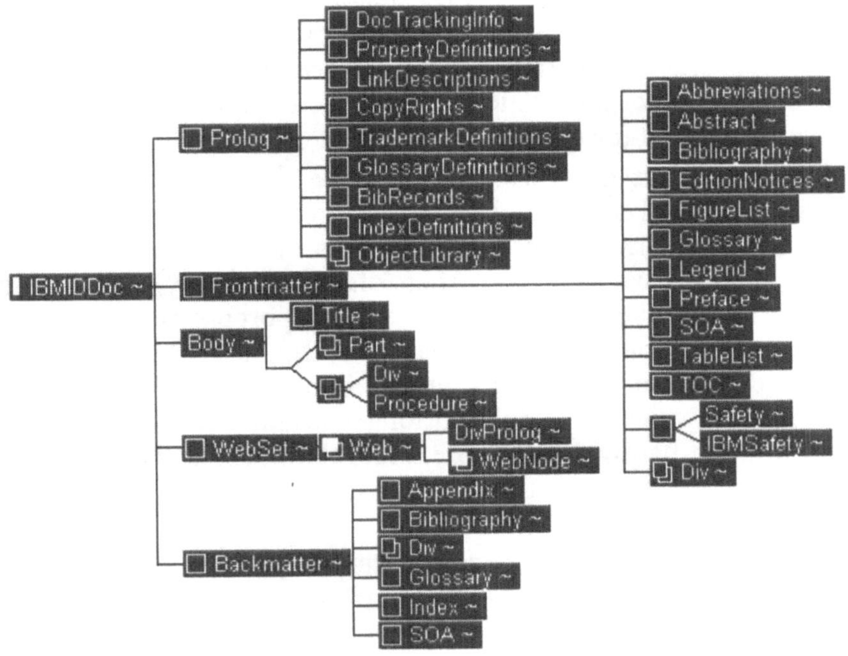

Figure 33. The IBMIDDOC DTD

Another more recent development is the CML (Chemical Markup Language), an XML DTD designed for chemists to use over the Web (see section 2.3.9.2).

2.3.6.1. The TEI DTD

```
-//TEI P3//DTD Main Document Type 1994-05//EN
http://www-tei.uic.edu/orgs/tei/
```

The TEI started from a meeting in 1987 as a project to create a method for the interchange of textual data between scholars in a form which would overcome the widespread incompatibilities between existing file formats. Because it uses SGML, use of the TEI has gone far beyond the interchange of data, and it is in widespread use for the permanent storage (archival) of important literary, historical, linguistic, and other texts in a form that can be put to multiple purposes for teaching and research. The project is managed jointly by Michael Sperberg-McQueen from the University of Illinois at Chicago and Lou Burnard from the University of Oxford, and benefits from contributions from scholars and technical experts from all over the world.

Despite its origins, it is by no means limited to the Humanities. The ultimate product of all academic endeavor, whatever the discipline, is almost always text: regardless of the quantities of other research products (raw data, for example, often numeric and of great complexity), the end result is still usually text: a thesis, an article, a conference paper, a book, or some other publication, often more than one, and perhaps on the Web as well as (or instead of) on paper.

The TEI DTD is geared towards serving the research community with a format for keeping and exchanging text, in a way which makes it immune to changes in technology and to the whims of commercial interests which have bedeviled other (often proprietary) data and text formats. Anyone who has worked in a user support position, in industry or in academia, is instantly familiar with the user who arrives with valuable data on antique media written in a format popular 10 or 20 years ago and which is simply no longer usable because no-one has the software or hardware any more. This, above all else in the research field, is where SGML can protect the investment of time and money in a way that no other system can.

The background to the encoding of text for academic research, and in particular for use with the proposals of the TEI, is well documented in the a number of places, notably the 'bible' of the TEI itself, the two big green volumes of the TEI' *Guidelines*[39], but also in a variety of publications about or referring to the TEI, such as Ide and Veronis' *The Text Encoding Initiative*[23] and a recent thesis by a student from my own institution[14]. A process of review for the TEI DTD started in 1996, and users can follow this and other discussions on the mailing list `TEI-L` (details in Appendix B).

The TEI DTD is among the largest DTDs, not alone in the number of elements available (although *DocBook* has even more) but in the richness of markup available at all levels. In many research texts, especially in literary works, it is important to encode items which have no distinct visual cue, but are needed for searching or analysis. The number of 'inline' or 'content-descriptive' elements (those which can be used to describe words in the content of running text) is thus very high, and the example of markup available for personal and place names gives some of the flavor of this (see the box). Eve Maler has described the TEI as enabling 'the effort to encode the sum of human knowledge in SGML'.

This provision of sufficient depth of markup for research purposes is accompanied by a careful construction of the DTD which allows the tagset to be tailored to the application. The DTD is composed of modules at several levels, so the exact features can be tailored to the application. Even within a single project, many different variants of the DTD can be in use, but all have an underlying compatibility. The model

Depth of markup in TEI texts

As an example of the kind of markup available, here is a fragment of text containing a name to be marked up:

> Through the door came Marius de Baer, Lord of the Bleak Peninsula, Scourge of Infidels, Scion of the House of Varuda, known to his friends as Mike .

Here you have a personal name made up of a forename, an honorific particle, and a surname; two formal titles, one of which contains a place-name; a sobriquet referring to a genealogical name; and a nickname.

```
Through the door came <persname key="BAER-M-01"
id="MDB"><forename>Marius</forename>
<namelink>de</namelink> <surname>Baer</surname>, <addname
type="political"><rolename>Lord</rolename> of the
<placename><geogname key="27.35.45 54.22.13">Bleak Penin-
sula</geogname></placename></addname>,
<rolename type="political">Scourge of
<genname>Infidels</genname></rolename>, <addname
type="dynastic">Scion of the House of Varuda</addname>, known to
his friends as <addname type="nick">Mike</addname></persname>.
```

For the purposes of retrieval, a researcher may wish to be able to identify the individual by any one or more of the names, or to search for similar references to parts of the name, or to follow the lineage of a family, or the line of political power, or locate the geographical reference on a map, or any of a thousand other uses that only become possible when content-descriptive markup is available.

which allows this has been nicknamed the 'Chicago pizza' model, as it lets the user choose a 'base' DTD on which they can then put 'toppings'. The bases you can choose from are:

Prose
Verse
Drama
Spoken text
Dictionaries
Terminological

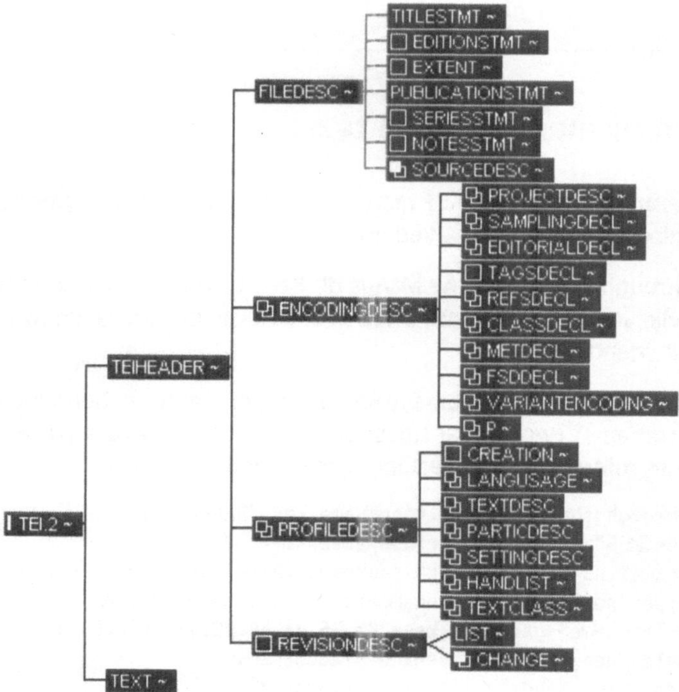

Figure 34. Structural markup in the TEI header

There are also provisions for a general-purpose (non-specific) base and for mixing several bases. These bases provide compatible markup facilities for the normal two-part construction of an SGML document: a documentary and bibliographic header; and a text body, with the conventional hierarchical division, paragraphs, lists, and a small amount of predefined inline markup.

Figure 34 shows the level of detail available in the TEI header, even without expanding on these structural elements. Figure 35 expands the elements of the `<filedesc>` container as an example. This level of detail is necessary to allow scholars to distinguish even very fine-grained information within a single text or between texts in a corpus.

On top of the selected base the scholar can then choose one or more 'toppings', which make available more specialized elements:

Linking, using an extended pointer notation
Text analysis
Feature structures
Certainty
Transcriptions
Text criticism

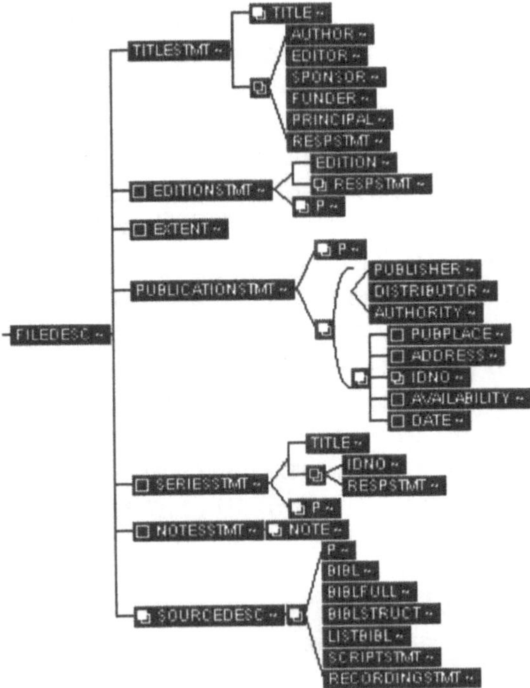

Figure 35. Details of the TEI file description header elements

Names and dates
Networks/graphs/trees
Figures
Corpora

The specification of all this is done in the ***DTD subset*** (the bit of a DocType Declaration that goes in [square brackets]) or in a new module of the ***external subset*** (ancillary files which can be modified by the user or designer). It is only possible to this level in the TEI because of the highly modularized design: it's not a feature available in most DTDs (*DocBook* is another example from a different field). The code for all variants is effectively already in all the files which make up the entire TEI DTD, but is 'switched off' by the use of entity-encoded `IGNORE` Marked Sections (see section 2.2.1.3), where the value of '`IGNORE`' is set in an entity declaration. To activate a particular topping, therefore, all that is needed is to switch it on by changing the value of the controlling entity from '`IGNORE`' to '`INCLUDE`'. An example of modifying the TEI is in section 2.6.1.

The content of the TEI text body is very complex, because the TEI is not a prescriptive DTD. Instead of enforcing a predefined sequential structure as would be the case with a business letter, technical report, or government submission, it encourages only a hierarchical one. This is not without problems, as some older documents simply don't have a hierarchical structure as we think of it today: the text just begins at the beginning and goes on until it comes to an end.

Nevertheless, it remains suitable for an extremely large class of documents which can use the section–subsection–subsubsection–subsubsubsection construct (in TEI terms, `<div0><div1><div2><div3>...`). In addition to this, the encoder has a set of other elements which can be used to model reasonably closely most of the structures of historical, literary, and even present-day documents. Whatever drawbacks there are in encoding documents this way, they are usually offset by the benefits of a reliable and common encoding between projects, which can make the use and reuse of documents across disciplines possible to an extent which was unthinkable even 10 years ago.

There are some problems with this scheme. Its flexibility means it is possible for users to be less than scrupulous about encoding information meaningfully, because most elements are optional. It therefore requires greater skill and discipline to encode in the TEI, in addition to the domain skills needed for the interpretation of the text itself, and the technical knowledge of SGML and an editing system. As Cournane has pointed out[14], knowing what to encode is of no use unless you know how to encode it, and *vice versa*.

An example of the difficulties faced by encoders of complex literary and linguistic texts (but usually absent from business or technical work) is the problem of ***crossed boundaries***. A fundamental principle of SGML is that markup is always nested inside markup, so a quotation which starts in one line of a poem and ends in another causes a problem if you need to encode the lines *and* the quotation. You therefore *can't* do this:

```
<lg type="limerick">
  <l>There was a young man from Tralee</l>
  <l>Who was stung on the bum by a wasp</l>
  <l>When asked did it hurt</l>
  <l>He replied, <q>Not at all,</l>
  <l>It can do it again if it likes.</q></l>
</lg>
```

(The verse is due to Spike Milligan, I think; the markup is mine.) The markup of the `<q>` element may not span the end-tag `</l>` of its containing element and the start-tag of a new `<l>` before the closing `</q>` has occurred. One possible solution is to use two `<q>` elements, with the `NEXT` and `PREV` attributes which can use the `ID/IDREF` mechanism to link them together; another would be to use specially-provided 'span-

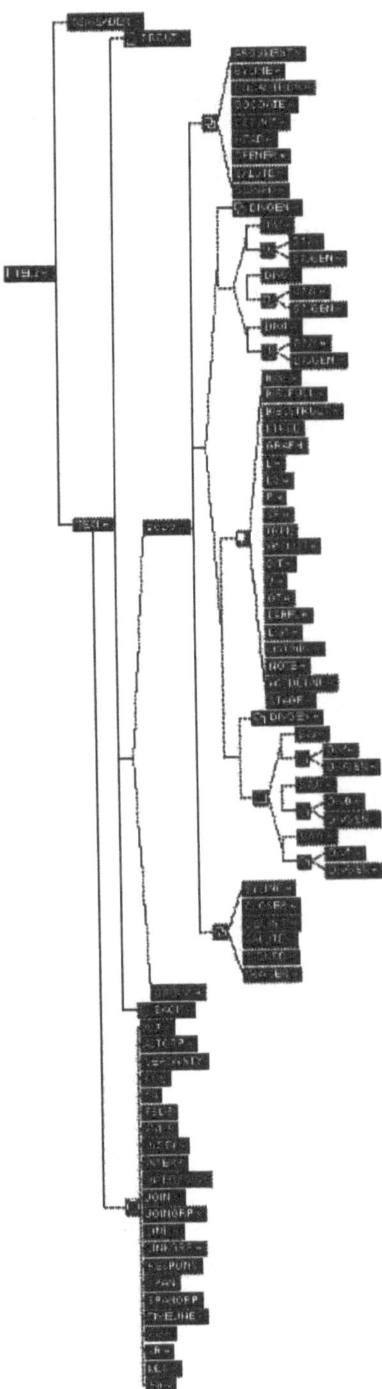

Figure 36. TEI DTD text body structure (outer level)

ning' elements which specify a pointer from the start to the end of the quote, again using `ID/IDREF` to link them.

Despite these problems, the TEI's major achievement has been the provision of a system which lets scholars share texts using a common format which is almost impervious to technological change. This in itself has encouraged and publicized the use of SGML markup, and some of the developments have contributed to further work: the TEI has had a significant influence on the design and organizations of many other SGML projects, from other DTDs to standards like HyTime, and from the problems of internationalization to new systems like XML (whose linking language uses the TEI's Extended Pointer Notation for complex hypertext links). As it is a large and complex DTD, it takes a while to get to know all the markup and what it's for. The 1,300 pages which make up the 'Green Book' master documentation repay a careful read. A formal process of review is examining comments and requests from users, and some further solutions and extensions will appear in a Technical Revision.

2.3.6.1.1. The TEI Lite DTD

```
-//TEI//DTD TEI Lite 1.6//EN
```

For many applications, the full power of the TEI DTD may be overkill. TEI Lite provides many of the basic features of the parent DTD but in considerably simplified form. It also amends a few of the misapprehensions apparent in the full version (for example it permits the use of `<GI>` to describe element markup, a necessity if you are trying to document what markup you are using elsewhere in a project).

The TEI Lite DTD does not use the pizza model: it's a single-file DTD with no options except one (empty) ancillary file to put user modifications into, so it's much easier to manage and much faster to compile. The header still provides plenty of scope for bibliographic description and documentation of what you are encoding, and the text body retains the standard divisional structure, but the descriptive inline markup is more limited (but still adequate for many scholarly purposes).

The TEI header, both here and in the full DTD, contains markup provision for an enormous amount of information *about* the document, as we saw in Figure 34 and Figure 35, and is worth close study if you are planning to create a DTD for information which will need this kind of metadata:

1. The header provides extensive bibliographic markup so that the exact edition or version of a document can be identified, with a

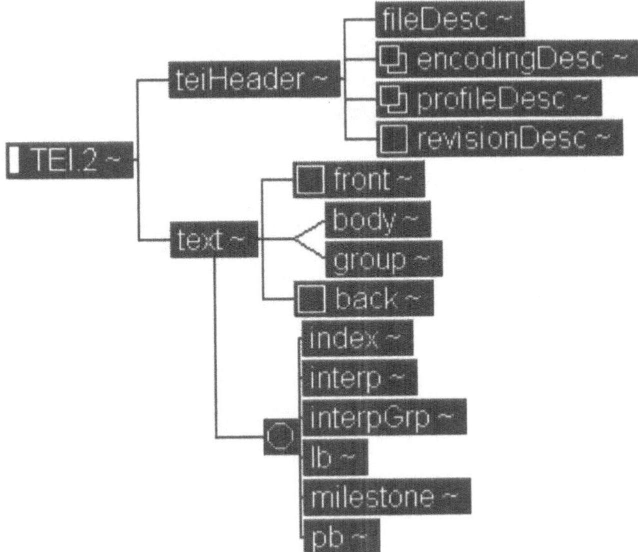

Figure 37. TEI Lite DTD structure

description of where it came from, how it was published, and where it 'belongs' in its field.

2. It provides a place for information about how the document was encoded: what the project is, what editorial decisions were made, how the encoding was done and what elements were used and why, and a referential mechanism to describe to processing software how to derive a correct textual reference from any location in the text.
3. There is a place to give a profile of the text itself: its creation, use of languages, content, classification, and even who wrote it and with what (important for manuscripts).
4. You can record who has worked on a file: the names and dates of people creating, scanning, typing, editing, marking-up, proofing, or otherwise being involved in the creation or production of the electronic document.

2.3.6.2. The Ebind DTD

```
-//UC Berkeley//DTD ebind.dtd (Electronic Binding (Ebind))//
EN
http://sunsite.berkeley.edu/Ebind/
```

The Electronic Binding Project at the University of California at Berkeley defines a DTD for 'binding together digital page images'. Although it is derived from the core tagset of the TEI, it differs significantly from

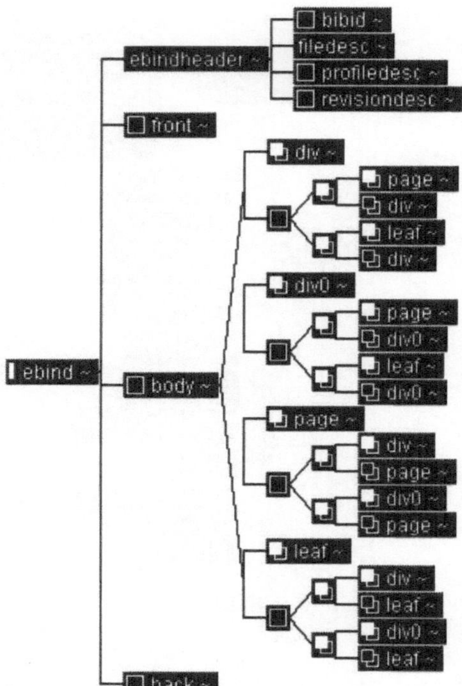

Figure 38. The Ebind DTD

the TEI in that its fundamental unit is the page or leaf (a leaf being exactly two pages, a front and a back) rather than the hierarchical descent to the paragraph.

It provides a documentary bibliographic header with a subset of TEI header elements, but the front matter, body, and back matter are constructed differently, with the divisional elements containing <PAGE> or <LEAF> structures (see Figure 38). Where TEI uses <PB> elements defined as EMPTY to mark pagebreaks, the Ebind DTD encloses pages with a start-tag and end-tag, avoiding the problem of using divisions which may end in the middle of a page.

```
<div0 type="chapter">
<head>XI - Les voiles de l'Orient tombent</head>
<page><image entityref="femin165" seqno="165" nativeno="147"></page>
<page><image entityref="femin166" seqno="166" nativeno="148"></page>
<page><image entityref="femin167" seqno="167" nativeno="149"></page>
<page><image entityref="femin168" seqno="168" nativeno="150"></page>
<page><image entityref="femin169" seqno="169" nativeno="151"></page>
<page><image entityref="femin170" seqno="170" nativeno="152"></page>
<page><image entityref="femin171" seqno="171" nativeno="153"></page>
<page><image entityref="femin172" seqno="172" nativeno="154"></page>
<page><image entityref="femin173" seqno="173" nativeno="155"></page>
```

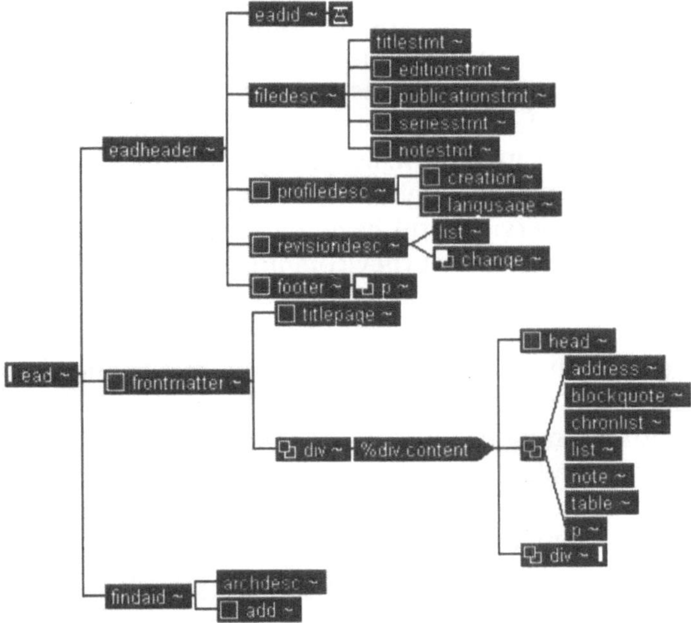

Figure 39. The Electronic Archival Description DTD (header and front matter)

```
<page><image entityref="femin174" seqno="174" nativeno="156"></page>
</div0>
```

Ebind is therefore simpler in construction (a small, single-file DTD) and is less restrictive in structure, although necessarily less descriptive of the text. Within a <PAGE> or <LEAF> element you can reference the image file of the page itself, and provide a caption, description, and the text itself, with elements for paragraphs, tables, lists, quotations and references. This approach gives great flexibility for holding page-based project data where the emphasis is on accessibility to the image, as the code example above shows (from Abensour's *Le problème feministe: un cas d'aspiration collective vers l'egalité* [1] available at the project Web site).

2.3.6.3. The Electronic Archival Description DTD

The EAD project, also at UC Berkeley, grew out of a 'Finding Aids' initiative aimed at investigating 'the desirability and feasibility of creating a platform-independent encoding standard for inventories, registers, indexes, and other finding aids, which are created by libraries, museums, manuscript repositories, and archives to describe and provide access to their holdings' (from their Web site).

The DTD is derives some of its components from the TEI, and provides a header and front matter for each holding (see Figure 39). With the growth of search engines on the Web, and the problems they demonstrate about the poor use of markup in HTML, the use of finding aids has become very important, especially in the library field. Although XML should help considerably by encouraging more relevant markup, specialist location services still have a need to make accurate indexes of where things are and what they contain.

2.3.6.4. CML: Chemical Markup Language

CML has the distinction of being among the first applications of XML (see section 2.4), and is aimed specifically at a vertical market (one which is entirely contained within a single product area or subject).

It allows molecular chemists to describe chemical structures in a way that can be transmitted over the Web and displayed interactively in a browser — something HTML would not be suitable for. For more details see section 2.3.9.2 and Figure 53.

2.3.7. DTDs for Tables

Tables have received a lot of attention, for something which to the outsider appears to be a simple rectangular grid of rows and columns. Only when you have worked with them for a while, in a variety of forms, can you start to see why they cause so much of a problem: every application is different, and every author, user, and publisher has their own view about how they should be encoded and how they should appear.

This has been apparent to many people who handle them on a daily basis. Indeed, as Knuth says:

> Printers charge extra when you ask them to typeset tables, and they do so for good reason: Each table tends to have its own peculiarities, so it's necessary to give some thought to each one, and to fiddle with alternative approaches until finding something that looks good and communicates well.
>
> *The TEXbook*[26], Chapter 22

Authors using non-SGML software usually type their tabular data into a spreadsheet-like system provided by the word processor (or into an actual spreadsheet, on systems which can link or pass data between such applications), and then pull rows and columns back and forth until the 'right' size and shape of table is achieved. While this works well for the purposes of printing once on a known size of paper, especially for small tables of a few rows and columns, it becomes tedious for larger or more complex tables, and pointless when publishing to a medium like the Web where you cannot know the geometry of the user's browser window. It also risks forcing the data to be stored in a possibly inappropriate format.

Bigger problems arise when dealing with column or row spanning, cells which contain text or image data rather than just digits, dynamically-resizable displays, and tables in which the cell location is related to the surrounding text in some way.

Even bigger problems are waiting if you want to use or reuse data which may or may not originally have been intended for tabular display, but which is marked up for content in such a way as to make it usable in a table (content-based markup). A simple example is a list of places and things to see, which could be presented in many different ways, one of which happens to be a table. Using non-table markup, you retain the ability to convert it to table markup as and when needed, while also being able to use the data for other purposes such as online query-based reporting, without the 'tableness' ('tabularity'?) interfering with the retrieval. For example, in this table, suppose a retrieval system finds the word 'sugar' that you were looking for in a plaintext file:

```
Fudge     Butter                   Brownies     Butter
          Sugar                                 Sugar
          Chocolate                             Chocolate
          Cream                                 Flour
```

Using simple unmarked text you get a single line containing the word 'sugar' twice, which is clearly meaningless. Even if the four 'columns' were marked up as columns, you'd get two lists of ingredients and no recipe name. Correct retrieval only follows if the lists are identified as lists first, complete with title or heading retrieved as a whole unit, and only then used as table cells for display.

The SGML implementations of tables usually start with the simplest definition, where each table is made of rows and each row is made of cells and each cell contains just text: TABLE ROW CELL . This is the model familiar to users of tables in HTML. But the demands of processing, especially for large tables, mean that formatting can be done much more efficiently if the processor can be told other factors beforehand, such as how many columns to expect, what the features or layout or content of each is going to be, and if there is a lengthy table heading section or footing section with totals.

Cells may not be just for classical numerical data: as shown above they may need to contain text, sometimes whole paragraphs, or titles, subheadings, and lists, or even other tables. This is not well handled by

CALS tables (see section 2.3.7.1) in their raw form, and some software vendors such as SoftQuad and ArborText support adaptations to handle this. Their table models are often used because they provide a practical solution to the choice of table markup when faced with matching your requirements to the table capabilities of an editing system. The SASOUT model (see section 2.3.7.2) also caters for cells with many (sometimes disparate) pieces of content, and with relationships between headers and the cells below or in line with them. Yet another model is provided by the tables fragment of the ISO TR 9573 Standards DTD (see section 2.3.7.3). In the aircraft and motor vehicle industries, there are some more specific table formats, ATA-1000 (Aircraft Maintenance) and J2008 (Motor Vehicle Maintenance), which are not covered here.

In the case of HTML, where tables are used to align large blocks of text to create the illusion of typeset columns, the content model for a cell can even match that of the document text body, including `<table>` itself.

2.3.7.1. CALS Tables

```
-//USA-DOD//DTD Table Model 951010//EN
```

The US military SGML initiative CALS (Continuous Acquisition and Lifecycle Support) generated a requirement for tabular material from MIL-M-38784B, the specification for technical manuals, to be available in SGML (see section 2.3.5). This specification was completed at a relatively early stage, and because of the nature of the imperative, software support from editors and formatters was soon available. This has meant that the model adopted by the CALS specifications has become the *de facto* model for other applications, as well as the *de jure* model in its own domain. The formal definition and explanation of the tables is in MIL-HDBK-28001, and the model has been updated by a Technical Recommendation of the OASIS organization (TR 9502:1995).

The CALS model requires specification (in advance) of the number of rows, and the contents or alignment of the columns. The number of rows is given in an attribute on the containing table element, but the column specification is done by including multiple `EMPTY` `<COLSPEC>` elements for each column in the table. These hold the remaining information about the columns in their attributes. They are often hidden from sight by graphical editors, as they have no data content, but the attributes are constantly updated by the editing software as changes are made to the visual layout and design of the table. Specification of any column spanning can be done in a similar manner with the `<SPANSPEC>` element.

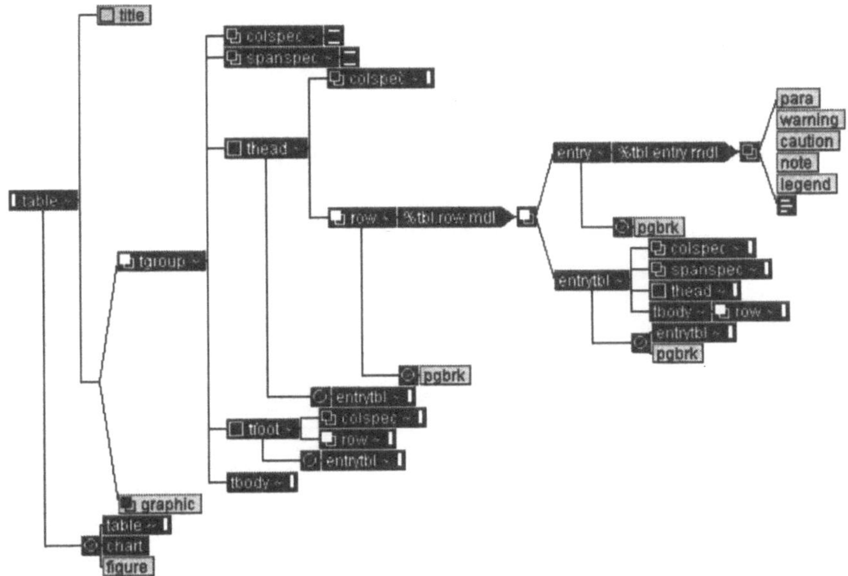

Figure 40. The CALS Table Model (OASIS Exchange version)

There are then three major segments to the rest of the table: `<thead>`, `<tbody>`, and `<tfoot>`, but the order is unusual: `<thead>` and `<tfoot>` come before `<tbody>`, so that a processor can read the totals and allocate column space *before* it reads the body of a large table. This also lets processors compute percentages or other statistics while reading the rest of the table, because the column sums are already known. Local modifications to column specifications can be done in `<thead>` and `<tfoot>` with additional `<COLSPEC>` elements, but not in the `<tbody>` element.

The principal content of all three is `<row>`, and this in turn contains `<entry>` as the cell element. Figure 40 shows this structure expanded, taken from the copy of the DTD which is included with *DocBook* (so tables in this book are done this way).

2.3.7.2. The SASOUT Table DTD

`-//Rincewind//DTD SAS Institute SAS-Out Table//EN`

In contrast to the head–body–foot model of the CALS table DTD, the SASOUT model presents a different approach. It was designed by Craig Sampson at the SAS Institute, well-known for their statistical software, in response to problems they detected when trying to use CALS for non-print presentation of tables. In particular, the SASOUT model allows the

AT&T Common Stock		
Year	Price	Dividend
1971	41–54	$2.60
2	41–54	2.70
3	46–55	2.87
4	40–53	3.24
5	45–52	3.40
6	51–59	.95*

```
<TGROUP COLS="3">
  <COLSPEC ALIGN="right" COLNAME="COLUMN1" COLNUM="1">
  <COLSPEC ALIGN="center" COLNAME="COLUMN2" COLNUM="2">
  <COLSPEC CHAR="." ALIGN="char" COLSEP="1" COLNAME="COLUMN3"
   COLNUM="3">
  <THEAD VALIGN="top">
    <ROW><ENTRY ALIGN="center" NAMEST="COLUMN1"
      NAMEEND="COLUMN3">AT&amp;T Common Stock</ENTRY></ROW>
    <ROW><ENTRY>Year</ENTRY>
      <ENTRY ALIGN="center">Price</ENTRY>
      <ENTRY ALIGN="right">Dividend</ENTRY></ROW>
  </THEAD>
  <TBODY VALIGN="top">
    <ROW><ENTRY>1971</ENTRY><ENTRY>41&ndash;54</ENTRY>
         <ENTRY>$2.60</ENTRY></ROW>
    <ROW><ENTRY>2</ENTRY><ENTRY>41&ndash;54</ENTRY>
         <ENTRY>2.70</ENTRY></ROW>
    <ROW><ENTRY>3</ENTRY><ENTRY>46&ndash;55</ENTRY>
         <ENTRY>2.87</ENTRY></ROW>
    <ROW><ENTRY>4</ENTRY><ENTRY>40&ndash;53</ENTRY>
         <ENTRY>3.24</ENTRY></ROW>
    <ROW><ENTRY>5</ENTRY><ENTRY>45&ndash;52</ENTRY>
         <ENTRY>3.40</ENTRY></ROW>
    <ROW><ENTRY>6</ENTRY><ENTRY>51&ndash;59</ENTRY>
         <ENTRY>.95*</ENTRY></ROW>
  </TBODY>
</TGROUP>
```

This table is quoted in *The TEXbook*[26] as deriving from a report by Michael Lesk[29], to whom I am grateful for permission to use it.

Figure 41. Canonical table example

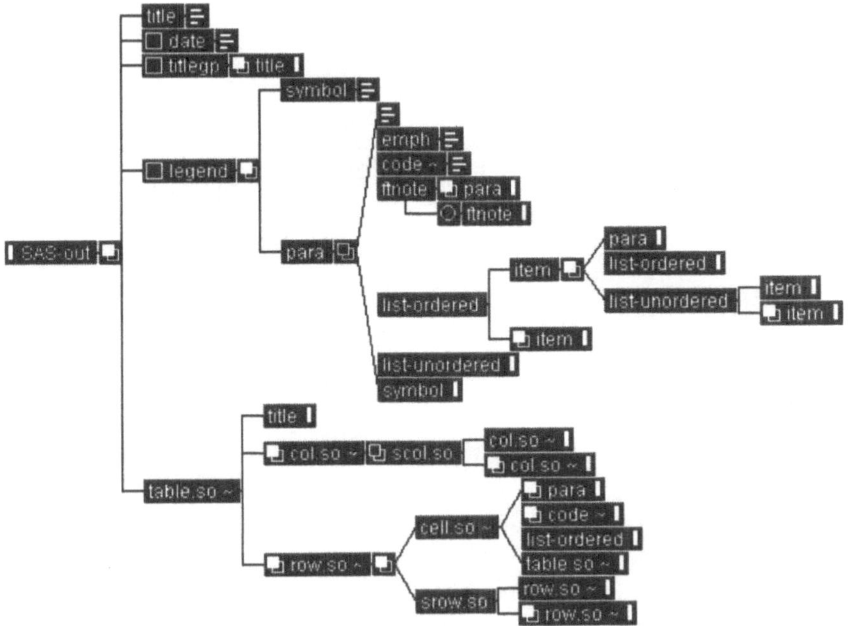

Figure 42. The SASOUT Table DTD

preservation of relationships between headers and cells, and supports more directly their formatting and presentation.

The DTD (Figure 42) has considerable markup richness available in the <LEGEND> element, where you can describe and label the table, at a level equivalent to simple documentation DTDs (paragraphs, lists, symbols, and footnotes, plus emphasis and computer-code elements). The table itself holds the column specifications as a separate block before the rows, with provision for split columns; and the rows and sub-rows contain cells which can hold the same kind of structural markup as the legend (lists and paragraphs).

This structure is important, bearing in mind the kind of tabular information typically produced by the canonical 'contingency table' output of statistics packages (crosstabulations), or those used for market research surveys, where each cell can have many items within it, displayed as a list of numeric values, as well as textual comment, flags, and other symbols.

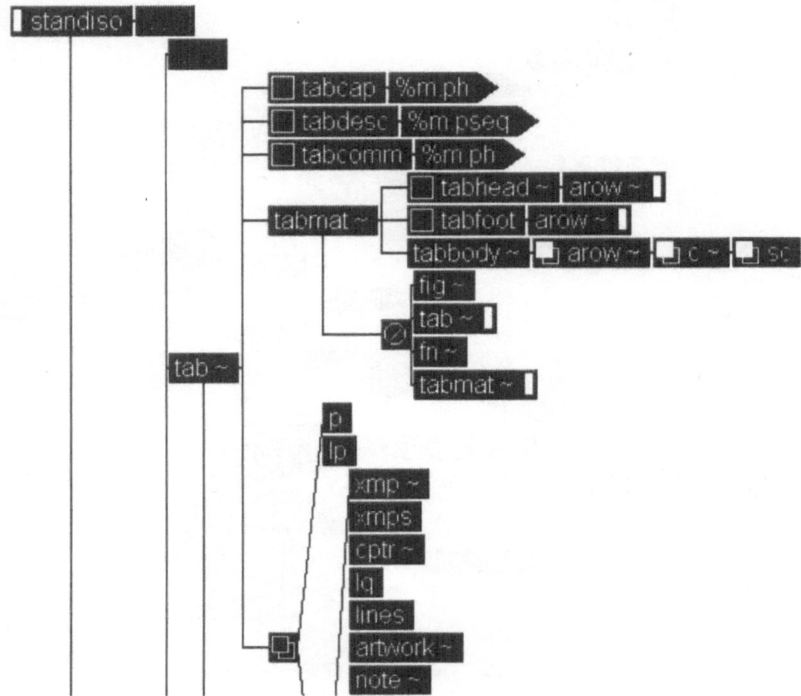

Figure 43. The ISO/IEC TR 9573 Table Fragment

2.3.7.3. The ISO/IEC TR 9573 Standards DTD table model

```
ISO/IEC TR 9573-11:1992//DTD for Standards//EN
```

The SGML support activity of the ISO has produced (among other things) a DTD for the documentation of ISO and other standards, part of which is a model for tables. This is shown in Figure 43 (the remainder of the DTD is not shown here, as it is intended for a rather specialized use).

The model provides for a caption, description, and comment, followed by head, foot, and body, each containing rows and columns in the conventional manner. However, the sub-cell element <SC>, which you can see terminating the cell in the diagram, can contain virtually the entire paragraph-level structural content model found elsewhere in the DTD (not shown here for simple reasons of space on the page). This gives great flexibility for the user, but implies the need for a fairly sophisticated formatting engine if an author can truly use almost arbitrary content at that point.

2.3.8. DTDs for mathematics

DTDs for mathematics are something of a special case. Indeed the discussion (or 'argument') about whether or not it is even possible to encode mathematics meaningfully in SGML still rumbles on, and those interested in debating it will find plenty of scope at the SGML/XML and TeX annual conferences.

Early attempts by the AAP and a number of other European scientific publishers resulted in DTDs aimed at encoding the appearance of the equation or expression, with heavy reliance on the concepts used in TeX's math-typesetting language. Later work between the AAP and by the European Physical Society has led to the current representative of these, the ISO 12083 Math DTD.

The American Mathematical Society has been an active player in the field of SGML and math for many years. Early work was done by former AMS experts Ron Whitney and Bill Woolf, and currently by Ralph Youngen, Barbara Beeton, and Patrick Ion, one of the co-chairs of the MathML group, who are involved in a project to define a comprehensive math symbol collection, with the ultimate goal being full support for the presentation of math notation on the Web.

Math print production, however, has in many places remained firmly wedded to TeX as the only viable automated math formatter of any significance: it has always seemed rather circular to take an author's TeX math and encode it in SGML, only to decode it back into TeX for printing. Some SGML systems like *DynaText* and *SGMLC*, allow you to embed TeX source code in the SGML markup, and render it in the display (this is similar to the way that IBM's Techexplorer plug-in for Netscape *Navigator* handles math within a browser screen).

Some mathematicians, though, have long wanted to be able to approach the storage and retrieval of math expressions analytically. It would clearly be useful if you could go to a math database and find all references to a specific expression, say the differential-difference equations for the probabilities $P_{m,n}(T)$ in papers on the general epidemic model for the diffusion of rumor[11], regardless of how they were expressed, or even when they formed part of a larger expression. Graphical equation processor systems like *Mathematica* and *Maple* have become standard tools for the visualization of mathematics, but depressingly large numbers of mathematicians, especially students, still struggle to position superscripts, subscripts, and symbols *by hand* in word processing systems (one university typographer proudly told me how he had helped a PhD student format his math thesis in 'only' two months using a manual system [a word processor], when it could have been done more accurately and with less pain in a matter of days using a system which understands math). However, a substantial amount of effort has now gone into math markup: the ISO TR 9573 Equation DTD represents some of work done on these lines by Anders Berglund, and its concepts now form part of many, if not most, math DTDs.

When the HTML+ proposal appeared (followed by the draft HTML3, see section 2.3.9.1), its math elements came under heavy scrutiny. Unfortunately, none of the then mainstream browsers felt able to include any mathematical capability in their products, so the only visible effect was the demonstration formatting provided by the *Arena* test-bed browser. Nevertheless, a number of math-oriented projects continued, and at least one at the commercial level resulted in the *Techexplorer* math plug-in from IBM for *Navigator*, which takes TEX code in an attribute value and formats it for display in real time. A project funded by the European Commission has resulted in the Euromath DTD and software (supported by GriF, see section 3.4.6).

In 1997 the World Wide Web Consortium (W3C) adopted a draft math DTD written for XML, called Mathematics Markup Language, or MathML, for use in the Web (see section 2.3.8.4). This is now set to supersede the previous attempts at embedding math in HTML, and is being supported by several manufacturers, including GriF and STiLO (see section 74), and is implemented in the W3C's *Amaya* browser (see Figure 50).

For the purposes of comparison in the examples here, the encoding is demonstrated for the simple expression (due to JL Bate):

$$b_4 i \sqrt{u} \frac{ru}{16} qt\pi$$

2.3.8.1. ISO 12083 Math DTD

```
ISO 12083:1994//DTD Mathematics//EN
```

This is actually a fragment rather than a free-standing DTD. It is designed to be incorporated into the ISO 12083 Book and Article DTDs wherever equations are required (see Figure 44), and provides a successor to the AAP Math DTD. The element names within a formula reflect the mostly presentational rather than structural intent. There are six purely typographic elements (font-styles), and each of them can contain the others recursively as subsidiary elements (the figure shows them unexpanded): the remainder of the elements are mathematical.

These remaining elements, with the exception of the spacing, line-breaking, and referencing elements, are also mutually recursive; that is, they can all contain all their peers *ad infinitum*. This is necessary in most

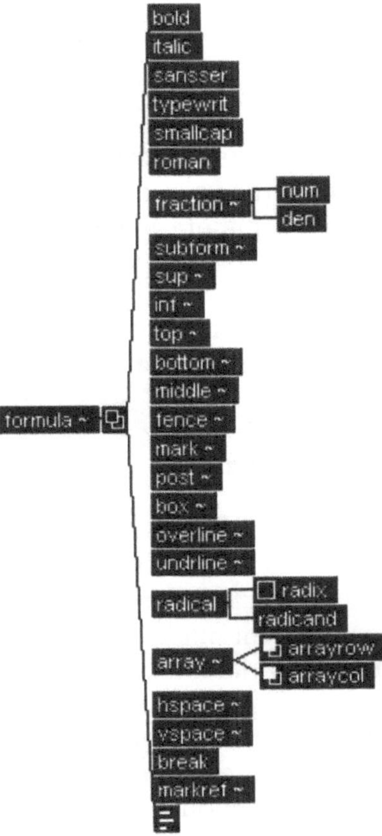

Figure 44. The ISO 12083 Math DTD

math structures, to allow bracketed or fractional expressions to contain bracketed and fractional expressions, which in turn contain bracketed and fractional expressions, which in turn contain...*etc.*

Box and fence elements are used to provide enclosures and to mark off the portions of an expression which need separate treatment, such as bracketed matter (the HTML3 math fragment uses a similar technique). The naming of the division of fractions into numerator and denominator, and of roots into radix and radicand is the extent of the structural provisions, so our sample expression looks like this:

```
<dformula>
  <italic>b</italic><inf>4</inf><italic><italic>i</italic>
  <radical>
    <radicand></italic>u</radicand>
  </radical>
  <fraction>
    <num><italic>ru</italic></num>
```

```
      <den>17</den>
    </fraction>
    <italic>qt</italic>&pi;
  </dformula>
```

The result is a reasonably robust model for the holding of basic mathematical data for print or screen presentation, and it is perhaps a little surprising that it has not been more widely used, especially by publishers, but this may be associated more with the adoption rate of SGML in general, rather than any specific fault in the ISO 12083 suite.

A number of editing systems also support the older AAP Math DTD (now nearly obsolete, in the process of being superseded by ISO 12083 and perhaps MathML).

2.3.8.1.1. ISO TR 9573 Equation DTD

```
ISO TR 9573-11:1992(E)//ELEMENTS Mathematics DTD//EN
```

This fragment is an attempt to make a less presentation-oriented tagset available for math. The distinction between 'formula' (inline) and 'display formula' remains, but font markup is limited to roman and italics, and there is more descriptive markup available within the more complex constructs like root and product.

There are nevertheless many mathematicians who would argue that this is still presentation-oriented — and many publishers who would argue that it does not contain enough presentation markup for it to be printed accurately. You can distinguish this from the ISO 12083 Math DTD by comparing the markup involved for our sample expression with the example in the previous section:

```
<df><italic>b</italic><sub>4</sub><italic>i</italic><root>
    <degree></degree>
    <of><italic>u</italic></of>
  </root><frac>
    <numer><italic>ru</italic></numer>
    <over>16</over>
  </frac><italic>qt</italic>&pi;</df>
```

2.3.8.2. The Euromath DTD

Euromath is a pan-European project funded by the European Commission to 'provide European mathematicians with a shared, enriched computing environment'. Among the tools produced are a common data model and a common user interface (editor), with an online support center at Bratislava. Access to the Euromath system is worldwide and is not restricted to Europe. See section 3.4.6 for details of the whole system.

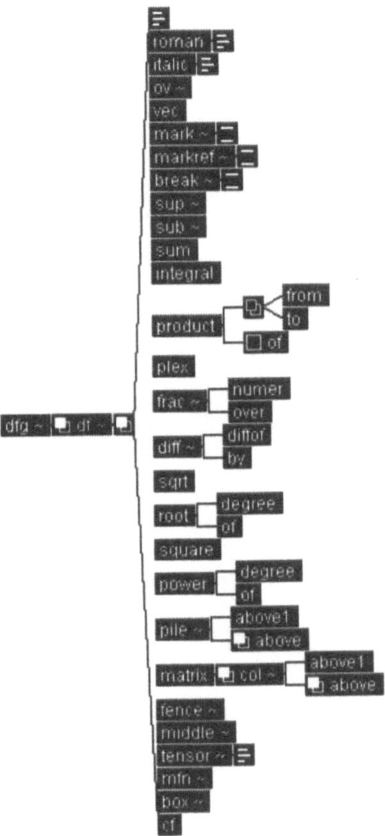

Figure 45. The ISO TR 9573 Equation DTD

The Euromath editor comes with a large number of DTD fragments which can be used to compose DTDs for several different tasks. The one I'm illustrating here is the Article DTD, as it is one of the commonest uses. If you're using the Euromath editor, you don't see the separate fragments, as it presents a graphical, formatted view instead. As this is an application where the math is an integral part of the whole DTD, rather than a subsidiary fragment, I have reproduced here the entire article structure (see Figure 46).

Instead of a single header containing the bibliographic data, it is separated out into its component elements at the same level of hierarchy as the sections. The body of text goes in the sectional divisions, with the usual section title and paragraphs for a preamble followed by subsections.

At paragraph level, there is actually no such element as <P> or <PARA>. Instead there is a choice of different kinds of structure, like plain para-

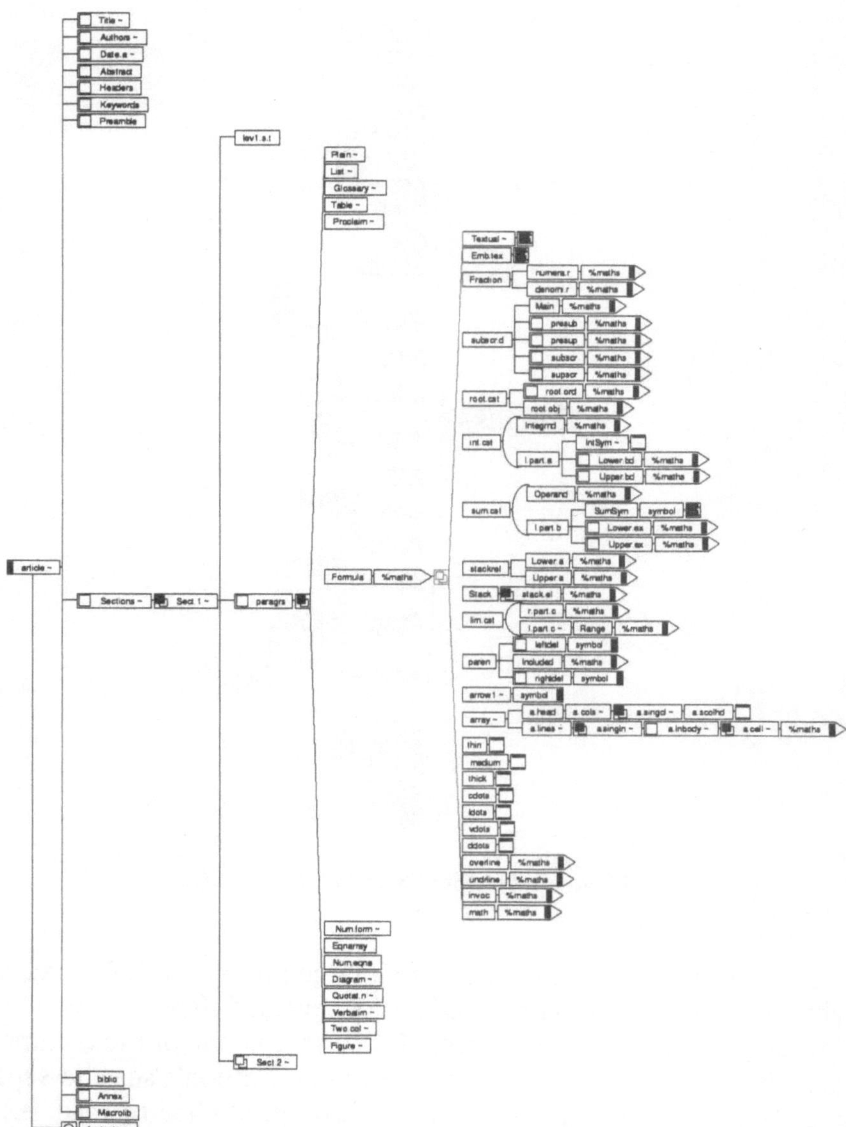

Figure 46. The Euromath Article DTD

graphs, lists, glossaries, tables, diagrams, quotations, verbatim text, two-column setting, and figures. In addition, there are math structures to proclaim theorems, formulas, and arrays (numeric and non-numeric).

```
<formula>
  <textual>b</textual>
  <subscr.d>
```

```
      <main>
        <textual>4</textual>
      </main>
    </subscr.d>
    <textual>i</textual>
    <root.cst>
      <root.obj>
        <textual>u</textual>
      </root.obj>
    </root.cst>
    <fraction>
      <numera.r>
        <textual>r</textual>
        <textual>u</textual>
      </numera.r>
      <denomi.r>
        <textual>16</textual>
      </denomi.r>
    </fraction>
    <textual>q</textual>
    <textual>t</textual>
    <textual>&pi;</textual>
  </formula>
```

Finally, within these structures, the inline markup provides for pictures, references (with very extensive bibliographic features), emphasis, in-line formulas, external references to other files and to Web and Gopher resources.

2.3.8.3. HTML3 Math

The early proposals for an expanded HTML including mathematics were contained in the HTML+ DTD, long since defunct, but were incorporated in the expired HTML3 Internet Draft which met with considerable popularity, and has formed the basis for most of those subsequent versions which do not use the flat content model (see section 2.3.9.1).

HTML+ introduced math markup for the first time, and the model has remained virtually unchanged in HTML3, although it has never been implemented outside the *Arena* and *Amaya* test browsers. It was introduced by using an exclusion exception to disable the normal in-line (paragraph-mode) text markup and an inclusion exception to add the math elements (see Figure 47), which made it possible to prevent recursion of `<math>` within `<math>` and allow for easier future modification (see section 2.3.9.1.6). It was also explicit in the design that this math model was intended to deal with relatively simple math, up to perhaps high school level, rather than for every possible contingency of the professional mathematician.

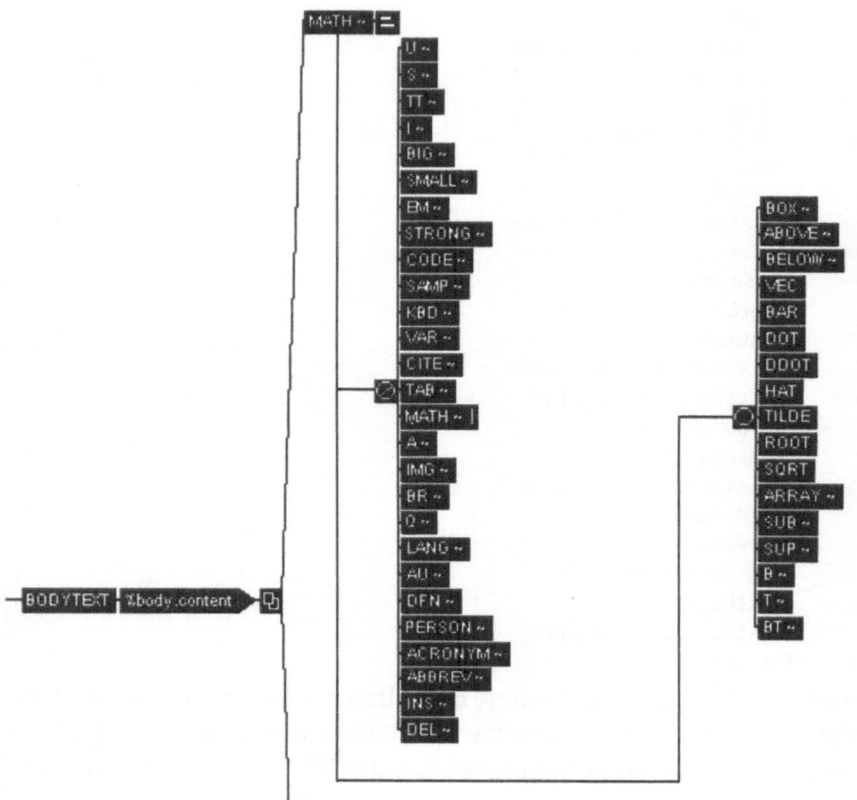

Figure 47. The HTML3 Math model

As in other DTDs, the <box> element can be used for enclosing expressions in brackets of various kinds, but the strong presentational nature is evident from the omission of a separate fraction element: instead, <box> has a complex content model which allows it to represent constructs which would otherwise need their own element (see Figure 48).

The influence of TeX on the research community where HTML originally evolved meant that visual indicators like <italic> were not considered necessary, as a browser or processing engine should easily be able to infer them from the notation of the expression (as does TeX). This has the big advantage that the markup is much lighter:

```
<math>b<sub>4</sub>i<sqrt>u</sqrt><box>ru<over>16</box>qt&pi;</math>
```

Although never implemented in a commercial browser, the possibility of math encoding for the Web contributed to the discussion on math in SGML, and ultimately gave rise to the latest proposal: MathML.

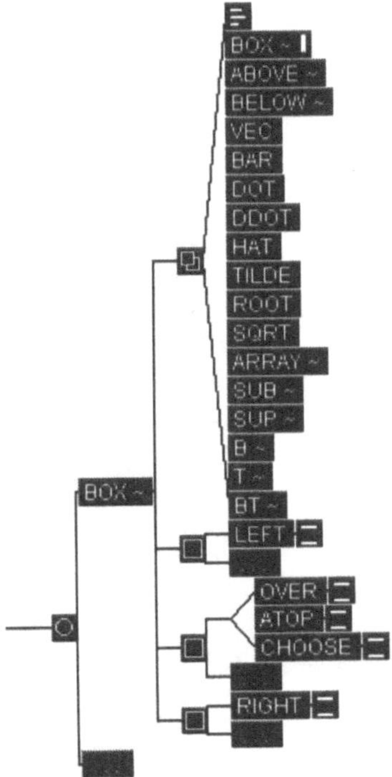

Figure 48. HTML3 Math: the box model

2.3.8.4. MathML

As XML provides users with the ability to design and specify their own markup, any of the existing math DTDs or fragments could be used in an XML version — provided browsers have the ability to display it.

Some math ability is already built into the Synex (now Inso) *ViewPort* engine which powers *Panorama* and *MultiDoc Pro* (see section 6), but further support from other browsers was needed to make it worthwhile for mathematicians to take this route. Microsoft's *Internet Explorer* now has some support for MathML, and the MathML project itself is also developing a browser independently. Both STiLO's and GriF's editors can do math, as can the obvious heavyweights like *ADEPT*.

The Mathematical Markup Language (MathML) is intended as an XML application (earlier versions were developed in regular SGML while XML was still being defined). The goal is 'to enable mathematics to be served, received, and processed on the Web, just as HTML has enabled this functionality for text'. MathML describes mathematical expression structure (the encoding of 'semantic notions', permitting the evaluation of mathematical expressions) as well as allowing presentational markup.

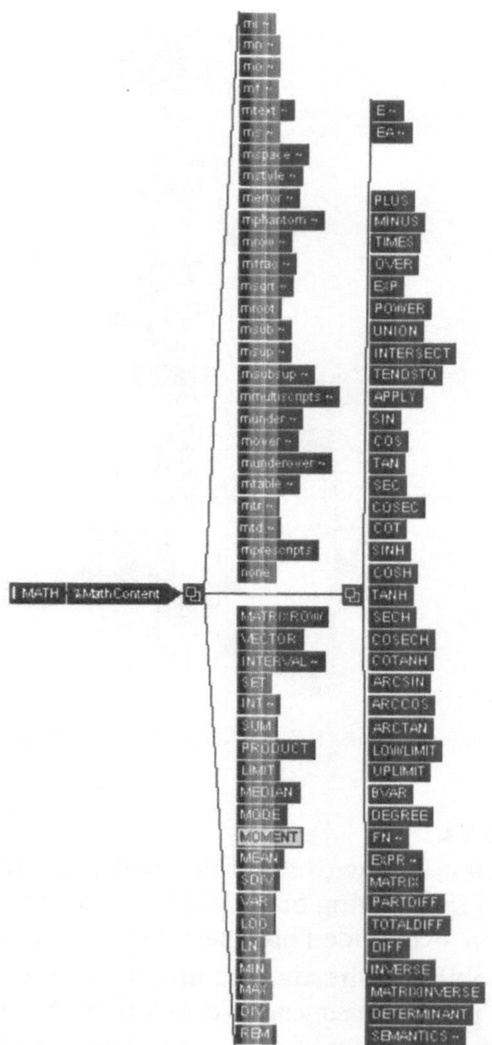

Figure 49. Mathematics Markup Language (MathML)

In Figure 49, the structural elements are shown in CAPITALS and the presentational elements in lowercase. The outer model is entirely flat, allowing any element to occur within `<math>`. Much of the design is recursive, as is normal with math DTDs, so many elements are themselves designed to hold almost any combination of other elements, but some functions (*eg* `<TAN/>`, `<COS/>`, *etc*) are defined as `EMPTY`, so they don't possess any content upon which to act, but work by imputation upon the formula following them.

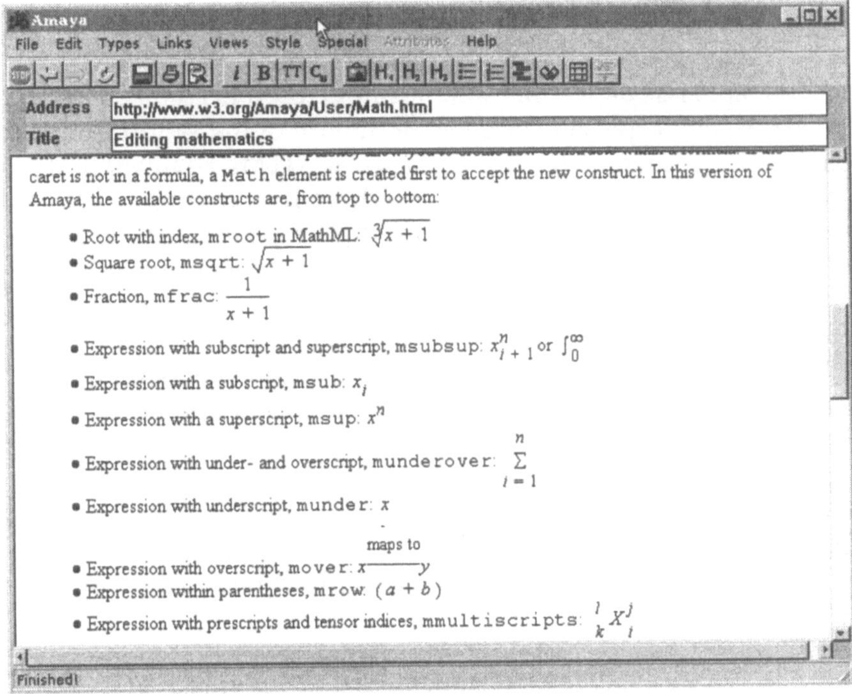

Figure 50. MathML displayed in the *Amaya* browser

```
<math>
  <msub>
    <mi>b</mi>
    <mn>4</mn>
  </msub>
  <mi>i</mi>
  <msqrt>
    <mi>u</mi>
  </msqrt>
  <mfrac>
    <mrow><mi>r</mi><mi>u</mi></mrow>
    <mn>16</mn>
  </mfrac>
  <mi>q</mi><mi>t</mi><mi>&pi;</mi>
</math>
```

The DTD is being developed by a Working Group of the W3C: a copy of the draft report is on the CD-ROM for reference, but you should check online at the W3C's site (`http://www.w3.org/Math/`) for further releases. It is supported by the W3C's testbed browser *Amaya* (see Figure 50).

2.3.9. DTDs for the Web

Since the rapid rise of personal and business Internet connectivity in the early 1990s, and especially because of the use of the World Wide Web, there has been growing interest in the use of HTML as an application of SGML (that is, in using HTML with validation). Although it was widely criticized in the SGML community as 'not proper' SGML, and despite some small oddities of design, it is in fact the *implementation* of HTML in browsers which has led to the misunderstandings over the way it is treated.

HTML nevertheless remains by a long way the most widespread application of SGML, and for most people it is the first and (so far) the only one they have met, even if they don't realize it. Its power as an introductory or enabling tool should therefore never be overlooked, and it is worth examining its development and versions in some detail, as they have had a major influence on the way subsequent SGML applications have been written, and particularly on the development of XML.

It was estimated in an HTML session at the SGML Conference in 1995 that perhaps 95–98% of the world's HTML files were either defective or just plain broken in SGML terms, as they were written without any kind of checking or validation. Since then the standard of HTML-only editors has improved considerably, and with it the quality of HTML code in Web documents, although (with a few obvious exceptions like SoftQuad's *HoTMetaL*) it is unlikely that such systems will ever produce completely valid HTML for anything except very simple instances.

In view of the virtual impossibility of bringing the world's existing base of invalid HTML 'back into the fold', and given the rapid progress of XML and the commitment to it by software vendors, it is clear that HTML is fast coming to the end of its useful life for the professional information provider, but it probably still has many years left as a simple, useful, and non-rigorous tool for marketing, domestic, and hobby use.

2.3.9.1. HTML

```
-//IETF//DTD HTML 2.0//EN
```

The invention of the HyperText Markup Language (HTML) as the method of identifying information in text files for the World Wide Web was a pragmatic one. It provided a way of marking structure, content, and appearance which was at once machine-parsable, non-proprietary, multi-platform, and editable by hand with any plaintext editor. The fact that it used the principles of SGML was not accidental, although the full implications did not become apparent until later: the benefits which HTML can provide are naturally those for which SGML itself is best known. The choice has nevertheless proved to be a useful one, particularly in terms of portability and scalability, although the management of future development has brought its own set of problems to bear.

2.3.9.1.1. Origins In 1992 it became clear that a small but increasing number of Web users and providers wanted to make more use of the structural editing, data retrieval and reusability facilities which SGML systems provide. To do this, a DTD and an SGML Declaration were needed, and draft versions were made available via the Internet from CERN (Conseil Européen pour la Recherche Nucléaire), the European Laboratory for Particle Physics, where the Web was invented.

From 1994 to 1996, responsibility for the development of HTML rested with the HTML Working Group of the IETF (Internet Engineering Task Force). This group produced the formal proposal of HTML 2.0 which was adopted as RFC 1866, as well as the drafts for HTML+ and HTML3, including subsequent revisions of the RFC (Request For Comments) documents for tables, file upload, and the use of multinational character sets. Development was done largely by volunteers, working either on their own behalf or with the support of their employers, many of whom had (and retain) a stake in the success of SGML as well as of the Web.

Current development is now being undertaken by the World Wide Web Consortium (W3C), an industry/research partnership based at the Massachusetts Institute of Technology Laboratory for Computer Science (MIT LCS) in the USA and INRIA (Institut Nationale de Recherche en Informatique et en Automatique) in France. The principal industrial players, including the two biggest browser manufacturers, Microsoft and Netscape, are among the 200+ members of the consortium. To date they have published recommendations and discussion documents on several topics, including style sheets, scripting, object insertion, and several revised versions of HTML (see section 2.3.9.1.2). The W3C is also responsible for XML (see section 2.4).

2.3.9.1.2. The HTML DTDs The HTML DTD is a simple description of a common and relatively non-rigorous class of office document or technical report, with features such as headings, subheadings, paragraphs, lists, and illustrations. It was designed to preserve and convey information for use via the World Wide Web in a portable format which could be created with the minimum of software.

The official standard is HTML 2.0 (RFC 1866). A more advanced version (HTML+) was never widely adopted: it formed the basis for HTML3, which expired as an Internet Draft in March 1995, but had enormous influence on subsequent versions. The W3C has issued a reference version (regrettably numbered 3.2, as it in fact contained mostly 2.0 material), and some experimental versions, resulting in HTML 4.x. The changes in these versions have been relatively small, updating features like inline scripts, stylesheets, and embedded objects from HTML3 with attributes invented by the browser makers, but they also added frames and better scripting support.

Browser makers have occasionally issued (or had written for them) versions or fragments of HTML which describe some of the additional features they support. There is also a draft composite DTD (*HTML Pro*) for professional use, compiled by my own consultancy. This contains all of the elements publicly known to be used in other versions, so the webpage developer can use the various extras added by different manufacturers, but use any SGML editor and retain conformance, thus providing a smoother upgrade path to XML.

The elements defined in HTML can be classed in three categories:

1. structural (sections, headings, paragraphs, lists, tables);
2. descriptive (emphasis, quotation, citation, hypertext, illustrations);
3. visual (bold, italic, spacing, fonts).

There is competition in the marketplace between the demands of graphic designers for more features like font changes, positioning, and animated illustrations, and the demands of information providers who need things like accurate context searching, reproducibility, portability, and durability. Many companies are under strong pressure to develop their Web presence, and are doing it for marketing and image purposes rather than as part of an information strategy, so software which concentrates on visual appeal tends to lead the market.

This is reinforced by the tendency of authors and creators of information to use the Web as simply another desktop publishing system. While this is a perfectly valid and unobjectionable use in itself, its promotion of HTML *solely* as another DTP format by browser and editor makers ignores the other benefits SGML could provide.

The 'black sheep' reputation which HTML had in the SGML field is partly due to the tendency by critics to confuse the specifications of the DTD with their implementation by browsers without a robust document model. This confusion over implementation rests not on any deficiency in the HTML DTD itself, but on the decision of most browser makers to ignore the DTD and to support the use of any element anywhere, and their consequent failure even to match start-tags

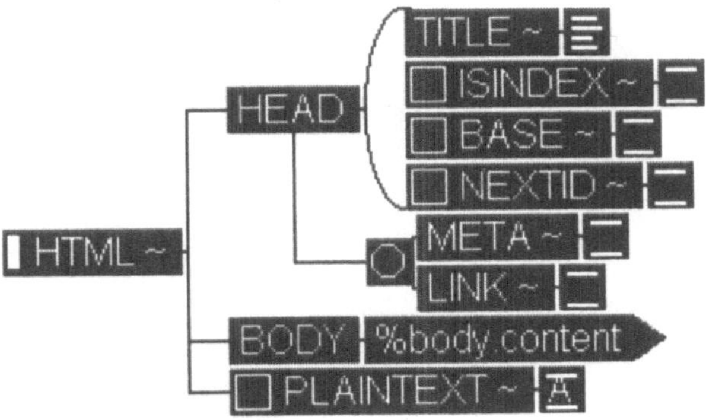

Figure 51. Header and upper body structure of HTML 2.0 (RFC 1866)

with end-tags. There are of course deficiencies in what is at heart a pilot system or experimental prototype, but it is a serious error to blame the DTD alone for the faults of the implementations. The question of markup to identify structure has already been addressed in the re-implementation of HTML3's `<DIV>` in recent browsers, and the appearance of the 'official' ISO-HTML DTD, with a list of amendments intended to rationalize and improve the design.

If the Web is to succeed in the long-term as an information system, the robustness of a formal means of modeling structure must outweigh the short-term gain of making pages look cute or clever alone, and bearing little or no actual information. Hence XML.

2.3.9.1.3. HTML 2.0 The DTD which made it to the official standard, RFC 1866, is fairly plain. It includes the basic structure of headings, paragraphs, lists, block quotations, and preformatted text, with some common inline elements for emphasis, citation, and computer documentation. Of the more advanced material that was being proposed at the time, only fill-in forms are included.

The body of an HTML 2.0 document follows a completely flat model, with mixed content throughout, except for one or two areas like lists, where the list elements themselves specify only list items inside them, and forms, where form-specific elements are involved. This enables the novice or naïve user to type `<P>` as if it were a separator (as originally specified), and not worry about content models, syntax, or validity because of the forgiving nature of Web browsers.

The `<A>` element used for hypertext can contain markup which includes headings and inline elements, but not whole paragraphs or other structural elements. Inline elements themselves have a recursive content model. As there is no division or section structure, headings sim-

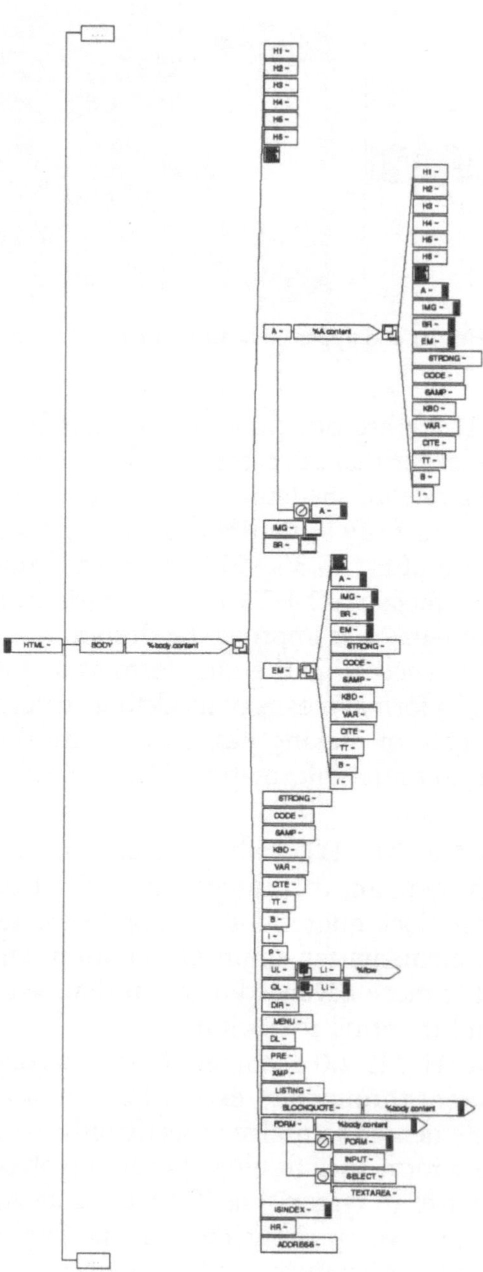

Figure 52. Body and text structure of HTML 2.0 (RFC 1866) showing the flat document model

ply act as separators between chunks of text, and may occur in any sequence (so there is no way to implement section numbering with any reliability).

A parameter entity switch enabled the DTD to be used in 'strict' mode, where some obsolescent elements were excluded (<XMP> and <LISTING>, for example). An experimental version with more facilities for inline markup and divisional structure was called HTML+, but this was superseded by HTML3.

2.3.9.1.4. HTML3 This pilot version developed from the experimental HTML+ in 1994 and 1995. It added <STYLE> and <RANGE> to the header as a way to handle stylesheets with the CLASS attribute, and an attempt at the specification of arbitrary spans of text for formatting or identification with the <SPOT> element (similar to the spanning elements of the TEI mentioned in section 2.3.6), identified with ID/IDREF values.

In the body, it added a number of structural elements:

- <BANNER> to allow a static portion of non-scrolling text at the top or side of the screen (now superseded by frames);
- <DIV> for dividing the document into sections;
- <MATH> for mathematics (see section 2.3.8.3) with <SUB> and <SUP> being allowed outside the math model as well;
- <FIG> for floating figures and other insertions (now superseded by <OBJECT>);
- <TABLE>, probably the most significant change in terms of the application of HTML, as it allowed alignments;
- <NOTE> and <FN> for notes and footnotes (never implemented).

There were some substantial additions to the inline markup model as well:

- <STRIKEOUT> , <INS>, and <DEL> for marking editorial or versioning changes;
- <BIG> and <SMALL> for affecting the type size;
- <TAB>, an ingenious 'set-tabstop' and 'jump-to-tab-stop' element, unfortunately never widely implemented;
- <Q> for reported speech;
- <LANG> for foreign-language matter, and a lang attribute on all elements;
- <AU>, <DFN>, <PERSON>, <ACRONYM>, and <ABBREV> for the names of authors; definitions (first terms); personal names; acronyms; and abbreviations. Only <DFN> was ever implemented.

Despite the poor implementation by browsers, the effect of HTML3 was substantial, and many of the concepts introduced have persisted in subsequent DTDs. The HTML3 Internet Draft was allowed to expire in 1995 when control of the DTD passed from the IETF to the W3C.

2.3.9.1.5. HTML 3.2 and HTML 4.0 When the World Wide Web Consortium took over the task of maintaining the HTML DTD, it eventually produced a version which was intended to codify existing practice, especially in respect of former markup introduced by the browser makers, rather than introduce anything new. In that sense, it was a pity that it was named HTML 3.2, as that implies that it is some kind of advance on HTML3, which it is not.

It reintroduced the `<SCRIPT>` element in both header and body, to allow the embedding of *Java* and other inline scripting languages; it added `<APPLET>` (but not `<OBJECT>` or `<EMBED>`) to handle the addition of plug-ins and applets; and it added the `<FONT>` and `<BASEFONT>` elements to allow arbitrary font changes.

Unfortunately this DTD was required to provide backward compatibility, which meant that:

- it declared — and thus perpetuated — some almost entirely obsolete elements (`<DIR>` and `<MENU>`, for example);
- it removed most of the content-descriptive elements introduced by HTML3;
- and it omitted the support for `ID`, `CLASS`, and `STYLE` attributes which would have enabled stylesheets.

HTML 4 finally introduced frames, which permit multi-paned displays, but the DTD continues to mix block-oriented elements (structural elements) with inline elements and character data in the content model for the text body. While this could be said very accurately to represent the current use of HTML, it is not a useful model for the future.

Some of the inline markup from HTML3 also reappears, but the lack of any kind of meaningful structure makes it (apparently deliberately) almost completely useless as a DTD for representing information: the data-entry elements for forms, for example, can appear outside the scope of `<FORM>` in order to enable their use by non-form scripts. Some attempt is made at internationalization, with the reintroduction of the `<BDO>` (bi-directional override) element and the theoretical support for Unicode, but the SDA `FIXED` attributes of HTML 2.0, specifically designed to allow use of browsers by those with visual disabilities, remained ignored (see section 6.3).

2.3.9.1.6. HTML Pro As an antidote to the progressively less structured DTDs noted above, I produced a version of HTML aimed at the professional information provider: *HTML Pro*. This is a composite of elements from all known versions, both those from the IETF and W3C, as well as the independent inventions of third and fourth parties such as WebTV (now a part of Microsoft). Where no content model was known (often the case with additions from companies consisting largely of a marketing department and with no technical knowledge), it was deduced or derived from examples of usage.

In the development versions, this does unfortunately mean the retention of precisely those obsolete and even meaningless elements which clutter other HTML DTDs, but they are carefully documented as such, and kept in places where they can do the least harm. As the DTD is intended for professional use, it is expected that users are capable of distinguishing the useful from the useless. Production versions can exclude the entirely obsolete elements.

The result is a DTD with a formal structure which encourages meaningful reuse of information, but which still allows the user to employ the latest additions supported by Web browsers. To date it appears to be the only DTD supporting `<CENTER>`, `<MULTICOL>`, `<NOBR>`, `<OBJECT>`, `<EMBED>`, `<MARQUEE>`, `<BGSOUND>`, `<SERVER>`, `<SPACER>`, `<AUDIOSCOPE>`, and `<SIDEBAR>`, however useful or not designers feel they may be.

This restructuring means that an author or markup specialist who wants to retain SGML conformance (or who is required to by a contract) can use any standard SGML editing or display environment and produce fully-conformant HTML, while remaining free to use whatever elements are most suitable (or prescribed) for the task.

2.3.9.2. Applications of XML

`http://www.w3.org/XML/`

The ability to define your own markup language appeals strongly to many widely divergent groups of users, particularly those who have run up against the limitations of HTML. The Extensible Markup Language (XML), which is described in the next section, is widely seen as a replacement for HTML, as it allows you to define your own markup, rather than have to squash your document into the confines of HTML's elements.

Even before the XML Specification was completed, many applications had been proposed, and DTDs had been written, and in some cases, software was implemented. The following are a few of the ones which appear (at an early stage) to be stable.

Chemical Markup Language (CML) was the first application of XML. It was developed by Prof Peter Murray-Rust at the Open Molecule Foundation as a generic tool for management of molecular and technical information. It can be used to process many of the `chemical/*`

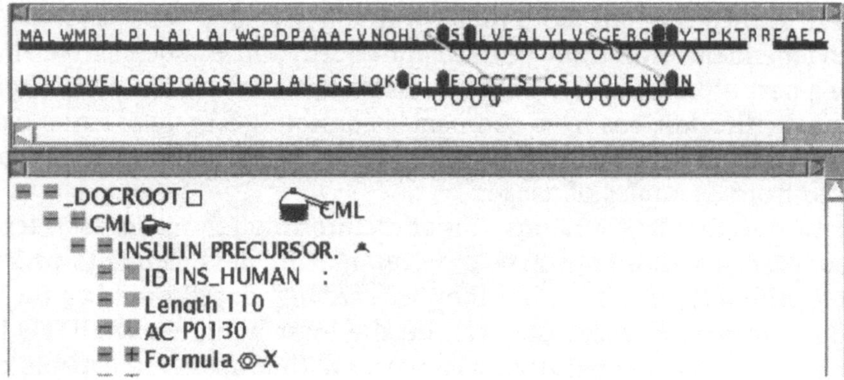

Figure 53. Chemical Markup Language used for insulin analysis, displayed with the JUMBO XML browser

MIME Content-Types used in chemical data transfer; to store spectra, sequences, molecules, crystal structures, and molecular bibliographies and hyperglossaries; and to support databases, instrumentation, publishing, and program postprocessing. The DTD and further details are at `http://www.venus.co.uk/omf/cml/`. There's even a browser to go with it, again the first for XML, *JUMBO* (Java Universal Markup Browser for Objects: see Figure 53).

Among others being developed are:

- MathML, an XML application for mathematics, which is described in section 2.3.8.4;
- Microsoft's CDF (Channel Definition Format), which defines the structure of 'push' Web broadcasts (no DTD is available, however); and OSD (Open Software Description), also endorsed by CyberMedia, InstallShield, LANovation, Lotus, and Netscape, which provides a data format to describe software components, versions, structure, and relationships to other components, so that 'smart' software downloading and installation can take place via the Web.
- RDF (Resource Description Framework) is a mechanism for exchanging metadata for arbitrary objects found on the World Wide Web: it places emphasis on facilities to enable automated decision-making about the kinds of processing to be applied to a web resource. RDF uses XML syntax but is not itself a DTD: instead it allows the definition of schemata to let an author or editor describe the data in a form which an XML processor can handle.
  Early candidates for this kind of description are the PICS (Platform for Internet Content Selection) rating scheme (see `http://www.w3.`

org/PICS/) and the Dublin Core metadata definitions (see http://purl.org/metadata/dublin_core).

Implementations such as Netscape's *Aurora* allow RDF information exported from many sources to be combined into new 'views', which can be tailored to the topic to which the information relates, rather than the source from which it came.

- OFX (Open Financial Exchange) is a unified specification for the exchange of financial data over the Internet, piloted by Check-Free, Intuit, and Microsoft, to remove some of the incompatibilities that financial institutions have to penetrate to exchange data with each other and with their customers (http://www.intuit.com/ofx/index.html).

  Apart from enabling the more reliable passing of data between banks, this project may also eventually provide a platform-independent and network-independent way for individuals to manage their bank accounts and investments.
- PGML (Precision Graphics Markup Language) is a draft of a 2D scalable graphics language 'designed to meet both the simple vector graphics needs of casual users and the precision needs of graphics artists'. It consists of suggestions for a DTD to describe all the graphical representations that a designer would typically need to be able to output, based on the way that PostScript and PDF currently work. This would enable a rendering system to use PGML as an output format for information stored in some other SGML or XML format, or for any information needing a graphical rendering, in the same way that PostScript print drivers currently exist for almost all text and graphics systems. Details are at http://www.w3.org/TR/1998/NOTE-PGML
- The Health Level 7 (HL7) initiative is developing standards for electronic information interchange among independent health care organizations' computer systems (see http://www.mcis.duke.edu/standards/HL7/hl7.htm).

  Among the projects being developed is a Health Care Markup Language. A number of participants, among them pharmaceutical corporations and Health Management Organizations, are researching ways of using XML to harmonize other aspects such as patient records or prescriptions. A pilot project, Kona, is gathering information on existing applications.

New proposals are surfacing almost daily as every industry sector sees the potential for their own markup language. This Balkanization is possibly a temporary state of affairs, however, as a large number of related industries may discover that they have more in common than they thought.

2.3.9.3. Other DTDs

Given the right tools, any SGML document in any DTD can be used over the Web. For years, the two major SGML browsers, *Panorama* and *MultiDoc Pro*, both of which use the same internal engine, have been able to accept any SGML files from a regular Web browser which has been configured to pass such files to them, and *MultiDoc Pro* can also act as a stand-alone SGML Web browser.

The way they work is explained in more detail in chapter 6, but in summary, the browser reads the DocType Declaration on the file it downloads, and identifies the DTD from its Formal Public Identifier, either in its own catalog, or by requesting a catalog file from the same place the instance came from. The DTD is downloaded, and a similar method (but using a different file) is used to locate the stylesheet, which is downloaded in turn and used to display the information. Although this mechanism works perfectly, the additional downloading is a performance penalty when using a DTD for the first time, especially when it is a very large one such as *DocBook* or the TEI is being used, but with an adequate cache or careful recording and storage of additional DTDs as they are encountered, this becomes less of a problem the more the system is used.

2.4. Extensible Markup Language (XML)

HTML's simplicity (some would say simple-mindedness) is also its Achilles' heel. It is adequate for short or transient documents or for those which don't have much need for structural or in-depth markup, but it was not designed to replace the much more robust DTDs needed in commercial, research, or academic work. This led to a polarization between using HTML for simple markup for the Web, and something much richer for other purposes.

XML (Extensible Markup Language) is a much abbreviated version of SGML. It is not a DTD or tagset like HTML, but a metalanguage like SGML: it's just been shorn of all the optional features which make SGML relatively difficult to write programs for. The idea behind it is to allow authors and providers of information the freedom to design their own document types and thus escape from the single-type model of HTML. The penalty is that some of the power and flexibility of SGML has been sacrificed for simpler design concepts and faster processing by parsers and browsers.

2.4.1. XML syntax

To achieve this greater simplicity, XML introduces a few small changes in syntax and one very significant but simple change in design. The changes are designed to make the syntax simple enough that it becomes easy to write programs to handle the language (one rough measure is that programming should be simple enough for the 'DPH' — the Desperate *Perl* Hacker who has a few hours against a deadline to get something working to read an XML file). The final specification agreed by the W3C in February 1998 is on the CD-ROM, but any more recent developments should be sought at the W3C's Web site (`http://www.w3.org/TR/`).

2.4.1.1. SGML Declaration

The SGML Declaration for XML is fixed in the specification and cannot be varied. As explained in section 1.5.1.7, it sets most of the quantities and capacities to their maxima, enables the use of ISO 10646 as the Coded Character Set for the Document Character Set, and makes element and entity names case-*sensitive* (see section 2.4.1.6).

2.4.1.2. XML Declarations and Processing Instructions

The most immediately noticeable of the syntactic changes is the use of modified SGML Processing Instructions (PIs) to convey information about the file to the software (parser, rendering engine, database, *etc*). The reason they are noticeable is that they go at the top of an XML file, before any DTD is declared, as they affect how the rest of the file is processed.

The format of a regular SGML PI is simple: it starts with a <?, the PIO (Processing Instruction Open) delimiter, and ending with a PIC (Processing Instruction Close) delimiter (the > character). The data content (between PIO and PIC) is opaque to SGML, and it simply gets passed through untouched to any subsequent software. Traditionally it has contained the name of the program it is aimed at, and the rest is in whatever command code format that program needs, for example: `<?typeset op413/op332>`. SGML parsers ignore the contents completely and just feed it to whatever program they are attached to.

An XML PI is symmetrical: it redefines the PIC to have a terminating question-mark before the angle bracket (?>). Part of the structure of the data content is specified in XML, in that anything to do with XML must have the letters `xml` immediately after the PIO, and the use of those three letters in that position is forbidden for any other purpose. (Because of the changed PIC, an XML PI may now contain the actual character '>' as part of its content, should you ever require it, which a regular SGML PI cannot.)

An XML PI is used as the first line of an XML document, where it is called the 'XML Declaration', and it provides the version number of XML (compulsory), the character set used (optional, defaults to UTF-8), and an SDD (Standalone Document Declaration), which tells XML software whether the document is DTD-less or not. For example,

```
<?xml version="1.0" standalone="yes"?>
```

specifies the version and states that this document has no DTD: it can stand alone. An SDD value of 'no' (the default) means that the software must expect to find a DTD specified and must read it. A DTD must be referenced in a standard DocType Declaration or supplied in the Internal Subset, *eg*

```
<?xml version="1.0"?>
<!DOCTYPE recipe SYSTEM "http://www.cooking.shop/recipe.dtd">
<recipe>...
```

An Internal Subset can also be used with a standalone document to specify attribute names and types, even though the element names are not declared, because the WebSGML Adaptations (see section 2.7.1.3) permit a new value of `#ANY` for the element name position in an `ATTLIST` declaration, *eg*

```
<?xml version="1.0" standalone="yes"?>
<!DOCTYPE recipe [
<!ATTLIST #ANY id ID #IMPLIED>
]>
<recipe id="abc123">...
```

The 'DTD-less' concept is explained in section 2.4.1.3, as the concept of 'no DTD' is alien to traditional SGML. Experiences with HTML have shown that the general public is far more familiar with the concept than the SGML community!

2.4.1.3. Validity and well-formedness in XML

The big change is in the definition of an additional class of document conformance. What have hitherto been 'valid' instances in regular SGML are now formally defined by the WebSGML Adaptations as 'type-valid', meaning their element types are declared, and the instance is valid in respect of them. The new document class is 'tag-valid' alone, which means in effect a nested hierarchy with all elements using start-tags and end-tags, conforming to some slightly more restrictive rules, but without necessarily having a DTD. Tag valid files are said to be 'well-formed' in XML terminology.

This means XML is able to introduce the concept of a file with no DTD, but instead defining its document structure purely by the existence, occurrence, and placement of its elements (much in the way that *Fred* can deduce a DTD from a file structure: see section 2.6.9). You can of course also operate XML *with* a DTD, in which case everything works almost identically to standard SGML.

What makes this possible is the concept that *type-valid instances must also be tag-valid*. In XML terms, 'valid' files must also be 'well-formed': a file *has* to be well-formed first, in order for it to validate correctly. Validity thus implies well-formedness: it is an error to speak of 'well-formed' files as if they were the opposite of 'valid' files.

A well-formed XML document has the following basic properties (there are a few other less significant ones):

- all start- and end-tags are properly balanced and nested (same requirement as for any normalized SGML document);
- all elements which are `EMPTY` must either use a special form of start-tag (`<name/>`) or be expressed as start-tag followed by end-tag with no content (`<name></name>`; see section 2.4.1.5);
- any attributes are deemed to be `CDATA` unless declared otherwise in the Internal Subset;
- there must be a value of '`yes`' for the Standalone Declaration (see section 2.4.1.2);
- the file may not use the proscribed features of regular SGML (see section 2.4.1.4).

These restrictions mean that it is a relatively simple task to write software to handle XML files, because almost all of the optional bits of regular SGML have been removed. Here's a tiny example which shows the XML Declaration, a `<text>` element nested inside a `<proverb>` element, and two attributes:

```
<?xml version="1.0" standalone="yes"?>
<proverb id="abc123" type="humorous">
  <text>Where there's a will, there's a lawyer<text>
</proverb>
```

Note that the `id` attribute can't be a real `ID` (referable from an `IDREF`), because without a DTD or other attribute list declaration, all attributes are taken as plain `CDATA`.

2.4.1.4. Restrictions in XML

When people say 'XML is simplified SGML', this is what they mean: these are the things which you may *not* use in XML. Removing these features from SGML is designed to make it easier to write programs for XML. Warning: this list mentions some aspects of SGML we have not covered yet, and some rarer ones not included in this book.

- No tag omission;
- Special tag form for empty elements;
- Comment declarations cannot have spaces within the markup characters of <!-- or -->;
- No comments (-- ... --) inside other markup declarations;
- Comment declarations can't therefore jump in and out of comments with -- and --;
- No name groups for declaring multiple elements or making a single ATTLIST declaration apply to multiple elements (but the WebSGML Adaptations do now permit multiple ATTLIST declarations);
- No RANK feature;
- No CDATA or RCDATA declared content in element declarations (use CDATA marked sections in the instance instead);
- No exclusions or inclusions on content models;
- No minimization parameters on element declarations;
- Mixed content models must be optional-repeatable OR-groups, with #PCDATA first;
- No AND (&) content model groups;
- No NAME, NUMBER, or NUTOKEN declared values for attributes (or their plurals: use NMTOKEN or CDATA with application-specific validation instead);
- No #CURRENT or #CONREF declared values for attributes;
- Attribute default values must be quoted in the instance;
- Marked sections can't have spaces within the markup of newline <![keyword[or]]>;
- No RCDATA, TEMP, IGNORE, or INCLUDE marked sections in document instances;
- Marked sections in document instances must use the CDATA keyword literally, not a parameter entity;
- No RCDATA, CDATA, or TEMP marked sections in the DTD;
- Comments, literals, and Processing Instructions in IGNOREd Marked Sections may not contain the delimiter string]]>; this helps ensure that the end-point of the conditional section does not change when the section is changed from IGNORE to INCLUDE;
- No SDATA, CDATA, or bracketed internal entities;
- No SUBDOC, CDATA, or SDATA external entities;
- External entities must have a System Identifier, which must be a URL;

- Parameter Entity references in the internal DTD subset may occur only between declarations;
- Parameter Entity references in the external DTD subset are restricted to certain positions in the grammar, and must replace whole non-terminals of the grammar; this ensures that all valid XML documents are valid SGML, and makes the restrictions on Parameter Entity replacement easier to understand and implement;
- No data attributes on `NOTATION`s or attribute value specifications on `ENTITY` declarations;
- No `SHORTREF` declarations;
- No `USEMAP` declarations;
- No `LINKTYPE` declarations;
- No `LINK` declarations;
- No `USELINK` declarations;
- No `IDLINK` declarations;
- No `NOTATION`s;
- No varying the SGML Declaration;
- Processing Instructions must be delimited by <? and ?>, and the first part of PI content is expected to be a token that indicates the application environment in which the rest of the PI has effect.

2.4.1.5. EMPTY elements in XML

In XML, the only major change to element markup is the alternate form for empty elements (like `<graphic/>`). This was developed originally to allow empty elements to be recognized under regular SGML, before the adoption of the WebSGML Adaptations, so in itself it is not new, but something of a hack. It meant that a program reading a DTD-less instance could immediately recognize an empty element as such: without it (and without a DTD as a guide) a program would *have* to assume each start-tag was matched by an end-tag, so `EMPTY` elements would be impossible, because programs would constantly be expecting end-tags for them which would never appear.

It is easiest to represent an 'empty' element simply as regular start- and end-tags without content (`<graphic></graphic>`), but this begs the question of whether the element was ever intended to have content, and just happens not to have it this time, or the element is genuinely only a 'single point' with no possibility of content. It is perhaps unfortunate that the distinction risks being elided: while in many cases there is no meaningful difference — no content is no content, period — there will be occasions when it is important to be able to represent dimensionless points in a document (bookmarks, for example, or the pagebreaks in a reference edition, or the points of inflection in stock trading data). The specification, however, makes no distinction:

> Empty-element tags may be used for any element which has no content, whether or not it is declared using the keyword EMPTY. For interoperability, the empty-element tag must be used, and can only be used, for elements which are declared EMPTY.

So if you're using a DTD which *declares* an element EMPTY, then you must use the singular form with the trailing slash, <graphic/>. Otherwise you can use either form.

2.4.1.6. Naming and case-sensitivity in XML

The colon is a valid NAME character in XML, and can be used experimentally to delimit namespaces, although a NAME cannot start with a colon. This allows developers to name elements after another DTD or convention such as

```
<!element ChML:Cocoa.Quality  (%text;)>
```

for some (hypothetical) markup language for the chocolate industry, or

```
<!element FT:finance:RATE-TO-DOLLAR (#PCDATA)>
```

for some borrowed element type names in the finance industry. The identity of the source of the names can be declared in a Processing Instruction:

```
<?xml:namespace prefix="ChML" ns="http://www.choc.an/"?>
```

This is recommended only for element names and attribute names, and as it is for experimentation, you should not make any XML files rely on its continued existence. The W3C working draft paper on namespaces is at http://www.w3.org/TR/WD-xml-names (a copy as at the time of writing is on the CD-ROM).

An important feature of XML is that it is case-sensitive. A regular SGML Declaration can state whether or not an application should fold NAME characters to upper-case (using NAMECASE to specify it: YES means treat lower-case the same as upper-case; NO means treat them as distinct). But XML's SGML Declaration is invariable: upper- and lower-case characters are *always* regarded as different, so an element <TITLE> and an element <title> and an element <Title> refer to *separate and distinct elements*.

This was done to ease the internationalization rules: case-*in*sensitive SGML folds everything to upper-case for internal comparisons, whereas modern computing practice, influenced by Unix, folds everything to lowercase. There is no universally applicable case-folding rule which will work with all languages, especially those using accented letters or symbols which don't have a single upper-case or lower-case form, or which switch between one and more glyphs (German 'ß' for lowercase double 'ss' is just two uppercase 'SS's when printed in capitals), or which don't use an alphabetic script with a case distinction.

2.4.1.7. White-space in XML

As explained in section 2.2.1.6, standard SGML has strict and rather complicated rules on white-space (line-breaks, spaces, and tabs) which allow applications to distinguish between two principal states (slightly simplified):

1. White-space *between* elements in a location where character data is not permitted, but only other element markup. This is sometimes called 'insignificant' white-space because it must be discarded without penalty by validating parsers, and has no effect on the document structure. (*Emacs* with *psgml*, for example, and SGML Systems Engineering's *TagView*, insert this class of white-space to tab-indent elements for ease of editing: see the example in section 2.3.8.4.)
2. White-space *within* elements with a mixed content or character data model. This is sometimes called 'significant' white-space because removing it would seriously affect the text: it is always retained by parsers and passed to the application. (This would be the normal case for spaces between words or inline markup in conventional running text like this).

In XML, a processor such as a parser must *always* pass *all* non-markup characters to the application, and if it is performing validation it must signal significance or non-significance as it does so.

To allow designers to vary this behavior, there is a reserved `xml:space` attribute which takes the values `default` (behave as above) or `preserve` (all white-space must be kept). Here's an example of adding it to a DTD so that the occasional poem can retain its linebreaks even though normal paragraph handling would reformat them:

```
<?xml version="1.0"?>
<!DOCTYPE novel PUBLIC "-//Joe's Personal//DTD Writing//EN"
"http://home.myserver.org/joedoe/scribbles/writing.dtd"
[<!attlist para xml:space (default|preserve) #implied>]>
<novel>
...
<para xml:space="preserve">Mary had a little lamb
When she was just a Deb
She kept it while at college
And sold it on the Web</para>
...
</novel>
```

2.4.2. XML Links

http://www.w3.org/TR/WD-xlink, http://www.w3.org/TR/WD-xptr

The linking technology of HTML provides simple one-way links using the 'anchor' element <A> with a HREF attribute containing a URL. It's 'one-way' because there is no way of knowing if a particular document is the target of someone else's link. Unwinding with the **Back** key the chain of links you have followed does not constitute two-way linking. A bidirectional link enables the target location or document to 'know', in effect, that it is pointed to by another location or document. You can see this already for regular SGML in the implementation of links in the Synex-engine browsers (*Panorama* and *MultiDoc Pro*), where elements that are pointed *to*, even by ID/IDREF links, are displayed with a symbol to mark the fact.

Links in XML retain HTML's <A>-and-HREF concept (although you can define other names for the elements and attributes), but there are also other more powerful linking features which draw on the principles of the HyTime standard (see section 2.7.2.1) and on the EPN (Extended Pointer Notation) of the TEI (see section 2.3.6).

Some of the terminology in linking requires careful reading, as it uses words from other fields but with different meanings (the precise nature of the terms 'one-way' and 'two-way', for example). A copy of the XML linking draft proposal is on the CD-ROM, but more recent versions are available on the W3C's Web site (http://www.w3.org/TR/WD-xlink), and these define all the terms in some detail. Although this work is closely bound to XML, it is not strictly speaking a part of the XML (language) specification, and is being developed separately, and at the time of writing is still officially just a Draft, so some of the mechanisms detailed below may change before being finalized.

You may see it referred to by its earlier name of XLL (XML Linking Language) but the draft distinguishes between 'XLink', the linking technology and how it fits into XML (how it represents the 'abstract structure and significance of links'), and the 'XPointer' language that XLink uses in conjunction with URLs (strictly speaking, with the URI structure), as fragment identifiers or queries, to specify sub-resources more precisely.

Overall, the most important features of XML linking are:

- You can point an XML link at one *or more* whole 'resources' (files, images, documents, and 'sub-resources' like document fragments or the results of queries). HTML can point at one resource per link, but one XML link can extend to point at several resources simultaneously;

- A link can be 'in-line' (containing one of its resources, like HTML's <A> element) or 'out of line' (residing somewhere else in the document, like HTML's <LINK> element, or even in another document entirely, but pointing to all the resources involved);
- XLinks use URIs (or URLs until URIs are fully defined). You can address a link target *within a document* in different ways (with an ID; by counting the sequential occurrence of an element ('width-first'); by hierarchical descent into the markup ('depth-first'); a span of text between two ID-bearing elements; by text search; or by one of several other methods described in the XPointer language);
- Links can bear an identification of the expected or recommended action: how to 'show' the link (a new browser window; replacement of the current page; or embedding in the current page), and when to 'actuate' the link (automatically or on request from the user).

Any element can be made into a simple link by adding the xml:link attribute with a value of simple. This lets an XML processor recognize that this element is a link resource (one end of a link). The address of the other resource goes in a href attribute just like HTML uses:

```
...see <XRef xml:link="simple" href="/help/explain.xml">the
explanations</XRef> for details...
```

The default behavior is to traverse the link only when the user actuates it (clicks on it), and for the linked document to replace the current one in the display: the same default as HTML. The href attribute is named purely for historical compatibility: its function can be mapped to another attribute name (in the Internal Subset) if you've already used HREF for something else:

```
<!ATTLIST XRef xml:link CDATA #FIXED "simple"
               xml:attributes CDATA #FIXED "href doc">
...
...see <XRef doc="/help/explain.xml">the explanations</XRef>
for details...
```

This specifies in advance that all <XRef> elements are 'simple' link elements and that their href value can be found in the attribute actually named doc. Because the values are specified as #FIXED, editors can be prevented from accidentally overriding the default values on each occurrence of the <XRef> element.

Extended links are done by using an outer containing element, identified by its xml:link attribute as an extended link, to hold a series of separate link elements each identified as a 'link locator'. These items each instantiate a link to a single resource, but because they are contained within an identifiable element, they can be referenced and managed as a unit.

```
<list xml:link="extended" actuate="user">
  <header>Check out the original versions online</header>
  <item xml:link="locator" show="new" href="thomas.html">The
fragment of Thomas's <title>Tristan</title></item>
  <item xml:link="locator" show="new" href="gottfried.html">The
MHG <title>Tristan</title> of Gottfried von Strassburg</item>
  <item xml:link="locator" show="new" href="eilhart.html">Three
versions by Eilhart von Oberge</item>
  <item xml:link="locator" show="new" href="beroul.html">The
version by B&eacute;roul</item>
  <item xml:link="locator" show="replace" href="hatto.html">The
English translation by Hatto</item>
</list>
```

Addressing with URLs means the ? query connector can be used to prefix data for a remote processor exactly as in an HTML environment. The # fragment connector can also be used in any meaningful way for non-XML resources.

For XML resources, however, the fragment connector must be followed by an XPointer which identifies the location in the target document. For example, this paragraph might be referenced from elsewhere as:

```
#child(2,chapter).(4,sect1).(2,sect2).(11,para)
```

or (given that this sub-section is all about XML linking and has 'xml-linking' as its unique ID):

```
#id(xml-linking).(11,para)
```

Other keywords ('descendant', 'ancestor', 'preceding', 'following', *etc*) provide for other directions and ways of navigating through the document structure: this paragraph could be identified as:

```
#id(xml-linking).descendant(-2,para)
```

being the penultimate paragraph in the section with that ID.

Identification is also possible based on the value of attributes (so `child(3,list,type,"numbered")` would be the third numbered list) and can also identify spans of text (thus `#id(summary).span(child(3,para),child(-1,para))` would be the third through last paragraphs within the element with ID 'summary'). Even finer addressing is possible with string searching, right down to the character level within an element.

2.4.3. XML Stylesheets

http://www.w3.org/TR/NOTE-XSL.html

Because XML lets you define your own DTD or use a well-formed element structure without one, browsers may have no clue as to the semantics of your design. A stylesheet is therefore likely to be essential, and there are several choices:

- DSSSL (Document Style Semantics and Specification Language), ISO 10179 (see section 2.7.2.3);
- CSS (Cascading StyleSheets), defined by the W3C and partially implemented in some HTML browsers;
- XSL (Extensible Style Language), a proposal to accompany XML;
- Other existing solutions (Synex stylesheets, FOSIs, editor stylesheets).

XSL stylesheets are written in a similar way to XML documents, and draw on both CSS/HTML and DSSSL (actually dsssl-o, the online subset) for their representation of styles. DSSSL is expressed in a syntax similar to the *Scheme* language, and is not immediately usable by people other than computer scientists. XSL stylesheets can express the same style information in a syntax which is more familiar to most XML and SGML users, and (from an implementor's point of view) can be processed by an engine the same as, or similar to, the browser used to read the XML documents they refer to.

The rules of XSL are straightforward: *every element in the user's document must be matched by at least one style rule of a higher 'importance' than any other matching rule.* This lets you specify several different ways to display an element, with the importance being some measure (attached to a rule in an attribute) picked by the designer to allow stylesheets to degrade gracefully between browsers of differing capabilities.

Selection rules enable the designer to specify a pattern for the selection of elements by descent or ancestry or occurrence. Here, a rule matches a `<title>` element within a `<section>` element within a `<chapter>` element.

```
<xsl>
  <rule>
    <element type="chapter">
      <element type="section">
        <target-element type="title"/>
        <children/>
      </element>
    </element>
  </rule></xsl>
```

As with DSSSL, a 'children' term enables a matching rule to state that all elements contained within it must also be submitted for processing at this point.

Once an element matches a pattern, ***style rules*** specify the appearance in conventional typographical or other terms.

```
<style-rule>
  <target-element type="productname"/>
  <apply font-posture="italic"/>
</style-rule>
```

XSL can represent 'flow objects' (a DSSSL term, meaning a collection or sequence of characters which can be treated homogeneously as they 'flow' onto the page) taken from HTML/CSS or DSSSL itself, so the CSS browser semantics of a former HTML element can be preserved in an XSL stylesheet.

You can write macros, with parameter substitution, and there is provision for attaching classes in *ECMAscript* (the formal version of *JavaScript*, see `http://www.ecma.ch`) so that in-browser manipulation can be carried out, much as with 'Dynamic' HTML.

2.4.4. XML Data

`http://www.w3.org/TR/1998/NOTE-XML-data`

If you have handled structured data (or if you are familiar with computer science or database engineering) you may have noticed that the concept of a DTD bears a close relationship to that of a ***schema***, the formal way of describing the features of objects in a database and how they relate to each other, and that XML syntax could be used to represent this, both at the syntactic level and the conceptual (semantic) level.

There is a draft Note at the W3C (URL above) which is a submission describing how this could be implemented, centered on two concepts:

- that XML document types can now be described using XML itself, rather than DTD syntax;
- that XML Data schemas provide a common vocabulary for ideas which overlap between syntactic, database and conceptual schemas.

The principle that you can describe the schema of your data in XML terms is not new (the question 'where is the DTD for DTDs?' is not uncommon). In this case, the XML Data submission document provides a DTD for the proposed method. It also recommends declaring the namespace from which the schema comes. It uses an `<elementType>` element to both define and describe the data items (=elements):

```
<?xml version="1.0"?>
<?xml:namespace ns="http://shop.foo.org/" prefix="shopping"?>
<s:schema id='myDataSchema'>
<elementType id="item">
  <string/>
</elementType>
<elementType id="list" occurs="ONE">
  <elementType type="#item" occurs="ONEORMORE"/>
</elementType>
</s:schema>
```

This is the equivalent of a traditional DTD which defines (in XML terms):

```
<!ELEMENT shopping:list (item+)>
<!ELEMENT shopping:item (#PCDATA)>
```

The document defines equivalents for all the syntax used in DTDs, so that a complete description of the data schema can be made in XML. It is important to note that this is only a submission document, not a formal proposal, and not a part of XML itself, so it should be regarded as experimental.

2.5. Identifying the DTD

In the preamble to this chapter we saw how an SGML file needed to declare the document type by using a Public or System Identifier. This section explains how the Formal Public Identifier and System Identifier mechanisms work, and how they can be resolved into actual filenames for the DTD that a program can read. This information, and the use of catalog files, is essential for getting DTDs to work in almost any system.

2.5.1. System Identifiers

The format of a DocType Declaration or other entity reference lets you provide a local filename, possibly with a path, to identify the file you are referring to. To do this, you prefix it with the keyword SYSTEM and the reference is then called a ***System Identifier*** (SI):

```
<!DOCTYPE article SYSTEM "/sgml/pubtext/Silmaril/DTD/article.dtd">
```

This is the simplest method of identifying DTD files and other entities, and is suitable when the author and user have already agreed about where to find the relevant files. When the instance is sent to someone, it must therefore be accompanied by all the relevant DTD files and other entities needed, or an an exchange methodology has to be established under which certain files can be assumed already to be present on all systems concerned.

In XML, however, the user can be presumed to have a connection to a network, so an explicit URL is always required:

```
<!DOCTYPE article SYSTEM "http://www.foo.org/dtds/article.dtd">
```

This format is also possible with regular SGML, of course, but a network connection may not always be available. One of the problems with URLs is that they are not persistent: a company can disappear, taking its Web server with it, or a file can be moved, or an organization or individual can change Internet Service Provider, leaving the user facing the infamous '404' error message, 'File not found'. The XML specification actually says URI (Universal Resource Indicator) rather than URL, but the work on URI definition is taking rather longer than expected.

The set of characters allowed in a System Identifier is restricted in regular SGML to letters, digits, spaces, linebreaks, and the characters '' ()+,-./:=?', but the provisions of the SGML Extended Naming Rules Technical Corrigendum (ENR: see section 2.7.1.2), and more recently the WebSGML Adaptations (see section 2.7.1.3) have extended these significantly, so in practice many parsers and other SGML systems now accept URLs in an SI, even if not all of them can perform network retrieval yet.

SGML does not impose any special format on the System Identifier as it does on the Formal Public Identifier (see below), which means any syntax or semantic can be used; but by the same token, an SGML processor cannot be assumed to know what to do with it. For example, while an XML browser may be able to recognize a URL and act accordingly, a standalone editor may only understand local filenames.

2.5.2. Formal Public Identifiers

As we have seen, it is usually not realistic for authors to use just local file paths and file names in a System Identifier for the DTD and other entity files as they exist on their own machine, because the recipient or user almost certainly will not have the same folders, directories, or file names. URLs too have their problems, as described in the previous section. As an alternative, ISO 8879 provides for an independent way of naming entities called the ***Formal Public Identifier*** (FPI), which looks like this:

```
+//Silmaril//DTD Article v3//EN
```

You have probably already seen these at the top of SGML, HTML, or XML files. This example tells a processor five things about the entity:

1. The plus sign means that the owner of this identifier is registered under ISO 9070 as a Public Owner (a minus sign would mean the owner is unregistered);
2. The name of the Public Owner of this identifier is 'Silmaril';
3. The Public Text referenced by this identifier is classed as a DTD;
4. It is named 'Article v3';
5. It is in English (the `EN` at the end).

It doesn't necessarily say or claim anything about who actually wrote or owns the DTD itself: what is provided here is just a *label*. It is what the author or supplier of the SGML file reckons you or your programs can use to identify uniquely and precisely what DTD or other resource is required. In fact most FPIs are of course generated by the creators of the resources they refer to, but the point needs to be made that they don't have to be: an FPI makes no statement of ownership of the resource, only of the label.

However, because it also contains nothing about the machinery, network location, filename, directory, or technology involved, an FPI has the potential to be a unique and resource-independent way of labeling entities for use in SGML systems.

The slightly unusual syntax of the Formal Public Identifier is the cause of some widespread misunderstandings, so it's worth getting to know it. There is a restriction on the characters available for the FPI in standard SGML, the 'minimum literal' set of characters, identical to that for SIs (letters, digits, spaces, linebreaks, and the characters '`'()+,-./:=?`') but the same relaxation also applies when the ENR or WebSGML Adaptations are in force, as for XML. In these cases the set of characters is the same as for CDATA, except that the double-slash cannot be used because it is the separator between portions of the identifier.

Registration The registration process is for the names of the Public Owners, not for the texts themselves or their identifiers. It is performed by the ISO 9070 Registrar, who is appointed by the ISO. The current Registrar is the Graphic Communications Association. The names of registered owners are listed on the GCA's Web site at `http://www.gca.org/`. There are three 'privileged' cases of a Public Owner which do not have any registration prefix (see below).

Public Owner Identifier This identifies the owner of the FPI. It may be subdivided by a double-colon into a Public Owner Prefix and owner-defined suffixes, for example `+//Acme Org::Sales//...` The three 'privileged' cases of a Public Owner which do not have any registration prefix are:

1. The ISO itself, notably for their character entity declaration files such as Latin 1, Latin 2, Greek, Cyrillic, math characters, publishers symbols, *etc.* These FPIs begin with 'ISO' and the standards number, for example

   ```
   ISO 8879-1986//ENTITIES Added Latin 1//EN
   ```

2. Identifiers beginning with 'ISBN' or 'ISSN' representing published texts, giving the relevant number, for example

   ```
   ISBN 82-7640-037::WWW//DTD HTML Level 0 Prescriptive//EN//2.0
   ```

3. Identifiers denoting an Internet Domain Name (introduced in the WebSGML Adaptations), for example

   ```
   IDN::ftp.falch.no//NONSGML The Whirlwind Guide: SGML Tools
   and Vendors (21 October 96)//EN
   ```

It is an error to prefix any of these three with '`-//`' or '`+//`'.

Public Text Class The Public Text Class gives the type of entity identified.

Class	Description
CAPACITY	a capacity set (as in an SGML Declaration)
CHARSET	a character set
DOCUMENT	an SGML document
DTD	a DTD subset
ELEMENTS	an element set (part of a DTD)
ENTITIES	an entity set (part of a DTD)
LPD	a LINK type declaration subset
NONSGML	a non-SGML data entity
NOTATION	character data for a NOTATION
SD	an SGML Declaration
SHORTREF	a short reference set
SUBDOC	an SGML subordinate document entity
SYNTAX	a concrete syntax
TEXT	an SGML text entity

This is followed by a compulsory white-space. An explanation of all of these in detail is beyond the scope of this book, but you may already have encountered `DTD`, `ELEMENTS`, `ENTITIES`, and `NOTATION`, however, as they are in frequent use in popular DTDs and DocType Declarations. Full details can be found in the text of Goldfarb's *SGML Handbook*[20].

Public Text Identifier This is a name chosen by the owner, usually descriptive of the text, such as the full name of the DTD, or the description of the module or entity set, or the short title of a document.

If the text itself is not publicly available (due to corporate or government restrictions, for example), this Identifier can be prefixed with the characters `-//`, for example:

```
+//Silmaril//ENTITIES -//Private Entity Set//EN
```

Public Text Language The language is identified by the relevant ISO 639 two-letter language code. Note that this has nothing to do with the two-letter country codes used in email addresses.

Public Text Designating Sequence In the case of an FPI for a character set, the language code is replaced by a designating escape sequence for the character set, as defined in ISO 2022:1994 (character code structure), which uniquely identifies it.

It takes the form of the keyword `ESC` followed by two pairs of numbers, each separated by a slash, and separated from each other by a space; for example `ESC 2/5 4/0` is the designated sequence identifying the ISO 646 IRV character set (ASCII).

Public Text Display Version This is to identify if the text is in a hardware- or software-specific version. The content is unspecified.

One of the problems users find with FPIs is that they don't say where to get the Public Text they identify: it is important to note that an FPI is a symbolic label, not an address. In many cases it is fairly obvious whom to ask (if the company or organization identified as Public Owner can be recognized or traced) but without the proper information it's a case of searching, asking, or going back to the author or provider of the file. They (or whoever they got it from) must by definition have had access to a copy in order to identify the file in the first place.

The standard method of resolving the FPI to a real file is to use a catalog entry in an OASIS catalog file (see section 2.5.4 for more details of catalogs). Thus instead of supplying all the DTD and ancillary files with every SGML or XML instance, you can simply provide the catalog entries. These may well point to URLs, but as we have seen, the advantage of this extra level of indirection is to provide a stable form for expressing the identity of an entity, and leave the current location of the file to an entry in a catalog.

2.5.3. Locating the DTD and other entities

Both FPIs and SIs can pose problems of location: an SGML program still needs to be able to find the file.

If the System Identifier is a simple filename, then a copy of the file should have been supplied with the instance, along with the SGML Declaration. If it was not, then you need to contact the author or owner and ask for copies of the files, because without them you cannot proceed. It is a common error to fail to supply the DTD and other files along with an SGML instance: make sure you don't fall into the same trap when you give SGML files to other people, and only provide local filenames in the SI.

If it's a URL instead, then a simple request to the Web can be used, and the returned file would be expected to contain the DTD or whatever entity file was requested. If it fails, and standard procedure for testing broken URLs is followed, then ultimately you need to contact the author or owner of the instance.

In theory, the FPI overcomes the problems of non-existent files, broken links, malformed URLs, *etc*, but it also raises its own set of problems about locating the text.

It would be possible, given a sufficiently large repository, to devise a lookup mechanism whereby a networked user could request a copy of a Public Text simply by sending the FPI. While no such global system exists at present, the author has written an experimental server at `http://www.ucc.ie/cgi-bin/public`, which resolves FPIs to the actual Public Texts they identify. Feedback on its applicability and development is welcomed (via the form provided online).

One method of identification was implemented in *sgmls* and in early versions of *psgml*, where spaces in the FPI are replaced by underscore characters, and the resulting Public Owner Identifier, Public Text Class, and Public Text Identifier are then treated as directory and file names in subdirectories below a configurable place on disk (by default `/usr/local/lib/sgml` on a Unix system). Thus on a PC, the FPI in the example at the beginning of this section would be expected to be a file called `c:\usr\local\lib\sgml\Silmaril\DTD\Article_v3`

Although this is simple to implement where users have write-access to the relevant directories so that they can install new files, it involves the remapping of those characters permitted in FPIs but not allowed

What to do when a URL doesn't work

When a URL (say, `http://foo.bar.com/pub/users/joe/docs/info.dtd`) doesn't work you can try the following, listed below roughly in the order of difficulty, easiest first:

1. Try the Reload or Refresh button, in case there was a temporary problem with making the connection;
2. Examine the URL for components with time significance, and if found, change them. For example, change `http://www.ux.edu/catalog/classes/fall1999/list.xml` to `http://www.ux.edu/catalog/classes/spring2000/list.xml` (of course we usually aren't lucky enough to have it this easy);
3. Take off the filename and directory name, to see if Joe has some kind of index: `http://foo.bar.com/pub/users/joe/`. This will load `index.html` [or some such file] in the `joe/` directory, if it exists. Otherwise it will show a listing of the files available for public access, or if the directory is not public, will give a message to that effect;
4. Progressively strip off the directory names on the right-hand end of the URL one by one, retrying at each stage, until you find a directory which *does* exist;
5. Take off everything but the root server name to see whether the site has a welcome page at `http://foo.bar.com/`;
6. Try the same thing without the trailing slash: `http://foo.bar.com`;
7. Many sites move machines around: try `www.*` and `web.*` machines;
8. Use a search engine to find the parent organization or Internet Provider of whoever created the resource, and try to find the resource through the links from the main page of that organization;
9. Find a person who might know the current status, and ask them.

Steps 1–7 take a little more time than doing a library catalog search. Step eight takes a bit longer, and step nine generally takes a day or two if the person responds to email. Still faster than postal mail, but the main problem is that success is by no means assured. After 1–7 are exhausted, eight might yield no results and nine might be impossible. So the problem still exists.

(I am grateful to Carlos McEvilly for permission to use the original of these helpful hints. Carlos is author of the document *How to make great WWW Pages*[31].)

in filenames (the slash and colon particularly). It is a useful method, however, where you have access to the directories (increasingly common with low-cost personal Unix systems) and a large or frequently-changing number of DTDs and a lot of *psgml* and *sgmls* or *nsgmls* users under Unix or on Windows 95/NT.

Where the DTD involved is a popular public entity, it is often a reasonable assumption that the experienced SGML user already has copies on a local disk, or knows where to obtain them. It would be expected, for example, that a publisher would have copies of the ISO 12083 DTDs, or that a Humanities SGML user has access to the TEI DTD, even if actually locating them the first time requires them to consult their local SGML expert or installer.

Providing a System Identifier as well as an FPI appears to be the choice of a lot of authors, possibly because of the lack of easily accessible documentation about the format of FPIs, which has tended to make them rather impenetrable (I hope the explanation above has helped this). The reality for users is somewhat different: many SGML systems, even stable and well-established ones, demonstrate unexpected behavior when faced with both FPI and SI. Some pick the Public Identifier and ignore the System Identifier, even if the Public one is then not found or cannot be parsed or resolved, or does not equate to a known local file name in a catalog (see below). Others pick the System Identifier and ignore the Public Identifier, even if one is provided and the SI turns out to be non-existent or the wrong type of file. Because ISO 8879 provides no guidance for attaching precedence to FPIs or SIs, there is no right or wrong here (although failing to try the other when one fails smacks of carelessness).

However, providing both identifiers is a good guide for any subsequent human user who may have to examine the first line of an instance to find out what's wrong. As mentioned above, XML cuts through this by requiring the System Identifier always, and requiting it to be a URL, so that a DTD or other entity may be located on the Internet. An FPI is optional (and I recommend it).

It is also possible to put the name of a binary (non-text) file in the System Identifier, whether or not a Public Identifier is specified. For example, SoftQuad's *Author/Editor* accepts

```
<!DOCTYPE html SYSTEM "c:\ae\rules\htmlpro.rls">
```

so that this can be used when a file is being passed between authors or editors sharing the same software on the same platform. This does make the file non-portable for others, though, so it is not a recommended solution for files expecting a wider currency.

The solution which overcomes a significant number of the problems of location and resolution is the 'catalog' file. Although catalog files have been in use for a long time, called variously 'Entity Managers', 'Resolvers', or 'Entity Catalogs', a formal proposal was made for a common catalog format by the OASIS organization, and this now becoming the most widespread solution, although regrettably a significant number of vendors still cling to their proprietary catalog formats.

2.5.4. The OASIS catalog (SGML Open catalog)

OASIS is an organization set up to promote and enable the widespread adoption of SGML. It was formerly called SGML Open. Among numerous technical papers, one of its most important products has been a definition of a simple catalog file format which lets you equate a Formal Public Identifier with a local file name on your system for any entity referred to in an SGML system. This has been widely implemented in many products, and removes the need to put System Identifiers in your entity references for regular SGML (XML requires an SI always but may have an optional FPI). The proposal is defined in OASIS's Technical Resolution TR 9401:1997, available at `http://www.sgmlopen.org/techpubs.htm#entity`.

Instead of the System Identifier you can therefore use a Formal Public Identifier, but you no longer have to worry about whether the a system will parse it correctly to a file name *à la sgmls*. If you or your users run software which understands the OASIS catalog format, all you need to supply are the entries for their catalog, either leaving space for users to fill in the name of the file where their local copy resides, or giving known file paths and names for the files you use or distribute.

Not all software uses this format. Many editors and other systems defined their own catalog format long before TR 9401, and have remained with it. In general, these private systems use a very similar format, but usually without the `PUBLIC` or other keywords (see below). Some also have restrictions on the use of spaces or linebreaks, and some introduce other separator characters, or require every entry to be on a single line (regardless of how long that makes the line), or require every entry to be split across two lines: all of which is a good reason why you should always use a reliable plaintext editor rather than a word processor to edit catalog files; or (under MS-Windows) use something like *CatEdit* (see section 2.5.4.2).

For an example of the OASIS catalog method, let's suppose you distribute a quarterly report to your investment clients, accompanied by a DTD that your company refers to as

```
-//Acme Corp//DTD Financial Report v7//EN
```

Inside this DTD there are references to some standard company boilerplate definitions:

```
<!ENTITY % financial "INCLUDE">
<![%financial;[
<!ENTITY % findefs
  PUBLIC "-//Acme Corp//ELEMENTS Financial Definitions v7//EN">
%findefs;
]]>

<!ENTITY % currsym
  PUBLIC "-//Acme Corp//ENTITIES Currency Symbols 1997//EN">
%currsym;
```

(Note the ability to switch the financial definitions on and off via a Parameter Entity, here set to INCLUDE). All you need to supply with the document instance are the SGML Declaration and the DTD and entity files, plus a catalog file containing the definitions required in OASIS format (the linebreaks here are for convenience on a narrow page):

```
SGMLDECL "/sgml/dtds/acme/acme.dec"
PUBLIC "-//Acme Corp//DTD Financial Report v7//EN"
       "/sgml/dtds/acme/fr7.dtd"
PUBLIC "-//Acme Corp//ELEMENTS Finance Definitions v7//EN"
       "/sgml/dtds/acme/fd7.mod"
PUBLIC "-//Acme Corp//ENTITIES Currency Symbols v7//EN"
       "/sgml/dtds/acme/cr7.ent"
```

Assuming you distribute this in some kind of self-installing compressed file format, so that the files always end up in the expected place, your clients simply point their software at the catalog file (usually called just 'catalog'), and it will find all the right files. Order is significant, however, so if you are updating a catalog, just appending to the end may not be the right thing to do.

SGML software which uses catalogs can often search a whole directory path for catalog files, so you may not be restricted to putting everything in a single catalog file.

If your clients are using a network with something like *MultiDoc Pro* or *Panorama*, you can make this catalog fragment, as well as the DTD and entity files, plus stylesheets and navigator accessories, accessible transparently, so the user just clicks on the document icon and everything else loads by itself, using URLs as the filenames.

It is important to remember that just providing a catalog on its own doesn't solve everything: the filenames you give in the second pair of quotes for each entry must still be in places the software can find. For this reason, most catalogs tend to contain absolute file paths and references after the FPI, just to make sure every program will find the right files.

The format of the OASIS catalog file is very straightforward: each entry begins with one of the keywords defined below, and is followed by one or more 'arguments' (values in quotes), depending on the meaning. SGMLDECL only has one, for example, meaning 'this file is the SGML Declaration', whereas PUBLIC has two, meaning 'when you see the first value as a Formal Public Identifier, use the file (System Identifier) named in the second value'. The more recent support for DTDDECL with two arguments lets you specify different declarations for different DTDs. You can use your regular plaintext editor to create the file, or a catalog maintenance program like *CatEdit* (section 2.5.4.2). The most commonly used entries are (the spacing here is just for neatness):

```
SGMLDECL "/usr/local/sgml/mdoc.dcl"
DTDDECL  "-//IETF//DTD HTML 2.0//EN" "/usr/local/sgml/sgmlhtml.dcl"
PUBLIC   "-//MDoc//DTD Letter//EN" "/usr/local/sgml/dtds/letter.dtd"
PUBLIC   "ISO 8879-1986//ENTITIES Added Latin 1//EN"
         "/usr/local/sgml/entities/isolat1.ent"
ENTITY   "fpanel" "frontpanel.tiff"
DOCUMENT "-//MDoc//DOCUMENT Annual Report 1997//EN"
         "mysgml/docs/annrep.sgml"
DELEGATE "-//Acme"
         "http://www.acme.ie/dtds/general.cat"
```

There are other keywords for document types, link types, and DocType Declarations (details are in the text of the Recommendation) and for SYSTEM (see section 2.5.4.1). The DELEGATE keyword is the most interesting from a networked point of view, as it enables the redirection of resolution requests for a specific case of Public Owner Prefix out of the current catalog into another catalog, which may be retrieved from another system.

The entries do not have to be on a single (sometimes long) line each, although this is convenient if your editor wraps lines neatly for easy viewing. They can be split onto two or more lines, but you need to check your applications, as not all programs support linebreaking in the same way. In theory you can break the line at any white-space, so for example, these first three entries are logically all the same

```
PUBLIC "-//IETF//DTD HTML 2.0//EN" "html2.dtd"

PUBLIC
    "-//IETF//DTD HTML 2.0//EN"
    "html2.dtd"

PUBLIC "-//IETF//DTD
HTML 2.0//EN" "html2.dtd"
```

Typing and spelling

For successful use of the OASIS catalog mechanism, the names of the Formal Public Identifiers and filenames must be exactly correct, character for character. I know it sounds odd to emphasize this, but if you find an SGML program failing to resolve a Formal Public Identifier, it's probably because there is no entry for it in your catalog, or the entry you think is there has a tiny but significant variation or typing mistake.

Some FPIs and file paths are long and complex, and it's easy to make mistakes in typing them, so where your system allows, use the copy and paste editor facilities to make sure the entry is copied correctly from the source document. If you have a problem resolving an FPI which you think is right, go and have a cup of coffee, and come back and examine it for typing errors again before looking for other solutions.

```
PUBLIC "-//IETF
//DTD HTML 2.0//EN" "html2.dtd"
```

but the last one is not, because there's a linebreak (which counts as white-space) between `IETF` and the following //, which is not there in the formal definition. Only break FPIs at real spaces, never immediately before or after a double slash.

Using catalog files you can build up a list of equivalences for every FPI you encounter, giving the file name on your system that an SGML program is to use.

There is no fixed name that the catalog file itself should have. The names `catalog` and `CATALOG`, `catalog.cat`, `sgml.cat`, `*.soc`, and so on, are all commonly used. Pick a suitable name, preferably one your software expects, and put the file in a location where you can easily find it, such as `c:\sgml` on a PC, or an `~/sgml` or `sgml` folder on a Unix or Mac system. It is possible, and occasionally useful if you use *Emacs*, to keep it in `/usr/local/lib/sgml/CATALOG`, as *Emacs* will seek it there if given no other information.

Each SGML program usually has a configuration option which lets you say where your catalog file is kept, so once you have established it, just set each program you use to point at the file, and ever thereafter all you need to do is keep the one file up to date with any new FPIs you

Warning: broken FPIs

There are a few FPIs which were unfortunately used in documents posted to mailing lists or newsgroups, or placed on Web sites, and which got a significant amount of exposure before errors were discovered. I don't think anyone is keeping track of them, but I have seen a TEI Lite FPI saying

```
-//TEI//DTD TEI Lite 1.6 //EN
```

(Note the space after the 1.6: this is exactly the error outlined earlier in this section). There are references in several places to FPIs with only one slash separating the Owner from the Class (some references to the Elsevier ART300 and ART400 DTDs exhibit this error).

A perennial problem is old references to `'ISO 8879-1986//ENTITIES Added Latin 1//EN'` and `'ISO 8879:1986//ENTITIES Added Latin 1//EN'` (and all the other character entity files). Look carefully and you'll see the first has a hyphen where the second has a colon. The hyphen was valid at the time (1986–89) but was superseded by the colon. Unfortunately there are still thousands of files out there still using the hyphen, so most catalogs need to support both formats.

You will also find many millions of files on the Web created by 'HTML editors' claiming to be HTML 2.0, 3.2, or 4.0 when they clearly are not, so you should approach with deepest suspicion any HTML file coming from a graphical HTML editor which is purporting to be conformant just by sticking a DocType Declaration at the top of the file (a pity, as there is an increasing number of authors who *are* creating conformant HTML, and a few editors like *HoTMetaL* which genuinely are conformant).

Finally, there are much smaller numbers of files put up on Web sites or posted to public discussions which have broken FPIs because the author has not come across the rules before. In these cases it is courteous to point out the error politely.

use, and your programs will always be able to resolve them and open the right files.

Unfortunately, some programs don't let you specify where the catalog is, or expect it to have a specialized name like `entref.lis`. In these cases, if you're using a filing system which allows aliases ('soft links' or 'shortcuts'), you can create a link to the file in a different directory with a different name, but still have only the one master catalog to maintain.

Some programs will also check the 'current' folder or directory (*ie* where the currently open document came from) to see if there is a file called `catalog` or `CATALOG` in there, and use that in preference to any other. This can be useful if you want to override your main catalog file on a directory by directory basis, but keeping a separate catalog file in each directory you use for SGML files is cumbersome, and prone to errors as the files get out of synchronization.

2.5.4.1. Making an entry in an OASIS catalog

Let's assume you have been given an SGML file to process, and it starts with the following DocType declaration:

```
<!DOCTYPE memo PUBLIC "+//Acme//DTD Office Report//EN" [
<!entity % abbrevs "+//Acme//ENTITIES Shortcuts//EN">
]>
```

You've been supplied with the SGML Declaration in a file `acmesgml.dcl`, and two files `acmerep.dtd` and `acmeabbr.ent` for the DTD and shortcut entities, all of which you've put into the `c:\sgml` folder. In order to point at the right files, the catalog needs the entries

```
SGMLDECL "c:\sgml\acmesgml.dcl"
PUBLIC "+//Acme//DTD Office Report//EN" "c:\sgml\acmerep.dtd"
PUBLIC "+//Acme//ENTITIES Shortcuts//EN" "c:\sgml\acmeabbr.ent"
```

You also need to check to see if the DTD and entity files themselves refer to any further identifiers: it is very common for DTDs to invoke other element definition fragments and common files such as the ISO character entities. Searching for the double slash is an effective way to check this. Let's suppose that `acmerep.dtd` turns out to refer to

```
<!entity % isolatl public
  "ISO 8879:1986//ENTITIES Added Latin 1//EN"
  "H:\ENTS\ISOLAT1.GML">
%isolatl;
```

and you haven't been given a copy of `isolatl.gml` because the ISO character entity files are commonly supplied ready-to-use with SGML systems, so it's assumed you already have it. You do have it, with your editor, but it's not called that, it's called `isolatl.ent` and it's actually in your `c:\sgml\entities` folder. You can make an entry in your catalog file (you may have it already from previous work):

```
PUBLIC "ISO 8879:1986//ENTITIES Added Latin 1//EN"
       "c:\sgml\entities\isolatl.ent"
```

but some systems will read the DTD, see the entry for `H:\ENTS\ISOLAT1.GML` and (depending on how they work), 'prefer' to use the System Identifier supplied within the DTD rather than check the catalog —

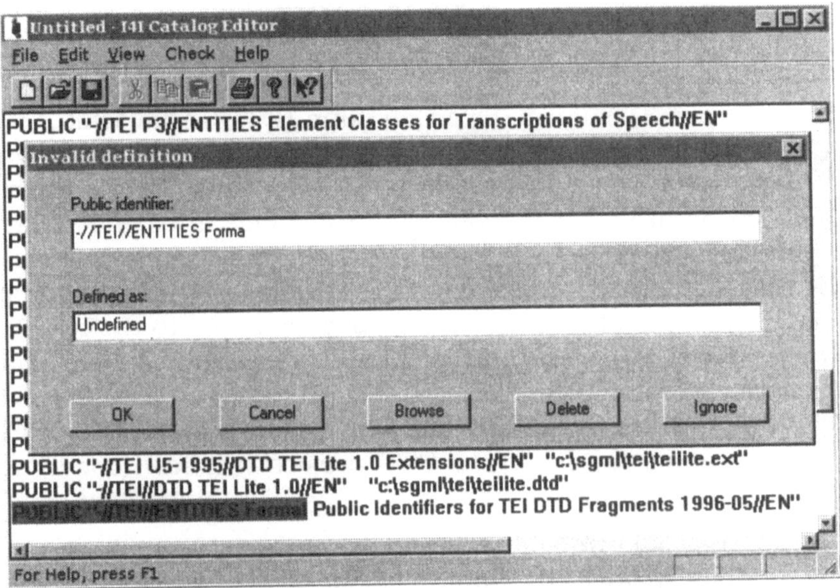

Figure 54. I4I's *CatEdit* editor for OASIS catalog files

and of course you don't have a file called `H:\ENTS\ISOLAT1.GML` on your system. To fix this, the OASIS catalog mechanism lets you make an entry in the catalog saying

```
SYSTEM "H:\ENTS\ISOLAT1.GML" "c:\sgml\entities\isolat1.ent"
```

so that a program looking for `H:\ENTS\ISOLAT1.GML` and failing to find it can look in the catalog file and see what file to open instead.

2.5.4.2. CatEdit (I4I)

Infrastructures for Information (whose *S4-Desktop* SGML libraries are covered in section 7.1.4) produce *CatEdit*, a free check-and-edit program for catalog files on MS-Windows systems.

As a checker, it reads a catalog and checks each `PUBLIC` entry to see if the System Identifier matches an existing local file. As a catalog editor, it displays the catalog in a plaintext edit window which lets you insert, change, or remove a `PUBLIC` catalog entry. It has no facilities for handling any of the other catalog keywords, which is a pity, but it leaves any existing other entries undisturbed.

This is a useful tool to run in conjunction with *RunSP*, the MS-Windows shell for the *nsgmls* parser (see section 4.3.5.1).

2.6. Writing and modifying DTDs

Writing your own Document Type Definition (DTD) from scratch is a non-trivial undertaking, although it is a skill worth developing if you are going to spend a lot of time with SGML systems. This is neither the place for discussing what you ought to include in or omit from a DTD, nor for how you design one: these things are dealt with in more detail in several books which discuss DTD design, of which the best by far (and at the time of writing the only one dedicated to the topic) is *Developing SGML DTDs: From Text to Model to Markup*[30] by Eve Maler and Jeanne el Andaloussi.

The process of creating a DTD can involve many stages. Maler and el Andaloussi summarize the typical DTD project workflow (condensed from their p.84 and §5.2):

1. launch, with a document recording the goals;
2. analysis and report on sample documents and existing systems (identify and define 'semantic components' (units of potential markup requirement) and classify them);
3. review and validation of the analysis report;
4. build a model and generate a design specification:
    - select the components that will serve as markup model requirements;
    - working from the requirements, build the document hierarchies (*eg* chapters, sections, subsections, *etc*) and the metadata;
    - build the 'information-level' units (structural markup that is not hierarchical, such as tables, figures, sidebars, *etc*);
    - build the 'data-level' elements (informational markup, usually found in mixed content);
    - populate all the contexts where the structure will have 'free mixtures' (*ie* where there is a choice of markup or types of markup);
    - specify linking relationships and other DTD 'connections';
    - specify any special processing markup.
5. specification reviewed by users;
6. make any changes in the light of this, and create document analysis report;
7. use this to create architecture report containing the technical information needed for implementation;

Making a DTD usable

Most parsers assume you are parsing a complete SGML document, that is, your document instance will indicate the DTD in its DocType Declaration, and your catalog will point both to the SGML Declaration and to the location of the DTD file[s].

When a DTD developer wants to parse a DTD, there's no DocType Declaration (they're not allowed in DTDs), so it is common to add one at the top of the DTD *file*, but *outside* the DTD code, enclosing it instead in the square brackets which denote an Internal Subset:

```
<!DOCTYPE foo [
...DTD declarations go here...
]>
```

If you don't have these two 'wrapper' lines when you want to parse the DTD file alone, you'll get error messages like `"ELEMENT" declaration not allowed in prolog` or `"ENTITY" declaration not allowed in prolog`.

Although this works for testing, many developers do not remove the DocType Declaration when distributing the DTD file, which makes the file unusable as it stands for parsing with document instances in the conventional way: if you try it by parsing an SGML instance which refers to such a DTD, you'll get the error message

```
/usr/local/bin/nsgmls:foo.dtd:1:2:E:
"DOCTYPE" declaration not allowed in DTD subset
/usr/local/bin/nsgmls:foo.dtd:999:0:E: character "]" not al-
lowed in
declaration subset
```

You can either remove the top and bottom lines from the DTD file, leaving the DTD declarations untouched, or you can concatenate the DTD file and your instance together (first removing your own DocType Declaration from the top of your instance), thus making the new file an instance-plus-its-own-DTD in a single file. The second method has the drawback that if the DTD needs updating, you may have to update *every* file that you have added it to in this way.

8. write the DTD and distribute to designers, users and documentors;
9. test and review, and report back to implementor;
10. documentation starts;
11. make any changes, update all reports, and distribute;
12. do documentation and training material, prepare for maintenance;
13. review and validate, and enter maintenance cycle.

There will always be unexpected surprises (requirements people never mentioned because they were 'too obvious to need explaining') but as with any project, the better the analysis before you start modeling or coding, the better the results will be.

However, not everyone creating DTDs has the luxuries of design teams, review panels, implementors, analysts, and documentation specialists. Small and medium-sized companies, research and academic projects, and sometimes just plain individuals, may all want to do themselves a DTD for some purpose, in which case the design team and all the other specialists may be one and the same person.

This is especially true now that XML makes it possible for anyone to implement a relatively simple DTD on the Web. You still need the analysis and planning — trying to cut corners here is a recipe for disaster — but the cycle is shortened because information has to pass through fewer hands. There are of course many consultancies who will help, either acting as external reviewers or analysts, or undertaking the entire job.

Tools usable for the latter stages, the mechanics of actually editing the code and validating it, are readily available and are dealt with in the sections on text editors and the chapter on parsing and validation. DTD designers, in common with specialists in all kinds of fields, tend to have their own personal toolkit or suite of utilities which they have built up over the years.

Tools for the earlier stages, however, are rare, and have more in common with data analysis tasks for database systems than with the business of editing or processing SGML text. This is one area where there are few obvious SGML-specific tools available yet. The notable exceptions are the tools developed for use with *Perl* (and to some extent with *Python*), especially Earl Hood's *perlSGML* (see section 5.1.3.1), which even includes a plaintext (ASCII) DTD structure view.

The only widespread commercial graphical system for DTD creation and display is Microstar's *Near&Far Designer* (their engine also powers Corel's *Graphical DTD Editor*). You will already be familiar with the symbol notation used in the *Near&Far Designer* display from the diagrams elsewhere in this chapter. The tree-graph display in the *Beca* program of the *Fred* system (see below) is also useful for small DTDs, although it is best-known for its ability to deduce a one-off DTD for the purpose of analysis or enabling a DTD-less document to be imported into an SGML system needing a DTD. This is useful where authors have made a (sometimes valiant) effort to create a document they believe to be 'in SGML', but where they have not been given (or have been unable to find) any information about the workings of SGML, availability of DTDs, or the need for validity.

Not everyone wants to write their own DTD, however: many users just want to make a few changes to an existing one to permit the occurrence of a certain element here, and remove another element there, and change the order of a content model or so. While this kind of modification is certainly possible, there are three caveats:

- you need to know and understand the meaning and use of the DTD, as well as its design philosophy: this means being aware that even very small changes may have quite significant knock-on effects in other parts of the DTD;
- you need to be very familiar with declarations, parameter entities, content models, and DTD syntax;
- the result should not be referred to by the same name as the original, otherwise other users may get confused about which DTD is intended, and the original author may object (on grounds of copyright, if nothing else). Create your own FPI!

The first section below deals with the mechanics of DTD modification, as its easier to start with something that already exists, rather than creating something from scratch. The remaining sections cover some of the available tools. The modifications discussed are restricted in scope, and are intended as examples only: if you are going to make anything other than trivial changes you may need to know quite a lot about formal SGML first.

2.6.1. Modifying a DTD

Modifying small DTDs is usually a matter of editing the source code and making the changes by hand, as they tend not to have the parameterized structure necessary to allow modification in the way described for the larger ones below.

Two examples of large DTDs being modified are given here: for the TEI and for *DocBook*. You should read the sections on these two DTDs first, if you haven't already done so (page 92 and page 82).

2.6.1.1. Changes to small DTDs

Changes to small DTDs usually involve the editing or replacement of element, entity, or attribute list declarations by modified versions. The principles are the same where parameter entities are involved, but require more study of the DTD beforehand.

To start, let's assume we have a DTD for an office memo (this one is based on the *Near&Far* Memo DTD discussed in section 20). Let's further assume we want to make three changes: add a category of priority called 'Low'; change the order of the headers to place the 'Copies to' headings at the end; and add a new element called <INET> so that memos can refer to Internet resources and have links work in the company's browser.

```
<!ENTITY % text  "((#PCDATA) | bold | italic | icon)" >

<!ELEMENT memo  - O (header,body) --top level of a memorandum-->
<!ATTLIST memo priority (Urgent,Important,Normal)  "Normal">

<!ELEMENT header    - O (to+,from,(cc* & bcc*),
                        (date | sysdate*)*,subject)>
<!ELEMENT body      - O (para+) +(footnote)>
<!ELEMENT to        - O (#PCDATA)>
<!ELEMENT from      - O (#PCDATA)>
<!ELEMENT cc        - O (#PCDATA)>
<!ELEMENT bcc       - O (#PCDATA)>
<!ELEMENT date      - O (#PCDATA)>
<!ELEMENT sysdate   - O  EMPTY>
<!ELEMENT subject   - O (%text;)>
<!ELEMENT para      - O (%text;)>
<!ELEMENT footnote  - O (%text;) -(footnote)>
<!ELEMENT bold      - O (#PCDATA)>
<!ELEMENT italic    - O (#PCDATA)>
<!ELEMENT icon      - O  EMPTY>
<!ATTLIST icon
          name  CDATA    #REQUIRED    --Name of icon file--
          type  CDATA    #FIXED "GIF" --Type of graphic format-- >

<!ENTITY % ISOlat1      PUBLIC "ISO 8879:1986//ENTITIES Added
                               Latin 1//EN">
<!NOTATION GIF          SYSTEM "/usr/local/bin/xv" >
<!NOTATION ADDBOOK      SYSTEM "/usr/local/bin/addlist">
<!ENTITY % AddressList SYSTEM "/u/d/jdoe/admin/addresslist"
                               NDATA "ADDBOOK">
```

If you look at the DTD, you'll see it falls into four parts (the indenting and formatting is just for clarity):

1. the declaration of a parameter entity called `%text;` which is used to define four things that make up the content model of the Subject,

paragraphs, and footnotes (the only places that running text occurs). We'll need this when we want to add <INET> to the elements you can use in such text;

2. the declaration of the <MEMO> element as containing a <HEADER> and a <BODY> in that order, and a single attribute called PRIORITY, which is the one we will need to edit to add 'Low';
3. the declaration of all the remaining elements starting with the <HEADER> (which we will want to edit) and ending with <ICON> and its attribute list;
4. four ancillary declarations to define a set of accented characters that can be used (Latin–1); two programs for the user's editor/browser to run (to display GIF images and to look up names in an address book file); and the location of an address book file.

The changes could be made as follows (edits are underlined):

1. The values for an attribute which can only take one of a restricted, predefined set of names are given in a list called a 'name token group' which appears in parentheses after the name of the attribute in the attribute list. Here, the <MEMO> element has the attribute PRIORITY, with the permitted name tokens Urgent, Important, and Normal declared in the line beginning <!ATTLIST MEMO. To add a category of priority called 'Low' you therefore just need to edit the name token group in parentheses to add a comma and the token Low, so it reads:

   ```
   <!ATTLIST memo priority (Urgent,Important,Normal,Low)
     "Normal">
   ```

   If you are doing this for an element with many attributes, you need to be aware that in regular SGML a token cannot occur more than once in a single attribute definition list for an element, even in different groups for different attributes. So if you had another attribute for <MEMO> called, say, IMPORTANCE, you could not use Low as one of its predefined values in a name token group. You could of course declare IMPORTANCE as CDATA, and allow it to hold any value, and Low could still occur as a name token on an attribute on another element. This restriction is removed in the WebSGML Adaptations provided that minimization is turned off, so it doesn't apply to XML DTDs.
2. To change the order of the headers to place the 'Copies to' headings at the end we need to examine the existing content model for <HEADER>:

   ```
   <!ELEMENT header - O (to+,from,(cc* & bcc*),
                         (date | sysdate*)*,subject)>
   ```

In the syntax of content models, the commas mean 'must be followed in sequence by'; the ampersand means 'in any order'; and the vertical bar means 'either/or but not both'. The plus sign means there may be more than one occurrence (*ie* you must have one <TO> element but you can have many); and the asterisk means the element is optional, but may occur many times if you wish (so you can have several <CC> [carbon-copy] and <BCC> [blind-carbon-copy] elements, and even more than one <DATE>).

To reorder the elements, we need to edit the line so it looks like this:

```
<!ELEMENT header - O (to+,from,(date | sysdate*)*,
                      subject,(cc* & bcc*))>
```

moving the cc* & bcc* group, together with its parentheses and the preceding comma, to the new location after the subject.

3. To add a completely new element is a little more work. We need to define what the new element is going to be called (<INET>), what it is going to contain, and where it's going to fit into the existing model. Assuming that we want it to represent the same function as HTML's <A> element, we probably want it to contain text, possibly with bold, italics, and even an icon, and to have mandatory start- and end-tags, so we could declare something like this (in the blank line after the end of the attribute list for the icon element, perhaps):

```
<!element inet - - (%text;)>
```

We want it to occur in %text;, however, so we also need to change the declaration in the first line to read:

```
<!ENTITY % text  "((#PCDATA) | bold | italic | icon | inet )" >
```

But wait! This would mean that <INET> could itself also contain another <INET> element, which is not desirable. We can use an exclusion exception to stop this by changing the element declaration to:

```
<!element inet - - (%text;) -(inet)>
```

Finally, we need to add attributes so that it can be used by a browser. Making the assumption that this browser will respond to the presence of a HREF attribute, we can follow the element declaration with:

```
<!attlist inet href CDATA #REQUIRED>
```

This makes HREF compulsory, and it can contain any character data, sufficient for a URL.

This is fairly short and easy, but you can probably already see that there are many more considerations, even to simple changes, than just adding a couple of names here and there.

Having made the changes, you now need to use a parser to validate the DTD itself, and if that's OK, then an SGML editor (and perhaps a DTD compiler if it needs it) to test the DTD by creating instances of the new Memo structure. Any errors and you go back to the code and fix them...

2.6.1.2. Modifying the DocBook DTD

Modification of the *DocBook* DTD is done by creating a new DTD driver which makes the changes using parameter entities, and then invokes the *DocBook* main DTD file, on the usual principle that entities can be multiply defined, but only the first definition is used (the opposite way round from programming languages, which tend to use the most recent value of a variable).

The worked example is for the DTD used for the XML FAQ, which implements HTML forms and math within *DocBook*. The *DocBook* DTD itself is discussed in section 2.3.3.2.

The new DTD file, which was named `dbhtform.dtd`, starts off with an explanation of what it's for and where it comes from.

```
<!-- This DTD fragment customizes the DocBook DTD V3.0
     by adding HTML forms and math so that files can be
     used in SGML browsers (Panorama, MultiDoc Pro, etc) -->

<!-- The resulting DTD (dbhtform.dtd) can be referenced as

     "+//Silmaril//DTD DocBook V3.0-Based Extension
         With HTML Forms//EN"

     This file is Copyleft 1997 by Silmaril Consultants under
     the terms of the GNU General Public License, a copy of
     which can be found at

         http://www.gnu.org/copyleft/gpl.html

     The DocBook DTD is Copyright 1992, 1993, 1994, 1995, 1996
     HaL Computer Systems, Inc., O'Reilly & Associates, Inc.,
     ArborText, Inc., and Fujitsu Software Corporation. -->
```

The next task is to identify from the `.mod` files the name of the content model entity for the place where we want `<form>` to be usable. In this case, we picked `%divcomponent.mix;` in `dbhier.mod` and `%component.mix;` in `dbpool.mod`, both of which place forms at the same level as paragraphs, lists, and other formal objects. Each such entity in *DocBook* comes with a blank %local...; entity for you to put redefinitions in, so we add form| to this (the vertical bar being needed to preserve the syntax of the content model to which it's being added):

```
<!-- Redefine entities where we want FORM to occur -->
<!ENTITY % local.divcomponent.mix "|form">
<!ENTITY % local.component.mix "|form">
```

The same principle is applied to the <math> element, added to the content model for inline and display equations:

```
<!-- Same with the ones for MATH -->
<!ENTITY % equation.content "(Math|Graphic+)">
<!ENTITY % inlineequation.content "(Math|Graphic+)">
```

The HTML element <item>, used in math arrays, is added to the CALS table model for a table row:

```
<!-- and an addition to the ROW model to include ITEM -->
<!ENTITY % tbl.row.mdl          "(entry|entrytbl|item)+">
```

In each case we have redefined an existing parameter entity, and this will prevent the one defined in the DTD itself being used.

The next thing to do is invoke the *DocBook* DTD via its existing driver file. Our new file thus becomes 'the DTD', and it simply incorporates the whole of *DocBook*.

```
<!-- Call the DocBook driver file -->
<!ENTITY % docbookmain PUBLIC
  "-//Davenport//DTD DocBook V3.0//EN">
%docbookmain;
```

The hardest bit was extracting all the definitions of the forms and math elements and all their content models from the HTML DTD. In this case *HTML Pro* was used, because the DTD already contained all the required elements. The files are on the CD-ROM in a subfolder of the *DocBook* DTD, or can be downloaded from http://www.ucc.ie/xml/ as formfrag.dtd and mathfrag.dtd.

For the forms fragment, the HTML non-form part of the content model of <form> was replaced by the relevant *DocBook* content model, %component.mix;, and the <option> element declaration was placed in an IGNORE marked section, as *DocBook* already defines an element by this name, which can be re[ab]used:

```
<!ENTITY % targetcontent "%component.mix;">
<!ENTITY % option.def "IGNORE">

<!ELEMENT FORM  - -  (%targetcontent;)
-(FORM)
+(INPUT , SELECT , TEXTAREA)>
```

```
...HTML forms elements defined here...

<![%option.def;[
<!ELEMENT OPTION  - O  CDATA>
]]>
```

In the math fragment, the same pattern was followed: the *HTML Pro* non-math part of the content model of `<math>` was replaced by the `%para.mix;` definition for `%text;` and `%para.char.mix;` for `%insertions;` (see section 2.3.9.1.6 for details of these content models).

These two files then get invoked, and this completes the construction of the new DTD.

```
<!-- Bolt on the HTML forms and math definitions -->
<!ENTITY % formfrag PUBLIC
  "+//Silmaril//DTD HTML Forms Fragment//EN">
%formfrag;
<!ENTITY % mathfrag PUBLIC
  "+//Silmaril//DTD HTML Math Fragment//EN">
%mathfrag;
```

It's important to note that you can only modify DTDs in this way if they have been deliberately designed to allow it. Most DTDs don't: they are hardcoded with highly specific declarations designed for their purpose, sometimes precisely because the authors do *not* want users modifying the DTD themselves.

2.6.1.3. Modifying the TEI DTD

This example uses the DTD of the CELT project, which deals with modern and historical Irish literary texts. They needed to encode prose transcriptions with an *apparatus criticus* (a complex analytical framework used in academic study) and provision for encoding names, dates, and hypertext links within the framework of the TEI, and add some extra attributes to some elements. The TEI DTD itself is discussed in section 2.3.6.

The TEI's mechanism lets you make these changes in the DocType Declaration Subset, so the first line of this reads:

```
<!DOCTYPE TEI.2 PUBLIC "-//TEI P3//DTD Main Document Type 1994-05//EN"
```

To change attributes, you need to mark an existing definition as ignored, and then redefine it, with new attributes, so the first thing to do is insert any new entity definitions to prevent existing ones being used:

```
<!ENTITY % TEI.extensions.dtd PUBLIC
  "-//CELT//DTD Extensions to the TEI//EN">
```

In this file there are new definitions of all the elements for which attributes are being changed:

```
<!ELEMENT %n.addSpan;   - 0  EMPTY>
<!ATTLIST %n.addSpan;        %a.global;          %x.celtsrc;
          type               CDATA               #IMPLIED
          place              CDATA               #IMPLIED
          resp               IDREF               %INHERITED
          cert               CDATA               #IMPLIED
          hand               IDREF               %INHERITED
          to                 IDREF               #REQUIRED
          TEIform            CDATA               'addSpan'     >
```

(and more). In each case the element declarations themselves are unchanged from the TEI originals, but the attribute lists add new attributes, using parameter entities like `%x.celtsrc;` which are defined in an entity file that gets invoked later.

The next stage is to decide on the bases and toppings needed:

```
<!ENTITY % TEI.corpus             'INCLUDE'>
<!ENTITY % TEI.prose              'INCLUDE'>
<!ENTITY % TEI.transcr            'INCLUDE'>
<!ENTITY % TEI.textcrit           'INCLUDE'>
<!ENTITY % TEI.names.dates        'INCLUDE'>
<!ENTITY % TEI.linking            'INCLUDE'>
```

and the ISO character entity sets required:

```
<!ENTITY % ISOlat1 public "ISO 8879:1986//ENTITIES
  Added Latin 1//EN">
<!ENTITY % ISOlat2 public "ISO 8879:1986//ENTITIES
  Added Latin 2//EN">
<!ENTITY % ISOnum public "ISO 8879:1986//ENTITIES
  Numeric and Special Graphic//EN">
<!ENTITY % ISOpub public "ISO 8879:1986//ENTITIES
  Publishing//EN">
<!ENTITY % ISOdia  public "ISO 8879:1986//ENTITIES
  Diacritical Marks//EN">
%ISOlat1; %ISOlat2%; ISOnum; %ISOpub; %ISOdia;
```

Finally the entity file referred to above, and the closing square bracket at the end of the internal subset:

```
<!ENTITY % TEI.extensions.ent PUBLIC
 "-//CELT//ENTITIES Extensions to the TEI//EN">
]>
```

Both the extensions files have predefined parameter entity references in the TEI, as the authors of the TEI foresaw exactly this kind of need for external modifications. In this case the entity file contains some renaming (these are just a few examples):

```
<!ENTITY % n.roleName  'rn'>
<!ENTITY % n.supplied  'sup' >
```

```
<!ENTITY % n.surname   'sn' >
<!ENTITY % n.unclear   'uncl' >
```

some additional character entities:

```
<!ENTITY tdot      SDATA "t" -- small t (dot-over)-->
<!ENTITY ampersir  SDATA "&" -- insular ampersand-->
<!ENTITY turnsemi  SDATA ";" -- inverted semi-colon-->
<!ENTITY aunderdot SDATA "a" -- small a, dot below -->
```

the ignoring of the elements for which new attributes are needed:

```
<!ENTITY % addSpan "IGNORE">
<!ENTITY % add     "IGNORE">
<!ENTITY % step    "IGNORE">
<!ENTITY % state   "IGNORE">
<!ENTITY % seg     "IGNORE">
<!ENTITY % text    "IGNORE">
<!ENTITY % sic     "IGNORE">
```

and the definition of the new attributes themselves:

```
<!ENTITY % x.celtsrc "source CDATA #IMPLIED">
<!ENTITY % x.celtref "
          gi                NAME            #IMPLIED
          attr              NAME            #IMPLIED
          freq              NUMBER          #IMPLIED
          label             CDATA           #IMPLIED">
```

Only some of the changes are given here, for brevity. The full file contents can be inspected at the project Web site, `http://www.ucc.ie/celt/dtd/`.

2.6.1.4. Really modify the DTD?

It can be infinitely annoying to discover that the DTD you are using doesn't permit text or some particular subelement or attribute in some location that you would have expected it to, or permits it in a place you wouldn't have expected. It is even more annoying when the rest of the DTD seems to do the job you want perfectly well. And it is tempting therefore to react by immediately changing the DTD to 'make it right'.

Maler and el Andaloussi and many others offer the sound advice that this usually means either you or the DTD designer has not paid sufficient attention to the document analysis or requirements. This may well be true, but it is small consolation to the user trying to edit a document against the clock, using a DTD which 'does things wrong'.

One rule of thumb I was given by a designer is that if you think you need to modify the DTD, you're probably wrong (assuming you are dealing with an otherwise competently-designed DTD: this was after I made some suggestions about one of his own DTDs!). In practice you may of course have to change a DTD on occasions (and recompile it if the application requires) in order to allow something to occur where it is needed, but when you are using a popular and well-tried DTD which involved many thousands of hours of design, it is sometimes better to consult the documentation or contact the authors or other users to see if there is some misconception about usage, rather than an actual design error.

Cultural differences can also cause 'design errors' which are not errors at all. One example was uncovered in the revision of a well-known DTD, where the element `<example>` was understood by North Americans to mean (specifically and invariably) 'an example of computer program code', but by Europeans to mean just a generic example of something, not necessarily programming at all.

2.6.2. Near&Far Designer (Microstar)

MS-Windows
`http://www.microstar.com/`

A graphical DTD display is a very useful tool for checking the structural logic of a DTD, as we have seen in the preceding sections. It is usually very clear exactly what elements are appearing in each content model, and it provides the ability to expand and contract the elements to hide or show their contents. As a result, *Near&Far* (now *Near&Far Designer*) has become a standard tool for some document type designers, even if their actual DTD editing and design takes place on another platform or using other software. It appears that *NFD* is currently the only technology of its type on the market: it is also used to power Corel's *Graphical DTD Editor*. A demonstration copy for viewing DTDs is on the CD-ROM.

However, its use as an editor is particularly appealing to users of graphical windowing systems (although it is available only for one, MS-Windows), because it uses the familiar point-and-click paradigm for adding, deleting and moving elements, parameter entities, and attributes. There are some severe limitations, though, in its ability to handle nested parameterized modules, particularly when the DTD resides in several separate files.

2.6.2.1. Installation

The software comes on diskettes or CD-ROM in two separate versions, one for Windows 3.1 and one for Windows 95 or NT. The setup runs in the usual way from `setup.exe` and installs by default into `c:\nfdesign`, occupying about 3Mb of disk space. It detects and avoids earlier versions of itself.

The installation includes two sample DTDs, Memo and NFTest, which are described in section 2.3.1 of this chapter. The only other file which a user will need to be directly aware of is the Entity Reference File `nearfar.erf`, which is *NFD*'s catalog file (see section 2.5.4 on how to manage these). This is where you put your equivalences between Formal Public Identifiers (FPIs) and local filenames.

There are two screen-grabbers included with the installation: Microstar's own *ClipWin* and a shareware copy of Software Excellence By Design Inc's *Grab It! Pro* (in `c:\nfdesign\addons\`). These are to help documentors grab screenshots of the *NFD* display.

The 100–page manual provides a 'quick start' tutorial as well as a stage-by-stage explanation of the design and creation process.

2.6.2.2. Operation

To display an existing DTD, run the program and open a DTD file with the **File|*Open*** menu (or use drag-and-drop, or double-click a DTD file if the filetype has been linked to *NFD* in your Registry). Assuming *NFD* can resolve any entity references, the unexpanded DTD structure will be displayed. If it's not, then you need to quit the program, examine the DTD with a plaintext editor and identify all the entity references; then add the references to the catalog file (see section 2.5.4) so they point at the correct disk files, and restart *NFD* so that it re-reads the catalog. Then open the DTD again. Be patient: a large DTD like the TEI or *DocBook* can take several minutes to load and resolve, even when loaded from a 'flattened' version.

The concept behind the display is that the tree-like hierarchical structure of a traditional DTD can be modeled on the screen like a family tree, with each node (an element) having branches leading to one or more others, which either have branches themselves, or terminate in a symbol for their data content. This is best explained with such a display in front of you (this chapter is full of them). In practice, the tree is best drawn sideways, as the long names of many DTD elements mean that a traditional vertical tree quickly overruns the width of the screen and needs a lot of horizontal scrolling.

Figure 12 earlier in this chapter contains a table of the symbols used. There are three groups of symbols:

1. the connector lines
2. the content model occurrence indicators
3. the data content or 'terminal' indicators

. An object (an element, entity, *etc*) is expanded or contracted by double-clicking it, or it can be selected for editing by clicking once and then pressing **Enter**.

In the HTML example in Figure 55 (repeated from earlier), you can see the following features:

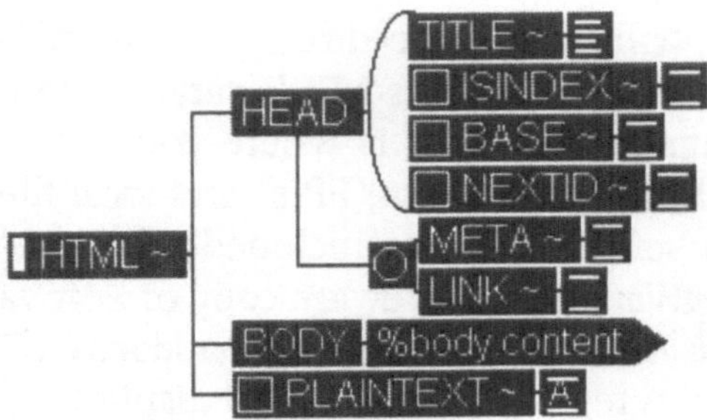

Figure 55. Header and upper body structure of HTML 2.0 (RFC 1866)

- the straight-line connector showing that the <HTML> element must contain <HEAD> and <BODY> in that order, and that <PLAINTEXT> must come after them, if used (the open square is for 'optional, but only one');
- the curved-line connector signifying that the component elements of <HEAD> (<TITLE>, <ISINDEX>, <BASE>, <NEXTID>) can occur in any order (and note that only <TITLE> is compulsory: no square);
- the square terminal symbols represent the data content of the elements: here they are all empty (the wide-spaced parallel lines) except <TITLE>, which may contain only PCDATA (text with no further markup), and <PLAINTEXT>, which may contain CDATA (character data, but further markup will go unrecognized);
- the open circle beside <META> and <LINK> shows they are included in <HEAD> as exceptions;
- the <BODY> element contains a parameter entity (symbol with a pointed right-hand end) which expands when double-clicked to reveal the elements which make it up (see Figure 52 in the section on the HTML DTD).

(The reason here for the different treatment of <META> and <LINK> is that they may occur multiple times, whereas the other elements in <HEAD> may occur only once. You cannot see from a graphical display, nor from the source code of the DTD itself, the reasons *why* a particular content model was chosen, only *how* it was done. For information on 'why', you need to read the documentation for a DTD, or the comments in the DTD source file, if any.)

A new element can be created by clicking the rectangular 'element' toolbar icon (see Figure 56 for the main screen layout) and dragging it to the place where you want it inserted into the DTD, either above or below an existing element in an existing content model, or to the right of an unpopulated element, to create a content model. This triggers a dialog where you give the element name and the occurrence, an

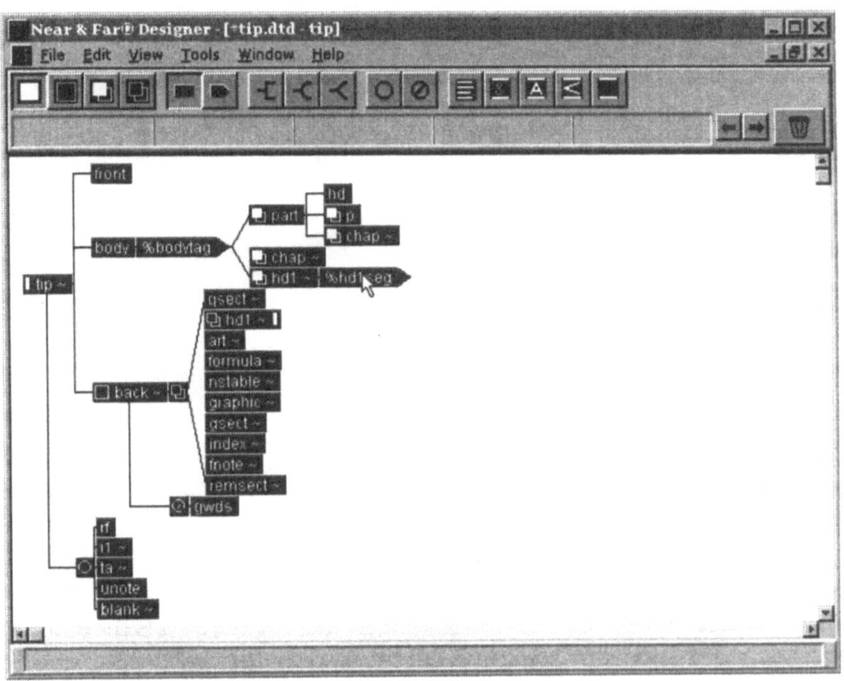

Figure 56. The Near&Far Designer screen

optional short title and longer description, and the start-tag and end-tag omission rules. Parameter entities are created in the same way with the relevant toolbar icon.

An existing element or parameter entity can be moved simply by dragging it to a new location (any descendent elements get moved with it). They can be reused by clicking and copying, and then pasting at another location, but this does not parameterize them: you have to do that by creating a parameter entity by hand. Data content ('terminals') can similarly be picked from the toolbar and used to populate elements.

Content models are constructed using the square, round, or angled bracketing symbols for ordered, unordered, or single choice (representing the comma, ampersand, or vertical bar of the DTD syntax).

Attribute management is done via menus and an attribute specification window (Figure 58). Attribute definitions can be reused from 'lists' which *NFD* maintains internally, so it is possible to pick graphically and apply attributes from other elements, even when there are many different meanings throughout the DTD for attributes of the same name.

There are many options for displaying the structure: vertically (as given here) or horizontally (family-tree style); the selected element can

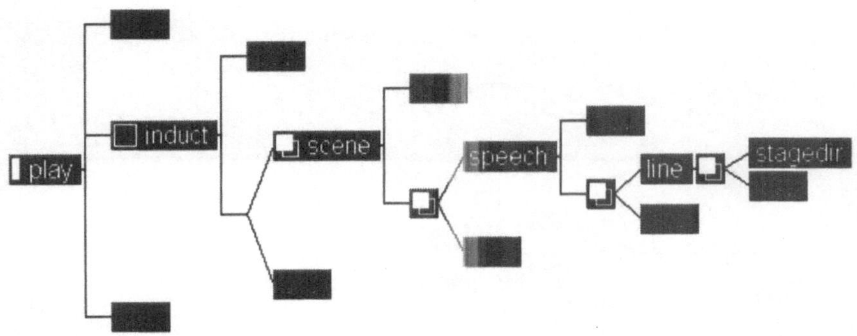

Figure 57. The 'path' to an element

be zoomed in on, or set as the focus by fitting the content model to the current window; and by pruning nonexpanded elements and trees, so that the 'path' to an element is all that remains on display (Figure 57).

The **File|*Reports*** option is used to produce printable tabular listings showing which elements each element contains, and which element they themselves are contained in; lists of attributes and which elements they occur in; supplemental objects like character entity references; the full descriptions of all objects (where entered); and a summary report of the whole DTD.

DTDs can be saved as binary files (`.mbf`) for faster reloading, or exported to ASCII (`.sgml`) files for use with other systems. The 'title' that can be supplied during element creation gets saved as a comment following the element declaration, but with an embedded piece of 'markup' that allows *NFD* to detect its presence on rereading:

```
<!ELEMENT TABLE - - (ROW+)
                --<Title>Simple table with rows--
                >
```

This means that reading an existing DTD which contains comments, and then saving it back as ASCII after editing, will make a mess of any formatting in the original comments. There is a view strongly expressed by some designers that *NFD* is a good tool for visualizing the DTD and for reporting on its structure, but the finished text file needs to be laid out and formatted by other means.

The drawback to the capabilities of *NFD* is that it does not handle external parameter entities correctly, so if you have a multi-file DTD it won't read it, and if you want to create one, you have to create it by hand. This means, for example, that both *DocBook* and TEI cause *NFD* to read the entire suite of files but then display nothing at all. The increasing trend towards the modular design of DTDs means that maintenance of the modularity will require manual editing.

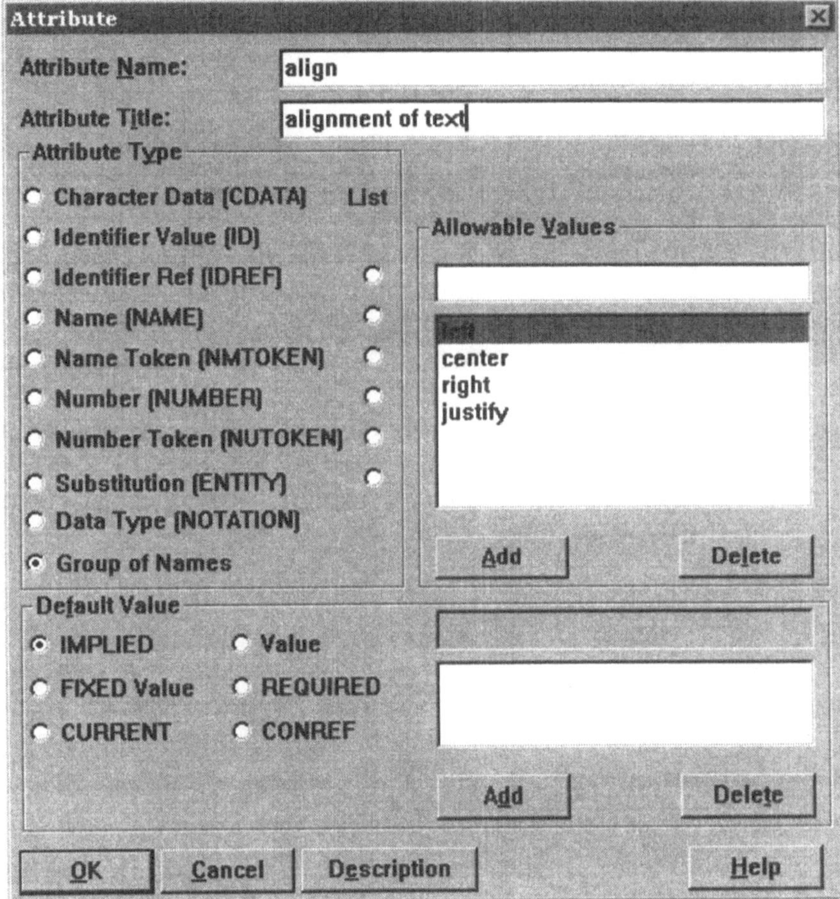

Figure 58. Attribute editing in *Near&Far Designer*

For reading existing DTDs, the solution is to 'flatten' the DTD with a program such as Richard Light's experimental *NormDTD* (see this chapter) or James Clark's *spam* (see chapter 4), both of which are included on the CD-ROM.

2.6.3. Graphical DTD Viewer (Corel)

This is a relicensed copy of *Near&Far Designer* which is supplied with Corel's *WordPerfect Suite* (Professional Edition only). The functions and use are identical to those described in section 2.6.2.

2.6.4. EasyDTD (Norm Smith)

DOS, Unix
`ftp://ftp.ifi.uio.no/pub/SGML/Demo/`

The syntax of SGML can be complex — perhaps understandably when you consider the complex task it has to perform. But there are occasions when a less demanding design of DTD means you can describe the structure more simply, or when you only need to create DTDs on rare occasions and the syntax eludes you. *EasyDTD* was written for these cases by Norm Smith, whose book on SGML Filters I refer to in section 5.

EasyDTD is a processor which takes a very simple form of SGML-like syntax to describe a document structure, and outputs a DTD in canonical SGML format. The syntax for *EasyDTD* resembles a document hierarchy rather than separate declarations for each element:

```
document
  fm
    title
    author+
    date
  body
    chapter+
      section*
        subsection*
          (p|
          list)*
            li
            li+
  bm?
    index
```

The indentation serves the purpose of defining the content model, and the bottom-most 'ends' of each hierarchy (in the above example, `<TITLE>`, `<AUTHOR>`, `<DATE>`, `<P>`, `<LI>`, and `<INDEX>`) are by default assumed to require `#PCDATA`. Occurrence indicators and model group delimiters and separators are used in the conventional manner.

Processing is with a simple command line which can be stored as a button-click in *PFE* or similar editors: typing `easydtd` *`input`*`.ezy` for the file above produces a DTD file like this:

```
<!DOCTYPE document  [
<!-- Skeleton DTD created by EASYDTD.
     CAUTION: This DTD probably needs editing before use!!!-->

                <!-- ENTITIES    -->
<!ENTITY % doctype "document" -- Document type GI -->
```

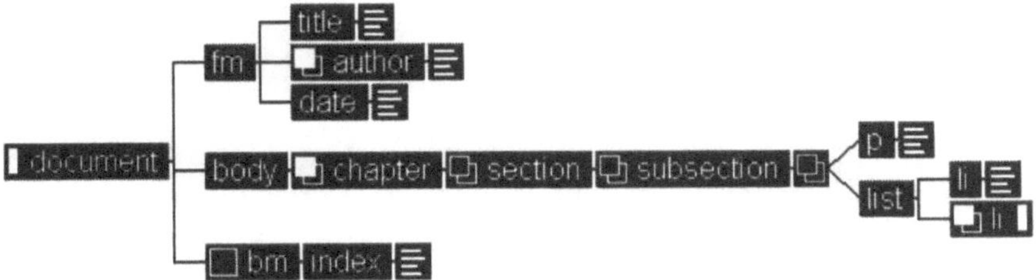

Figure 59. Sample DTD produced by *EasyDTD*

```
                    <!-- ELEMENTS     -->
<!--        ELEMENTS         MIN  CONTENT -->
<!ELEMENT %doctype;          - - (fm,body,bm?)  >
<!ELEMENT fm                 - - (title,author+,date)  >
<!ELEMENT title              - - (#PCDATA)  >
<!ELEMENT author             - - (#PCDATA)  >
<!ELEMENT date               - - (#PCDATA)  >
<!ELEMENT body               - - (chapter+)  >
<!ELEMENT chapter            - - (section*)  >
<!ELEMENT section            - - (subsection*)  >
<!ELEMENT subsection         - - ((p|list)*)  >
<!ELEMENT p                  - - (#PCDATA)  >
<!ELEMENT list               - - (li,li+)  >
<!ELEMENT li                 - - (#PCDATA)  >
<!ELEMENT bm                 - - (index)  >
<!ELEMENT index              - - (#PCDATA)  >

                    <!-- ATTRIBUTES  -->
<!--        ELEMENT        NAME          VALUE           DEFAULT -->
]>
```

The DTD in this case requires no further editing for testing, despite the warning. As this is not an application containing a formal parser, any more robust usage will need proper validation. The structure is nevertheless very clear (see Figure 59).

There is considerably more sophistication available, however, including more complex modeling, the use of parameter entities, and the specification of attributes. One interesting feature is that the program can output a skeleton *Omnimark* program to process instances using the DTD, and *awk* programs to do searching and replacement. In view of the application of XML without a DTD, where the document structure is defined by the occurrence of the elements, this provides a simple way to start building a DTD from a simple indented hierarchy. There is no XML version planned, but for simple, non-parameterized DTDs it's not

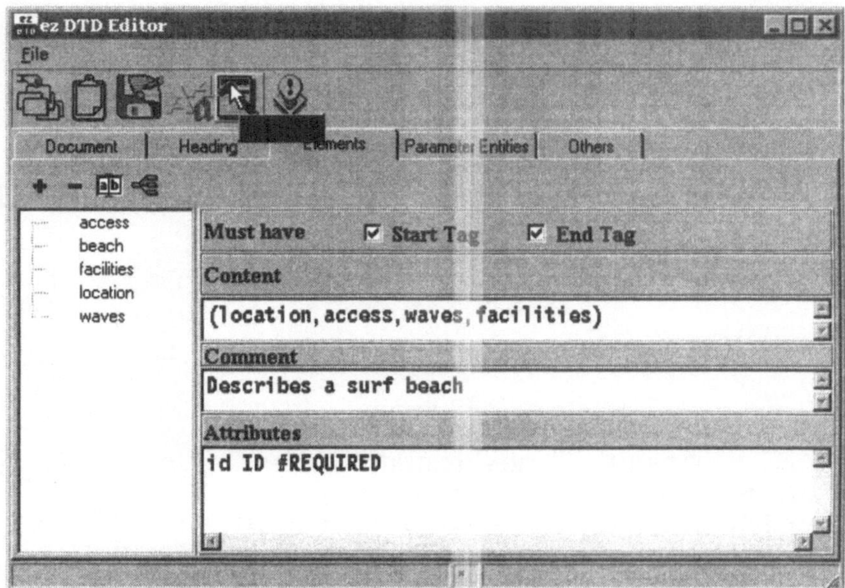

Figure 60. The *ezDTD* DTD editor

hard to edit out the minimization parameters and check the content models by hand.

2.6.5. ezDTD (Duncan Chen)

MS-Windows
`http://www.geocities.com/SiliconValley/Haven/2638/ezDTD.htm`

This is a simple program which provides a graphical interface to typing in the details of element and attribute list declarations. It is non-validating (non-parsing, even), but it's a good example of what could be done to make life easier for those who want to make their own very simple DTDs.

The 'Document' tab asks for the Document Type, version, author, organization, and date. A 'Heading' tab allows entry of Processing Instructions and a DocType Declaration (the aim is clearly to support XML, but there seems to be confusion over the role of the DocType Declaration).

The central tab allows the entry of element names, content models, attributes, and control over minimization. The root element can be set, and because there is no validation, element declarations can be added and removed (or renamed) at will — the assumption being that you are going to use an external parser/validator from time to time.

Other tabs allow the entry of entity declarations and notations. The whole DTD under development can be stored in binary form or exported to the standard plaintext file for inspection and saving. The program is at an early stage of development, so there are some rough edges, but the concept of a simple graphical interface to schematic-style entry is an attractive one.

2.6.6. NormDTD (Richard Light)

MS-DOS
`ftp://ota.ox.ac.uk/pub/ota/TEI/software/`

This is a public domain DOS program written by Richard Light (author of the *SGML Tagger*, see section 3.4.4) to handle those occasions where an SGML system cannot accept the complexity of large DTDs with deeply nested marked sections and parameter entity references to external files.

It 'flattens' the DTD to a single file, duplicating where necessary all the references that were previously handled by parameter entities. The element content models in this normalized DTD will not contain any references to elements that are not declared, and so it can be used by highly-strung packages such as *RulesBuilder* (see section 3.3.2.3) that refuse to process such applications (the TEI in particular: see section 2.3.6) for this reason.

2.6.6.1. Installation

NormDTD is supplied for download as a self-extracting executable, `normdtd1.exe`, from the Oxford Text Archive's public FTP server, in the TEI software directory. This program expands in the same directory where it is run to the application itself, `normdtd.exe`, a low-memory version `normlow.exe`, and a subsidiary executable `taggerrd.exe` with an overlay for use where memory constraints require the process to be run in separate stages.

2.6.6.2. Operation

The command line for execution is `normdtd` *`dtdfile outputfile`* If the output file exists, the program stops, so any output from a previous run of the same name must be deleted manually first. If you don't give an output file name, one will be created with the same name but the filetype `.dtn`

```
Normalizing DTD TEITEST
10: PHR normalised version being output
11: S normalised version being output
12: W normalised version being output
13: ATT normalised version being output
14: GI normalised version being output
15: TAG normalised version being output
16: VAL normalised version being output
17: FORMULA normalised version being output
18: ETREE normalised version being output
19: GRAPH normalised version being output
20: TREE normalised version being output
21: CAMERA normalised version being output
22: CAPTION normalised version being output
23: MOVE normalised version being output
24: SOUND normalised version being output
25: TECH normalised version being output
26: VIEW normalised version being output
27: CASTLIST normalised version being output
28: FIGURE normalised version being output
```

Figure 61. NormDTD normalizing the TEI DTD

There are some uneven patches in *NormDTD*, so the author suggests 'you should run a parser over the resulting normalized DTD to check for hanging separators and ambiguous context models'. In practise this means checking that there are no content models ending

```
<!ELEMENT LG - 0
((HEAD)*, (L | LG)+, )
>
```

where the extra comma is left 'hanging' after the plus sign, and needs removing. This takes only a few seconds with the repeat-replace function of any text editor (and for the whole TEI it occurred just twice).

The software has been reported to hang when presented with an invalid DTD, so it is wise to parse and validate your application and check that it is 'clean' before trying to normalize the DTD.

2.6.7. SP (James Clark)

Unix, DOS/Windows
`http://www.jclark.com/sp/`

James Clark's *SP* package contains several programs which can be used in DTD development, but as the core of the package is concerned with parsing, the tools are dealt with more fully in section 4.3.5. I'm confining this section to the validation and processing of DTDs, rather than instances, although the program used is the same (*nsgmls*, the principal component of the *SP* suite).

Many DTDs are still written or maintained by hand in a plaintext editor, for a variety of reasons, not the least of which is the lack of software for large-scale DTD project development and code management. Parsing and validating a DTD frequently and rigorously during development is vital, in order to catch any errors before they become compounded.

To validate a DTD, you can just use *nsgmls* with the option `-p` (only parse the Prolog, and suppress any output), and `-f` (to redirect error messages into a file for examination):`nsgmls -pf`*`mydtd.err my.dtd`*The `-s` option, used when parsing instances to suppress the output, is implied by the `-p` option.

The options specifying the use of ancillary files require the filename *directly* after the letter (no space after the option). *Nsgmls* assumes the default catalog file is called `catalog` in the current directory, or in the location specified by the `-c` option:

```
nsgmls -pfmydtd.err -cmycat.cat my.dtd
```

If you are using *Emacs* and *psgml*, you can press **Ctrl–C Ctrl–V**, which runs *nsgmls* on the current buffer (file) and traps the error messages to a window, but you'll have to edit the command line to put in the `-p` by hand, as the default is intended for validating whole documents. If there are errors, a keyclick on an error message will jump you to the file in question and place the cursor at the point of error. If you're using MS-Windows, you can install *RunSP*, which is a windowing shell for *nsgmls*: see section 4.3.5.1.

Because *Emacs* expects a DocType Declaration at the top of the file, if you get the following message when using *nsgmls* this way:

```
c:\sp\bin\nsgmls:my.dtd:20:2:E: "ENTITY" declaration not
allowed in prolog
```

it means you're probably trying to validate a DTD file. Instead, create a 1-line SGML file containing the DocType Declaration, referencing your DTD file with a System or Public Identifier (in effect, a document with a missing instance) and validate that instead.

XML parsing is slightly different. Quite apart from the additional constraints of XML syntax, a DTD may or may not be specified, and if it is, it may be retrievable from the Internet using a URL, rather than from a local file. The version of *nsgmls* distributed with the *Jade* converter/formatter (see section 5.2.4) has XML support, and this is on the CD-ROM. James Clark has also written *XP*, an XML parser in *Java* (see section 4.3.7.2)

The method of normalizing or 'flattening' a heavily parameterized DTD that I have referred to elsewhere for several DTDs can partly be done with the *spam* program using the following options:

```
spam -mms -ppxxfmyfile.err myfile.dtd >newfile.dtd
```

The `ms` value for the `-m` option removes all `IGNORE`d Marked Sections and unmarks all `INCLUDE`d Marked Sections; the `-p` option (twice) outputs the Prolog (SGML Declaration and DTD) and expands any entity references between declarations; and the `-x` option (also twice) expands all references to entities that contain tags. The error output (if any) is redirected into a file with `-f`, and the output (the flattened DTD) is written to the final filename (the > is a Unix and DOS technique to redirect output away from the terminal screen and into a file).

2.6.8. Carthage (Michael Sperberg-McQueen)

> **Unix**
> `ftp://ftp-tei.uic.edu/pub/tei/sgml/grammar/carthage/`

Michael Sperberg-McQueen wrote *Carthage* to overcome one of the problems encountered when compiling the full TEI DTD in systems which object to elements being referenced but not declared. The problem is explained in more detail in section 3.3.2.

This is a C program written for Unix, called `carthago` (for elements which are to be deleted; a subtle scholarly joke for those who know Latin: 'delenda est Carthago'). It reads a DTD and rewrites it, syntactically omitting from content models any elements which are not declared, where this is possible (on some occasions it cannot do all of them, for example if an element is marked as compulsory: further corrections have to be done manually). It can also delete `IGNORE` Marked Sections, detect entities declared more than once, and expand all parameter entities.

The software is offered 'as-is' (unsupported, and for regular SGML only at the moment) from the TEI FTP server at the University of Illinois at Chicago.

2.6.9. Fred (OCLC)

> **Unix**
> `shafer@oclc.org`

Before the days of easily obtainable (and especially, networked) information about SGML, misconceptions such as those explained in section 1.5.3 were even more widespread than they are today. Among the most pernicious was (is still, perhaps) the belief that SGML is just the act of making up some 'tag names' in pointy brackets and putting them in a file with your text. While XML goes a long way towards making it this simple, there are still some rules to be followed, but surprising numbers of projects have created files with arbitrary tag names believing that they are creating SGML, and there have also been projects and individuals who have used the tagset of a real DTD, but without access to information about how SGML works, and without access to any software, leading to much grief over misplaced tags when the file is eventually parsed, and sometimes to untested and unsupportable claims about 'using SGML'.

This phenomenon was noted early on by the OCLC (Online Computer Library Center), dealing with bibliographic and other material which was tagged in an 'SGML-like' manner, but without a DTD. *Fred* is a suite of programs which the OCLC wrote to help overcome the problem: it can deduce a grammar from a sample document, and compose a DTD which represents it. This means that a special one-off DTD can be generated for a file which uses SGML syntax (nested matching start- and end-tags, with attributes with values in quotes, using angle brackets to enclose them, a format almost identical to an XML file).

The DTD thus generated usually applies only to that one file, and not to anything else, although if there are other files done by the same author in the same way, they may well also 'fit'. Because it is machine-deduced, it may (probably will, for anything but trivial use) contain constructs which no human would dream of making, but it can be used as a starting-point for the generation of a grammar to be applied as a DTD elsewhere because the output can be edited, used, tested, and refined. In many cases, however, the 'sample document' is the only actual instance of the set of tags in existence (having been made up by an enthusiastic but untrained user), so there may be no need for the DTD to be generalized.

More importantly for those trying to coerce an SGML-like document into action, *Fred* also means that the file can eventually be parsed and validated as SGML, and passed through a regular SGML processing system for conversion or import into another document type.

Fred is available under license from OCLC for some Unix platforms and for Windows NT. The *Fred* engine is the basis for a number of processing interfaces which make up the whole system. The principal ones are *Austin* and *Beca*.

Austin This is the program which does the grammar generation. You open an SGML-like file (one with tagging but no DocType Declaration or DTD), and click on 'Generate Grammar'.

Assuming the file can be parsed with a reasonable degree of reliability, a structured grammar is generated, and can be displayed

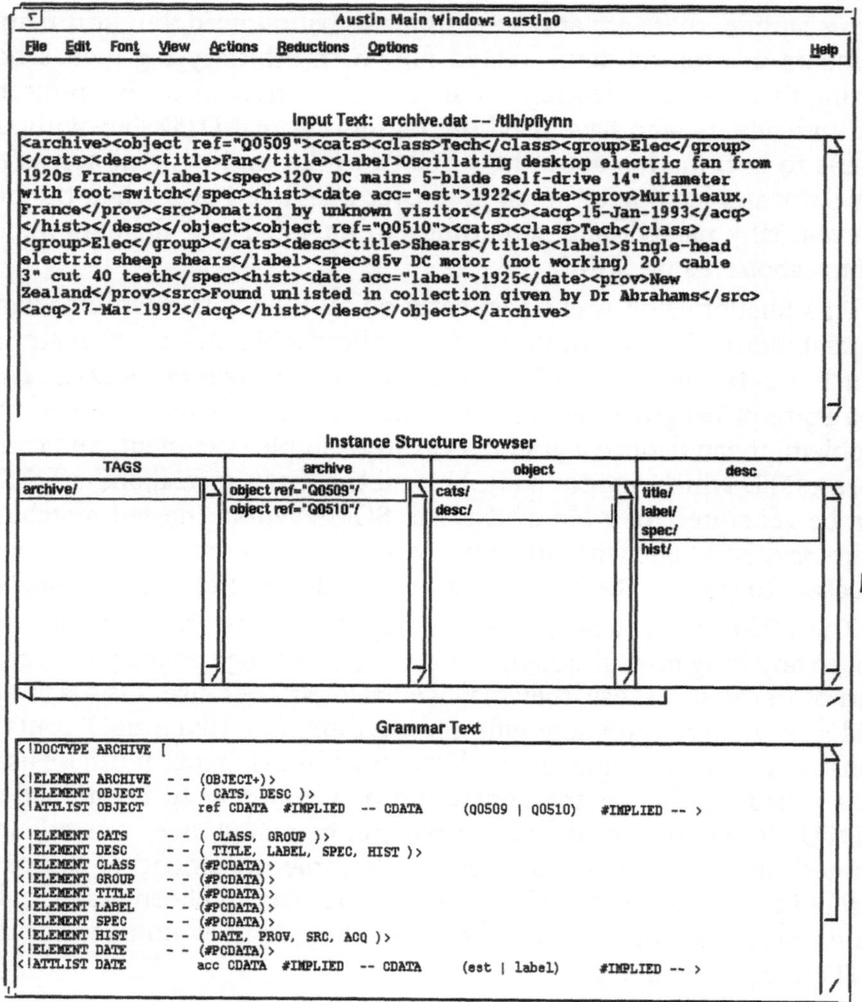

Figure 62. The *Austin* program generating a grammar from a tagged file

and saved in several formats: DTD, BNF (Backus-Naur Form), or 4–tuple form (a bounded symbol/state table).

Beca Once the grammar has been generated and saved, this program can read it, display it in graph form, and allow modifications. This way you can intervene manually to fit the grammar more closely to other models of the text.

The remaining programs in the *Fred* suite are concerned with the refinement of the grammar model, with special reference to its usability in a corpus of texts. This is a tool with very significant powers, espe-

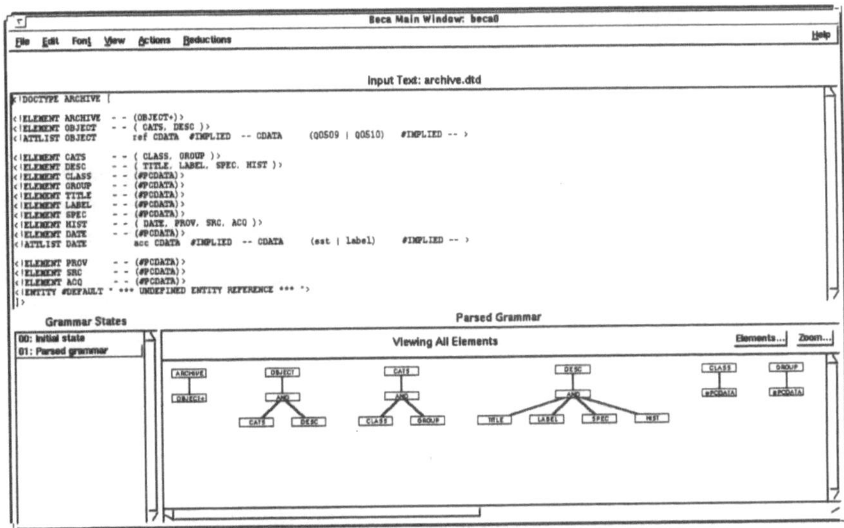

Figure 63. The *Beca* program modifying a generated grammar

cially in the light of other research into the automated generation of grammars (for example the paper by Ahonen *et al*[2]), and the move towards DTD-less usage in XML.

2.7. SGML update

`http://www.sil.org/sgml/topics.html#revision`

Since the publication of the SGML standard, there has been an ongoing process of development, both for the ISO 8879 standard itself, and for other standards associated with it.

This section lists some significant additions, amendments, and proposed amendments which may affect users directly. There are many other suggestions under review in the pipeline, some of which are simply 'enabling legislation' rather than structural modifications, but changing an international standard is not a simple task, and full consideration has to be given to the impact on users of each change.

There is a detailed section on the status of proposals and reviews in the SGML Web pages at the address given at the start of this section.

2.7.1. The SGML Standard

`http://www.sil.org/sgml/topics.html`

The text of ISO 8879:1986 is not in the public domain, so it is not available for download on the Internet, unlike the Internet's own standards. As with all International Standards, you have to buy it either as the formal document from your national standards body, or in the case of SGML by buying the book, *The SGML Handbook*[20] by Charles Goldfarb, editor of the standard.

2.7.1.1. The Standards review process

`http://www.ornl.gov/sgml/wg8/wg8home.htm`

International standards are subject to a formal 5–yearly review. Like the rest of the standards procedure this involves ballots at every stage — development and approval, periodic review, and amendment/correction. The ISO procedure, while it can be cumbersome and has been criticized for being slow, is designed to protect due process for as many interested parties as possible: formal international standards should not be changed on a whim. As with any international agreement, ISO standards are ultimately voted on by your country's representative (contact your national standards body to find out who this is).

Changes are posted in the form of a TC (Technical Corrigendum), which is the term used to describe a revision of one or more discrete aspects of a standard on technical grounds. TCs are proposed by the relevant Working Group of the ISO and voted on by national representatives before they can become an extension to the standard. When successful, the TC is incorporated into the body of the text of the standard.

The Working Group with responsibility for SGML is ISO/IEC JTC1/WG4: Document Description Languages. (This was formerly ISO/IEC JTC1/SC18/WG8: Document Description and Processing Languages but the WG has in effect been 'promoted' so it now reports directly to Joint Technical Committee 1 rather than to its Sub-Committee 18). The convener is James Mason (Lockheed Martin). Your national standards body can tell you the name of your national representative on WG4 if you want to contact them. For stability, the URL of the WG8 Web site continues in use for WG4 at the present time.

The publication of DSSSL (ISO 10179) triggered a Technical Corrigendum to the HyTime standard (ISO 10744) that resulted in the publication of a second edition of HyTime in the fall of 1997. Corrigenda to

DSSSL itself are likely to result from some of the investigations into alternative stylesheets for XML (see section 2.4.3). The SGML standard was amended once (long ago) but an accumulating list of proposed changes resulted in two important ones coming to the fore:

- the Extended Naming Rules TC (ENR) in 1996 (see section 2.7.1.2) enables changes to the rules governing the SGML Declaration to allow extended character sets such as ISO 10646 (Unicode) to be used;
- the 'WebSGML Adaptations' (rather more extensive than a simple TC) in 1997 (see section 2.7.1.3) is a group of several changes to the SGML Declaration needed to accommodate the demands of using SGML over the Web.

To make use of these you therefore have to make some changes to your SGML Declarations, so that processing software can identify the changes you want. The SGML Declaration must also reference the changes in the way it names itself on the first line, to tell processing software that you expect the new behavior or facilities. Finally, you do need to use software which can handle the new way of working. Older software will need to be replaced with versions that will cope with the Adaptations.

The ENR TC is now subsumed into the WebSGML Adaptations, so what was previously required in the SGML Declaration (WWW+ENR) should now be written more simply:

```
<!SGML "ISO 8879:1986 (WWW)"
...
>
```

The default without these changes is to perform exactly as specified in the unmodified standard.

2.7.1.2. Technical Corrigendum for Extended Naming Rules (December 1996)

http://www.sgmlsource.com/8879rev/n1896rev.htm

This extends the naming rules in SGML Declarations to handle large character sets, and to cope with character sets which do not distinguish case.

The problem was those parameter values in the SGML Declaration which are in the 'NAME' class were subject to the limitations of the Reference Concrete Syntax, which meant that values could not exceed eight characters in length; or in the case of numbers, eight digits. It was therefore impossible to specify long numeric values like the ones needed to implement some types of character encoding under ISO 10646 (Unicode). The Technical Corrigendum extends the length of these values to accommodate this.

As with many internal technical changes, this is invisible to the average SGML user: knowledge of it only becomes necessary if you need to write SGML Declarations for applications using an extended character set. For the general user, using a pre-written DTD, this task should have already been undertaken by the document type designer.

2.7.1.3. The WebSGML Adaptations (June 1997)

`http://www.sgmlsource.com/8879rev/n1929.htm`

This Technical Corrigendum, now formally known as a set of 'adaptations', significantly extends the facilities of the SGML Declaration to cope with the needs of use on the Web (some of them specifically for XML) and introduces some variation of the rules for DTDs. The principal internal change is that the Adaptations define two classes of validity for parsers to work to:

Type-validity This is 'validity' as defined in the unmodified standard, ISO 8879:1986, in the way it has always been applied in the past. You must have an SGML Declaration (explicitly supplied, or implicitly using the defaults and the Reference Concrete Syntax), a DTD, and an instance, and they must all conform to SGML.

Tag-validity This is what enables 'DTD-less' operation: the SGML Declaration is either the implicit Reference Concrete Syntax or an implicit declaration fixed and expected by an application specification (such as the one for XML); the document type may be implied by the first element; the 'DTD' is in effect self-defined by the very occurrence and location of the elements in the instance; and the instance must conform to some more restrictive rules than type-valid SGML (in the case of XML, this is the concept of 'well-formedness', to which 'XML-valid' documents must also conform: see section 2.4).

Documents that are type-valid are necessarily also tag-valid, but documents that are tag-valid do not have to be type-valid.

There are some general changes outside the declarations and document markup itself to support tag-validity:

- Internet Domain Names are added to the list of privileged Public Owner Prefixes for Formal Public Identifiers, which means it does *not* take a registration prefix (`-//` or `+//`). The privileged prefix `IDN::` is followed by an FQDN (Fully-Qualified Domain Name) as the Public Owner. This means that URLs could be expressed in FPI syntax, as the character set for FPIs has also been extended:

```
IDN::www.foo.com//DTD dtds/general/gendoc.dtd//EN//http
```

[ab]using the Display Version to identify that this is available using a specific protocol.

- The DocType Declaration may be of the form:

  ```
  <!DOCTYPE #IMPLIED SYSTEM>
  ```

  which allows the root element to default to the first element encountered. An optional System Identifier for a DTD may follow the `SYSTEM` keyword. This is implicit for XML, and is what enables DTD-less operation.
- Element markup and Marked Sections must be wholly contained in the entity (usually the file) in which they start: you cannot have the start-tag in one entity and the end-tag in another as you can with regular SGML.
- External entity sets referenced with a Formal Public Identifier using the `ENTITIES` Public Text Class can now contain `ATTLIST` declarations, not just `NOTATION`s.
- `SUBDOC`s are no longer subordinate documents but can have their own SGML Declarations and be parsed in a separate, self-contained parser subprocess.

The changes in what you can declare or use in DTDs are:

- Multiple `ATTLIST` declarations are permitted, with the first taking precedence, as with entity declarations. This makes it possible to provide a variant attribute list in a DocType Declaration subset.
- An `ATTLIST` declaration may take the 'wildcard' argument `#ALL` if it is to apply to all elements, or `#IMPLICIT` if it is to apply only to implicitly-defined elements in tag-valid mode.
- Empty attribute lists are permitted, for example if parameter entities defining them evaluate to the null string. If the parameter entities contained connectors (for example, vertical bars in the expectation of there being values to separate), the occurrence of adjacent connectors with no value between them is no longer an error.
- Duplicate name tokens are permitted in a single attribute list but only when there is no minimization allowed. This allows two attributes on the same element both to have the same permitted values like `YES` and `NO`, something which the standard SGML rules on attribute value minimization prohibited.

- In tag-valid mode, undeclared element model content defaults to `ANY`, and attributes are always `CDATA` and `#IMPLIED`. Entities and notations are always `SYSTEM`.
- An End Of Reading marker `!EOR` may be placed between declarations in a DTD to allow processing down that far but no further, for use in checking.

The changes to the SGML Declaration itself are:

- Empty elements may have end tags when the parameter `EMPTYETG` is set to `YES` (turned off by the value `NO`).

  The Null End-Tag (`NET`) is separated out into the NET-Enabling Start-Tag Close, `NETSC` (/), and the `NET` delimiter itself (>).

  The value `SHORTTAG NO` can be distinguished by a new `STARTTAG YES` and values for a new `ENDTAG` of `EMPTYTAG`, `NETANY` or `NETEMPTY`, `BOTH`, or `REQUIRED`.
- Both `CAPACITY` and `QUANTITY` can now have a setting of `NOLIMITS`.
- A new `ENTITIES` section predefines character entities for `&`, `<`, `>`, `"`, and `'`.

  Hexadecimal numeric character references are enabled by a new Hexadecimal Reference Character Open (`HRCO`) delimiter, to allow the specification of values as '`&#xhhhh;`', where the `h`s are the hex value. (The `x` is XML's fixed choice, but regular SGML applications can use another character such as `U` for Unicode.)
- White-space handling can be defined by the `WSCON` (White-space Construct) keyword as `SGML1986`, which works as before; or `KEEPALL`, by which all white-space is passed to the application, even white-space occurring between tags in element content.
- In the `APPINFO` section, a new keyword `SEEALSO` allows values of `NONE` or a Formal Public Identifier to identify further constraints specific to a particular domain of usage (*eg* XML).

There are some other changes which are supporting or enabling mechanisms for the above. Most of the effects of these changes are hidden from end-users: you just see HTML and XML work without needing to know what made it happen. But if you write DTDs, modify other people's DTDs, or create or reference FPIs, you should be aware of these changes.

The specific version of James Clark's *SP* parser suite which accompanies his *Jade* DSSSL engine already implements these changes.

2.7.2. Associated standards

HyTime and DSSSL
`http://www.sil.org/sgml/related.html`

Among the many applications of SGML, there are two major standards which have been very influential in affecting the way people design and build their own SGML systems: HyTime and DSSSL.

HyTime (ISO 10744) defines a method (actually several methods) of implementing hypermedia and time-based applications. It originally grew out of work done on SMDL (Standard Music Description Language, now ISO 10743), and is now being used in many systems, from the hypertext linking found in browsers like *Panorama* or *MultiDoc Pro*, to the huge and growing field of interactive online technical and other documents, and in XML.

The hypertext components can be applied to almost any SGML system where you need formal data management facilities for linking resources together. The time-based components are used in hypermedia and other systems where real-time synchronization or elapsement is required (music being one obvious field).

DSSSL (ISO 10179) is best known for having brought a stylesheet language to SGML, but it also introduced two other languages: a transformation language that can be used for file conversion between DTDs, and a search language for expressing the location of objects within the grove created by a parser.

Stylesheets or style files have been used in DTP and word processing applications for decades, but the problem with them is that there were very few standards to let them be commonly transferable between different applications. DSSSL's formatting language opens the way for applications to achieve portability at the presentation level.

These advances made clear the necessary convergence of several aspects of the technology which were shared between SGML, DSSSL, and HyTime, some of which were developed since the announcement of HyTime and during the writing of DSSSL (the HyTime TC brings many of these into line between itself and DSSSL). The most significant of these have been the General Architecture and Extended Facilities (due to HyTime) and the development of the concept of ***groves*** and ***property sets*** (formalized in DSSSL but represented in both standards).

Groves and property sets

The twin concepts of **groves** and **property sets** are key to an understanding of the operation of the languages specified by DSSSL, and to some of the addressing and hypertext concepts in HyTime, but they are defined at a level of abstraction intended for the computer scientist or programmer rather than the user of SGML tools, and a detailed discussion of them would be outside the scope of this book. There is extensive information about groves and their definition on the SGML Web site (`http://www.sil.org/sgml/topics.html#groves`) and in several books such as the one by DeRose and Durand already mentioned[17], and in *Practical Hypermedia*[25] by Eliot Kimber. A graphical example of a fragment of a grove appears in Figure 64

In essence, a grove is an abstract representation of the model of what a parser should be able to 'see' once it has parsed a complete SGML document. It's what used to be called the 'parse tree', until it was realized that the tree is fractal — even an attribute value can be a tree[21] — and a grove is really a group of such trees. A grove has been described as the 'in-memory result of parsing a document'[24].

The SGML property set is the complete repertoire of objects and their properties that may occur in SGML, categorized into a number of classes. For any given document, the property set therefore defines the set of possible classes and their properties that each component can be allocated as it is parsed.

For practical implementations an application can define a 'grove plan' which identifies the subset of all this possible information that the application needs for its immediate purpose (the parse tree and the property set). A grove is said to be populated by 'nodes', which are the objects the parser identified on its way through the document, and each node is given its class and properties from those available in the grove plan. The point about groves is that the value of a property is itself just a further list of nodes, each of which also has a class and properties of its own, and so on.

This abstraction makes it possible for programmers, document architects, and system designers to make references or comparisons to processes or models of the document or document type, knowing that everything can be defined and labeled independently of how any particular parser may happen to implement it. But more importantly, it provides a means by which SGML programs themselves can refer to the various objects they encounter in a document or a DTD so that they can communicate information about them independently of their internal way of operating.

Given this trivial SGML document:

```
<!doctype simp [
<!element simp o o (bit*)>
<!element bit - - (#PCDATA)>
<!attlist bit name id #required>
]>
<bit name=one>1</bit>
<bit name=two>2</bit>
```

This is a picture of part of the grove that a conformant SGML parser should produce:

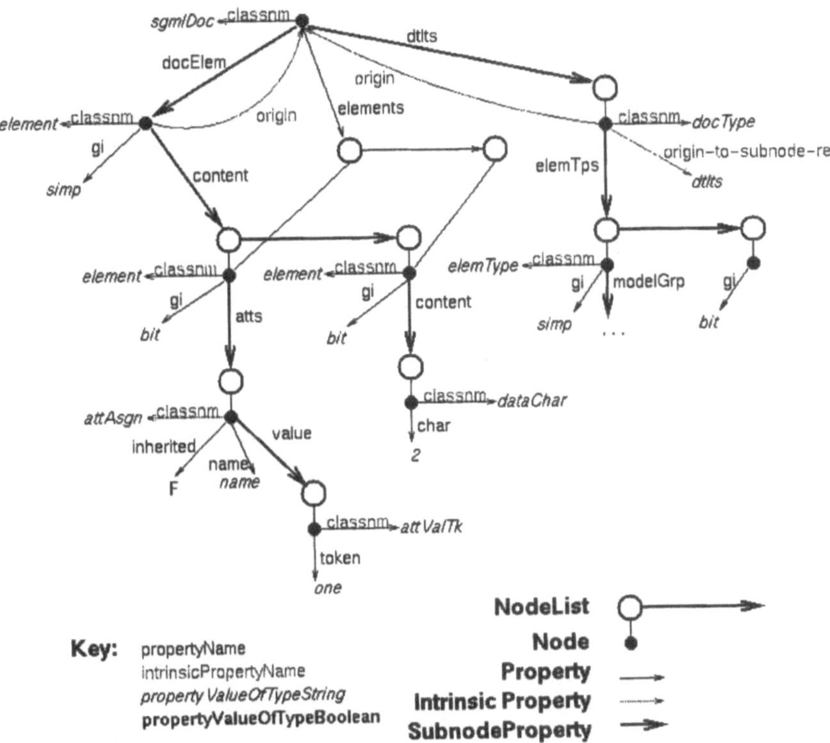

Figure 64. Graphical representation of a part of a grove (by kind permission of Henry Thompson, Edinburgh University)

2.7.2.1. HyTime (and its Technical Corrigendum)

http://www.hytime.org/papers/htguide.html

HyTime is ISO 10744, the Hypermedia/Time-based Structuring Language, an SGML application (strictly, a 'document architecture') which provides enabling facilities for handling non-text and time-sensitive data in SGML. As with SGML, the formal standard document itself is obtainable from the ISO or your national standards body, but there is a large quantity of documentation available on the Web, both at the HyTime pages references at the head of this section, and at the SGML pages. There is also the excellent book by Steve DeRose and David Durand, *Making Hypermedia Work: A User's Guide to HyTime*[17].

The revision of HyTime through its Technical Corrigendum exposed a number of new concepts, but most importantly it gave expression to the idea of Architectural Forms (AFs: see section 2.7.2.2), which let a DTD designer implement or reuse a set of definitions for features common to several (or many) DTDs, which will be recognized by a conforming processor. In the case of HyTime these are the hypertext linking/addressing and the scheduling definitions, and an example of their use is in the following section; but AFs are not limited to HyTime: any common architectural feature could be portably encoded in this way, such as form-fill features, tables, database keyword tagging, *etc*, right down to general everyday concepts such as paragraphs, lists, sections, or headings.

The wider concept of architectures found its expression in the Revised HyTime Standard (HyTime 2), which separated the General Architecture, which defines small set of architectural features usable in any SGML DTD, from HyTime's own architectures (linking, addressing, and scheduling), which are what is needed for hypertext and time-based work. It also codified some Extended Facilities, four sets of definition requirements which specify the enabling rules:

- AFDR (Architectural Forms Definition Requirements), which defines the rules by which AFs can be used;
- PSDR (Property Set Definition Requirements), for defining the general mechanism whereby property sets are defined;
- FSIDR (Formal System Identifier Definition Requirements), which defines the way in which FSIs can be declared;
- LTDR (Lexical Type Definition Requirements), which specifies the requirements for the character strings used for defining attribute values, text data content, and search strings.

The enabling of Formal System Identifiers lets you use (among other things) URL syntax in an external entity declaration or a DocType declaration, for example:

```
<!DOCTYPE html SYSTEM "http://host.foo.org/~blort/dtds/html6.dtd">
```

although the enabling of the Internet Domain Name prefix for Formal *Public* Identifiers makes it possible to do the same in FPI syntax, as explained in section 2.7.1.3.

2.7.2.2. Architectural Forms used to enable HyTime Linking

HyTime makes it possible to superimpose its linking facilities on an existing DTD without making structural alterations. It does this by defining generic meta-elements with predefined names and values which are recognized by HyTime processors. They can be referenced in your DTD as part of the declarations for your own elements and attributes, which lets the processor identify which attributes and which elements you want to be treated as hyperlinks. This way you don't have to change any of your own declared names, but only add the relevant attributes. With attribute list redefinition now enabled in the WebSGML Adaptations, this will be even easier to do in a DocType Subset.

As an example, we'll use the HyTime Context Link (`clink`) to enable hyperlinking in bibliographic footnotes. This is a form used in many fields, from financial reports to disciplines in the Humanities. A citation points at a short bibliographic reference in a footnote, with the extended details in a bibliography elsewhere. Suppose we have in our DTD the following declarations:

```
<!element fn - - (note|para|table|list)+>
<!attlist fn id  ID     #IMPLIED
             n   NUMBER #IMPLIED
             sym CDATA  #IMPLIED>
```

so we could make a footnote like this:

```
<fn n="1"><note>HyTime standard, p.55</note></fn>
```

A processor would typically produce the superscripted number[2], and move the footnote content to the bottom of the page, or into a pop-up window on the screen.

But in the online version, let us suppose we also want the footnote to be a link to the full reference. To invoke HyTime, we need to add the application information to our SGML Declaration:

```
FORMAL YES
APPINFO "HyTime"
```

and supply the HyTime declarations themselves as Processing Instructions between the end of the SGML Declaration and the start of the DTD:

```
<?HyTime version "ISO/IEC 10744:1992" hyqcnt=32>
<?HyTime module base>
<?HyTime module locs>
<?HyTime module links>
```

HyTime lets us add two attributes to our footnote element attribute list, `HyTime` and `linkend`, so it now reads:

[2]HyTime standard, p.55

```
<!attlist fn id       ID     #IMPLIED
             n        NUMBER #IMPLIED
             sym      CDATA  #IMPLIED
             HyTime   NAME   #FIXED  "clink"
             linkend  IDREF  #REQUIRED>
```

This identifies our `<FN>` element to a HyTime processor as conforming to the Architectural Form it knows as a 'Context Link'. If we now encode our footnote as `<fn n="1" linkend="iso10744"><note>HyTime standard, p.55</note></fn>` and make sure our bibliography has an entry with the ID value `iso10744`, a HyTime processor can detect and enable the hypertext link between the footnote and the bibliographic entry and include that cross-reference as part of the footnote automatically.

More complex HyTime links can be multi-headed (pointing at more than one target object) and bidirectional, can point outside the current document, and can provide information in other attributes about the nature of the link, for the processor to act upon. HyTime also provides another format of link, the Independent Link, which does not reside within or around the author's text at the point of reference, but can exist elsewhere in the document, or even in a separate document, so you can maintain collections of links between many locations without this information being held inside any of the referenced documents (see section 6.2.2 for how this is implemented in some browsers).

2.7.2.3. DSSSL

`http://www.sil.org/sgml/related.html#dsssl`

The introduction of DSSSL (ISO 10179:1996, Document Style Semantics and Specification Language) gave the SGML community a public, standardized method of specifying how to treat the markup in an SGML file when you want to output it, or transform it in some way. Until then, viewers, print programs, converters, and other tools had to rely on inventing their own specifications (such as the CALS FOSI, or the *DynaText*, HTML CSS, or Synex *ViewPort* stylesheets), or on borrowing those inherent in a processor (such as the LaTeX styles for *LinuxDoc* [now *SGML-Tools*]). Most tools still use their existing stylesheet syntax, but James Clark's *Jade* processor has demonstrated how powerful the use of DSSSL can be (see section 5.2.4).

DSSSL specifies three internal languages: a Formatting Language, for writing stylesheets; a Transformation Language, for writing conversions from one DTD to another; and a search language, SDQL (Standard Document Query Language), which can be used by applications to navigate a document structure. The formatting language and the

Here is a small but complete document and DTD:

```
<!DOCTYPE HTMLLite [
<!ELEMENT HTMLLite O O (H1|P)* >
<!ELEMENT (H1|P) - - (#PCDATA|EM|STRONG)* >
<!ELEMENT (EM|STRONG) - - (#PCDATA)>
]>
<HTMLLite>
<H1>This is a heading</H1>
<P>This is text</P>
<P>This is <em>bold</em></P>
<P>This is <strong>strong</strong></P>
</HTMLLite>
```

And here is a small but complete stylesheet to go with it:

```
<!DOCTYPE style-sheet system "style-sheet.dtd" >
<!-- you must have James Clark's style-sheet.dtd for this parse to cor-
rectly. -->

 (element HTMLLite (make simple-page-sequence))
 (element H1
  (make paragraph
        font-family-name: "Times New Roman"
        font-weight: 'bold
        font-size: 20pt
        line-spacing: 22pt
        space-before: 15pt
        space-after: 10pt
        start-indent: 6pt
        first-line-start-indent: -6pt
        quadding: 'center
        keep-with-next?: #t))

(element P (make paragraph
        font-family-name: "Times New Roman"
        font-size: 12pt
        line-spacing: 13.2pt
        space-before: 6pt
        start-indent: 6pt
quadding: 'start))

(element EM (make sequence
    font-posture: 'italic))

(element STRONG (make sequence
    font-weight: 'bold))
```

Figure 65. Simple example of DSSSL applied to HTML (from Paul Prescod's tutorial, with permission.)

transformation language share a large amount in common, as they are both based on an underlying Expression Language. The Formatting Language is covered in more detail in the section on *Jade* referred to above.

The languages are expressed in a syntax resembling that of the SCHEME language, which in turn derives from LISP. These will be familiar to most computer scientists but not to most users, which may account for the slow uptake by implementors. An alternative syntax, proposed in the XML stylesheet language XSL, is being developed as DSSSL2, and this has the advantage of being expressed in the XML dialect syntax of SGML. As an example of the native DSSSL expressions, see Figure 65.

A subset of DSSSL called DSSSL Online ('dsssl-o') specifies base-level features required for two purposes: formatting for online delivery for formal publication; and more informal print-oriented delivery from browsers and viewers. This subset probably marks the entry-point for SGML systems seeking commonality of stylesheet specification.

A good example of a DSSSL stylesheet is the one produced for *DocBook* by Jon Bosak with assistance from James Clark, Anders Berglund, Tony Graham, and Terry Allen. This is on the CD-ROM in the `dsssl` folder or you can download it from `http://sunsite.unc.edu/pub/sun-info/standards/dsssl/stylesheets/docbook/docbook3.dsl`.

There is a mailing list for discussing DSSSL (details in Appendix B): see `http://www.mulberrytech.com/dsssl/dssslist/index.html`.

3. Editors

Editors are ghouls and cannibals.

Dorothy L Sayers, *Busman's Honeymoon*

- Editors and DTDs
- WYSIWYG and the use of stylesheets
- General-purpose SGML editors
- SGML extensions to non-SGML editors

If you have to enter information into a computer, you will at some stage almost certainly have to use an ***editor***. It may be hidden from you (for example, when entering data into a database field or Web form), or it may be your most important piece of software. The religious wars surrounding editing and word processing software are the stuff of legend, and any devotees of a particular system can regale you with tales of the amazing abilities of their pet program and the appalling indignities you have to suffer when using competing products: rather like the PC *vs* Mac disputes, or whether you should open a boiled egg at the big end or the little end.

In the Unix field, where some of the wars started, the argument is between *Emacs* and *vi*, the two most common editors in that environment. Among DOS and MS-Windows users, it tends to be among *Word*, *WordPerfect*, and your own personal favorite; on the Mac between *Word* and *Claris Works*; under VMS between *EDT* and *TPU*; and so on with occasional mentions of other products relegated to the fringe. In most cases the argument is that product X can do something with the text that product Y cannot, or that product X's behavior is worse than product Y's in some specific circumstance, or even in general. Rarely does the business of storing and preserving the text itself get mentioned, and most word processors, including the biggest names in the market, have an appalling record of bungled upgrades, version incompatibilities, and non-existent 'facilities' — and that's before you even start to consider moving text *between* systems.

Using SGML, however, you can take some comfort from the fact that your choice of a platform-independent system means that files can be moved from one machine to another, across manufacturers, operating systems, versions, and even between applications — and back again! — with zero loss of information. But for a long time the choice of SGML editors was small, exceptionally expensive, and (with one or two notable exceptions) the interface was sparse, even Spartan.

The choice has now widened significantly and because a common core of facilities has evolved over the years the choice can usually be made on pragmatic grounds: operating system, price, support, usability, *etc*, rather than on whether an editor performs a particular task or not. There are admittedly a few SGML editors around with somewhat unusual characteristics or idiosyncratic behavior, but even here there are usually sound reasons behind them. There is a checklist in section 3.3 which covers most of the things you may want to look for in an editor, both in terms of SGML and with respect to general text-editing facilities.

If you are new to editing in SGML, there are two aspects to it which need to be isolated carefully before you start as they are the cause of a very large number of questions among newcomers: how does the DTD fit into all this? and what do SGML and an editor do about appearance and output styles? The first two sections below deal with these areas.

3.1. Editors and DTDs

All SGML editing is governed by the DTD you use. While this is obvious to anyone who has done it before, it is entirely non-obvious to those coming to SGML for the first time: if you have an SGML editor, it handles most of the technicalities for you; if you have a non-SGML editor, you have to do it mostly by hand.

The previous chapter has explained what the DTD is and how it works, and has given examples of the varied document types available to use, and even mentioned writing your own. This section deals with how you get an editor to use the DTD, something which most manuals tend not to cover in much detail (why they gloss over this critical step has never been fully explained). The exception to this requirement is XML editors being used on DTD-less documents, and this is covered separately in section 2.4.

One feature of most SGML editors is that they use a ***compiled*** DTD. 'Compiling' is the term used in computing to describe turning a designer's (or programmer's) human-readable instructions into a form readable by a computer, so that it's ready for use. Just as a regular computer program has to be compiled before you can run it, so a DTD usually has to be compiled before a program can make use of it. Compiled DTDs, like compiled programs, also load faster because they are already in the internal code expected by the computer. The first time you use a DTD that you haven't used before (or if an existing DTD is being updated) you usually have to spend a few minutes compiling it for use with your software (some more detailed reasons are explained in the box).

Most editors come with a selection of precompiled DTDs, which can be very useful, but these include tests, cut-downs, early versions, or demonstration samples as well as production DTDs. In any case, you may want to use a private DTD or make changes to a standard DTD before you use it to suit it to your environment (see section 2.6), or you may want to download a more recent version of a public DTD and compile that instead.

Sometimes the routine for compiling is built into the editor; sometimes it is a separate program. Where compiling is required, I have explained separately how to do it for each program, but the next section contains some general guidelines that apply to all the tools.

A few editors don't require separate DTD compilation prior to use: they do it 'on-the-fly' as each SGML file is loaded for editing. Where this is the case it is noted and explained.

3.1.1. Resources needed for compilation

Before you start compiling a DTD, you should be familiar with the rules explained at the end of chapter 1.5.1.5 concerning:

- the SGML Declaration;
- the DocType Declaration (with Public or System Identifiers);
- the catalog file or other method of ***entity resolution*** used by your editor (that is, the process by which components a DTD or document instance refers to get identified as actual files on your computer).

Each SGML program which uses a compiled DTD can only use those which have been compiled by its own compiler, so you cannot 'share' a compiled DTD between different applications from different vendors. The format of compiled DTD files is usually proprietary, and not normally accessible to the user (the *Emacs psgml* `.ced` format is an exception, being in the public domain).

Why use 'compiled' DTDs

There are two reasons for the use of stored compiled DTDs: convenience and control. Many DTDs describe large and complex document types, and until recently, desktop computer processing speeds simply weren't up to rereading and reparsing the full DTD every time you loaded a file using it. On a 66MHz 80486 PC (now obsolete, but a staple of businesses for many years), compiling the *DocBook* or TEI DTD took many minutes, whereas a precompiled version loaded in a couple of seconds. This requirement became less prevalent as faster processors became available: a 300MHz Pentium does the same compilation from scratch in under four seconds.

However, keeping compilation separate from distribution also enables large organizations or distributed projects to have one person or group in charge of DTD development, and to distribute working copies of the DTD to all the other people in a precompiled form which cannot be modified (accidentally or deliberately). If you are trying to keep large numbers of users in step with a single master DTD, 'binary' (compiled) distribution is a very convenient way — possibly the only way — of preventing unauthorized or accidental changes or additions which might invalidate a user's text.

The documentation for each program specifies, more or less intelligibly, where its compiler looks to find DTD files, entity files, the SGML declaration, and any other resources needed. In some cases this information is less than obvious from the documentation, so I have tried to explain it more clearly in each section.

There is an unfortunate tendency among some vendors to skate over the business of compiling in the documentation as if it were a sideline activity not worth troubling too much over. Unfortunately, it's critical to the use of the editors. It is true that it can be a very simple task if you're using a small, single-file DTD with the default SGML Declaration using the Reference Concrete Syntax and no external character entity sets, but one hallmark of a good editor is the ease (or otherwise) with which it can handle even large and complex DTDs. I have come across systems claiming 'full' SGML conformance which simply won't handle big or multi-file DTDs with configurable options like TEI or *DocBook* as they stand, and need substantial massaging before they will compile. It was perhaps acceptable in the days when DTD compilation was undertaken by a high priestess and the result distributed to the users: it is less so now that many users want to be able to devise and compile their own DTDs, particularly for use with XML.

You may find it useful to have a file manager window and a plaintext editor window open during compilation, especially for the first time, as there may be unexpected edits to be made to some files. This is particularly true if:

- you have put the various files belonging to the DTD in folders that the compiler is not going to look in (this may be forced on you if you are on a multi-user system);
- your files have different names to the ones expected by the compiler or the catalog (often true when using material native to the Unix, Mac, or Windows 95 world on a machine with short filenames);
- the DTD file(s) refer to Formal Public Identifiers (see section 2.5) which are not yet in your catalog file (or you don't yet have a catalog file: see section 2.5.4);
- this is the first time you have compiled this DTD with this SGML Declaration.

3.1.1.1. The SGML Declaration

Occasionally problems arise in compilation because of different ways systems have implemented the use of the specifications, capacities, and quantities expressed in the SGML Declaration. As a result, some compilers may complain that values are out of range, too high, or too low. These ought to have been preset correctly by the authors of the DTD, but sometimes DTDs get shipped without their proper SGML Declaration, or the file gets mislaid or deleted.

However, many DTDs use the defaults (SGML's 'Reference Concrete Syntax': see section 1.5.1.7), so if you haven't got an SGML Declaration specifically for your DTD, it may mean it doesn't need any special facilities, and the default values and limits will work. There is more on how to handle errors detected in the SGML Declaration in section 4.2.1.

If you want more information on the content, construction, and editing of an SGML Declaration, Omnimark have produced a very useful document called *Understanding the SGML Declaration*[8], which is on the CD-ROM in the `sgml/doc/dec` folder, and is also available at `http://www.omnimark.com/resources/white/dec/` on the Web.

3.1.1.2. Catalog files

It is quite common to encounter errors in locating files on the first few compiles of a new DTD, especially when dealing with the ISO character entity files, or a DTD with many components. This can normally be fixed by the use of 'catalog files'.

Although every SGML system tends to come with its own set of character entity files, just for safety, different applications often expect different physical filenames for them in their catalogs, and even more so on systems with case-sensitive filenaming mechanisms. For example, the filenames

```
isolat1
isolat1.ent
isolat1.sgm
isolat1.gml
ISOlat1
ISOlat1.ent
ISOlat1.sgm
ISOlat1.gml
ISOLat1
ISOLat1.ent
ISOLat1.sgm
ISOLat1.gml
ISOLAT1
ISOLAT1.ENT
ISOLAT1.SGM
ISOLAT1.GML
```

all refer to the same object: the official ISO 8859–1 declarations for the Latin–1 character entities, known as '`ISO 8879-1986//ENTITIES Added Latin 1//EN`' (to use its Formal Public Identifier or FPI: see section 2.5). This should not be a problem if your DTD refers to the entities using this standard format, because catalog files (see section 2.5.4) exist precisely for the very purpose of resolving the FPI to a local filename. You fix the local filename once in your catalog and it will work for all time or until you move your files around.

If the filenames are hardcoded as System Identifiers (local filenames) you don't need a catalog to resolve them, but your files are then less portable, as other people will almost certainly not keep the same files under the same names in the same directories as you do. The recent adaptations to SGML (see section 2.7.1.3) make it possible to use URLs as System Identifiers (and compulsory to do so in XML), so files can be fetched over the Web more easily.

If you are using several different SGML applications on the same computer it's worth spending a little time rationalizing all the multiple copies of ISO character entity sets that came with each application into a single copy of each file in a central folder, and a shared catalog file.

This is particularly important if you are managing a multi-user system with other people running SGML software, such as a central shared file server or a Unix system providing login, because it minimizes the problem of multiple, disparate versions. The same principle holds for keeping a single centralized copy of frequently-used DTDs, so that there's only one copy to update when a new version is issued.

This does *not* apply to cross-platform use, unfortunately, because these files are designed to be platform-specific: they hold the specific character data (SDATA) required to represent each character *on that system*, nowhere else.

If a file referenced by a DTD isn't on your system, you will have to get hold of a copy before you can go any further: compilers will not work if some of the files needed are missing. If it's a public DTD and you are connected to a network, you may want to hold a browser or file transfer window open while you do the compilation for the first time, so you can find and get any missing files.

If a requested file is there on your disk, but the compiler is complaining it still cannot find it, check, re-check, double-check, triple-check, and quadruple-check the spellings of references in the catalog, the DTD, and anywhere else they occur: I was once held up for a whole day by an obscure two-character typing error in an entity reference for one of the components of the TEI DTD, which only became obvious when I finally asked publicly about it, and had it pointed out to me within minutes by a dozen people, including one of the editors of the TEI!

In these circumstances it is valuable to have a system which will point the cursor at the exact location where a reference went astray. For example, *Emacs psgml* (see section 3.4.1) running *nsgmls* as a subtask will let you place the cursor on an error message and press **Enter**, and it will take you to the exact character position on the line of the file that caused the error.

3.1.2. What to do with compiled DTD files

If the DTD is compiled with an external program that you run separately (*ie* not built into the application program itself), the compiled copy will need to be saved to disk in a folder where it can be found by the application itself. In most cases the compiler will prompt you to do this, suggesting the folder where it normally looks for compiled copies, or perhaps the folder where the master DTD file was stored. It's important that the compiled copy gets saved to the right folder.

In the case of experimental DTDs, or perhaps a test compilation of a DTD to see if it will suit a particular task, you may want to save the compiled version in a different directory to normal. This applies especially if the saved file has the same name as an existing compiled DTD, which is a frequent occurrence if you are evaluating different DTDs for common document types like 'report', 'book', or 'article': you don't want to overwrite a production copy with an experimental one.

Applications which do *not* use an external program for compilation can usually use the compiled DTD immediately in an adjacent edit window, sometimes without the need to save it. It clearly makes sense to save it if a lot of work is going to be done using the DTD, because the compiled version will load faster, but it also means that editing can be done on files which use small DTDs without the need for running a separate program, and this can be very useful in testing DTDs under development.

Not every system uses stored compiled DTDs: *InContext* and *STiLO* are examples of editors which reread the DTD afresh each time an SGML file is loaded. With a modern processor the time delay is usually insignificant except on very large DTDs.

3.2. Stylesheets and WYSIWYG

Before we examine some editing software, we should be clear what to expect in terms of WYSIWYG (What You See Is What You Get). This once useful but now over-used phrase was coined by the marketers of desktop publishing systems in an attempt to explain why real-time on-screen typographic formatting, which rearranges the lines, paragraphs, and pages each time you press a key, is 'better' than preview-mode formatting, which formats a whole document or section separately after you have typed it, or when you want to print it. In fact, both methods can be WYSIWYG: the difference is actually in the interactive reformatting rather than in the quality of the display or printed copy.

Both approaches have their merits, but it is worth remembering that there is no such animal as 'true' WYSIWYG unless you have at a minimum a 300dpi A4 or Letter size paper-white screen and a processor fast enough to run a dynamic type manager as well as handle your editing and the formatting engine. Few machines achieve anywhere near this: most of us mortals have to make do with WYSIAYFWG, or What You See Is All You're Damn Well Getting (substitute the expletive of your choice).

In SGML terms, the guiding principle of most document design is to keep the presentation formats and data formats separate as far as possible, because it is this which gives SGML its ability to act as guardian of your data across technological change. But on-screen typographics are not just expected by users: for most of us they play an important part in making the task of editing easier, so it is natural for this separation of data and its visual instantiation to become blurred.

Almost all SGML editing systems have some form of graphical display in a windowing system, with the obvious exception of those specifically designed to run in a character-cell window or terminal screen (*eg* DOS and Unix command line programs). Over the course of several years, the basic toolset of graphical representation for editing (for SGML and other systems) has settled down to a common core shared by almost all the programs which use the conventional windowing paradigm:

Typographic style A typographic style can be attached to any element, either by name alone or according to a specific hierarchic ancestry or sequential occurrence, or according to a set of attribute values, or any combination of these. Formatting attached to an element's existence or place in the parse tree or hierarchy in this way is known as 'context-sensitive' formatting.
For example, `<title>` as the first element within `<div1>` can be given a distinct typographical style from `<title>` as the first element within `<table>`, which would be quite different from the third consecutive occurrence of a `<title>` element in a land registry application.

Inheritance By default, elements and character entities usually derive their style from their containing element (this behavior may be switched on or off in some systems). This is known as 'inheritance'. For example, if `<table>` was set to display in Univers 8/10pt, it would normally be expected that the `<row>`s and `<cell>`s within it would use the same style unless specified otherwise.

'Paragraph' or 'block' style Paragraph-level markup ('block' or 'structural' markup) is typically identified with having or causing a line-break or vertical white-space before and after, although categorizing markup purely on the basis of appearance is not a reliable practise. Conventional styling parameters include:

- vertical white-space before and after (above and below) the element;
- page-break control before and after;
- left and right margin settings;
- indent or undent on first lines;

- hanging indentation (for whole phrases as well as for numbers or bullets);
- flush-left, flush-right, centered, or justified setting;
- plus all character-level styles as given below;
- in-memory processing (such as holdover for floating matter like figures).

'Character' or 'inline' styles Character-level markup ('inline' or 'descriptive' markup) is typically identified with occurring in mixed content, for example *within* a paragraph. Conventional styling parameters include:

- typeface (font), leading, weight, slant, shape, design size, scale, and spacing;
- color (foreground and background), variant shadings or distortions;
- position (subscript or superscript), overlap, transparency, rotation, and float;
- prefix and suffix text or symbols ('generated text'), especially autonumbering or sequencing, with separate character styles for the prefix or suffix;
- the replication, calculation, or deduction of attribute values from markup *elsewhere in the document* (using ID/IDREF linking, for example);
- Character entities can be given their own typographic style in a similar way.

With the exception of separate styles for character entities, the above set of features is now so common in graphical editors and display systems that I will assume them unless otherwise specified. The two-level model (paragraph- or block-level and character- or inline-level) is also used by almost all word processors and DTP systems. The major differences between editors' styling approaches are:

- the ease and speed of use of the menus or keystrokes;
- the dimensional accuracy of the results;
- the accessibility and reusability of the format in which style information is stored;
- the level of flexibility and reconfigurability;
- the availability of macros to perform more complex or repetitive formatting.

(As an example of what I mean by flexibility, it is surprisingly difficult in many systems to obtain a character-level format for an inline list: the kind that goes (a) first item; (b) second item; and (c) third item; without breaking the paragraph. Doing vertical lists, with the items one underneath the other, is usually trivial; doing them inline is often a little trickier, even assuming the DTD allows lists to occur within paragraphs.)

Some editors let you change styles at will while you are editing. Others use an externally-defined stylesheet which is assumed to have been set up previously and separately, usually along with compiling the DTD. In this case changes cannot be made by the user in the editor (apart from final adjustments or 'tweaking' for the purposes of printing).

The drawback of the first method is that any user can change the appearance of anything whenever they want, which may be extremely undesirable from the viewpoint of maintaining a fixed corporate or institutional standard. The second method prevents this by keeping the styling specifications under separate control.

The advantage of the first method is that where the typographic display is purely for ease of editing and not for prescribed presentation such as final printing, there would seem to be no good reason why the users should not be at liberty to arrange a style which suits themselves. You need to decide if these ergonomic advantages outweigh the problems of allowing user control over formatting.

The use of SGML for military applications led to the development of stylesheet systems which adhered to the standard known as the FOSI (Formatting Output Specification Instance) described in section 2.3.5. But not all editors use FOSIs, however: many developed their own stylesheets, often based on those used in *DynaText* (see section 6.2.1). The arrival of DSSSL as an international standard means that there is now a standard for representing stylesheet information which can be used between conforming systems. DSSSL is not yet widely implemented in editor stylesheets, but its use in the *Jade* conversion formatter (section 5.2.4) has already demonstrated its power. The HTML stylesheet language, CSS, and the XML stylesheet language, XSL, have added to the choice, and XSL in fact incorporates the ability to represent styles in DSSSL and CSS. Until a single standard becomes available evenly across most SGML systems, we are left in the unenviable position that stylesheet data cannot easily be exchanged or shared between editors, although there are a few stylesheet converters now becoming available.

3.3. General-purpose editors

These systems range from the fairly basic to the very sophisticated, but they are all straightforward and reliable, and will handle any DTD; some are also available on more than one platform. In some cases they really are just editors, and do not make any claim to perform more than rudimentary formatting, suitable for proofing; others are very close to being full-scale publishing systems.

Three of them (ArborText's *ADEPT•Editor*, SoftQuad's *Author/Editor* and GNU *Emacs* with *psgml*) have acquired something approaching cult status with their users: *ADEPT•Editor* because it's been around for a long time and has a reputation for power and stability; *Author/Editor* because of its relatively low price and the popularity of its little sister, *HoTMetaL* (one of the very few conformant HTML editors); and *Emacs* because of its strong Unix and PC following, the fact that it's free, and its ability to do much more than just edit.

However, almost all SGML editors have a similar set of core features and modes of behavior which are important for structured editing. Apart from being able to use a DTD, which is an essential characteristic of all SGML systems, the following should be regarded as the minimum needed for SGML editing (even if you don't use all of them immediately):

- Context-sensitive recognition of markup
- Hiding and revealing markup
- Markup-sensitive searching and replacement
- Attribute value entry and editing
- Context-sensitive selection (marking), cut/copy, and paste
- On-demand validation without leaving the editor
- Import and export of SGML files prepared (or for use) elsewhere

The following are apparent only when you are using a graphical system (as opposed to a character-cell system like a terminal window):

- Graphical start-and end-tag symbols to distinguish them visually from text data (character-cell editors may use color instead)
- Context-sensitive typographical styles for any element as an aid to editing (or as the output style for printing)
- Structured view of the document as opposed to a typeset view (may be in a separate window)
- Graphical view of tables
- Inclusion of illustrations (graphics) in the edit window

Some facilities are needed in almost all editing systems, SGML or otherwise. It's sometimes hard to remember what life was like without all this:

- Multiple files open simultaneously
- Cut-and-paste between the editor windows and other applications
- Multi-level 'undo', macro, and keystroke-recording facilities
- Spelling dictionaries and thesauruses in multiple languages
- Full documentation available online within the editor
- Automatic backup or safety copies of files you edit

Finally, some specific features which you may want to consider:

- Unix-style Regular Expressions in the 'find' and 'replace' function;
- Does it have a separate DTD compiler or is it built-in?
- Are there less-used features of SGML which you need, which may not be supported in all editors (*eg* `SUBDOC`, `CONCUR`)?
- Does it work with XML as well as regular SGML?
- Can stylesheets be created and edited from within the editor, or is it done by a separate program?
- Is there online (Internet) support, either in a Usenet newsgroup, on a mailing list, or by email to the authors or vendors?

Obviously, not everyone is going to want or need all of these, and there may be specialist services you want like interactive links to databases or the Web, which need platform-specific tailoring (some editors have a scripting language to implement this kind of function).

3.3.1. ADEPT•Editor (ArborText)

MS-Windows and Unix/X Windows
`http://www.arbortext.com/editor.html`

ADEPT•Editor is a comprehensive and widely-used editor and screen formatter in the *ADEPT* series of SGML software from ArborText, a company with a long history in text-handling software, based in Ann Arbor, MI. The editor is also used as an embedded display and editing platform inside some database systems. It presents a rich editing interface with extensive toolbar and customization support, so it can be used for individual or bespoke applications as well as in highly structured environments where you may have many users working on the same application.

Design control is managed separately from editing: the companion product *Document•Architect* compiles DTDs and manages the creation and maintenance of stylesheets, so that appearance can be controlled separately from the editing process. The *ADEPT* series uses FOSIs, the stylesheet specification created as part of the CALS initiative (see section 2.3.5). Operators can 'touch up' the styles by affecting linebreaks, spacing, and inline font sizes or colors, in order to smoothen out any small irregularities caused by mechanical formatting, but the design format of the document is managed separately and cannot be changed by operators using the editing module alone.

ADEPT software uses a compound document technology developed for database applications, combined with the *Java* language and its own scripting language, to allow customization of the interface and of the editor behavior. It can handle both regular SGML and XML (see section 2.4) as well as allow specification of *Java* functionality from the editor interface.

ADEPT•Editor comes with a variety of precompiled DTDs and FOSIs to match:

DocBook, for technical (computer) documentation
HTML
MIL-M-38784C, for CALS technical manuals
ISO 12083 Book, modified
ISO 12083 Article, modified
Memo, Letter, Report, and Slide, sample business DTDs

Installation is from CD-ROM, and includes a license key manager for fixed or floating licenses, so it can be installed on standalone or networked machines.

3.3.1.1. Operation

In addition to the conventional buttons for filing, printing and editing, there are controls for element split and join; structure hiding (collapsing and expanding element content); entity, table, and graphic insertion; element insertion, deletion and changing; and access to a DTD structure viewer and a hypertext-generated table of contents. These last two make editing considerably faster for complex material, as they provide navigation between different parts of the document with a keystroke or mouse-click.

The edit screen displays the DTD structure synchronized with the text (see Figure 66) and the element markup can be hidden or revealed. It is possible to set the editor to permit mouse marking to span across element boundaries (to start in the middle of one element and end in the middle of another, for example): in most editors marking is constrained by the start- and end-tags. It is also possible to display the text with graphical tag icons pointing inwards to the element content.

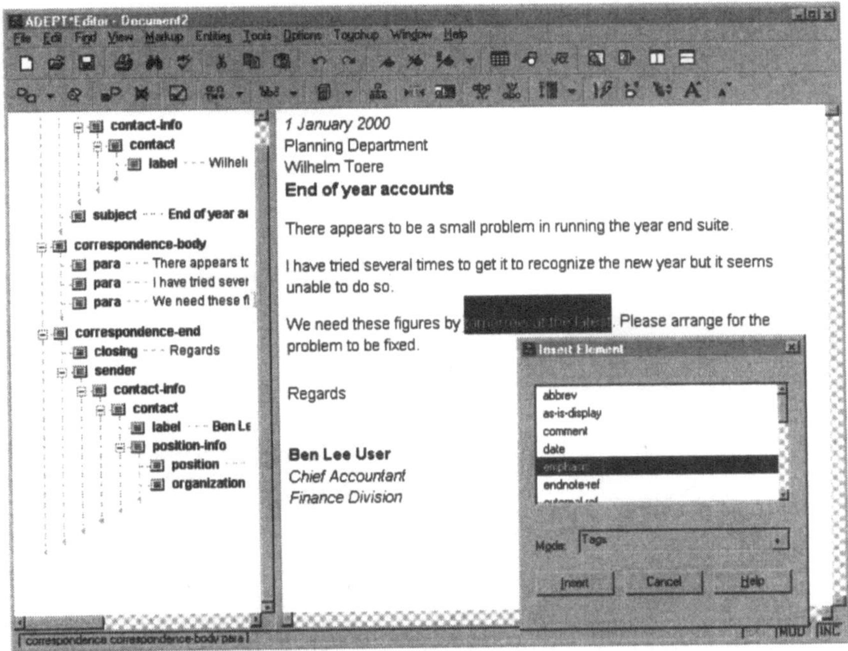

Figure 66. ArborText's *ADEPT•Editor*

The toolbar is context-sensitive, so a different one appears when editing tables, with a collection of table operations and support for CALS tables and for ArborText's own table model, which provides finer control over formatting. The custom toolbar is useful, as handling tabular data can be one of the trickiest and most time-consuming things about SGML editing. The table edit interface has a ruler bar to help with column widths, and it can handle fixed and stretchable row and column dimensions. Rules and cell shadings are available (where they are supported by your DTD). *ADEPT*'s model of table editing is probably the most reliable and comprehensive of the common graphical editors, although it has been around, relatively unchanged, for a very long time: the graphical equivalent, perhaps, of the Elsevier *Pandora* editor (an SGML-ized DOS *WordPerfect* derivative formerly supplied to Elsevier's typesetting houses).

Graphics support is available both for direct file references (as in HTML, for example) and for general entity references (where the graphic is referenced via a declared entity using a System Identifier or FPI).

Support for mathematics has been added to the MS-Windows version (previously it was only available in the Unix version). This pro-

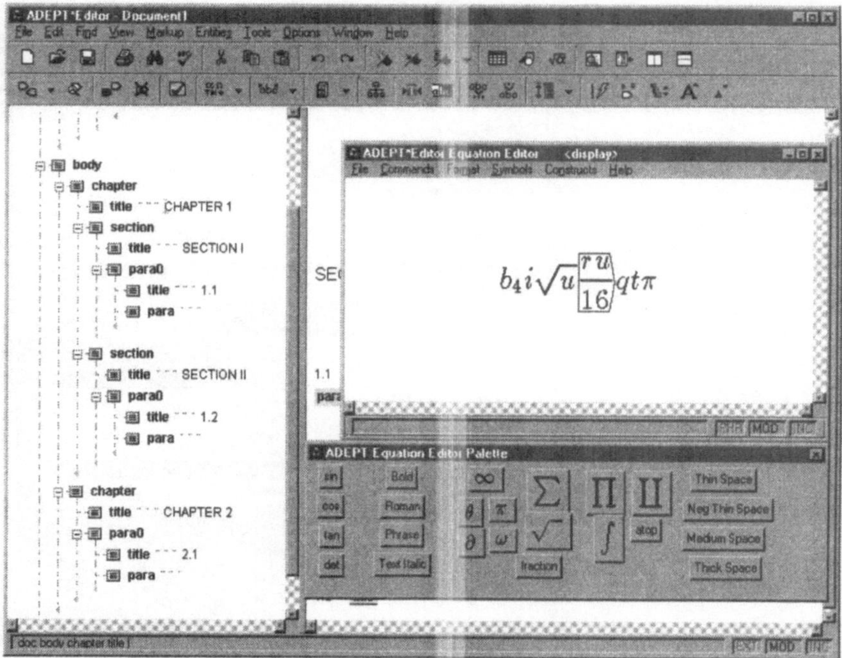

Figure 67. Math editing in *ADEPT•Editor*

vides a graphical math editing window where an equation can be built up from components (see Figure 67). The test expression we saw in section 2.3.8 took only a few seconds to put together, as the editor can treat syntactic groups like fractions as a single unit.

Support is available for user-defined character sets (non-Latin alphabets) and for element-specific help files which you can write to provide online help about how or when to apply every element in the DTD you are using. This level of customization is the tip of the iceberg: there is a hefty layer of Command Language available to let you modify most aspects of *ADEPT*'s behavior.

In general the interface is fast and comfortable to use, although as with most large systems, training is advisable in order to become familiar with all the facilities. The manuals are clear and well-illustrated:

- the editor user guide, which takes the form of an extended tutorial, introducing SGML concepts in their *ADEPT* environment and explaining all the edit facilities from simple insertion to tables, graphics, hyperlinks, and importing and exporting SGML;
- an editor reference guide, which lists the behavior of each item on each menu and toolbar;
- a manual for the *ADEPT* Command Language (see below);

- the manual for *Document•Architect*, which covers DTD compilation and the creation and maintenance of FOSIs.

3.3.1.2. Handling DTDs and stylesheets with Document•Architect

Document•Architect is the DTD compiler and stylesheet editor for the *ADEPT* series. It runs as a separate task in its own window, but once a DTD has been compiled, a sample instance can be brought up in an edit window so that the facilities of *ADEPT* can be used to help in the creation and maintenance of the FOSI. A compiled DTD also has an Auxiliary Tag Data (ATD) file, which stores information about the way in which you want the DTD to be used and lets you customize various aspects of editor and formatting behavior such as identifying which elements are for graphics or how to format out-of-context pasted text.

To compile a new DTD you supply the DocType name, DTD filename, SGML Declaration, and the directory path to search for entity files. *Document•Architect* asks for the Formal Public Identifier (if there is one). It uses a temporary OASIS catalog file while compiling, so if you have a DTD with external references which need catalog resolution, you can supply your own catalog, and once compilation is successful, its contents get added to the main *ADEPT* catalog for future reference. It is instructive that *ADEPT* alone of all the windowing editors I have used was able to compile my privately-modified version of *DocBook* first time without error.

Once the DTD is compiled, you answer a series of further dialog questions which enable *ADEPT* to gain some knowledge of the nature of the DTD. It asks you to supply the element names your DTD uses for:

> the document title, title block, and title page
> regular paragraphs
> graphics, and attribute names for assorted graphical manipulation features
> divisions (chapter/section/subsection *etc*)
> lists (numbered/bulleted/definition)
> figure blocks and page breaks

This is what enables *ADEPT* to display the hypertext table of contents, to 'understand' where you are in the DTD, and to help generate a 'starter' FOSI if you don't have one yet, so that you get an immediate draft screen appearance that will help you create test instances for use in the layout design process.

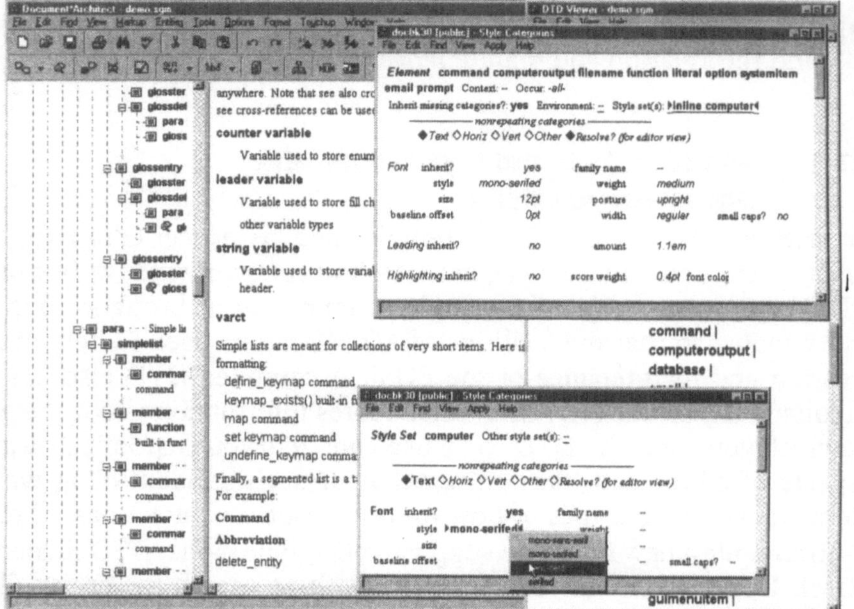

Figure 68. Editing a FOSI in *Document•Architect*

The final — and often longest — stage of DTD setup is to use the FOSI editor to define the typographic styles for each element that will be used. The features here are very extensive, up to the level of a typesetting system (perhaps not surprising given ArborText's long association with TEX, elements of which underlie the composition engine). Although it takes time to set up the FOSI from scratch, there are existing FOSIs in specific areas which can be used as templates, such as the US Navy FOSI Repository at `http://navycals.dt.navy.mil/dtdfosi/`.

The style palette (see Figure 68) identifies the element and any conditional factors (its context or attributes), and lets you define the appearance characteristics for inline and block-mode use (discussed in the introduction to this chapter, but with many more options than most programs provide).

The FOSI structure is a fairly rigid definition of a stylesheet. Normally you don't see any of it, as the FOSI editor provides the graphic interface through which you set it up and make changes. A FOSI itself is an SGML file, however, with a DTD of its own, so it is possible (sometimes desirable) to edit it manually, or to import FOSIs from other applications and use them modified or unmodified.

3.3.1.3. ADEPT Command Language (ACL)

The customization layer of the *ADEPT* Command Language allows you to control the editor from the command line, and to write programs in ACL which modify the behavior of the editor. Command-line control means you can customize the way the program starts up (special commands, enabling or disabling checking, loading different FOSIs).

Being able to write programs in an internal editor language means you can do almost anything from changing the behavior of a keystroke to virtually rewriting the interface. You can tailor-make commands and ship them with files for editing by specific users or customers, and provide 'hooks' tied to specific events which trigger certain actions such as pop-up dialogs when the event occurs.

ACL has variables, loops and conditions, arrays, math and string evaluation and functions, and external file reading and writing, but its main power source is the built-in functions which allow it access to the document parse tree (the 'grove'), so it can locate child or parent elements, test attributes, and manipulate the text in its context, even interacting with the user via a window dialog.

This level of API means *ADEPT* can be integrated with other applications such as databases in order to give them an SGML editing environment. Texcel's *Information Manager* database (see section 6.6.1.1) is an example of this kind of embedding.

3.3.2. Author/Editor (SoftQuad)

Unix/X, MS-Windows, Mac
`http://www.sq.com/`

Author/Editor is among the best-known SGML editors for windowing systems. It comes from SoftQuad in Toronto, Canada, and is available for Macs, Unix, and MS-Windows. It is big sister to the popular *HoTMetaL* editor for HTML, which has been many a Web users' introduction to SGML and structured editing, and to the more recent *Xmetal* for XML.

Author/Editor implements a simple graphical interface for editing SGML along traditional word processor lines: the button-bar contains the conventional filing, printing, editing, and searching tools and provides dictionary and thesaurus buttons. There are five additional buttons for the most common SGML edit functions: hide/reveal markup, insert element, remove markup, validate, and insert table.

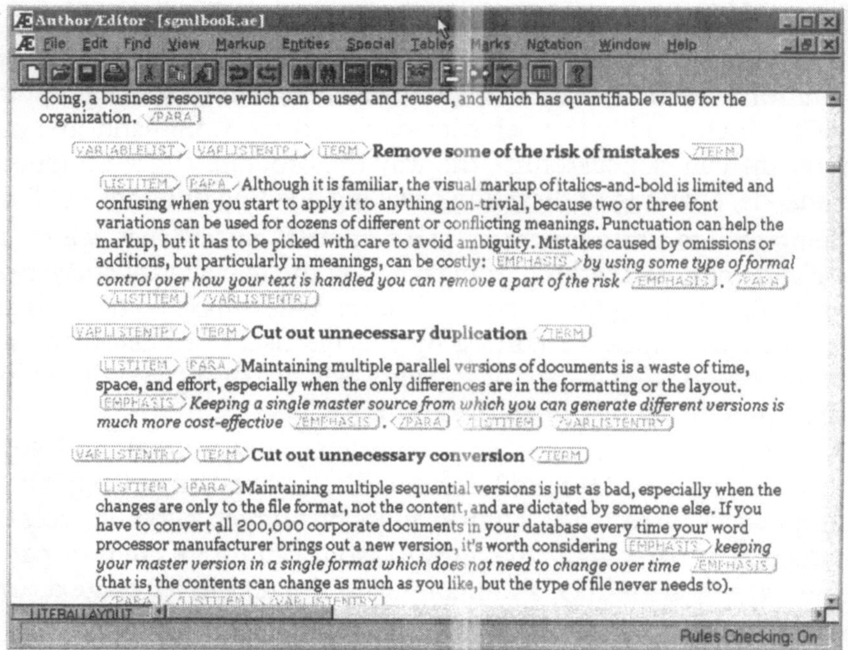

Figure 69. The *Author/Editor* edit screen, markup revealed

3.3.2.1. Installation

Author/Editor is supplied on CD-ROM. Installation follows the standard Windows pattern, and requires the activation of a software license key after installation, by typing in a code supplied with the package.

The system comes with several precompiled DTDs including samples from CALS and ATA (and a table fragment to go with them), the old AAP DTDs, a small book DTD, and some generic office-style memo, letter, minutes and press release DTDs. Others you have to compile yourself with *RulesBuilder* before use.

Sample style files are included for all supplied DTDs, as well as some sample SGML files to illustrate usage. The manual is clear and includes a tutorial which uses the sample SGML files provided. The entire manual text is also accessible as a help file.

3.3.2.2. Operation

The graphical interface follows the usual MS-Windows and X Window conventions for menus, marking, cutting and pasting, and use of the button-bar. Creating a new file brings up the list of precompiled DTDs ('rules files') for you to pick one: if you want to use one of your own, or one of the public DTDs, you have to compile it with *RulesBuilder* (see section 3.3.2.3).

Importing an existing SGML file is straightforward provided it is valid. Invalid markup causes *Author/Editor* to display the file in plaintext form, highlighting the location of the first error. There are two parsing options: 'validate', which conducts a formal validation, and 'interpret', which parses the file but pauses at each error and lets you correct it until the file is valid. *Author/Editor* files are stored in a binary format, and can be exported to plaintext SGML with or without the SGML Declaration and/or the DocType Declaration.

The action of adding markup is sensitive to mouse marking, so when no text is highlighted *Author/Editor* inserts an element, and when text is highlighted it surrounds it. Cut-and-paste follows the markup strictly: you cannot bridge over the close of one element into the next element.

Styles can be changed directly from the edit screen at any time and the stylesheet is automatically updated. You can create context-sensitive styles and give them user-defined style names, but these cannot themselves be used as the ancestors of other context-sensitive styles.

As *Author/Editor* is used extensively for text entry, with the text created being destined for use in some other system, typeset-quality formatting is not provided: SoftQuad sells a separate product, *Sculptor*, which is a publication-quality formatter companion for *Author/Editor* (not covered here).

Graphics are inserted by using attributes of a suitable element: one for the filename and one for the file type (as a `NOTATION`), so your DTD needs to make provision for this. A registry then binds the notation to an internal or external graphic display program. Graphics are initially hidden: double-clicking on the element pops up the image, and double-clicking again hides it away.

Author/Editor has its own internal table model, for which they provide one DTD fragment, and they also provide another which maps it to the CALS model. The internal table model fragment can be used on its own in any DTD just by including it, and a similar but slightly more complex process for the CALS fragment lets you add CALS table compliance to your own DTD. Table markup and data entry is done with floating toolbars, which is more convenient than menus. The table-handling produces validly marked-up tables, but the on-screen formatting is poor for anything other than very trivial tables.

3.3.2.3. Compiling a DTD with RulesBuilder

There is a separate program for compiling DTDs for use with *Author/Editor*, called *RulesBuilder* (*RB*). This produces a binary 'rules file',

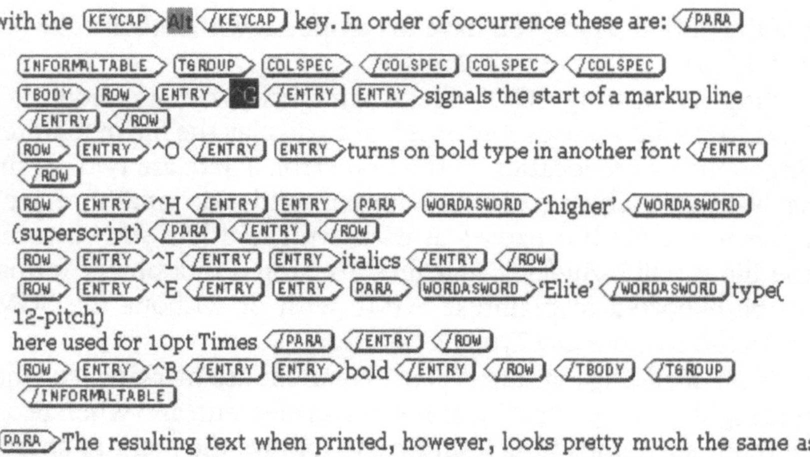

with the <KEYCAP>Alt</KEYCAP> key. In order of occurrence these are: </PARA>

<INFORMALTABLE> <TGROUP> <COLSPEC> </COLSPEC> <COLSPEC> </COLSPEC>
<TBODY> <ROW> <ENTRY>^G </ENTRY> <ENTRY>signals the start of a markup line
</ENTRY> </ROW>
<ROW> <ENTRY>^O </ENTRY> <ENTRY>turns on bold type in another font </ENTRY>
</ROW>
<ROW> <ENTRY>^H </ENTRY> <ENTRY> <PARA> <WORDASWORD>'higher' </WORDASWORD>
(superscript) </PARA> </ENTRY> </ROW>
<ROW> <ENTRY>^I </ENTRY> <ENTRY>italics </ENTRY> </ROW>
<ROW> <ENTRY>^E </ENTRY> <ENTRY> <PARA> <WORDASWORD>'Elite' </WORDASWORD>type(
12-pitch)
here used for 10pt Times </PARA> </ENTRY> </ROW>
<ROW> <ENTRY>^B </ENTRY> <ENTRY>bold </ENTRY> </ROW> </TBODY> </TGROUP>
</INFORMALTABLE>

<PARA>The resulting text when printed, however, looks pretty much the same as

---

inserts with the Alt key. In order of occurrence these are:

^G	signals the start of a markup line
^O	turns on bold type in another font
^H	'higher' (superscript)
^I	italics
^E	'Elite'type(12-pitch) here used for 10pt Times
^B	bold

The resulting text when printed, however, looks pretty much the same as any

Figure 70. Simple table in *Author/Editor*

which is what *Author/Editor* needs in order to work. If you are a first-time user of *Author/Editor*, you will need to buy *RB* as well if you want to use your own DTDs or anything other than the sample DTDs supplied. Installation is similar to *Author/Editor*, and a license string is also required for activation.

RB has a reputation for being one of the pickiest DTD compilers around. For this reason, some complex DTDs may fail to compile unless given special treatment. The most common symptom of this is the warning that some elements have been referenced but never declared (the TEI DTD is probably the best-known candidate for this, and solutions are discussed in section 2.3.6). It is important to note that this is an entirely different situation to having elements which have been declared but never referenced. Both situations are legal SGML.

The catalog mechanism used by *RB* is based on a file called `rb.map` in the directory where the *RB* program was installed. This is not quite an OASIS catalog but is very similar, each entry consisting of line containing the FPI, a tilde character, and the filename to use, for example:

```
"-//USA-DOD//DTD Table Model 951010//EN" ~ c:\sgml\cals-tbl.dtd
"\+//Silmaril//DTD HTML Forms Fragment//EN" ~ c:\sgml\formfrag.dtd
```

(The way *RB* reads the catalog file involves the use of some Regular Expression code (see section 5.1.1.1), so a leading plus sign on a FPI from a Public Owner registered under ISO 9070 must be escaped with a backslash.)

To compile a DTD, you run *RB* and use the **File|*Open*** menu to open your DTD file (or the 'driver' file in the case of a multi-file DTD). The file is opened in a plaintext edit window. You pick **Special|*Build Rules*** from the menus, and fill in the entries as prompted (see Figure 71):

1. the name of the document type (the name of the top-level element for the document type you want to use);
2. the Formal Public Identifier;
3. the System Identifier (usually the DTD filename);
4. the SGML Declaration for this DTD, picked from a file dialog;
5. reporting options

Clicking on **Build Rules** starts the compilation. Successful compilation results in a 'Save' dialog box where you give a name and directory for the new Rules File.

If an error is detected in compilation, one of two things occurs:

- If the error was in the syntax of the DTD, compilation stops, and an error message is displayed, and you can edit the DTD and try again;
- If the error was in resolving an entity file, *RB* pops up a dialog box which lets you navigate to the right directory and specify which file to use.

This last facility is one of the best features of the *RB* interface, and one sadly lacking on many DTD compilers and other SGML programs, which tend to abort and make you start over. Because of the unspecified nature of FPI resolution (see section 2.5.4) and the assumptions DTD authors and SGML software authors make about file types, it is not uncommon for DTD compilers to fail to find a file where they expected. Being able to point at the right file and have the process continue is very useful.

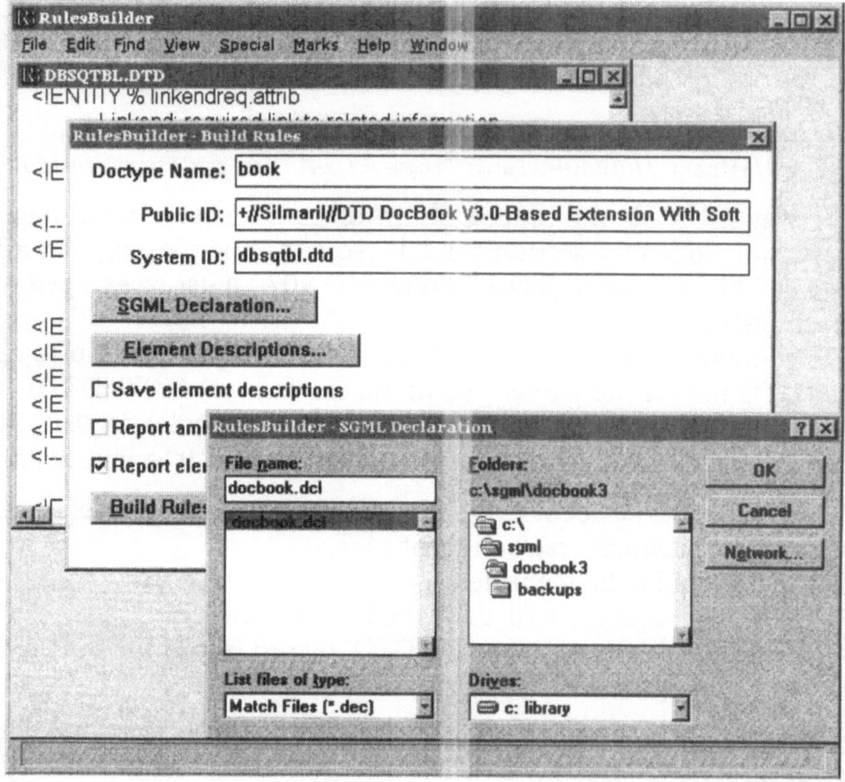

Figure 71. Compiling a DTD into a Rules File with *Rulesbuilder*

3.3.3. SGML Editor (GriF)

MS-Windows, Unix, Mac
`http://www.grif.fr/`

The GriF *SGML Editor* has one of the least complex interfaces to editing SGML. It provides a simple WYSIWYG-style screen in the manner of a word processor, with conventional controls for files, printing, fonts, alignment, spellchecking, and searching.

Compiling the DTD and creating a stylesheet are tasks administered separately from the editor, using the *Application Builder* program, but the screen controls still allow the user to impose local (non-element-based) styles on a document. In addition to being used in business and publishing applications, GriF's is the interface used in the Euromath editor (see section 3.4.6).

The only trace of SGML on view in the editor is the one-line display showing the current context by descent from the root (the sequence

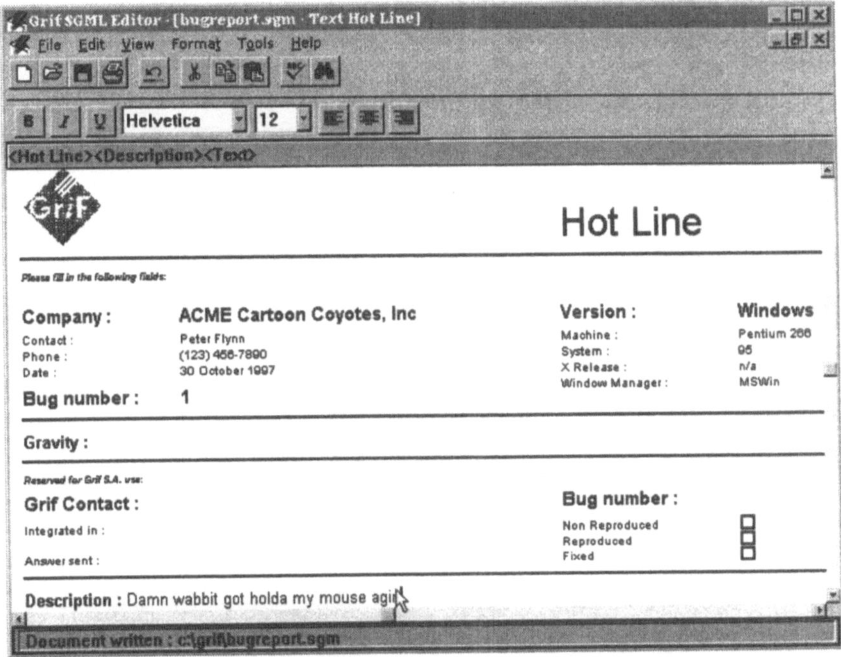

Figure 72. GriF's *SGML Editor* using a form-fill report format

of elements which lead to the element currently open at the cursor). Display styles are dictated by those established when the application is built (by compiling the DTD and writing the stylesheet), but the traditional screen controls for formatting all still operate in the normal way.

This approach allows almost complete word processor-style WYSIWYG control with complete independence from the markup: a stylesheet may cause a particular element to default to bold type, for example, but you can override that manually by using italics, for example, or changing the size, on an entirely independent basis, without affecting the element markup in any way. The effect is achieved internally by using Processing Instructions to record the *ad hoc* styles within the markup, so that these operator-controlled styles are not tied to an element.

Locations on the screen where data content is required are identified by gray squares, so text entry for very prescriptive DTDs can be made almost as simple as a form-fill application, and it is immediately apparent if any required element is left unpopulated.

By default, the **Enter** key creates a new instance of the current structural element, if the DTD permits this (for example, pressing **Enter** at

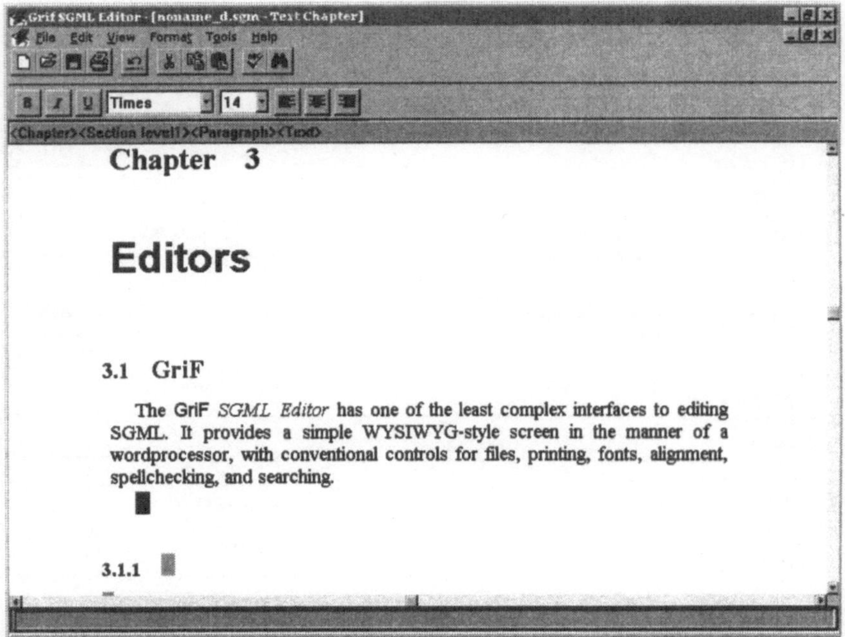

Figure 73. Editing text using GriF's *SGML Editor* (see style programming code in text)

the end of an <PARA> would create another element of that name). If the current content model is at an end (all required elements are present, and no further optional elements are wanted), the **TAB** key moves to the next content model where input is possible. The **Edit** menu gives access to the usual element-insert and element-surround items, and you can specify insertion before or at the current point or after it, which is how you add more elements to the current model, or open a new element after the end of the current one. There is a built-in parser to validate the document.

3.3.3.1. Additional software

GriF's approach is that each document type is presented to the user as a self-contained 'application'. To compile a new DTD and provide a template for editing (stylesheet), you therefore need the *Application Builder* product which is sold separately. It works from a DTD file named after the root element, either with or without a DocType Declaration in the DTD, and needs a catalog in `entity.pub` in the DTD directory. Compilation produces a lot of files, all with the same base name but different file types, for structure, presentation, translation, features, the binary DTD itself, the styles, and the compiled presentation that is delivered to the user.

To establish a style for presentation in the edit window, you have to write a style file (called a presentation schema) and compile it using *Application Builder*, along with the DTD, into the form that *SGML Editor* can use. The presentation schema language is, in effect, a typographic programming language, and provides very high-level control over the formatting and design of the screen and the page:

```
 CHAPTER:
BEGIN
Create(CHAPTER_S);
Create(CloseTag);
CreateLast(CHAPTER_E);
Page(PageBody);
Create(BoiteChapter);
        Create(BoiteNumchapitre);
Create(Section_TabMat);
Size: CORPS_PARAGRAPHE;
Font: Times;
Style: Roman;
ForeGround: BROWN;
HorizPos: VMiddle = Enclosing . VMiddle;
VertPos: Top = Enclosing . Top;
Indent: INDENT_PARAGRAPHE;
Justify: Yes;
LineSpacing: 1.2;
Depth: 1;
IN C_VTABLEOFCONTENTS
   BEGIN
   Page(PageTableMat);
   Justify: no;
   END;
IN C_VBOOKTBLCONTENTS
   BEGIN
   Page(PageTableMat);
   Justify: no;
   END;
END;
```

Every aspect of *SGML Editor*'s actions can be controlled from the internal language, not just the formatting of the display or the print, but also interaction with the user, menus, and even the buttons on the screen. There is, however, no graphical interface to these design scripts: the programming language is preciely that, and needs to be written using traditional plaintext editing tools.

There is a simple read-only interface to SGML, *Active Views*, which is a delivery tool in the form of a browser for viewing documents created by *SGML Editor* and the stylesheets of *Application Builder*. It provides the same WYSIWYG interface but without edit controls; instead, it adds hypertext and bookmark abilities.

GriF also have some XML support in their Web editing software *Symposia Pro* and *Symposia Doc+*, with CSS style sheet editing, but these are not a part of *SGML Editor*. The original GriF company was taken over in 1997 by I4I (see section 7.1.4) but the GriF product lines and name are being retained and actively developed.

3.3.4. Document Generator and WebWriter XML (Stilo)

MS-Windows and Mac
`http://www.stilo.com/`

STiLO's *Document Generator* is one of the few editors supporting both Macs and PCs. It comes on diskettes, and installs into 7.5Mb (5Mb for *WebWriter*, the XML version, which shares an almost identical interface). The documentation is available in PDF format for Adobe *Acrobat*.

These editors don't require a precompiled DTD: they parse the DTD and the instance when you open a file (in the case of *WebWriter* with well-formed files, by reading the instance alone), but it is possible to save the DTD in compiled form in either case.

To create a new file in *Document Generator*, you need a 'template' containing the DTD or a DocType Declaration, which you have to create externally (with a plaintext editor or similar) the first time you use a new DTD.

With *WebWriter* you have a choice of opening an existing XML-conformant DTD in the same way as for *Document Generator*; or an XML well-formed document (from which a DTD will be generated). You may also use **File|*New*** menu item to start from scratch and create an XML document and DTD by adding new elements yourself as you edit.

External entity references encountered during parsing cause a dialog to be opened where you can specify the location of the file: this is automatically recorded in a catalog file for future use.

Opening a file displays the text in recessed rectangles for each element (see Figure 74) in a similar manner to *InContext*. A new file contains only the root element. The editing model has some similarity with GriF's, being based on pressing the **Enter** key at the end of text entry for an element: this creates another instance of that element (the normal behavior for continuous writing) if the content model allows, otherwise it moves to the next required or available element of the next structure in the DTD.

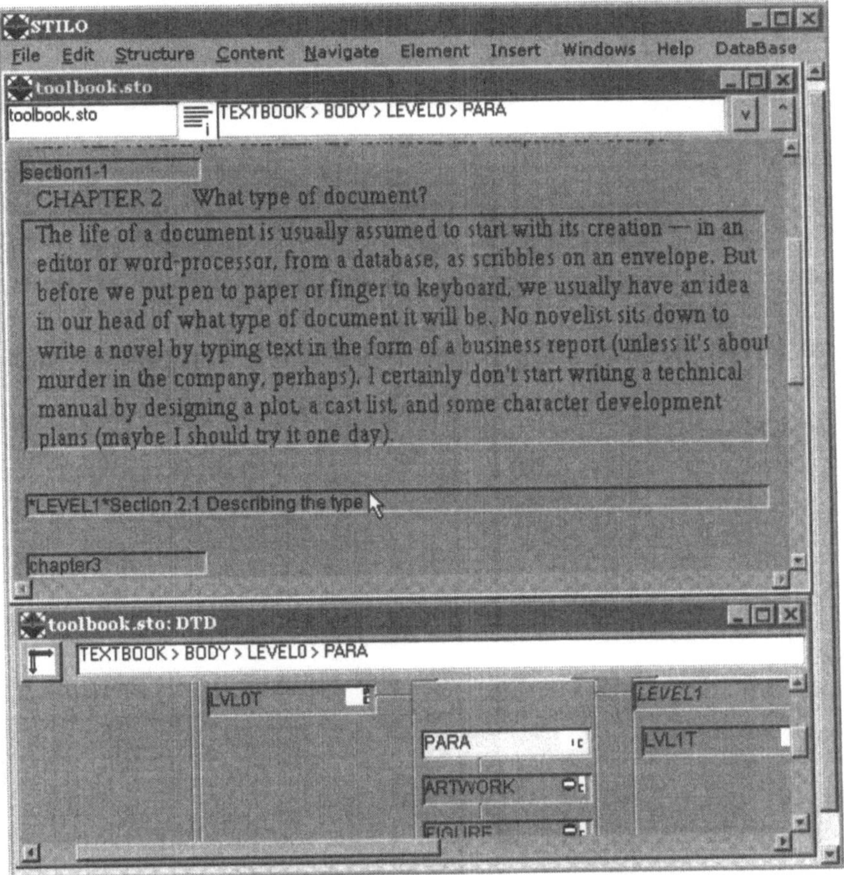

Figure 74. The STiLO *Document Generator*

There is a DTD navigation window which provides a graphical display of the DTD linked to the edit window, so it can be used to select the next element for insertion, as well as for moving around the document. Elements which are contextually available at the current cursor point are always in the **Insert** menu, and elements outside the current element (siblings or parent) are available from the **Elements** menu.

In addition to the usual windowing edit functions, you can display comments from the DTD separately for the document type, each element, and each attribute, which provides for a useful method of implementing a self-documented DTD. The XML version allows the creation of new elements and attributes for use with well-formed documents, and the resulting structure can be saved as a DTD for future use (see section 75).

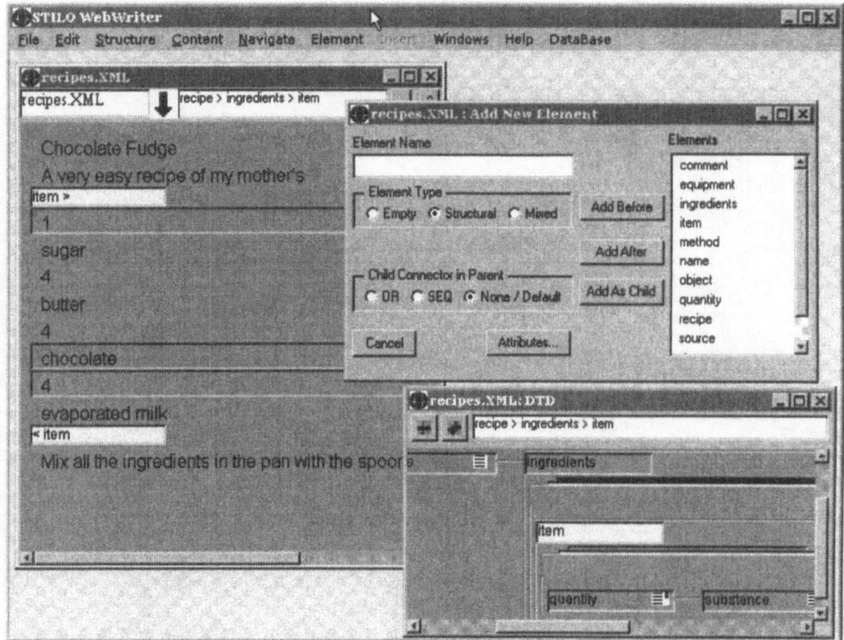

Figure 75. STiLO *WebWriter*

In *WebWriter*, you can create the markup while you write. A 'new element' function lets you name a new element, and position it as the child, parent, or sibling of an existing element. It's then available for use just as if it was in a DTD all along (in effect, it *is* in the 'virtual DTD' that *WebWriter* is maintaining on your behalf. Having created a file using this method, you can choose to save it with or without the DTD, and if you pick 'with', then it writes the DTD that it deduces from the element structure you have used.

You create display styles separately from elements, and give each a name, then link them to the desired elements, so they are easily reusable. As *STiLO* is an editor only, the styles are for editing convenience rather than for typographic printing, and there is no way to distinguish between inline and block-oriented elements: all elements occupy their own rectangle.

3.3.5. InContext 2 (InContext)

MS-Windows
http://www.incontext.com (http://www.incontext.ca)

InContext is a text-based SGML editor for MS-Windows from InContext Corp in Mississauga, Ontario, also known for their diagnostic software for the Web. The edit display provides a navigator window in parallel with the text editing window, which displays the location where you are in the document at any time, as well as showing the surrounding structure, and it also provides the element insertion/deletion functions. The text window displays the text being edited as a series of structural blocks, as with the STiLO editors, rather than in word processor or WYSIWYG format.

Installation is from three diskettes, and a copy of the Adobe *Acrobat* reader is also provided on a fourth diskette for using the online manuals. The installation routine pops up a check for Microsoft's *Excel* spreadsheet, because this is used for table data entry. The installed software takes up about 5Mb of disk space.

3.3.5.1. Editing and display

The initial screen is sparse, containing just the **File** and **Help** menus. You open an existing file in the normal way, from the **File**|***Open*** menu and a dialog box, but there is a short pause while it reads the associated DTD: *InContext* is one of the few editors which does not require a precompiled DTD. The file is then displayed for editing. Because the default display is structural, this approach makes starting to use a new DTD very fast: there's no stylesheet definition required for editing, only for printing.

Figure 76 shows the two-panel approach: the element context is shown in nested graphical rectangles in the left-hand pane, called the 'Logical Editor', and the corresponding text is shown opposite it in the right-hand pane, called the 'Content Editor'. The distinction between those elements which may contain character or mixed data and those which may contain only element markup is shown by the data-bearing elements having a raised dot in the open square to the left of the element name.

The Logical Editor displays only structural markup by default: inline markup is symbolized in the Content Editor with a variety of configurable graphical tags (see the little triangles in the date in Figure 77), but the Logical Editor can be configured to display content markup as well.

Elements containing other markup can be collapsed and expanded, as with an outliner: in this case their presence is shown in the Content

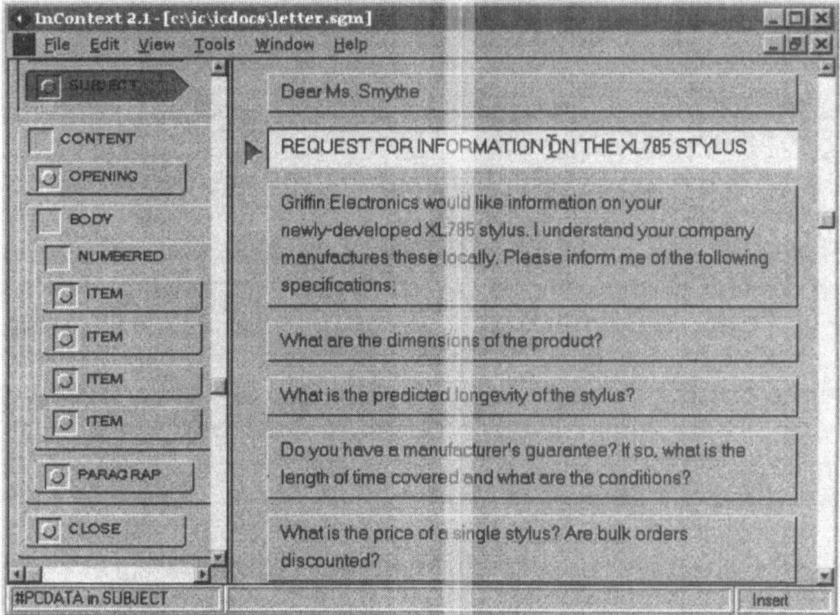

Figure 76. The *InContext* main edit screen

Editor by an elongated plus sign. The display can be toggled between 'fielded' and 'inline' views at any level, so the structure as presented for editing can be changed to suit the task: largely structural 'form-fill' applications require a different ergonomic to largely content-oriented applications such as scholarly text.

Graphics are handled as entity references, so the DTD has to be able to provide the `NOTATION` mapping needed. Windows OLE is used to link and activate display from external sources, so the file format you use must be supported by an OLE-compliant program or library.

Tables are handled by Excel, as noted earlier. *InContext* has support for CALS tables, but they also provide for ATA-1000 (Aircraft Maintenance) and J2008 (Motor Vehicle Maintenance) table formats. The path for establishing the linkage is a little cumbersome, going from `.dcl` file to DTD to 'ATD' (Auxiliary Tag Data) files via the `ic.ini` file and into Excel, but the result is the flexibility of editing in a well-known and strongly supported environment.

3.3.5.2. Stylesheets and printing

The approach of keeping element content in closely defined panels within the Content Editor means that *InContext* achieves almost 100% separation of presentation from markup, as there is no means of af-

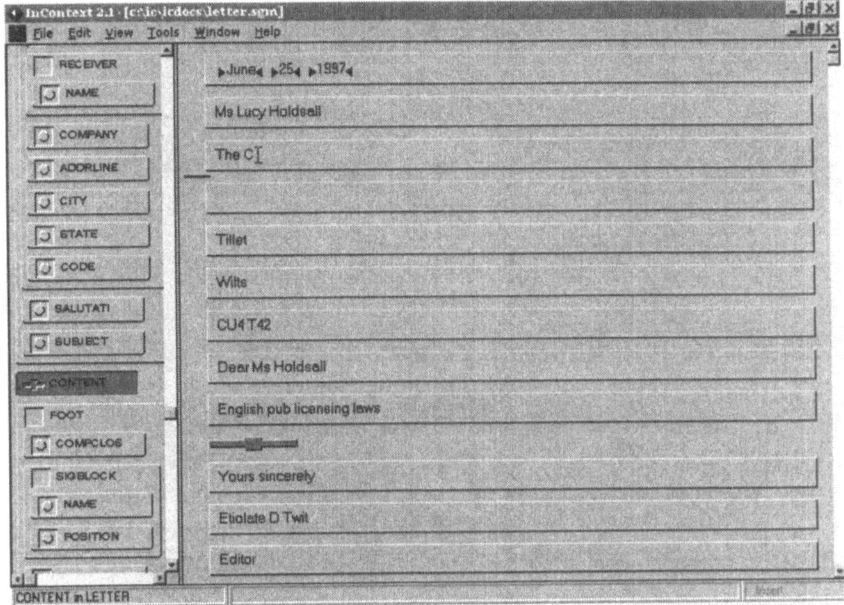

Figure 77. InContext editing with partially collapsed markup and some elements set 'inline'

fecting the formatting of the data content as it is displayed on-screen while editing. In this sense, the edit window is not WYSIWYG, which is either a curse or a blessing, depending on your viewpoint.

There is an extensive style-sheet mechanism to associate the formatting needed for printing. One useful feature of this is that it allows the designer reverse access to element attachments: you can list what elements a particular style name affects, as well as seeing which style names can be applied to a particular element.

Print preview and printing itself are done via the Windows *Write* or *WordPad* programs, spawned on demand, but there is an option to create an RTF file for export to other systems.

3.3.5.3. Catalogs and DTDs

There is a catalog for *InContext*'s entity manager in the file `c:\ic\entity\enttable`, so installing a new DTD means editing this file to add the equivalences between each FPI and filename on disk. This file does not use OASIS format: instead, you place each entry on pairs of adjacent lines:

```
-//ATA-BOEING//DTD SB-BOEING-VER2-LEVEL3//EN
C:\IC\ATA\sbboe02.dtd
```

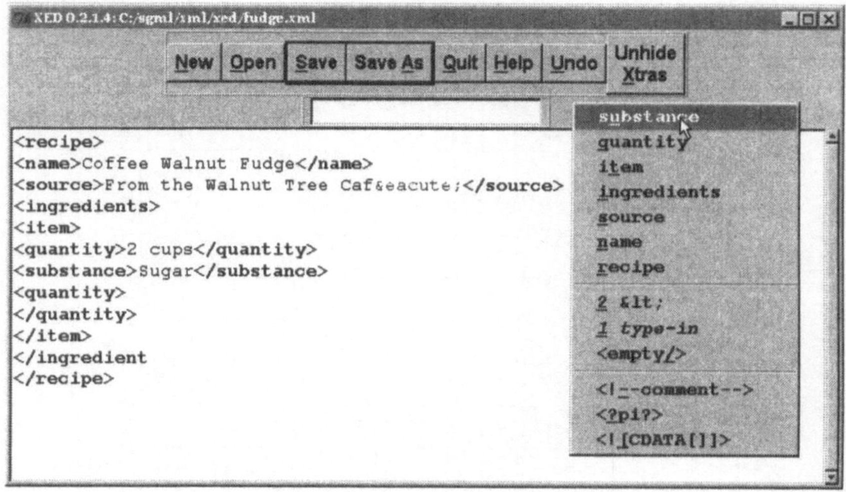

Figure 78. XED showing element menu

Adding the relevant lines will allow you to open an existing SGML file which refers to that DTD. To create a new file with a new DTD, you also need to supply a Declaration File, giving a the FPI and the name of the DTD file, plus an SGML Declaration, if there is one, and give this the filetype `.dcl`, so for HTML 3.2, for example, you would create a file `html32.dcl` containing:

```
<!DOCTYPE HTML PUBLIC "-//W3C//DTD HTML 3.2 Final//EN" "html32.dtd" []>
```

If the DTD is a single file, you can add the filename as the optional SYSTEM identifier after the FPI, as shown, and make sure the file is in the same directory as this `.dcl` file.

3.3.6. XED Henry Thompson

Solaris 2.5, Windows 95/NT
`http://www.cogsci.ed.ac.uk/~ht/xed.html`

XED is a simple, standalone, text editor for well-formed XML document instances. It does not parse a DTD or validate an instance, but keeps track of your document structure so that your instances are always well-formed.

The editor was built on *Python* and *Tk*, using the *LT XML* toolkit (see section 7.1.3). It is designed for small, hand-authored files, and supports a number of useful features like pressing '<' to get the element menu, and '&' to get the entity menu.

Like the nascent *ezDTD* (see section 2.6.5), this is new software, and subject to further development, but it's an example of easy, fast editing when you don't need or want the complexity of more powerful systems.

3.4. SGML extensions to non-SGML editors

We are beginning to see word processors take an interest in adding SGML capabilities to their products. Both Microsoft *Word* and Corel *WordPerfect* both have SGML facilities, the first via conversion and the second as a native feature. DTP systems like *FrameMaker* have versions for SGML, and some like *3B2* can import and export SGML as a built-in operation. A number of smaller WP systems are reported to be investigating SGML, including *Nota Bene*, the 'academicized' version of *XyWrite*. The careful reader will not be misled by claims of SGML conformance from systems which purport to output valid HTML.

Some of the move towards SGML is undoubtedly due to the enormous increase in demand for HTML editing for the World Wide Web. Although HTML is defined as an application of SGML, the acceptance by browsers of completely arbitrary tagging with no validation has meant that fully SGML-conformant HTML import and export is currently limited to derivatives of SGML editors: even the most careful 'Save As HTML' function cannot create meaningful markup where none was provided by the author in the first place, so all you get is mixtures of paragraphs and fonts designed to mimic the word processor screen.

The most famous and most widely-used extension to a non-SGML editor is Lennart Staflin's *psgml* ('Parsing SGML') mode for *Emacs*, but Corel's *WordPerfect Suite* contains a complete SGML editing environment, and Microstar's *Near&Far Author for Word* uses Microsoft *Word* as the edit tool in tandem with its own graphical DTD technology.

At the end of this section is a more specialist editor, not in fact an add-on to a non-SGML system, but a full SGML editor in its own right but for a specialist market: mathematics. Although several regular SGML and XML editors handle mathematics, the Euromath editor is specifically designed to do so.

3.4.1. GNU Emacs and psgml-mode

> Unix, X, DOS, MS-Windows, VAX/VMS,
> `http://www.gnu.org/software/emacs/emacs.html`

Emacs is a large and powerful program for editing text. The name is short for 'edit macros' because it is a programmable editor: you can define your own commands as macros in a Lisp-like language, which is what *psgml* does.

Emacs was written by Richard Stallman, formerly of the MIT AI Lab, as part of a project to produce a complete suite of portable software, from operating system up to application, which would not be dependent on any particular make or model or manufacturer, and which would be freely distributable (see the box).

Emacs in its plainest form looks and works much like any other character-cell plaintext editor in a standard 80–character by 25–line terminal screen. However, *Emacs* runs under Unix and the X Window system (in a separate version, not by GNU), DOS and MS-Windows, and also under VAX/VMS and on Apples (these tend to lag behind the Unix/DOS versions) so it can use mice and menus in the usual way. Like most windowing applications, it retains the ability to use keyboard shortcuts, which many frequent text users prefer, as you don't have to move your hands off the keyboard to do editing. It is also very easy to rebind any key to any function, so you can customize *Emacs* very substantially (you can make the F-keys behave the way the gods intended, for example).

Apart from editing files, *Emacs* can act as an email program (*RMAIL*), a Usenet newsreader (*GNUS*), Web browser (*GNUscape Navigator*), calendar/diary, file manager, and shell (command line) interface. It can also manage file compilations (C, TEX, SGML DTDs, *Jade etc*), play games, and do pretty much anything else except make the coffee (I expect someone is working on that). Even though the world of terminal-only access to centralized computers is a part of history in most places, many Unix users still run *Emacs* immediately they start up each morning, and keep it active all day, using it for almost every task they do.

3.4.1.1. Operation

In a windowing system, you double-click the *Emacs* icon to start; in a command-line environment (Unix without the windows, or DOS or VMS) you just type `emacs` optionally followed by the name of the file you want to edit.

The window is uncluttered, losing only three lines: the menus (at the top); and a status line and an input or echo area (at the bottom), which acts as a dialog box for error messages and prompts for filenames or other values. The native X-based version (the non-GNU one) uses additional space at the top for a toolbar.

The command and control set for *Emacs* is very large, and includes features such as incremental search and Regular Expression replacement otherwise found only in a few of the large-scale commercial editing systems. The 450–page manual is fairly comprehensive, but does assume that the reader is capable of absorbing technicalities at a fairly high rate. There is also a reference card giving the most frequently-used commands, and large numbers of other training and help documents are available on the Internet.

The CD-ROM has versions for Unix, DOS/Windows 3.1x, Windows 95/NT. The Apple and VMS versions are there also but they do not support SGML editing with*psgml*. The manual and reference card are supplied in PostScript format as well as their source code. I have tried to make the installation of the *NTEmacs* version for Windows 95 as fully-working as possible, by including a catalog file and copies of most of the public DTDs discussed in chapter 1.5.1.5.

3.4.1.2. psgml-mode

The programmable features of *Emacs* which allow for SGML editing are provided by the concept of 'modes'. Each different application has its own mode, for example mail mode, web mode, news mode, C mode, TeX mode, or SGML mode. There's also a mode for writing *Omnimark* programs (see section 5.2.1) and for writing DSSSL for *Jade* (see section 5.2.4).

The basic `sgml-mode` is included in the *Emacs* distribution, and was written by James Clark to speed tag entry and file management: it provides recognition of the syntax of SGML. The *psgml* mode is an addition written by Lennart Staflin which uses the DTD to enable parsing of the file. The result is context-sensitive editing, element insertion and deletion, syntactic indentation, and attribute editing. Access to an external parser such as *nsgmls* is available for validation. *Emacs* can be set to switch automatically into *psgml* when you load a file ending in `.sgml` (or other filetypes such as `.html`).

Psgml-mode will locate the DTD using an OASIS catalog in the directory where your SGML file is (and if it's not there, in the directory pointed to by the `_SGML` environment variable, or, failing all else, in `/usr/local/lib/sgml/CATALOG` or its equivalent like `c:\usr\local\lib\sgml\CATALOG`). Parsing starts automatically the moment you do something which requires a knowledge of the DTD, like inserting an

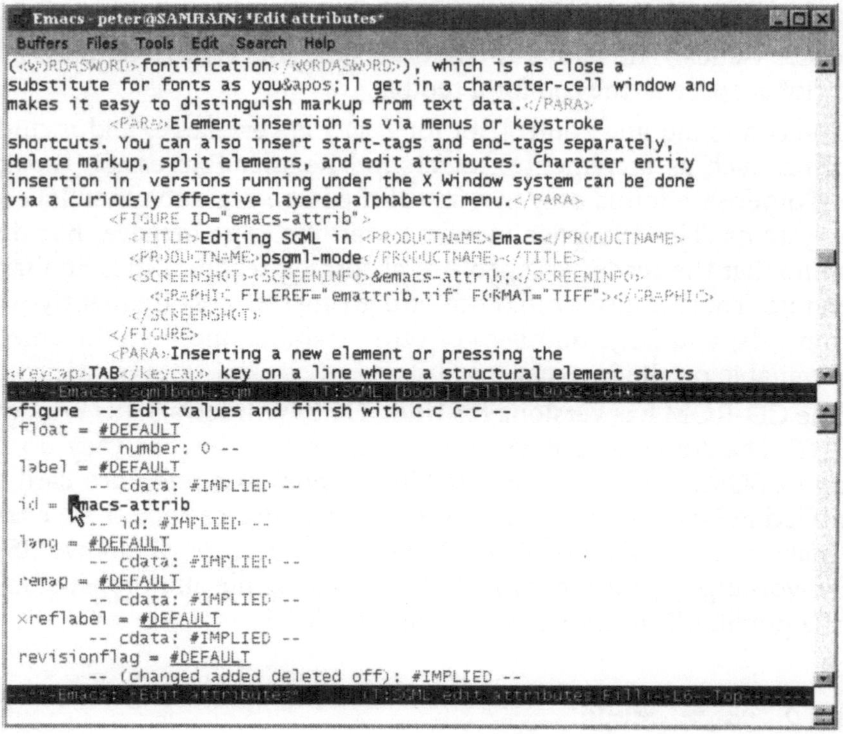

```
Emacs - peter@SAMHAIN: *Edit attributes*
Buffers Files Tools Edit Search Help
(<WORDASWORD>fontification</WORDASWORD>), which is as close a
substitute for fonts as you&apos;ll get in a character-cell window and
makes it easy to distinguish markup from text data.</PARA>
        <PARA>Element insertion is via menus or keystroke
shortcuts. You can also insert start-tags and end-tags separately,
delete markup, split elements, and edit attributes. Character entity
insertion in  versions running under the X Window system can be done
via a curiously effective layered alphabetic menu.</PARA>
        <FIGURE ID="emacs-attrib">
          <TITLE>Editing SGML in <PRODUCTNAME>Emacs</PRODUCTNAME>
          <PRODUCTNAME>psgml-mode</PRODUCTNAME></TITLE>
          <SCREENSHOT><SCREENINFO>&emacs-attrib;</SCREENINFO>
            <GRAPHIC FILEREF="emattrib.tif" FORMAT="TIFF"></GRAPHIC>
          </SCREENSHOT>
        </FIGURE>
        <PARA>Inserting a new element or pressing the
<keycap>TAB</keycap> key on a line where a structural element starts
--**-Emacs: sgmlbook.sgm      (T:SGML [book] Fill)--L9052--64%--------
<figure  -- Edit values and finish with C-c C-c --
 float = #DEFAULT
         -- number: 0 --
 label = #DEFAULT
         -- cdata: #IMPLIED --
 id = emacs-attrib
         -- id: #IMPLIED --
 lang = #DEFAULT
         -- cdata: #IMPLIED --
 remap = #DEFAULT
         -- cdata: #IMPLIED --
 xreflabel = #DEFAULT
         -- cdata: #IMPLIED --
 revisionflag = #DEFAULT
         -- (changed added deleted off): #IMPLIED --
--**-Emacs: *Edit attributes*      (T:SGML edit attributes Fill)--L6--Top----
```

Figure 79. Editing SGML in *Emacs psgml-mode*

element. You can also force it to re-parse the DTD (if you have changed it, for example), and save a binary copy for fast loading later.

If you are using regular *Emacs* in the X Window system or *NTEmacs* under Windows 95 or NT, you can turn on syntactic color ('fontification'), which is as close a substitute for fonts as you'll get in a character-cell window and makes it easy to distinguish markup from text data.

Element insertion is via menus or keystroke shortcuts. You can also insert start-tags and end-tags separately, delete markup, split elements, and edit attributes. Character entity insertion in versions running under the X Window system can be done via a curiously effective layered alphabetic menu.

Inserting a new element or pressing the **TAB** key on a line where a structural element starts will cause the start-tag to indent ('structural' in this case means 'in element content'). This makes it possible to have a very useful syntactically-indented file, with the indent level representing the depth of markup (see Figure 79).

The TAB key also performs another of *Emacs*' standard features, 'completion'. Using this, whenever there is input to type (opening a new file, giving the name of an element to insert), you can type the first few letters and press TAB to complete it, provided the abbreviation you have typed is minimally unique. This makes element insertion very fast, even using keystrokes rather than menus, and you can in any case customize frequently-used keystrokes to individual F-keys or control keys.

A character-cell editor is not for everyone: many users feel uneasy without the word processorized 'feel' of a typographical editor. A fuller graphical interface is certainly possible using *Xemacs*, but the portability and robustness of *Emacs* is a big advantage if you are working cross-platform, or in circumstances where commercial software is unavailable.

The *NTEmacs* installation included on the CD-ROM has a special setup program to install a full copy of *Emacs* on Windows 95, with *psgml* included, plus a catalog file and copies of all the publicly-distributable DTDs referred to in chapter 1.5.1.5, so on this platform at least you should have a complete free SGML editor ready to run. There is an enhancement to *psgml* for supporting XML from David Megginson, which is included in the setup. This operates as a major mode of *psgml*, and requires the version of *nsgmls* that comes with *Jade* (the one that does XML parsing and validation).

3.4.2. WordPerfect Suite 8 (Corel)

MS-Windows
`http://www.corel.com/products/wordperfect/cwps8pro/`

Corel are well known in the word processing, graphics, and DTP field, especially in the Macintosh environment. Having taken over from Word Perfect Corporation, Corel took the earlier SGML interface, *WordPerfect SGML Edition*, and created a fully-fledged SGML environment in their revised *WordPerfect Suite* product.

The old DOS/Unix *WordPerfect* was the word processor you either loved or hated. It was robust, reliable, and delivered exactly what it promised; but nothing more, and its interface was forbiddingly unmemorable. A late foray into the MS-Windows environment never caught on.

The new *WordPerfect Suite* series (which started with 7), however, is a quite different animal. A direct competitor to *Word*, it offers similar facilities, but is also a complete SGML editor, with DTD compiler, stylesheet support, and a graphical DTD viewer.

> **WordPerfect on CD-ROM**
>
> **A full copy of the *WordPerfect Suite* editor for MS-Windows 95 is on the CD-ROM, on a 90-day time-lapse trial. To install it, double-click the `setup.exe` program in the Corel folder.**

Installing the software with the SGML option checked adds an |*SGML* item to the **Tools** menu, from which you can operate the SGML-related functions. You need to start from here if you want to create an SGML file, as the regular **File**|***Open*** menu is only for non-SGML documents.

The *Graphical DTD Viewer* is a copy of *Near&Far Designer* licensed by Corel. It is only available with *WordPerfect Suite Professional* as it is aimed at the document type designer, not the general user. For an explanation of the functionality of this, see the description in section 2.6.2.

3.4.2.1. Compiling a DTD

As usual, you will probably need to compile a DTD to use, as *WordPerfect Suite* comes with a precompiled copy of HTML 3.2 only: anything else must be added. If you have access to a PC you can use the demonstration version on the CD-ROM to compile any of the DTDs included on the disk.

The system refers to compiled DTDs as 'Logic Files' (`.lgc` files), and there's a directory for them: all the relevant files for a new DTD can be copied into a subdirectory of their own within it: for example `c:\corel\suite8\programs\lgcfiles\recipes`. The installation adds several Corel items to the Start Menu, apart from the word processor itself: among them is the 'WordPerfect DTD Compiler' item in the 'Tools' menu, which provides a panel where you can give the path and filename of the DTD, where to put the `.lgc` file when it is created, and where to find the SGML Declaration and 'map file' (their term for a catalog). Figure 80 shows this panel set up to compile my modified *DocBook* DTD.

The parser/compiler seems to produce more warnings than anything else, but it is very fast, and compiled my modified DTD in about six seconds on a 200MHz Pentium. Interestingly, it did apply some of its own limitations to some of the quantities in the SGML Declaration,

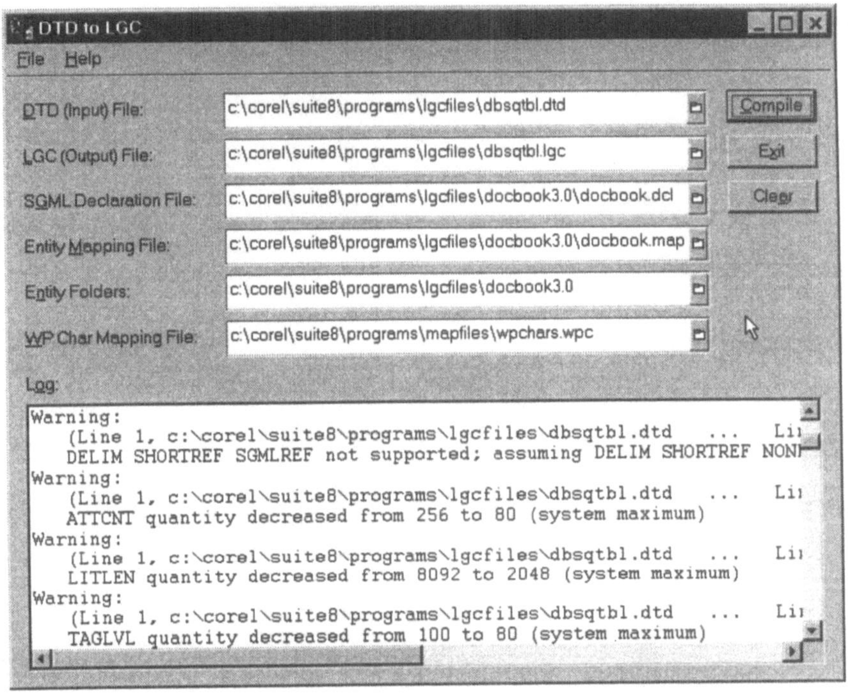

Figure 80. WordPerfect Suite compiling the *DocBook* DTD

as shown in Figure 80. Saving the compiled DTD makes it available in the **Tools|*SGML*|*Document Types*** menu of the actual word processor (all SGML items are under this menu: doing a regular **File|*Open*** on an SGML file will not bring the SGML modules into action). Once the menu has been used, it creates an **SGML** drop-down button on the toolbar.

The catalog file format is almost OASIS (*Suite 9* will move to full OASIS conformance). It requires the addition of a document type keyword (*eg* `DTD`) between the Formal Public Identifier and the System Identifier, so it's not hard to take an existing catalog entry and edit it into this form.

3.4.2.2. Styling

Creating a stylesheet is done with another separate program: the SGML Layout Designer (again from the 'Tools' section of their entry on the Start Menu). This reads an `.lgc` file and lets you pick each element in turn and specify the formatting items. The formatting window (see Figure 81) has three places for formatting information, rather than two: when the start-tag is encountered; when the end-tag is encountered but before the element is closed; and after the end-tag has been processed.

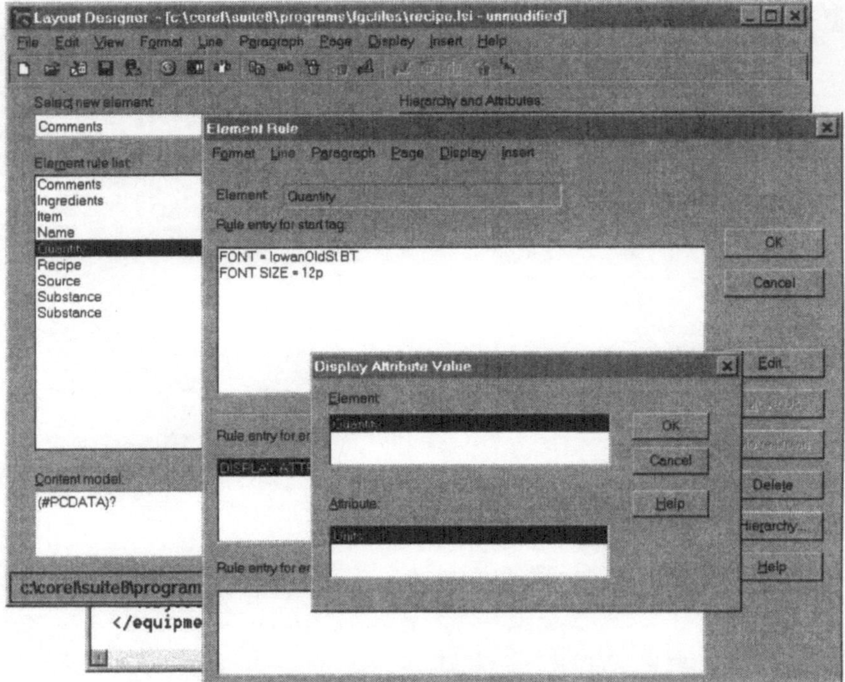

Figure 81. Creating a stylesheet in *WordPerfect Suite*

The styles are fairly comprehensive and easy to apply, but as the word processor display is not synchronized with the stylesheet, you have to save the stylesheet and go to the editor window and re-pick the stylesheet again from the SGML menu to make it re-read the file and apply changed styles. This means a chicken-and-egg situation for a new DTD, in that it's useful to have an instance to use for testing the stylesheet — but it's nice to have the stylesheet set up before editing an instance. In fact you can edit an instance without a stylesheet: you just get unformatted stream SGML.

3.4.2.3. Editing

Having got the DTD and stylesheet set up, and added to the Document Type and Stylesheets menu items, picking a Document Type opens a new file (there's a separate item for opening an existing file). The editing interface to *WordPerfect Suite* uses the standard word processor 'document layout' screen but you can pick the **Elements...** menu item which places a floating DTD-based element menu on the screen (see Figure 82).

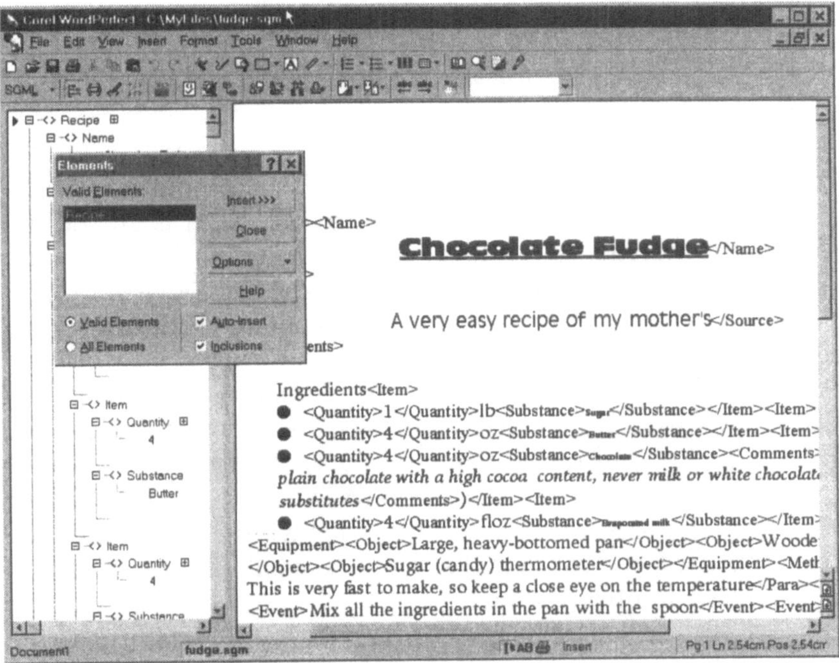

Recipe
Name
Elements
Valid Elements:
Insert >>>
Close
Options
Help
Valid Elements
All Elements
Auto-insert
Inclusions
<Name>
Chocolate Fudge</Name>
A very easy recipe of my mother's</Source>
Ingredients<Item>
<Quantity>1</Quantity>lb<Substance>Sugar</Substance></Item><Item>
<Quantity>4</Quantity>oz<Substance>Butter</Substance></Item><Item>
<Quantity>4</Quantity>oz<Substance>Chocolate</Substance><Comments>
plain chocolate with a high cocoa content, never milk or white chocolat
substitutes</Comments>)</Item><Item>
<Quantity>4</Quantity>floz<Substance>Evaporated milk</Substance></Item>
<Equipment><Object>Large, heavy-bottomed pan</Object><Object>Woode
</Object><Object>Sugar (candy) thermometer</Object></Equipment><Meth
This is very fast to make, so keep a close eye on the temperature</Para><
<Event>Mix all the ingredients in the pan with the spoon</Event><Event>
Item
Quantity
Substance
Butter
Document1
fudge.sgm
Insert
Pg 1 Ln 2.54cm Pos 2.54cm

Figure 82. Editing SGML in *WordPerfect Suite*

The tags appear on the screen in a sans-serif font but not in graphical form: you can hide them or shrink them to nested square brackets, in the same way that *Frame+SGML* does. The DTD structure, however, remains on display in the adjacent window, so you can see where you are in the hierarchy at any time. Provided you remember not to stray back to the word processor menus for formatting, and stick to the elements provided by the DTD, this makes a very easy and comfortable edit interface.

Element insertion can be done in two ways: one is to position the cursor at the point where you want the element inserted, which causes the element menu to reflect the valid elements at that point, and then picking the right element from the menu. The other is the 'Enter key' method also used in STiLO's *SGML Document Generator* and *WebWriter*, and in GriF's *SGML Editor*, and in some other editors: press the **Enter** key, and (if allowed by the DTD) a new instance of the current element will be created (this would be the case if you were editing a paragraph, for example); if no further instance of the element is allowed by the DTD, a new instance of its parent will be created (for example, you were editing a list `<item>` this would have created a new, empty `<list>` container).

3.4.3. Near&Far Author for Word (Microstar)

MS-Windows
http://www.microstar.com

Microstar make the *Near&Far* graphical DTD editor and viewer (*NFD*) described in section 2.6.2. The *Author* product (*NFA*) is an add-on for MS-Windows systems which lets you use Microsoft *Word* for writing your SGML files under the structural control of *NFA*. Although *NFA* uses some *NFD* technology, they are two separate products: you don't need to buy one to run the other.

NFA comes in two versions (Windows 3.1x and Windows 95/NT). Installation is from floppy disk, and puts the files in `c:\nfauthor` (to parallel the directory of its sister product). You need to have *Word* already installed before you start, as *NFA* expects to find it, and won't install without it. Because it uses an existing word processor to provide the edit interface, the additional software is small (4.5Mb installed) by comparison with other systems.

3.4.3.1. Operation

You run *Word* first, and you'll find an additional menu on the top line called **N&F Author**. This provides an 'import' and a 'create' function for SGML which parallels the 'open' and 'new' functions for other files. Creating a new file causes a menu of sample DTDs to appear, but you can navigate to any directory where the DTD you want to use lives. Selecting a DTD makes the *NFD* program load and run, parsing the DTD and displaying it graphically in its own window.

A Word template window guides the selection of elements: it displays a list of all valid elements for the location where the cursor is currently in the edit window. It doesn't apply any hierarchy to the list: you use the graphical DTD display to identify what you want next, which is much easier than picking from a list, as the graphical display is a tree-like structure for the DTD (see Figure 83: the same principle as all the DTD diagrams I have used in this book).

The graphical DTD display in effect drives the parser/manager, which keeps track of what element you are currently 'in', and passes that information through to *Word*. Picking an element makes *Word* display a shaded block where you start typing: pressing the **Enter** key brings up the element selection panel again, for the next element to be picked.

Styling is handled by stylesheets attached to the *Word* document in the normal way, but driven by the DTD. You need to turn off *Word*'s own formatting toolbar, however, because the styles are managed by the mapping from the DTD.

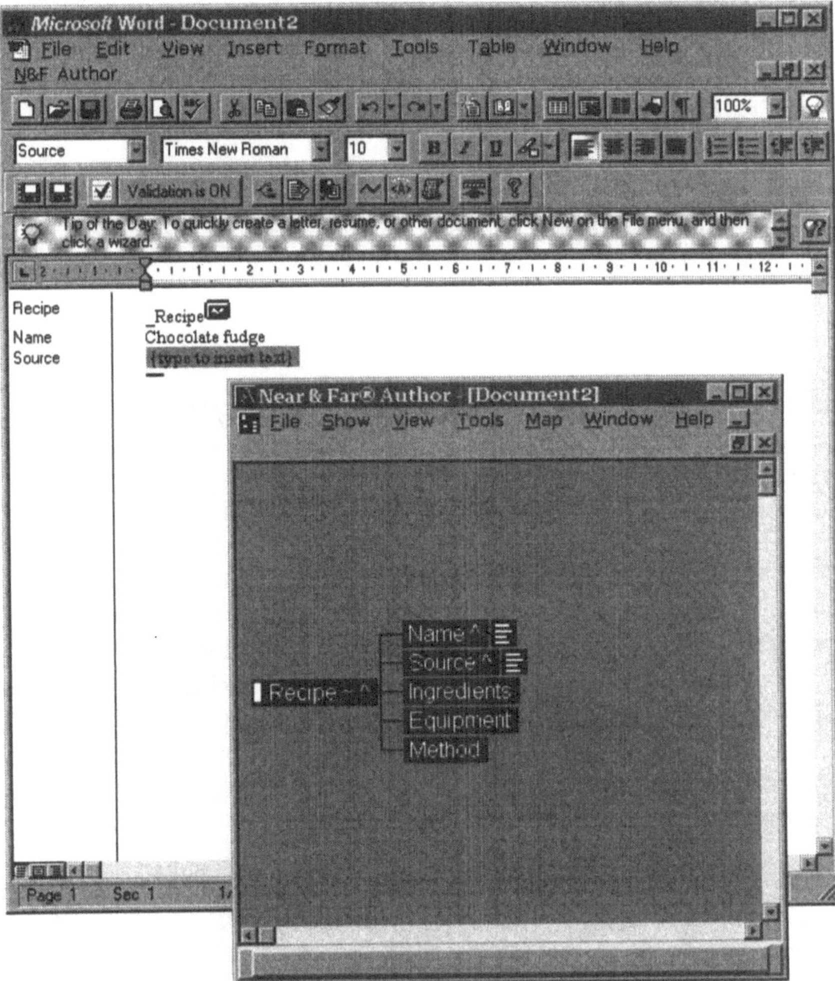

Figure 83. Near&Far Author for Word creating a new document with the graphical DTD display

3.4.3.2. Setting up a new DTD

NFA comes with a similar set of DTDs to *NFD*, for simple articles, press releases, letters, and memos.

To set it up for a new DTD you create a new sample document and pick the new DTD. *NFA* reads and parses it, and creates a default template. This can be edited to create the mappings between element (and context) and the styles to use in *Word*. The creation of the template generates a lot of 'first-occurrence-in-context' maps, which are useful in some cases (for example, turning off indentation on a paragraph following a list) but tend to clutter the menus and require some careful editing.

Once the styles are established, they can be applied to any file using that DTD. Because the whole of *NFD* is present, users can modify styles themselves if they wish.

3.4.4. SGML Tagger (OUP)

DOS

Oxford University Press, Oxford, England

'Taggers' is a name given to programs which let you add markup to a file without necessarily conducting a formal parse and validation of the entire file. There are also some highly specialist applications from the academic environment, using linguistic tools to identify words which require tagging, which are outside the scope of this book.

The *SGML Tagger* is the commercial version from Oxford University Press of a program originally by Richard Light which can turn a plain DOS character-based editor or word processor into a non-validating SGML editor. It is a memory-resident pop-up facility which you run, and which then sits in the background awaiting your call: a TSR (Terminate and Stay Resident) program in DOS jargon. You then run your DOS editor or word processor, and the *SGML Tagger* can be activated whenever you need SGML. This is a strictly DOS-only program: it will not run under MS-Windows.

As it's not a part of your editor, it doesn't control your editor, so it is restricted to reading the screen and deducing your whereabouts in the DTD tree, based on the markup it can 'see' on the screen, which it does pretty well. At the start of a document, it can read the DocType Declaration, so it knows where it is; however, if you are in the middle of a long paragraph such that no markup is actually displayed on the screen, it has a harder time guessing.

Because of this, it provides no guarantee that the text you are creating is fully conformant, so it sensibly comes with a copy of a parser (*sgmls*), and the manual recommends you validate your file after each edit session.

3.4.4.1. Setup

The installation is typical of DOS programs, using `install.bat` from the single floppy disk. This creates a directory `c:\tagger` containing the executable, some overlays, and a copy of `taggerrd.exe` which also forms part of the same author's *NormDTD* (see section 2.6.6). A sample

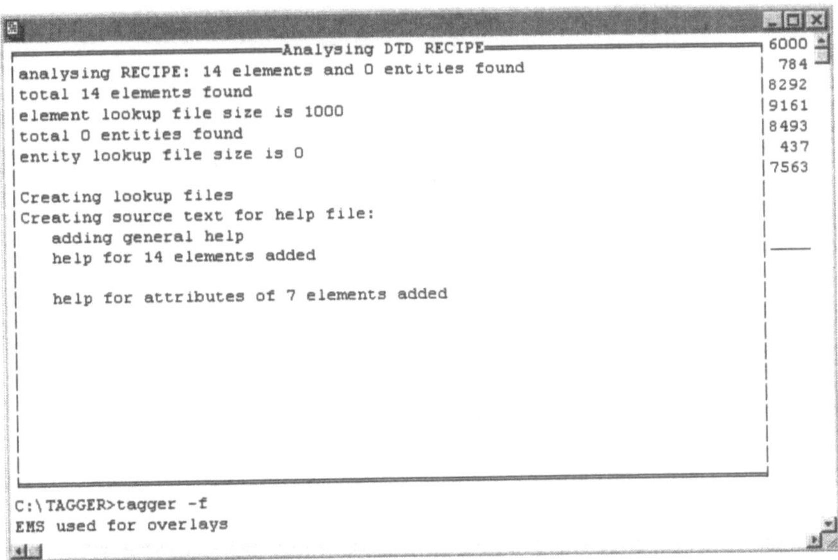
Analysing DTD RECIPE
analysing RECIPE: 14 elements and 0 entities found
total 14 elements found
element lookup file size is 1000
total 0 entities found
entity lookup file size is 0
Creating lookup files
Creating source text for help file:
adding general help
help for 14 elements added
help for attributes of 7 elements added
6000
784
8292
9161
8493
437
7563
C:\TAGGER>tagger -f
EMS used for overlays

Figure 84. Loading a DTD in the SGML Tagger

DTD for letters is included (see section 2.3.1.2.2) to test the installation with. If you want to run the program outside the `c:\tagger` directory, you need to configure it into your path and add an environment variable.

Because the *SGML Tagger* is a TSR, you must run it and load the DTD you want *before* running your DOS editor. After the splash screen, you press **Enter** and a pattern for your DTD filenames appears, suggesting `*.dtd`. Pressing **Enter** again lists all the files in the current directory with the given pattern, and you can pick the one you want with the arrow keys. A third **Enter** parses the selected DTD and saves the compiled image to disk for reuse. The first time you use it with a new (or modified) DTD, it parses and saves it, but doesn't load the tagging code into memory. Run the DTD through a second time to do this.

Now the program terminates but stays resident in memory, and you can run whatever DOS editor you use. The big restriction is memory: the *SGML Tagger* uses conventional DOS memory, and it doesn't appear to be possible to load it into high memory, so available memory for a word processor is limited to around 400Kb. This effectively prevents some big old word processors from running at all (*Nota Bene*, for example, and *PC-Write* 4.15, although *PC-Write* 4.0 or earlier works fine). The manual offers a service to registered users to make it work with any commercially available text editor that fits in this space.

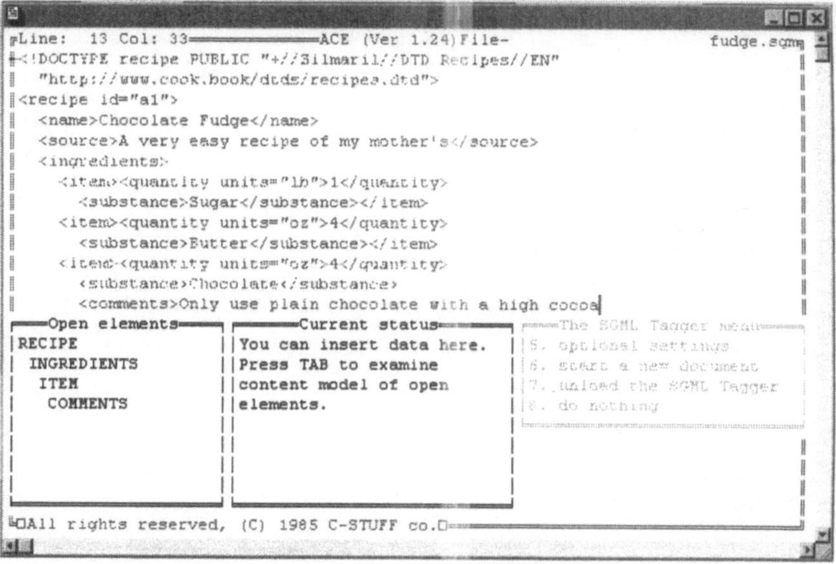

Figure 85. Editing in the SGML Tagger

3.4.4.2. Operation

With a file open in your editor or word processor you hit **Ctrl-Space** and the *SGML Tagger* wakes up and parses what is on the screen. If it's a new, empty file, it will suggest the root element of the DTD, and if you confirm this, it will insert the DocType Declaration, and open the root element, leaving the cursor inside it.

Subsequent presses of **Ctrl-Space** cause the same action, and each time, the menu of available elements is displayed, based on the cursor location, exactly as with a graphical editor, but without the graphics. If the only permitted content is character data, it says so, and it warns against text in empty elements.

The choice of **Ctrl-Space** is obviously to avoid conflicts with editor or word processor keystrokes: clearly it's going to conflict with some of them, so it's possible to make the hot key configurable, but not to Function keys or arrows.

You can get help on SGML by pressing the **F1** key, and you can build your own help text into DTDs so that the user can get customized help: insert a comment immediately before the closing '>' character in an element declaration:

```
<!element note - - (title?,(para|list)+)
  --Use this for notes other than footnotes-->
```

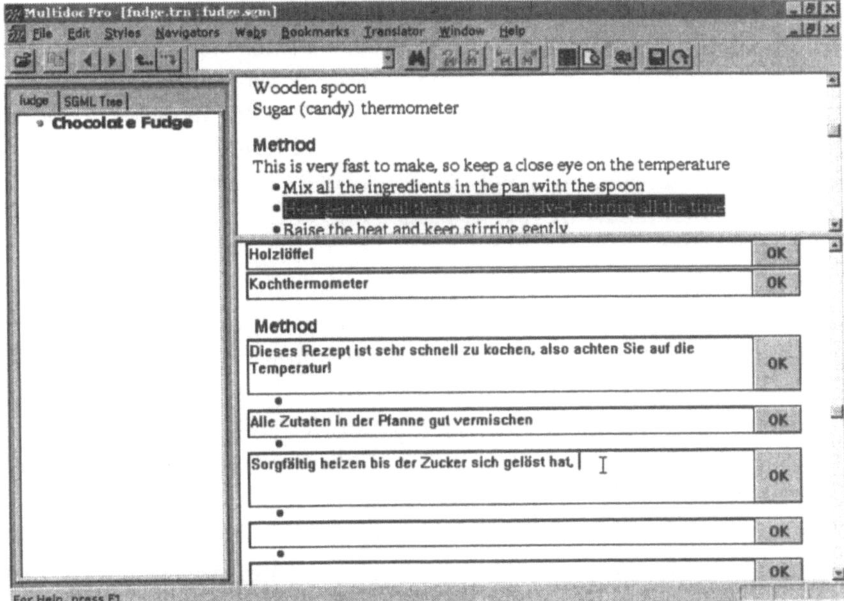

Figure 86. MultiDoc Pro Translating Editor in mid-translation

and it gets recorded when the DTD is compiled, and popped up as online help with the element wherever it is valid. There are additional data-entry panels for attributes and character entities.

3.4.5. The MultiDoc Translating Editor (Citec)

MS-Windows
`http://www.citec.fi/`

The *MultiDoc Pro* browser (see section 6.2.4) forms the basis for this program which is designed to let translators produce versions of an SGML file in another language while maintaining strict control over the file structure. Keeping an identical element structure means better control over the quality and accuracy of the translation, and also allows indexing or hypertext linking systems to refer to the same `ID`/`IDREF` values and even to the same ancestor, child, or sibling elements (see section 2.4.2 for details of how this kind of linking works in XML).

The *Translating Editor* installs from CD-ROM in the usual MS-Windows manner, and requires a licence key to activate it. The core of the program is the same as *MultiDoc Pro*, and it will display an SGML file in the same way, using the same (Synex/Inso) stylesheet and navigator files, and even connect to the Web the same way.

To set up a new translation, you specify which elements will need translation, which ones *may* need it, and which ones must not be translated. This lets you retain the source language for things like copyright statements, actual quotations in a third language which you may or may not want retained, and (in the technical field) objects like examples of computer output which must be kept untouched. The system then creates a translation (`.trn`) target file, containing an almost exact copy of the source file, ready for translation.

The text screen splits in two, with the master copy at the top and a series of edit boxes at the bottom, corresponding exactly to the element structure of the master document (see Figure 86). The translator can select any of these by clicking in it, and the source element is highlighted for reference. All the normal Windows edit facilities can be used, and as you move from box to box, the scrolling of the master copy is synchronized.

You can save and leave the translation at any time and come back to it, and you can preview the result, which displays the master and the translation side by side, using the same stylesheet.

There are a few restrictions on the content of the SGML files you can use: because it parses and validates the master file, it resolves things like entity references and marked sections, so the 'duplicate' created to hold the translation would not represent them: you need to work from a 'sanitized' copy of your source document if it uses these features.

3.4.6. The Euromath editor

Unix/X (Sun)
`http://www.dcs.fmph.uniba.sk/~emt`

The editing of math for SGML has been a thorny problem for many years, as the discussion of DTDs for math (section 2.3.8) has shown. Part of the problem is the very popular use of TeX and LaTeX by mathematicians, as it provides a robust method of automatically formatting math correctly. Until recently this has therefore meant less interest in other systems (such as SGML) than would otherwise have been expected.

The abortive attempt at math in HTML3 highlighted both the need for math on the Web and also the mainstream vendors' judgment that mathematics was not a market worth serving. Conversion was one option, using systems such as *LaTeXtoHTML*; another was to use plugins like IBM's *Techexplorer*. In the meantime, the Euromath project of the

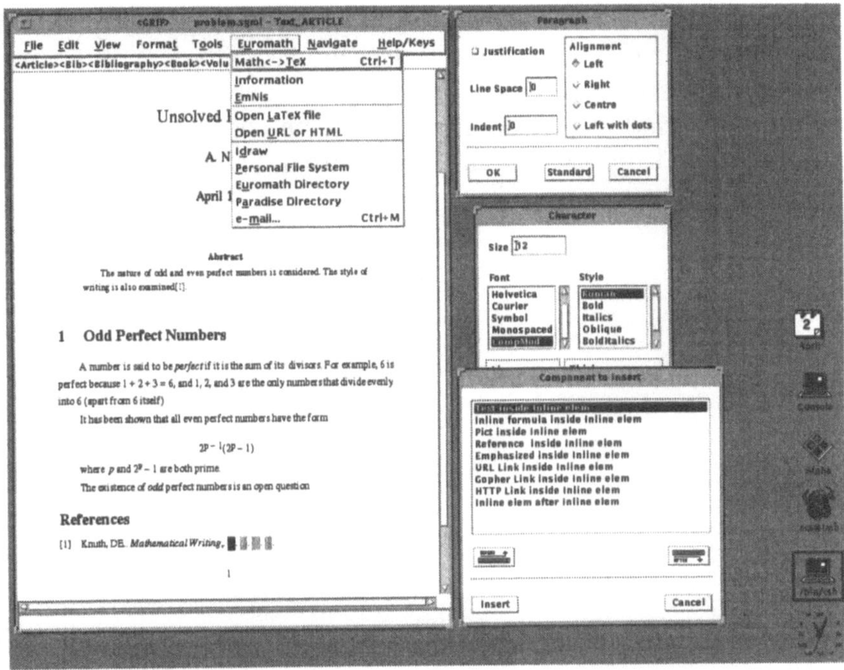

Figure 87. The Euromath editor (*GriF*)

European Commission was defining the editing problem and providing a solution, at least to markup and editing, if not to Web delivery.

The current version of the Euromath system includes the editor and DTDs, a LaTeX translator, new math fonts, an email service with X.500 directory support, online help, and support for computer algebra systems. It is only available for Unix with the X Window system. Installation is straightforward, from downloaded *tar* files, and well documented in the manual. A license key is required to enable use of the editor, and this uses a license server program to manage multiple users.

The editor is actually a modified version of GriF's *SGML Editor* (see section 3.3.3), but with additions to the menus to handle TeX conversion. Opening a new file involves just typing a name: there are several DTD fragments provided for embedding elsewhere, but the main document type is preformatted for a mathematical journal article (see section 2.3.8.2).

The edit screen presents the typical GriF view of shaded areas where data entry is required, making it very simple to type in the title, author, date, abstract, and section heading in the conventional manner for a research article.

The element insertion menu leaves a floating window open which always shows the elements valid at the cursor. Math data entry can be either in highly structured form, using the element markup directly, or by typing TEX math code and clicking on the conversion menu item, which converts from TEX to the Euromath DTD and back (see Figure 87).

4. Parsing and validating

CHECKER — Officer entrusted with seeing to it that one or a group of citizens remains loyal to the State. Checker's responsibility includes the actions, attitudes, and well-being of his charges.

Larry Niven, *The Integral Trees* and *The Smoke Ring*

This dog don't parse.

Lapel button from the SGML University

- The need for parsing
- Using a built-in parser
- What to do with parser output
- Using a stand-alone parser

Almost all SGML software comes with a ***parser*** which is used to prove the structure of a file against the specifications in the DTD. This test is called 'validation', but it is also often called just 'parsing', although strictly speaking that is just the act of identifying and describing the component parts of a grammatical structure, without trying to say if they are meaningful or not. A ***validating SGML parser*** is one which can detect and report on errors in the document syntax or structure when compared with the DTD and SGML Declaration. XML parsing and validation is similar but simpler, and can also handle DTD-less operation.

Validation by parsing is necessary as the only secure way of maintaining the integrity of a document between applications and platforms. ISO 8879 mandates a number of requirements for a system claiming to be a validating parser (§15.4): it must find and report errors which are classified in the standard as 'reportable', and it mustn't report errors when there aren't any; it can report other errors or potential errors if it wishes; it must identify error messages separately from other output;

and it must give enough detail to let you find and correct the errors. The XML Specification carries a similar mandate (see section 4.3.7).

The first commercial parser program for SGML was *Mark-It!* in 1986–87 (see section 4.3.3), and the first public domain one was Jos Warmer's *Amsterdam SGML Parser* (*ASP* for short: still available, but regarded as obsolete). Others soon followed, and are discussed below in their own sections, the most notable being *ARC-SGML* by Charles Goldfarb, *sgmls* by James Clark and the *YASP* toolkit by Pierre Richard and others. These have been supplemented by a third-generation suite of programs, also from James Clark, called *SP*, of which the parser itself is called *nsgmls* (the package also includes a normalizer and a markup stream editor: see section 4.3.5).

A validating parser can be used on its own to check the validity of the SGML markup in a single file or group of files in isolation, but almost all SGML applications such as editors, formatters, browsers, or databases have a parser built in or closely bound to them, sometimes based on the source code of one of the above programs.

Validating an SGML instance is much more than just parsing, therefore, and includes checking all element and entity names to see that they appear in the DTD; testing them against their 'place' in the document structure; checking all the `IDREF`s against `ID`s to see that they match up; expanding all entity and other references; checking marked sections; and a host of other tasks related to the integrity of the document instance. The objective is to guarantee that the file conforms strictly to the rules of ISO 8879, so that it can be passed between SGML systems in the knowledge that the markup, and thus the structure, conforms to the DTD. Parsing and validation say nothing at all about the data content of the file: only a human can check that and say if it makes sense or not, although there have been several proposals for the identification of data content so that an SGML or XML application can carry out its own checks[35].

SGML systems vary in their approach to parsing and validation: some perform a constant check on everything the user does, all the time, keystroke by keystroke; others allow the temporary input of anything, and keep validation as a separate task which you can initiate by clicking a button or typing a command; yet others are designed so that it is impossible even to see the existence of anything other than what is strictly required or permitted.

In most cases the parser is invisible, in the sense that it snaps into action the moment you do something like import a file, move something around, or try to insert a new element, and it checks that what you are doing fits within the structure laid down in the DTD you are using. In editors, this technique is referred to by various names, including 'interactive parsing', 'inline parsing', and 'constant parsing', but it usually only invokes a syntax check in the immediate context, rather than a full validation of the whole file every time. The effect of an error varies, but it usually means a beep or an error message if you try to do something which is not meaningful, like insert a chapter heading in the middle of a paragraph. To avoid allowing the insertion of partially-valid markup, editors can usually be configured to insert any elements that are required within a new element (such as the first <ITEM> in a <LIST>, for example), and to prompt for compulsory attribute values. Details of how to interpret and react to parser/validator error messages are in section 4.2.1.

The most crucial aspect of all full SGML parsers, though, no matter whether they are standalone or attached to another system, is that they all need access to the SGML Declaration, the DTD (and all its entity files) as well as your instance. XML parsers have different but allied requirements: DTD-less instances may refer to external entities, and those with a DTD may use FPIs as well as SIs, so an application may choose between using a local catalog or going out onto the Internet to locate the URLs.

This is where it starts to be come obvious why using an OASIS catalog file is A Good Idea — you can maintain one catalog, referencing all the files you ever encounter using SGML, and all your applications can share it: all you have to do is add new document type FPIs as and when you use them. If you only ever use one document type, it may not be a problem to use half a dozen applications, each with its own private catalog file format. But when you typically use more than two or three DTDs, especially when some DTDs are spread over multiple files, you need to keep them all synchronized carefully. If you are planning on anything other than trivial use of SGML, I suggest that keeping an accurate and up-to-date catalog will save considerable amounts of time in all your SGML activity.

4.1. Using a built-in parser

Editors and other interactive file-creation programs for SGML and XML usually check what you type as you type it. Attempting to type text into an EMPTY element, for example, will cause a beep or error display, as will trying to insert text or an element in a place where it can't be used. The built-in parser keeps track of where you are in the structure of the document instance, so it knows what elements are valid at any given point (and in the case of DTD-less XML, allows you to create new element types).

There is little that can be said about the physical operation of built-in parsers. Mostly you click the **Validate** button or menu item (or type the command) to validate the whole of a file. In an editor you can often also highlight a region of the file (usually restricted to whole elements, like an entire section, or paragraph, or list) and validate just that, rather than all of the document. The result will either be success (the document or region is valid) or it will give you a list of one or more errors. Some means of navigation is provided to let you position the cursor at the point where the next error occurred, so you can fix it. Reading the error message is only part of the solution: recognizing what went wrong and knowing how to fix it is a common problem: examples of frequent errors and how to approach them are in section 4.2.1.

Validation also takes place when you import (and sometimes export) an SGML instance. In these cases it is more like stand-alone parsing, except that applications will again usually position the cursor at the relevant place (or as close as possible) when an error is found. Systems like databases or indexers which do not use an editor display all the time may have to run an external editor to do this. On finding an error, the import or export process usually stops, as conformant systems will not go further until the error is resolved and the process restarted from the beginning, in order to avoid importing/exporting invalid or corrupt data. You should be able to override or ignore this restriction in order to let you use an external (plaintext) editing system to fix errors before reprocessing the file.

This behavior highlights the major difference between SGML-conformant systems and the general run of World Wide Web (HTML) browsers and editors. The latter usually plow on regardless, absorbing or ignoring faulty markup, illegal characters, and unknown elements and attributes, and coping as best they can. Their primary task is seen as being to display the text, whether the HTML markup is valid or not (and perhaps 95–98% is invalid). The result is that many browsers are unable to take full advantage of SGML (although the move from HTML to XML should alleviate this position considerably, see section 4.3.7), but the main problem is that they all 'cope' differently and incompatibly.

4.2. Interpreting and reusing parser output

Parsers produce two kinds of output: errors and the data stream. You can usually turn off the data stream (the -s option in *nsgmls*, for example), but you cannot turn off the errors.

In a large number of cases, the error messages let you know exactly what's wrong, and it can then be fixed. Even if it is tedious and time-consuming to do so, it does at least mean you end up with a valid file. A few of the errors can sometimes be difficult to locate, or even difficult to understand why they are classed as errors in the first place (for example the infamous 'pernicious mixed content' error: see section 2.2.1.6).

4.2.1. Understanding parser errors

The error messages from parsers represent the state of the document *from the parser's point of view*, not yours. Frequently, you will know the textual context of the error location because you are familiar with the document (maybe you wrote it): but the parser only knows the location with respect to the markup. Bearing this in mind can sometimes make it much easier to see what is wrong. The errors identified by validating parsers fall into four groups (from the user's perspective: this is slightly different from the formal list in ISO 8879 at §9.3):

- errors in specifying or locating external files, either via System Identifiers or Public Identifiers;
- errors in the SGML Declaration;
- errors in the DTD;
- errors in the document instance.

As an SGML user, you may or may not have edit control over the SGML Declaration, the DTD, or the instance, depending on the nature of your work, who 'owns' the DTD, and who has authority to make changes. If you are using a well-tried industry or research DTD that thousands of others use, it's unlikely that you'll hit errors in the DTD or SGML Declaration: if you're developing your own system, or adapting someone else's, then such errors may occur.

Errors in resolving FPIs Errors such as these:

```
cannot generate system identifier for public text
cannot open file "finance.dtd"
cannot resolve entity "%mydtdmods;"
```

are usually due to one or more of the following:

- the FPI simply isn't in the catalog;
- typing mistakes in the DocType Declaration or the catalog (check, check, check again);
- accidental deletion of the file from disk (or moving it elsewhere and failing to update the catalog).

Check the spelling and punctuation first, both in the instance and the catalog. Then check the file exists on disk in the place the catalog (or System Identifier) says it does. Then check the spelling again.

Errors in the SGML Declaration A very common class of error with a DTD (and its SGML Declaration) that you haven't used before involves the values of some of the capacities specified in the SGML Declaration. Errors like `Value of NAMELEN is too low (8)` refer to the default maximum permitted length of the value, which (in this particular case) means the length of names of elements. If the DTD declares something like `<PARAGRAPH>`, that's nine letters, so `NAMELEN` needs increasing to 9 in the SGML Declaration.

If the DTD declares a very large number of attributes, you may get similar complaints about `ATTCNT` being too low. Again, it's easy to fix: just edit the SGML Declaration file and increase or decrease the value given; but in all events it may be worth reporting the change to the DTD authors in case there are reasons for the values being set as they were.

For some strange reason, a few otherwise compliant SGML systems require settings for these values which can vary dramatically. As quoted elsewhere, the parser with the old*PAT* retrieval system required `NAMELEN` to be over 80 (!), and it required `TAGLVL` (the depth of nesting) to be over 1000.

None of this should apply to XML, where there is no limit on quantities and capacities.

Errors in the DTD The most common errors in DTDs appear to be (from personal experience):

- syntax, punctuation, or spelling (missing brackets, missing or duplicated model group connectors, wrongly-nested brackets, mis-typed element names, *etc*);
- ambiguous content models: when an element can occur in two or more different content model groups, depending on usage, its must be in such a way that it would never be ambiguous when parsing, as to which of the content model groups was being represented;

- inclusion and exclusion exceptions which affect whether or not an element is permitted or required;
- accidental multiple `ATTLIST`s: this is permitted under the Web-SGML Adaptations to SGML (see section 2.7) but not in the original standard;
- elements being defined twice, or not at all: it is *not* an error for an element to be *referred to* but never defined, so long as it never gets *used* in the instance (see section 3.3.2.3); it *is* an error to use elements without declaring them, except when using XML in DTD-less mode.

In all these cases, it is usually a simple edit to fix the problem. If it goes deeper than that, then it may be a case for redesign.

Errors in the instance This is the most common class of error, especially when the instance has been created by hand in a non-SGML system or translated by a non-conforming processor. Mistranslation and simple human error are possibly responsible for the majority of non-SGML character errors.

If you (or the document author) have used a regular SGML editor the document should already be valid, but editing systems sometimes permit 'slightly' invalid markup, such as when a document section must contain a heading followed by one of (say) a paragraph, a list, a table, or a subsection, but the editor does not enforce the entry of any of the subsequent elements at the point where the section is created, because it has first to deal with the insertion of the section heading.

Common errors are:

- elements wrongly-placed, mis-spelled or just plain missing when they are compulsory;
- missing or unmatched quotes round attribute values;
- wrongly-matched or overlapping start- and end-tags;
- leaving out tags which are OK to leave out in some cases but not others: it's an error to omit them if they then cause an ambiguity in the content model; and in XML they simply can't ever be left out at all;
- missing initial values for `CURRENT` attributes (TEI's `<DIV1>`, `<DIV1>`, *etc* are prime candidates for this);
- unmatched `ID`/`IDREF` values, common in complex documents;
- unresolved entity references;
- running foul of 'pernicious mixed content': see section 2.2.1.6.

```
% nsgmls -s sgmlbook.sgml
/usr/local/bin/nsgmls:sgmlbook.sgm:7519:9:X: reference to
 non-existent ID "SGMLREV"
/usr/local/bin/nsgmls:sgmlbook.sgm:7508:15:X: reference to
 non-existent ID "PAT"
/usr/local/bin/nsgmls:sgmlbook.sgm:7113:15:X: reference to
 non-existent ID "UNIX"
/usr/local/bin/nsgmls:sgmlbook.sgm:5707:15:X: reference to
 non-existent ID "RCS"
/usr/local/bin/nsgmls:sgmlbook.sgm:7272:30:X: reference to
 non-existent ID "SMPOOX"
SGML validation finished at Wed Dec 31 22:50:48
```

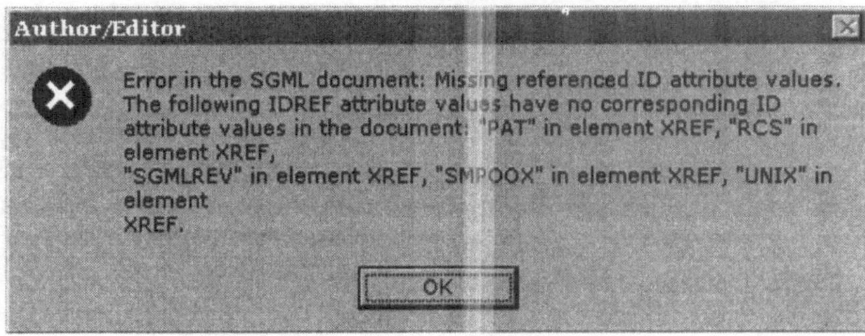

Figure 88. Unresolved ID/IDREF values detected with *nsgmls* (using *Emacs/psgml*) and with *Author/Editor*

Most error displays in graphical systems are clear (graphically if not logically) on what is wrong and where to fix it. However, if you hit a validation error in a system using a graphical interface that does not let you see exactly what is wrong, and it's not obvious from the error message what needs fixing, you may find it easier to export the instance to an external plaintext file and run one of the standalone parsers, edit the file, and import it back into the graphical application.

The error message texts try hard to be self-explanatory, often in the nature of 'you can't do this here' where you've made a mistake, or 'missing a required value' where something has been left out, but they do assume (they have to assume) that you know something about SGML markup and your document. In the example in Figure 88 you can see the results in two editors of validating a file containing five broken `ID`/`IDREF` cross-references: I had referred five times to sections or subsections that I hadn't written yet, giving them names I hadn't yet used, so the parser rightly objected to this. It may also be instructive to note that the free parser (*nsgmls*, used from inside a free editor, *Emacs/psgml*) provided me with more information about the location of the errors than did the commercial product.

Some of the more abstruse errors, however, result in messages from parsers which can sometimes be less than helpful, especially to the beginner. There are two reasons for this:

1. because of the necessity for strict conformance to the rules of SGML, the error messages are worded to describe things *from the point of view of the parser, not the reader*;
2. although validating parsers will sometimes give the line number or screen location where the error was *detected*, this may not be the place where the error was *caused*.

Parsers do try to make it obvious what you have done when such an error occurs, but a working knowledge of the DTD is a necessity. 'Hard' errors like wrongly-placed elements, missing markup, unknown element names, or cross-nested tags may cause the validator to halt and describe the error, and refuse to go any further until it's fixed. 'Soft' errors like unmatched IDs and IDREFs may be stored up and displayed in a group after validation of element markup has been completed. Where an application has the ability to hide or display markup at the user's request, it is always a good idea to have the markup on display during validation so that it is more obvious where an error has occurred.

4.2.1.1. Normalization

Ambiguity in parser errors becomes particularly evident when elements are defined with optional end-tags or mixed content, and even more so when the author has used minimization, because the markup can become ambiguous when hand-edited, and it may not then be possible to identify precisely *which* apparently still open element is in error.

If you have to deal with instances created or edited in a non-SGML system, bear in mind that an error may have occurred many screens before the place where the parser detected it. The following fragment has a missing end-tag: it's not an error in the minimized version:

```
<DIV2 N="U432.1" TYPE=entry><P><FRN LANG=LA><PS><FN
TYPE=saint>Patricius</></> peruenit ad <PN
TYPE=country>Hiberniam</> <NUM VALUE="9">nono</> anno regni
<PS><FN>Teodosii Minoris</></>, primo anno <TERM
TYPE=episcopate>episcopatus</> <PS><FN>Xisti</></> <NUM
VALUE="42">xl.ii.</> <TERM TYPE=bishop>episcopi</> Romane
&Eogon;clesie. Sic enumerant <PS><FN TYPE=saint>Beda</></>
&ampersir;<PS><FN>Marcillinus</></> &ampersir;
<PS><FN>Issiodorus</></> in Cronicis suis.</></>
```

It's certainly not clear if you were to look at a formatted version of the file , because much of the markup (here TEI) does not have a visual instantiation:

> 432.1] Patricius peruenit ad Hiberniam nono anno regni Teodosii Minoris, primo anno episcopatus Xisti xl.ii. episcopi Romane Eclesie. Sic enumerant Beda ⁊ Marcillinus ⁊ Issiodorus in Cronicis suis.

But it *is* an error if the markup is normalized:

```
<div2 n="U432.1" type="entry"><p><frn lang="LA"><ps><fn
type="saint">Patricius</fn></ps> peruenit ad <pn
type="country">Hiberniam</pn> <num value="9">nono</num> anno regni
<ps><fn>Teodosii Minoris</fn></ps>, primo anno <term
type="episcopate">episcopatus</term> <ps><fn>Xisti</fn></ps> <num
value="42">xl.ii.</num> <term type="bishop">episcopi</term> Romane
&Eogon;clesie. Sic enumerant <ps><fn type="saint">Beda</fn></ps>
&ampersir; <ps><fn>Marcillinus</fn></ps> &ampersir;
<ps><fn>Issiodorus</fn></ps> in Cronicis suis.</p></div2>
```

If you are confronted with an instance which uses extensive minimization, it may seem like a good idea to try to ***normalize*** it first, so you can see where you are. Unfortunately, normalization can only be done on fully valid instances, so validation has to come first. (It is possible to use *Emacs psgml* to normalize without a formal validation, as its internal parser usually catches enough of the errors to allow you to fix those and then normalize the file (`M-x sgml-normalize`) before conducting the validation.) In the case above, validation gives the clue, when normalized:

```
nsgmls:G100001.sgml:506:6:E: end tag for "FRN" omitted, but its
declaration does not permit this
nsgmls:G100001.sgml:500:31: start tag was here
```

In case you're curious, it's the missing `</frn>` which causes the problem: but when the markup is minimized, the first `</>` is taken as the `</frn>`, and because the paragraph element is declared with minimizable end-tags in the TEI, its end-tag is elided, and the second `</>` is taken as the required `</div2>`. This is the kind of reason why you need to know the DTD in order to understand why some classes of error occur.

Once you have a valid instance, you can use *SP's sgmlnorm* or similar to normalize it for future use. While it is permissible, and perfectly valid, to keep minimized instances, I feel it is safer in an interchange environment to use fully normalized instances except where special circumstances dictate (such as massive tabular work, where there is so much more markup than data that it becomes almost impossible to hand-edit, or cases where disk space is critically tight). One way to improve matters is to check the SGML Declaration to see if `OMITTAG` is set to `NO`, and if not, make it so. Then parse, validate, and normalize...and if the Declaration is not yours, edit it again and set `OMITTAG` back to YES. Fortunately, almost all modern editors automatically include all end-tags when saving or exporting files, so the problem arises only when a file has explicitly been minimized, or it it has been created in a non-parsing environment.

4.2.2. ESIS (Element Structure Information Set)

Successful parsing with most standalone parsers produces a lengthy default output stream. In the case of *sgmls* and *nsgmls*, for example, this shows every element instance preceded by *all* its attributes fully normalized, each on its own line, and the element data content printed on a line by itself (see the example below).

Each element or attribute name printed in the output is prefixed by a special character as the first character on the line, and the data content is prefixed by a minus sign (hyphen), so a subsequent process can easily identify which lines are which.

This format is *[n]sgmls*'s text representation of the ESIS (Element Structure Information Set), which we will come across again in later sections. The ESIS is a set of information intended for use by 'structure-controlled' applications (such as most SGML software): it describes the location and boundaries of elements, attributes and their values, *etc.*

ESIS was defined in RAST (Reference Application for SGML Testing), ISO 13673 as a standard for testing the equivalence of two parsed streams (*ie* the output of two parsers run on the same file), so it omits a few things which are essential for other uses, notably the identity of EMPTY elements andID/IDREF attributes. Nevertheless, it forms the basis for many other SGML systems because it identifies the features that an application can use for navigation, editing, transformation, or formatting: the text format as output by parsers like *nsgmls* is very easily reusable.

For an example, take this little HTML file:

```
<!DOCTYPE HTML PUBLIC "-//IETF//DTD HTML 2.0//EN">
<html>
  <head>
    <title>About me</title>
  </head>
  <body><p>See my <a href="/index.html">personal Web page</a> for
details.</p></body>
</html>
```

and use the command nsgmls me.html to pass it through *nsgmls*. The ESIS representation will be as follows (HTML 2.0 was chosen for the example because of its relatively low complexity):

```
AVERSION CDATA -//IETF//DTD HTML 2.0//EN
```

```
ASDAFORM CDATA Book
(HTML
(HEAD
ASDAFORM CDATA Ti
(TITLE
-About me
)TITLE
)HEAD
(BODY
ASDAFORM CDATA Para
(P
-See my
AHREF CDATA /index.html
ANAME IMPLIED
AREL IMPLIED
AREV IMPLIED
AURN IMPLIED
ATITLE IMPLIED
AMETHODS IMPLIED
ASDAPREF CDATA <Anchor: #AttList>
(A
-personal Web page
)A
- for\ndetails.
)P
)BODY
)HTML
```

Each element start-tag is represented by an open parenthesis and the element name, and each end-tag is shown the same way but with a closing parenthesis. Attribute names *precede* their element and are prefixed by a capital A. Text (character data) content is regarded as a pseudo-element and also kept to a line by itself and prefixed with a minus sign. Linebreaks within character data are symbolized by the Unix convention of `\n`.

This makes it very simple to handle with any of the standard Unix tools, or with multiplatform scripting languages like *Perl* or *Python* (see section 5.1 for all these). For example, to print the text data only (in effect performing a parsed, validated strip of the markup), you could use the *awk* command:

```
nsgmls me.html | awk '/^-/ {print substr($0,2)}'
```

You can refer to section 5.1.1.3 for the syntax, but put simply, this is picking only the lines which start with a minus sign, and printing everything from the second character onwards in those lines.

With a sufficiently powerful pattern-matcher and some reformatting capability (*Perl* and *Python* are obvious candidates) it is possible to perform a huge amount of processing on output formats like ESIS, saving you having to write your own parser. *Perl* in any event now incorporates an XML parser of its own.

ESIS is being replaced for XML use by a standard conceived by James Clark, called ‘Canonical XML’, based on the fact that every well-formed XML document has a unique structurally equivalent canonical XML document. As with RAST, this makes it possible to compare two outputs: two structurally equivalent XML documents have a byte-for-byte identical canonical XML document.

James Clark has in effect reduced the grammar of XML to the following canonical format (from `http://www.jclark.com/xml/canonxml.html`):

<table>
<tr><th>Production</th><th>Grammar</th></tr>
<tr><td>CanonXML</td><td>::= Pi* element Pi*</td></tr>
<tr><td>element</td><td>::= Stag (Datachar | Pi | element)* Etag</td></tr>
<tr><td>Stag</td><td>::= '<' Name Atts '>'</td></tr>
<tr><td>Etag</td><td>::= '</' Name '>'</td></tr>
<tr><td>Pi</td><td>::= '<?' Name ' ' (((Char - S) Char*)? - (Char* '?>' Char*)) '?>'</td></tr>
<tr><td>Atts</td><td>::= (' ' Name '=' '"' Datachar* '"')*</td></tr>
<tr><td>Datachar</td><td>::= '&' | '<' | '>' | '"' | '	'| '
'| '
' | (Char - ('&' | '<' | '>' | '"' | #x9 | #xA | #xD))</td></tr>
<tr><td>Name</td><td>::= (Letter | '_' | ':') (NameChar)*</td></tr>
<tr><td>Char</td><td>::= #x9 | #xA | #xD | [#x20-#xD7FF] | [#xE000-#xFFFD] | [#x10000-#x10FFFF]</td></tr>
<tr><td>S</td><td>::= (#x20 | #x9 | #xD | #xA)+</td></tr>
<tr><td>NameChar</td><td>::= Letter | Digit | '.' | '-' | '_' | ':' | CombiningChar | Extender</td></tr>
</table>

`Letter`, `Digit`, `CombiningChar`, and `Extender` are defined in detail in Appendix B of the XML Specification (see copy on CD-ROM or at `http://www.w3.org/TR/REC-xml`). `Char` is any Unicode character, excluding the surrogate blocks, `FFFE`, and `FFFF`. Attributes are in lexicographical order (in Unicode bit order). A canonical XML document is encoded in UTF–8. Ignorable white space is considered significant and is treated equivalently to data.

4.3. Stand-alone parsing

The simple existence of a file on disk, or sent to you through email, or downloaded from a network server, claiming to be SGML, is in itself no guarantee of validity. Even if you use software with a built-in parser, and while you may know on some occasions from external sources that the file *is* valid, and therefore needs no further checking, there are many occasions when you may want to validate the file without having to open a (possibly large) application, or use some parser output (see section 4.2.2).

Stand-alone parsers are usually plain executable programs which just check the file and don't do anything else with it. They normally run from the command line of a DOS, Unix, or VMS task and are therefore especially useful when handling large numbers of files in sequence, because a script or batch file (command file) can be set up to process a list of filenames. They are also useful for files which are very large and won't load easily into a graphical display application like an editor.

There are now also several MS-Windows interfaces to the *nsgmls* parser, so that SGML files can be parsed by drag-and-drop, for those users who are unfamiliar or uncomfortable with using DOS commands (see Figure 89).

One of the the reasons for using a stand-alone parser, particularly *Mark-It!*, *sgmls*, or *nsgmls*, is that a special format of output can be passed into other programs or stored in another file for reprocessing. In the case of the latter two, this output data is an ESIS format described in section 4.2.2, which is designed so that you can construct your own applications as simple shell scripts under Unix (batch files under DOS, or command files under VMS), without having to write or embed your own parser. The ESIS output from *nsgmls*, for example, is a stream of parsed text, with markup flagged using special characters in the first position on each line (so that subsequent processors can identify it), and the parsed character data (your text) on separate lines. This makes it easy to link together a variety of subsequent utilities so as to arrange the output in the desired manner, especially under Unix where such programs are easy to connect together (see the examples in section 5.1.1).

Almost all the current parsers now support XML as well as standard SGML. In addition to the common ones presented here, parsers are also being embedded in browsers and other XML products, and often the parser is in fact one of these very systems. Microsoft's *Internet Explorer* has in fact had two XML parsers built into it from version 4.0 onwards, although use of them is experimental and undocumented, and intended for the programmer, not the user. Netscape's *Navigator* v.5 uses James Clark's *expat* parser (the same as embedded in *Perl*: see section 4.3.7.3).

4.3.1. ARC-SGML (Charles Goldfarb)

ARC-SGML was the first public domain parser, written by Charles Goldfarb, editor of the SGML standard, at IBM's Almaden Research Center (ARC). It formed the basis for *sgmls* (see below), and is no longer in general use.

4.3.2. ASP (Jos Warmer)

DOS, Unix, Mac
`http://www.sil.org/sgml/publicsw.html#asp`

The *Amsterdam SGML Parser* (ASP) by Jos Warmer was another early public domain parser for SGML. It is now mainly of historical interest, but it is still possible to download it from a number of sites on the Internet (see URL for details).

4.3.3. Mark-It! (SEMA Group)

DOS, Unix, Siemens
`http://www.sema.be/sgml-web/products/`

Mark-It! was the first commercial SGML parser, and it has developed into a more general SGML processing system which can be used for data location and conversion tasks, although the core remains the parser. It is available as a standalone program or as an API (Application Programming Interface) to build into your own software. Sema do a 'Limited Edition' of *Mark-It!* which is available for free for MS-Windows (32–bit versions) and Linux systems. A copy is on the CD-ROM.

The standalone parser is a single program with a very large number of command line options to control its action on your files, including stopping and starting output at certain points, stripping markup, importing subdocuments, and many varieties of event tracing. The parser can perform non-SGML functions as well, such as applying Regular Expressions (see section 5.1.1.1) to identify text structures, and there is an application development backend which lets you use the parser output in conversions to other formats.

There is a rather unusual catalog: twin files, one holding the Formal Public Identifiers with all internal white-space removed, the other holding the System Identifiers. In each file there is one entry per line, so you need to ensure that each FPI in one file is matched by the corresponding SI on the same line in the other file: get them out of synch and you're sunk. FPIs are 'minimum literals' in SGML terminology, which (among other restrictions) means that all spaces, TABs and linebreaks are collapsed to single spaces before use: in fact this FPI catalog file strips all white-space completely instead.

The output is in two streams: the parsed token list (SGML Declaration, complete DTD, and instance) and the document text output. The parsed token list comes with error messages enclosed in SGML comments `<!-- like this -->`, which is useful for editing, in that the errors are embedded in the markup and visible right at the point where they were detected.

The `-d` option to remove all markup from the document output is also useful if you want a parsing, validating strip at binary executable speeds, compared with the rather rudimentary versions shown in sections page 290 and page 298.

The *Mark-It!* API is incorporated into a companion product, *Proof-It!*, a simple MS-Windows parser with an edit window to let you edit corrections and [re]parse SGML instances. It has almost the same functionality as *Mark-It!*: a demonstration version is on the CD-ROM with some precompiled DTDs (*DocBook* and HTML3.2). The parser API will also form the basis for a new version of Sema's earlier DOS/Unix editor, *Write-It!*.

4.3.4. sgmls (James Clark)

DOS, Unix, Mac
`http://www.sil.org/sgml/publicsw.html#sgmls`

James Clark's *sgmls* was the mainstay of standalone parsing for many years but has now been replaced by *nsgmls* (see section 4.3.5). I'm including some details here because it is still available, there are many copies of *sgmls* still in daily use, and its operation had a formative effect on a number of other SGML systems. It is still bundled with a number of SGML packages, such as the *SGML Tagger* and *LinuxDoc* (*SGML-Tools*).

Sgmls is free, and comes as a precompiled single binary executable or as source code for you to compile yourself. It is a command-line program and uses the standard Unix format of control arguments (minus sign

Sgmls and the hunt for entity resolution

As a way of providing several methods for *sgmls* to identify and locate the file referred to by Formal Public Identifiers and System Identifiers, you can use the SGML_PATH environment variable (you have to double all % signs when typing this when using DOS):

```
c:\usr\local\lib\sgml\%O\%C\%T:%S:%N.dtd
```

This setting provides three ways for *sgmls* to resolve the identifier, which are tried in sequence:

1. by splitting the Formal Public Identifier into Public Owner, Class, and Text (%O, %C, %T) and using those strings in the directory format specified to locate the file;
2. by using the System Identifier (%S) if any.
3. by using the Document Type name (%N) with `.dtd` added to the end.

Thus for the DocType Declaration

```
<!DOCTYPE report PUBLIC "-//Corporate//DTD Re-
port//EN" "rep.dtd">
```

sgmls would look for:

1. `c:\usr\local\lib\sgml\Corporate\DTD\Report` (the 'Corporate' replaces the %O, the 'DTD' the %C, and the 'Report' then %T;
2. if that failed, it would look for `rep.dtd` in the instance directory;
3. if that failed, it would look for `report.dtd` in the instance directory.

and letters). The program is robust and very fast, and formed the parser core of many commercial products until replaced by *nsgmls*.

To run the program, just type `sgmls` followed by your filename. The default action is to output the entire document in an ESIS format intended for subsequent reprocessing by another program (see section 4.2.2). Possibly the most common command line option is therefore `-s`, which suppresses this output and gives only the error messages (if any). You use this to parse a file when you just want to check the syntax and validity. See the box for an example.

This was the first parser which tackled the problem of resolving Formal Public Identifiers algorithmically: it looks in an environment variable for directory/file patterns containing symbolic 'slots' where the pieces of the FPI can be placed: commonly the Public Owner Identifier, the Public Text Class, and the Public Text itself, but also the System Identifier, if any. This allows

```
+//Silmaril//DTD Financial//EN
```

to be resolved to

```
/usr/local/lib/sgml/Silmaril/DTD/Financial
```

under Unix, or

```
c:\usr\local\lib\sgml\Silmaril\DTD\Financial
```

under DOS, and its equivalent on other operating systems. You can see the pattern in the box. The component parts are specified in the environment variable to let you specify whereabouts in your own directory structure the file can be found. Unfortunately this method will not work for long FPIs on operating systems without long filename support, and problems occur with FPIs whose mapped filenames would contain spaces, slashes or colons, as these are not valid characters in filenames on some systems. I'm including it as an example, however, as it illustrates why the use of catalogs for entity resolution is so important.

Sgmls `-c` warning

If you're used to *nsgmls* and you accidentally use the `-ccatalog` option to *sgmls* instead, it will overwrite your catalog. The `-c` option in *sgmls* means 'capacity': it writes a report on what capacities were used (very useful, but not what you were expecting!).

Line numbers are given in the error messages, but as with all parsers, this is the location where the error was *detected*: the actual markup error may have occurred on an earlier line. A more sophisticated detection of error source is included in *nsgmls* (see section 4.3.5).

Included with *sgmls* is a copy of *rast*, an implementation of the RAST (Reference Application for SGML Testing) standard defined in ISO 13673. This program parses an SGML document and outputs the result format of the ESIS, which is defined in the standard.

4.3.5. SP and nsgmls

MS-Windows and Unix
`http://www.jclark.com/sp/`

This is the successor to a previous parser by James Clark, *sgmls*. It runs faster, due to several internal code changes, and it uses only OASIS catalogs to resolve FPIs. The ESIS representation is modified slightly, and some new options have been added, especially in the version of *nsgmls* distributed with the *Jade* converter which now includes XML parsing. The error messages have been improved, and now include (where possible) a pointer back to the last known location at which everything parsed OK, which is possibly the place where an error had its root. *Nsgmls* is now the default parser expected by *Emacs psgml*, and is replacing *sgmls* in the many other products which use it.

Nsgmls is a part of the *SP* package, which also contains a normalizer (*sgmlnorm*); a program called *spam* ('SP Add Markup'), which is a stream editor for SGML (and *nothing whatever* to do with the term for unsolicited junk email!); and a program called *spent* ('SP Entity Printer') for extracting a list of entities from an instance.

As mentioned above, there is a slightly different release of *SP* distributed as part of *Jade*, in `http://www.jclark.com/jade/`, and this is the place where the newest facilities are tested, including the XML parsing.

Operation of *nsgmls* is almost identical to that for *sgmls*, and many of the options are the same. A straightforward parse and validate of a single document, suppressing the ESIS output, is thus done with the command `nsgmls -s` followed by your filename. A file called `catalog` is expected to exist in the same directory, which provides the standard OASIS format catalog entries, but if the catalog is elsewhere, it can be specified with the `-c` option, *eg*:

```
% nsgmls -s -c/usr/local/lib/catalog.cat recipes.sgml
```

You can specify multiple input files on the command line (such as chapters of a book) and they will be concatenated to form a single document. If they have been used as separate documents for editing (and therefore each have a DocType Declaration) they can be parsed separately with the `-B` option (although this will defeat `ID/IDREF` resolution between files). Other options let you control various levels of output and warnings and a variety of different behaviors (such as parsing only the DTD, as explained in section 2.6.7).

Nsgmls parsing a file and finding an error in the markup

This is a short SGML instance in a file called `custrep.sgm`

```
<!DOCTYPE report PUBLIC "-//Corporate//DTD Report//EN">
<report><title>Liaison Visit to ACME Ltd</title>
<date>23 August 1998</date><rep>Claire MacDonald</rep>
<sec M="1"><head>Objectives</head>
<p>The objective of the visit was to re-establish the client
relationship after last year's legal proceedings.</p>
</sec></report>
```

Here's the DTD it uses from a file called `Report`:

```
<!ELEMENT report                - - (title,date,rep,sec+)>
<!ELEMENT (title,date,rep)      - - (#PCDATA)>
<!ELEMENT sec                   - - (head,(list | p)+)>
<!ATTLIST sec                   N     NUMBER     #IMPLIED>
<!ELEMENT head                  - - (#PCDATA)>
<!ELEMENT list                  - - (head?,item+)>
<!ELEMENT (p,item)              - - ((#PCDATA) | emph)*>
<!ELEMENT emph                  - - (#PCDATA)>
```

The user types the command and *nsgmls* parses the file, finding an error:

```
C:\clients\> nsgmls -s custrep.sgm
nsgmls:report.sgm:4:7:E: there is no attribute "M"
C:\clients\>
```

The parser identifies that `M` is not a valid attribute name (for the `<SEC>` element). The user must have mis-typed it instead of an `N`, one of the problems with not using an SGML editor!

4.3.5.1. Runsp

This is an MS-Windows interface to *SP* from Richard Light which provides drag-and-drop parsing: just configure it for your copy of *SP* and your catalog using the menu and dialog screens, and you can then open an SGML file or drop one onto the icon. It provides control over the identification of errors and places the cursor into an edit window for the instance so you can correct simple errors and re-parse.

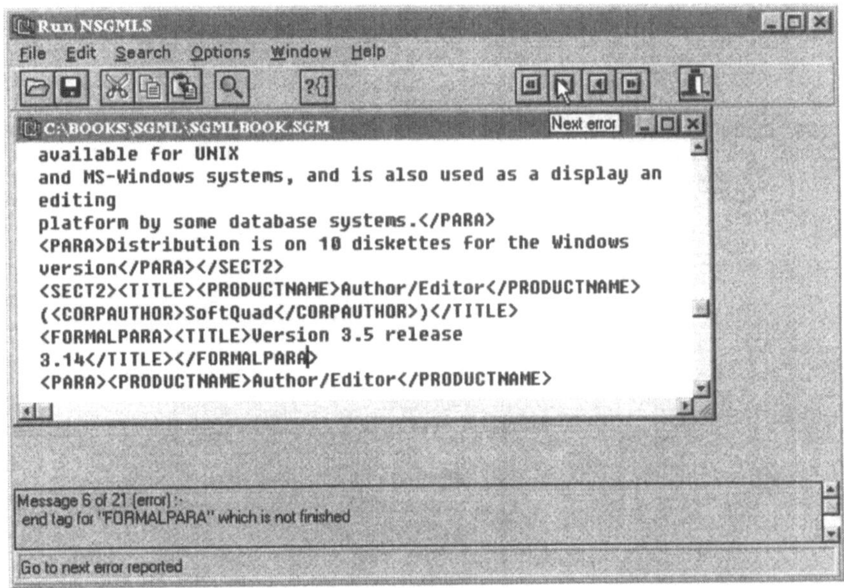

Figure 89. The *RUNsp* interface to *nsgmls*

Used in conjunction with the *CatEdit* program from I4I (see section 2.5.4.2), this makes a simple and effective way of managing a catalog and performing validation, avoiding the need to open a DOS task within Windows and have to remember the typed commands.

4.3.6. SMPOO (YASP)

Unix, Mac, DOS/Windows, Windows NT/95, OS/2, MVS/VM
`ftp://ftp.edf.fr/pub/SGML/YASP`

YASP provides a library of SGML functions in C for writing parser applications (see section 7.1.1). The sample application called *SMPOO* which is included in the package is a ready-built parser with an output format which can be reused in a similar way to *nsgmls'* representation of the ESIS (see section 4.3.4). The example in Figure 90 shows a fragment of the documentation and the output from the parser.

4.3.7. XML parsers

Among the design objectives of XML is that it shall be easy to write programs to process XML documents. The reason for stripping most of the optional features out of SGML was to make XML simpler to parse,

```
  <body>
    <h1>
      <h1t>Concepts</h1t>
      <h2>
<h2t>What is an SGML Parser?</h2t>
<p>Electronic text formatting for publishing has been evolving
steadily over the years, from an early base of formatters that
...

C:\sgml\smp00\nt\smp00\release> smp00 test.sgm

YASP V1.35/NT 08/09/96 07:25:02 GMT -- IBM Corp. 1993
An SGML System Conforming to
International Standard ISO 8879 --
Standard Generalized Markup Language

=> Start BODY
=> Start H1
          *dfl* ID=(#IMPLIED)
          *dfl* STITLE=(#IMPLIED)
=> Start H1T
=> Data |Concepts|
=> End H1T
=> Start H2
          *dfl* ID=(#IMPLIED)
          *dfl* STITLE=(#IMPLIED)
=> Start H2T
=> Data |What is an SGML Parser?|
=> End H2T
=> Start P
=> Data |Electronic text formatting for publishing has been evolving|
=> Record End
=> Data | steadily over the years, from an early base of format-
ters that|
=> Record End
```

Figure 90. SMP00 with instance fragment and output format

and therefore easier to write programs for than 'full' SGML. In the discussions on the proposals by the XML SIG (Special Interest Group), the concept was used of the 'DPH', the 'Desperate *Perl* Hacker'. This is a perhaps not-so-mythical figure in the backroom, on whom the boss has just dumped an urgent request for information to be extracted from XML files. Armed with the XML specification and a programmer's knowledge of *Perl,* it was felt it should be possible to write a script to process the files sufficiently to extract the data needed, without recourse to reading the entire SGML standard.

To a large extent this requirement seems to have been met. Even while XML was only part-formed, four or five parsers were produced, so that XML instances and DTDs could be written and checked, despite some areas not being fully-defined. The parsing model envisaged by the XML developers has been called 'draconian', because it admits of no quarter when an author fails to produce conformant text. The XML Specification (1.0) says:

> **Error**
>
> A violation of the rules of this specification; results are undefined. Conforming software may detect and report an error and may recover from it.

Although the rules are not actually written in blood, this has already been widely misinterpreted to mean that a browser should completely refuse to accept faulty documents, whereas it actually means that *the parser within the browser* should object to them, and make the browser aware of the problem. A browser can thus be programmed, as it says, to recover from an error, even a fatal one: it is fatal only to the parser, which must stop parsing normally when such an error is found.

> **Fatal error**
>
> An error which a conforming XML processor must detect and report to the application. After encountering a fatal error, the processor may continue processing the data to search for further errors and may report such errors to the application. In order to support correction of errors, the processor may make unprocessed data from the document (with intermingled character data and markup) available to the application. Once a fatal error is detected, however, the processor must not continue normal processing (i.e. it must not continue to pass character data and information about the document's logical structure to the application in the normal way).

The makers of browsers know only too well what to do when erroneous data is processed: reputedly half the entire code in big HTML browsers is given over to handling more or less gracefully the random assemblage of tag-like objects masquerading as HTML that authors and editor programs have created. One of the reasons for the early support of XML by the browser makers was that they saw at last an opportunity to get rid of this millstone around their necks: having to support every garbled variant of pointy brackets posing as HTML syntax merely because to fail would mean the opposition would be seen as 'better'.

With hindsight, of course, it's easy to claim that had the coders taken time to learn more about SGML and parsing at an early stage in the Web's development they could have jointly avoided the entire problem, simply by refusing to handle broken files at all: authors would have learned to make valid files very quickly (and perhaps XML would never have been thought of!). In fact, in November 1993 some TEI experts met some browser authors and recommended exactly this, but most of the authors felt SGML was 'too complicated' for a Web they saw more an a networked DTP system; but in reality a full parse every time a file was loaded would have made the Web quite unusable on the equipment on most users' desks at the time. The absence of any normative framework for error-handling in HTML provided part of the reasoning behind the XML model.

A formal parse is therefore central to any use of XML, whether or not it also needs validation. With modern system speeds, DTD-less operation, almost no optional features to code around, and the experience of a decade of SGML processing, the parsers described below can rip through a megabyte of XML in a few seconds, which is quite fast enough for JIT (Just-In-Time) delivery of parsed text to the browser's other modules (formatting, rendering, interaction, *etc*).

Among the jockeying for positions among API vendors, SAX (Simple API for XML) from David Megginson has attracted the attention of many parser authors although it is still a draft at the time of writing. SAX is an event-based interface for XML parsers written in object-oriented languages such as *Java*. The idea is that it should be possible to plug in any SAX-conformant XML parser, either at compile time or even at run time, so that your application is not tied to a specific one. The SAX definitions and requirements can be found at `http://www.microstar.com/xml/sax/`.

The programs listed here represent only a sample of those available. As parsers tend to be the first applications written for a new language, every university computer science department in the world seems to be implementing an XML parser in *Java*, C or C++. Details of those which are notified to the W3C appear on `http://www.w3.org/XML/`, and those which survive eventually make their way into Steve Pepper's *Whirlwind Guide*[34].

4.3.7.1. Lark and Larval (Textuality)

http://www.textuality.com/Lark

Lark and *Larval* were written by Tim Bray, a co-editor of the XML specification. *Lark* is a non-validating XML processor, designed for speed and compactness; *Larval* is built on top of *Lark* and provides full validation. Both are implemented in *Java*, so they require the presence of a *Java* run-time processor, and are small enough to be delivered with XML applications. The package comes as just over 100 *Java* classes, with source code.

Lark is just over 45Kb, so it is usable over the network. It reads a document and its DTD and checks for well-formedness, and passes the document structure to the application. It implements all of XML, including the requirement to stop formal parsing the moment it finds any violation of well-formedness constraints (but it continues to look for further errors and report them). *Larval* performs full validation including error reporting, but at the time of writing is regarded as experimental.

4.3.7.2. XP (James Clark)

http://www.jclark.com/xml/xp/

XP is an XML parser in *Java* from the James Clark, author of *SP*, *Jade*, and other well-known SGML software. It is completely conformant to the XML 1.0 specification, in that it it detects all non-well-formed documents, but it does not (at the time of writing) perform validation.

It handles all external entities (DTD subsets, parameter entities and general entities) and aims to be the fastest conformant XML parser in Java — the author's notes make it clear that it relies on the more recent (v1.1) features of the JDK (Java Development Kit). It provides two levels of API, one for normal work and one to support the construction of different kinds of XML parser (such as incremental parsers).

It comes as some 60 class files, and is designed more for applications that applets (so keeping class file size small was not an objective). As it is intended for production use, error handling is 'brutal'.

4.3.7.3. expat (James Clark)

This is an XML parser in C, written on top of the earlier *xmltok* library which tokenizes an XML stream. It is blindingly fast, one of the principal reasons it has been chosen for incorporation into both *Perl* and Netscape *Navigator* 5.

It is fully conformant to XML, but at the time of writing is a parser only, not a validator. Included in the packages is the *xmlwf* program,

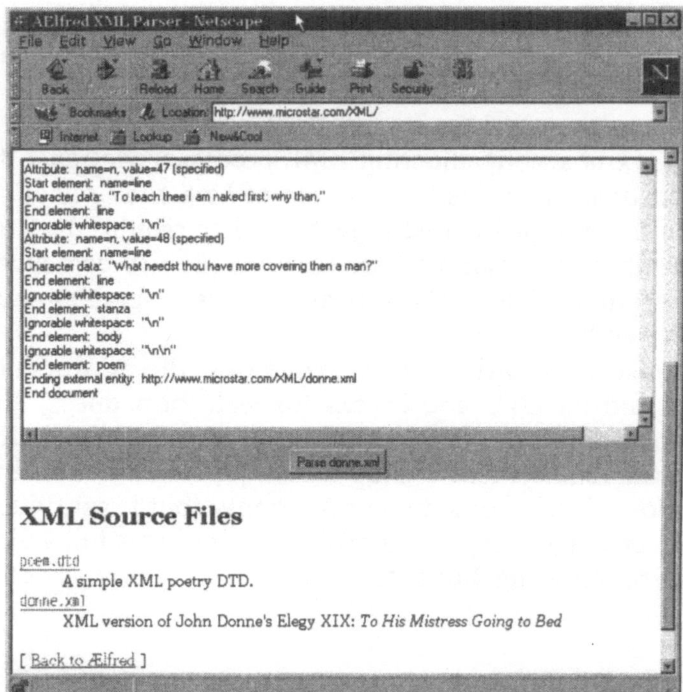

Figure 91. *Ælfred* demonstration running live in a browser window

which parses XML files for well-formedness, and writes those files which pass the test to a nominated directory in 'Canonical XML' format, making it easy to use as a 'sorter' application to distinguish a sequence of well-formed files from those with errors.

There is a copy on the CD-ROM: it is subject to the 'Mozilla Public License Version 1.0', which applies conditions similar to, but distinct from, those for the GNU General Public License, so if you apply or modify it, you are required to read and act on the terms of the license (read the license documentation in the *expat* directory).

4.3.7.4. Ælfred (Microstar)

`http://www.microstar.com/XML/`

Ælfred is a free DTD-aware Java-based XML parser from Microstar, makers of *Near&Far* (*Designer* and *Author*: see sections page 172 and page 244).

It is designed for use in *Java* applets, and the system is aimed at *Java* programmers who want to add XML support to applets and applications without a size penalty: *Ælfred* consists of only two core class files with a total size of about 26K. There is also a complete SAX driver available for interoperability.

The *Ælfred* Web page has a live demonstration which you can test online with any *Java*-enabled browser (see Figure 91). This shows the trace of information passed to the application as the file is parsed. Note especially the description of the quality of white-space, in accordance with the XML rules (see section 2.4.1.7).

It makes a feature of supporting Unicode to the fullest extent possible in Java (the ligature in the name is intended as a reminder of this), and according to the documentation it handles XML documents encoded using UTF-8, UTF-16, ISO 10646-UCS-2, ISO 10646-UCS-4 (as far as surrogates allow), and ISO 8859-1 (ISO Latin 1/Windows).

5. Manipulation and conversion

Bend me, shape me, any way you want me.

American Breed, 1967 Top Ten

- **Quick and dirty: non-SGML tools**
- **Programmable conversions**
- **Import and export without programming**

Among the benefits of SGML most often quoted is the ease with which files can be converted to other formats. 'Keep the master source in SGML, and you can generate everything else from it' is a paraphrase of advice frequently given to those considering SGML.

SGML is a publicly-defined, formal structure, with a (by now) well-documented and robust structural model which can be used to define the 'rules' for a document type once and reuse the definition many times. But precisely because those rules can be defined separately for each different type of document (different DTDs), it is not yet possible to have 'an SGML-to-everything' converter which you just click on. A target format (the format you want to convert into) may simply not possess enough smarts to be able to represent the things described in an SGML file (for example *Word* has no markup to represent `<placename>`); or an SGML DTD may simply never have been designed to represent all the things a particular target format can do (my `recipe.dtd` has no provision for multicolor printing, which my formatter can do trivially).

(In fact, there probably *is* a market for a 'click to convert' product, giving a one-time one-way conversion from a few common DTDs to a few popular word processors, using predefined office-style target page layouts, and doing everything in a completely prescriptive, lowest-common-denominator format providing no options at all. There are perfectly genuine occasions when ephemeral documents need conversion in this manner. But converting in the other direction is much less certain: see section 5.3)

Yet despite this, there are clearly certain common objects we use in documents which occur time and time again: sections, headings, paragraphs, lists, tables, forms, references, notes (the list could go on and on). It seems an obvious step to create a once-and-for-all list of these forms which could be used as labels in each DTD, and thus passed between document types, even between SGML and non-SGML applications, regardless of the names given to the elements in the DTD or the facilities of the programs used.

However, document designers and document architects argue convincingly against casting this kind of list in concrete, because we can never know what structures will be invented in the future. The closest we come at the moment is the concept of Architectural Forms devised for the HyTime standard (see section 2.7.2.1). We're therefore going to need converters for the foreseeable future.

The first section of this chapter is a look at the various non-SGML tools available which people use with SGML files. These are almost all for Unix operating systems, as Unix provides the most extensive built-in facilities for text file manipulation.

The remainder of the chapter covers the programming and non-programming methods of conversion, into and out of SGML, and between different DTDs. There are many ways of converting documents, and only a selection is show here. For a more detailed analysis, with programming examples, see Norm Smith's *Practical Guide to SGML/XML Filters*[38].

5.1. Quick and dirty: using non-SGML tools

If you've arrived here via the scenic route through the other chapters, you will have gathered that parsing is normally considered a prerequisite to any kind of work with SGML files, and is built into most SGML systems (or tightly bound to them). The idea, therefore, of using generic non-SGML tools on SGML files may come as a bit of a surprise: if they don't parse, you say, how can they do anything useful?

In fact there is quite a lot that you can do without either parsing or groves, if you are careful. SGML files are mostly available in plaintext format, so they are suitable for manipulation by all kinds of programs, especially by the standard tools which come with every Unix system.

There are also more advanced programmable tools which can parse, and there are several systems and packages developed in *Perl* and *Python* which use both parsing and non-parsing methods.

5.1.1. Unix utilities

This term is used to describe the standard set of file handling programs that are the staple of all text processing on Unix systems, whether for SGML or not. Many of them are also available in DOS versions, so they can be run on a PC, but the fixed-memory environment of DOS may restrict their use to small files or a small amount of processing. Windows and Mac versions are also available commercially. More advanced packages like *Perl* and *Python* are slowly taking over, but the standard utilities will be with us for a long while yet.

If you don't use Unix or feel you are not likely to, you may be tempted to skip this section. Please don't. Even if you never touch Unix systems, you should at least be aware of the existence of these programs, as they are frequently referred to in computing discussions, and there is often an assumption by experts that listeners understand the shorthand terms used. Case-hardened Unix users probably *should* skip this section, as I have made some deliberate simplifications for the sake of explanation.

The commands I describe here are the ones that I have found most useful in text handling for SGML, but everyone who uses Unix develops their own personal favorite ways of doing things: the absence of specific programs here should not be taken to mean that they are not used for SGML, and there's nothing to say that the way I use these programs is the only way to do the job. There are many other utilities in Unix which are described in much more detail in the dozens of books on Unix systems management and shell script programming in the computing sections of any large bookstore.

Non-Unix users should also note that a crucial factor in using Unix commands comes from the ability to chain ('pipe') many commands together. This technique lets you pass the output of one command into the input of another: some DOS programs have a similar ability. By storing commands which use this technique in a file, you can create a new program (called a 'script': see the box) in a few minutes just using the standard utilities: I give some examples below.

The basic syntax of almost all the Unix utility commands follows this pattern: `command` *`-options arguments filename`* which is a mnemonic notation meaning:

Command lines don't bite

If you have never used a command line system before, you may want to examine a Unix or DOS command window on someone's computer before you read any further, as the paradigm is quite unlike clicking on icons.

A command window is a dialog: the computer prompts you when it's ready to accept a command from you, by displaying a word or symbol (%, $, `#`, and `C:\>` are all common): this is called the 'command prompt'.

You type your instructions on the keyboard and they appear on the line to the right of the command prompt. When you have completed the command you press the Enter key and the system processes the command and displays the output (see Figure 92). Then it displays the command prompt again, ready for you to type another command.

If the command is longer than one line, you can just keep typing, but it's regarded as better practice on Unix systems to type a backslash (\) at a suitable place just short of a full line, press the Enter key, and continue typing on the next line.

Most command line interfaces have little or no editing ability, so if you make a mistake there is no such concept as using the up, down, left, or right arrows to correct it like a word processor. You probably *can* use the BackSpace or Delete key to erase things *while still typing a line*, but the moment you move onto another line, anything typed before is committed and no longer editable. (Some systems do better than this: ask a local guru).

Finally, **scripts**. A script is a file containing a useful collection of commands in sequence, such as 'list all files created yesterday, parse the ones belonging to my book, and write them to the backup device'. It enables the commands to be run as a suite, by typing the name of the file (in effect becoming a new command in itself).

- each element of the command is separated by a *space* (and there may be many repetitions of options and arguments and filenames in a single command);
- the *command keyword* (the name of the program) comes first;
- if there are any *options* you wish to use (normally single letters symbolizing a specific modification to the program's behavior), they must be preceded by a minus sign (hyphen);

```
% ls -l *.sgml

-rwxr--r-- 1  pflynn   37465  9-Oct-1997 13:45 register.sgml

% nsgmls -s -cnew.cat register.sgml
/usr/local/bin/nsgmls:register.sgm:235:25:X: reference to non-
existent ID "UCC"

% emacs register.sgml &
[2345]

% grep -i '<authorgroup' bibliog.sgml
<BOOKBIBLIO><AUTHORGROUP><AUTHOR><FIRSTNAME>Steven</FIRSTNAME>
<SURNAME>DeRose</SURNAME></AUTHOR></AUTHORGROUP>

% omle docbook.dcl faq.sgml -source db2html.xom -of faq.html
faq.sgml done

% grep -i title faq.html
```

The user is currently typing a command at the bottom of the screen which starts with the command keyword grep. Scrolled up above the command line you can see previous commands and their output. For the sake of clarity, commands the user has typed are shown *underlined*: on a normal screen this distinction is not made.

Figure 92. Unix commands being typed (taken from a terminal window)

- the options may be followed by *arguments*, which are values that the options may need to work with: there may be several options and arguments interleaved;
- finally you type the *filename or filenames* to search.

The exact values for the options and their arguments (if any) are always given in the manual page for each command (type `man` followed by the name of the command), but these can be confusing for beginners because they use a very terse and compressed jargon aimed at the experienced user. Any of the dozens of books on Unix for beginners will explain them in far more detail than is possible here.

It's easiest to see in an example: I'll use the command *grep* (explained more fully below) to search all SGML files in the current directory for the keyword 'DocType' (in any mix of upper- and lower-case letters), and give the number of the line in each file where the word occurs:

```
grep  -in  doctype  *.sgml
```

The component parts of the command can clearly be seen:

- the command name 'grep' comes first;

- followed by the options 'i' (ignore the difference between upper- and lower-case) and 'n' (display the line numbers of the lines found);
- followed by the expression to search for: 'doctype';
- and finishing with the file specification for the file[s] to search: here the asterisk prefix and `.sgml` means 'all files ending in `.sgml`'.

The output from this command might look like this (searching multiple files automatically causes *grep* to prefix the matching lines with the filename they were found in):

```
draft1.sgml:1:<!DOCTYPE BOOK PUBLIC "-//Davenport//DTD DocBook V3.0//EN
draft1.sgml:373:when using a DocType Declaration that you have not ever
yr2k.sgml:1:<!doctype html public "-//IETF//DTD HTML 2.0//EN">
xml.sgml:1:<!DocType Article Public "+//Silmaril//DTD Article V2//EN">
xml.sgml:129:especially for those DocTypes which are not intended for
ispde.sgml:1:<!DOCTYPE Bericht PUBLIC "-//Zotty//DTD Bericht//DE" [
ispde.sgml:69:was damaligen DocTypen nicht vorhanden hatten, da&szlig;
```

You can see on each line the filename where the 'hit' was found, the line-number of the line in question, and the text of that line. Note that in this example it has located every occurrence of 'doctype' regardless of whether it was part of a DocType Declaration or not.

Explanations of the various options to this command can be found in the Unix online manual pages. These are plaintext descriptions of the meaning and usage of every command: they are, however, intended for reference purposes, not as a tutorial, so they presuppose a considerable understanding of Unix. The command for reading a manual page is just `man` followed by the name of the command, so if you type `man grep`, you will see all about the `grep` command, including the following, which relates to the options we used above:

```
SYNOPSIS
     grep [ -bchilnsvw ] [ -e expression ] [ filename... ]
...
     -i   Ignore the case of letters in making comparisons -
          that is, upper and lower case are considered
          identical.

     -n   Precede each line by its relative line number in
          the file.
```

Output of the manual pages pauses at the bottom of each screenful: to go to the next page, press the spacebar (type a **Ctrl-C** to abort it and return to the command prompt).

Unix command input and output can be 'redirected': many Unix programs expect data to be typed at the keyboard unless a filename is given, and they display their output on the screen. Prefixing a filename with the '>' character means 'send the output of this command into this file instead of displaying it on the screen'; prefixing a filename with the '<' character means 'read the data for this command out of this file, instead of expecting it to be typed at the keyboard'. In these cases, the less-than and greater-than signs have nothing whatever to do with SGML: it is pure coincidence that Unix uses them.

Finally, many other non-letter characters in Unix have a special meaning when used in a command you type, depending on what 'shell' (Unix command processor) you are using (*sh, csh, ksh, tcsh, bash, etc*). For example, the ampersand (&) means 'perform this command in the background; let the user carry on typing something else while it is processing' (useful for commands which will take a long time to run); and the semicolon means 'this command is complete, but don't do it yet, expect a further command on this line'. To escape from these restrictions, you need to prefix such characters by the backslash or enclose the entire expression in single quotes. Other characters to watch out for are '$', '*', '[', '^', ']', '(', ')', and the backslash (\) itself. Most of these have one special meaning to the shell (when typed unescaped) and another, quite different, meaning to each command (when typed as part of an argument).

While these commands are a standard part of all Unix systems, it is worth noting that there are GNU versions of many of them which tend to have expanded capabilities, and may fix some known bugs in earlier versions which may still exist on older machines.

One of the commonest uses of these utilities in file analysis is for the reprocessing of the ESIS output of parsers, but as that involves some foreknowledge of parsing, it is dealt with in chapter 4.

5.1.1.1. grep

This is the standard Unix searching tool: it reads a text file line by line and extracts for display or reuse all the lines which match a pattern supplied by the user. The pattern is given in an expression in a very regularized syntax known as a ***Regular Expression*** (also called an 'RE' or 'regexp'), which allows anything from very simple to very complex pattern-matching, and it has become the almost universal standard for pattern-match searching.

The example given earlier of Unix command syntax used `grep` as the illustration. Here's another one, this time searching for any lowercase acute accent, by using the syntax of Regular Expressions to create a pattern to match SGML character entity references like `á` or `ú`:

```
grep '&[aeiou]acute;' mybook.sgml
```

We're not using any options here, so the Regular Expression follows right after the command keyword, and it is in quotes to escape from the special interpretation of characters by the shell. Here's how it's formed in this case:

- it begins with an ampersand, to match the one which starts character entity references;
- square brackets in a Regular Expression are used to enclose alternatives, of which *only one* can match on any particular occasion: so the second 'character' of the overall pattern will be any of the vowels enclosed in the brackets;
- letters on their own in a Regular Expression are matched just as they stand, so the next part of the pattern is the word 'acute';
- finally, let's assume we only want those fully-formed character entity references which end with the semicolon.

Last of all comes the filename we want to search. The output is all lines from the file containing any acute-accented lowercase vowel, and will be displayed on your terminal screen.

However, it won't match the floating accent `´` from the ISO diacritical marks character entity set, because that does not have an initial vowel between the ampersand and the word 'acute'. To overcome this, we can use one of the Regular Expression 'occurrence indicators', the asterisk, immediately after the closing square bracket: `[aeiou]*` which makes it mean 'zero or more occurrences of the preceding Regular Expression' (very close to SGML DTD content model syntax). It's this aspect which lets us match both `´` as well as `ú` (and `&aeacute;` if such an entity were defined).

Finally, we need to allow for character entities which do not terminate with the semicolon. We can't easily follow strict SGML syntax here, because *grep* does not read the SGML Declaration or the DTD (it doesn't even know it's processing SGML), so it doesn't know about 'name characters' or the SGML `REFC`. For practicality and simplicity, we'll assume the character entities we have used in the file are followed by a space or another ampersand if they don't end with a semicolon. This means we need to allow for the Regular Expression `[;& ]` to occur, so our revised command is:

```
grep '&[aeiou]*acute[;& ]' mybook.sgml
```

Regular Expression syntax is a little convoluted, although strictly logical. It is principally defined in the Unix manual pages for the *ed* line-mode editor (type `man ed` to see these), but several programs extend it with additional facilities. To get the full benefit of its power, you need to be using it frequently for a while, but it is documented in almost

Regular expressions in markup searches

Although Regular Expressions are a powerful and compact way of expressing a search term, they have their dangers when used with markup. It's not just the fact that the '<' and '>' characters mean different things to SGML and the Unix shell, and thus need careful handling: there are hidden problems with white-space and with minimization as well. If you search for `'<partno type="a"'` to retrieve all automobile part numbers you may miss some if the spacing in the file is different from a single space (such as a linebreak):

```
<partno
type   = "a"
num    = "123456"
>
widgets
</>
```

As we saw in sections page 63 and page 139, white-space, including line-breaks, between elements in element content is normally treated as irrelevant in regular SGML, and is removed by a parser (XML, however, retains them). In addition, some white-space *within* markup (between attributes, for example, but not within attribute values) is functionally equivalent to a single space. Minimization, if used, may mean that you cannot do a simple search for `</partno>` because it may return no hits at all. Because most Unix-style commands using Regular Expressions also work on the basis of the 'line' as the unit of the file to be searched, whole elements split across a line boundary may not easily be searchable.

The Regular Expression searches inside SGML editors usually have ways around this, because they already have access to the document markup, and the Regular Expression search in *Emacs/psgml* usefully matches a space to any of a space, TAB, or newline.

every book on Unix, and you should read one or two of these if you are going to be using the operating system at anything other than a trivial level.

Here are a couple more examples for SGML. The first one searches for any element with an ID attribute set to 'PF':

```
grep  -i  'id *= *"*pf"*'  mybook.sgml
```

We use the `-i` option again because markup and ID values are often case-insensitive; the Regular Expression matches the attribute name `ID` followed by optional space, an equals sign, more optional space, optional quotes, the initials, and more optional quotes. There are some problems and assumptions here, though: it won't match anything if the attribute and its value are split over two lines, because *grep* reads the file one whole line at a time; it doesn't handle the cases where the file uses single quotes around attribute values; and if you search SGML documentation which uses `id="pf"` as an example, it will find that as well, because it is not distinguishing between markup and data. See section 5.1.2 for a command line search program which can make more use of SGML (and other) markup.

The second example searches for all lines starting with an element start-tag (the reason for this will become more apparent later):

```
grep '^<[a-zA-Z]' myfile.sgml
```

There are two things to note here:

- the caret (^) at the start of the Regular Expression means 'this Regular Expression only matches the starts of lines': it does not mean there must be a caret in the text (ending a Regular Expression with a dollar sign ($) will make it match at the ends of lines);
- the hyphens in the content of the square brackets make the a–z and A–Z into *ranges* of characters: here this means that any line beginning with an open-angle bracket followed by any upper- or lower-case letter will match.

5.1.1.2. sed

This is a stream editor, a program which reads a file line by line and allows pattern-match editing changes to be applied to the lines as they pass through. Changes can be done repetitively or recursively on consecutive lines, and are usually employed to change one pattern of characters into another. All lines which are unaffected by the editing are passed through to the output unchanged.

There is an extensive language of pattern and buffer specifications for holding and modifying patterns and data between lines, but we will look here just at the simple use, the `-e` ('edit') option. This is followed by a 'script' command (the letter 's'), made up of the string of characters to be changed and the string of characters to change them to, delimited by some otherwise unused character (the plus sign or the slash are common characters to use for this). For example:

```
sed -e s+Smith+Jones+g myfile.sgml >newfile.sgml
```

would change all occurrences of 'Smith' in `myfile.sgml` into 'Jones', and put the result into `newfile.sgml` (leaving `myfile.sgml` untouched). Note the plus sign used as a delimiter to separate the 's' from the 'Smith' from the 'Jones', and from the trailing 'g', which makes the change 'global': without it, only the first occurrence of 'Smith' on each line would be changed. You can also use a number instead of the 'g' to specify the maximum number of changes per line. The strings are case-sensitive, so accidentally typing

```
sed -e s+smith+Jones+g myfile.sgml >newfile.sgml
```

would have the effect of changing (for example) 'ironsmith' into 'iron-Jones' and 'smithereens' into 'Jonesereens' while leaving 'Smithers' untouched. The first example would have changed 'Smithers' into 'Jonesers', too!

The power of *sed* comes from the fact that the first string (the one you want to change) can be a Regular Expression (see explanation under *grep* above). So to change any occurrences of 'Smith', 'Smithe', 'Smyth', or 'Smythe' into 'Jones', you could say:

```
sed -e s+Sm[iy]th[e]*+Jones+g myfile.sgml >newfile.sgml
```

but this will still upset Mr Smithers. There's a way around this but it involves using a very much more complex pattern, to accommodate matches for 'anything except' a character.

Regular Expression syntax also lets a command 'memorize' the pattern which actually matched the Regular Expression on each occasion, and reuse it in the replacement string. This is done by enclosing the piece of the pattern which you want to reproduce in escaped parentheses (backslash-parenthesis, otherwise all it does is search for an expression including regular parentheses themselves), and by representing the place where you want it reproduced in the second string by an escaped digit: 1 for the first such string to be memorized, 2 for the second, *etc*:

```
sed -e 's+<\(/*\)[Pp][Aa][Rr][Aa]+<\1P+g' *.sgml
```

Here, we are changing all `<PARA>` *and* `</PARA>` tags to `<P>` and `</P>` in a single command, by matching an optional forward slash (note the asterisk) before the element name (which can be any combination of upper- or lower-case letters). The slash is enclosed in `\(` and `\)`, which are the escaped parentheses, and the `\1` in the replacement pattern marks the place where any slash (if it occurred) will be replicated. Thus when a paragraph start-tag is encountered, with no slash, there is nothing to memorize, and the output will be just `<P`, but when a slash occurs (as with the paragraph end-tag), the output will be `</P` instead.

This is admittedly complex, but done with care to make sure the pattern you search for to change really is unique and cannot occur anywhere you don't want it changed, so that the files are not corrupted or invalidated, it is one of the most powerful ways to make changes to a file on an automated basis. If you perform it inside a script which controls its application to a list of files, you can convert even very large document collections very fast.

You can have many such edit changes in a single pass of *sed*, and it is common for the 'script' specifications to be put in a file, one per line, and referenced in the command with the `-f` option instead of the `-e`. In this case the scripting never reaches the shell, so special shell characters do not have to be escaped (parentheses for memorization-replacement still do, and ampersands have a special meaning to *sed* itself). Thus for example if we put the following lines in a file called `unsgml`:

```
s/&/\&amp;/g
s/</\&lt;/g
s/>/\&gt;/g
```

and used the command `sed -f unsgml example.html >example.txt` we could change all ampersands, open-angle and close-angle brackets to their conventional character entity equivalents, thus 'unsgml'-ing a fragment of SGML suitable for inclusion in a coding example such as HTML's `<PRE>` element.

A similar technique could be used to strip an SGML file of all element markup. This relies on there being no start-tag with so many attributes that it spans more than two lines, and it won't handle angle brackets embedded in attribute values, or features like Marked Sections, `CDATA`, comments, or Processing Instructions, so it nicely indicates some of the many limitations of using these text utilities rather than a parser-based SGML system. It also shows the use of Regular Expressions which specify a list of characters *not* to match (start the list inside the square brackets with a caret). Here's the *sed* program:

```
s+<[^<>]*>++g
s+^[^<>]*>++
s+<[^<>]*$++
s+&acute;+'+g
s+&\([ACDEGIKLNOTUYacdegiklnostuy]\)[EHJTabcdeghjmnorstuz]\
[HOabceghilmnoprt][NRacdeghiklnorstuv]*;+\1+g
```

The first line replaces all text between angled brackets, which does not itself contain other angled brackets, with nothing (the final two delimiters together with nothing between); the second line does the same, but for lines starting with any number of characters not including angled brackets, but with a close-angle bracket occurring on the line; and the third repeats the same procedure but for lines containing an open-angle bracket but no subsequent open- or close-angle bracket. The fourth line replaces the floating acute accent with an apostrophe (readers can concoct equivalents for other members of the `isodia.ent` file, should they wish); and the final line (here printed broken across two lines of type for reasons of space; the break is heralded by the trailing backslash) contains a Regular Expression which matches all fully-formed character entity names in the ISO Latin–1 and Latin–2 character entity sets, and replaces them with their first alphabetic character, so `í` becomes just ‘i’. (It may match others that the user has declared separately, so it should be used with caution.)

5.1.1.3. awk

Awk is a processing tool which reads lines from a file and divides them into ‘fields’ (by default this means words, or at least, strings of characters separated by spaces) which can then be accessed separately (word 1, word 2, word 3, *etc*) and extracted in a different order, or changed in some way, or selected by using Regular Expressions, or otherwise manipulated.

The syntax is to enclose each action you want taken in curly braces and put the whole mini-program in single quotes. An action can be preceded by a Regular Expression between slashes if you want to restrict it to lines matching a pattern. For example:

```
awk '/^<\![Ee][Ll]/ {print $2}' myfile.dtd
```

could print the element names from any element declarations in a DTD, assuming they always started at the beginning of lines (remember the caret mark at the start of the Regular Expression which forces this). The Regular Expression needs to match an open-angle bracket and an exclamation mark (the latter has to be escaped because it has a special meaning in *awk* when used alone) followed by an E and an L (in upper- or lower-case). Lines which match this Regular Expression are passed to the following action in curly braces, which prints the second field on the line, which in this example will normally be the name of the element (or parameter entity reference) being declared. Unlike *sed*, lines which do not match are *not* passed through to the output: only matching lines get processed.

Awk programs can extend over many lines, and as with *sed*, lines of *awk* code can be stored in a file and referenced in the command line with the `-f` option. You can include ‘if’ statements in the actions inside the curly braces, so code can be doubly conditional, depending once on the pattern-matching of the Regular Expression and a second time on action conditions. If there’s no Regular Expression before an action, then all lines get passed to the action for processing. There are also facilities for accumulating and holding values during processing, even arrays (tables) of values. Here’s a simple program to process the output of the Unix *ls* command which lists all your files: this command will tell you the total size of all your SGML files:

```
ls -lg *.sgml | awk '{tot = tot + $5} END {print tot}'
```

The END keyword means the action following it only gets performed once, after all lines have been processed.

Here's an example of *awk* processing a catalog file and printing out the names of all the regular Public Owners of FPIs. It makes the reasonable assumption that the FPI occurs on the same line as a PUBLIC keyword, and it uses *awk* twice, both times using a special keyword BEGIN to do some preliminary status-setting. The first time it sets the field separator (FS) to the double-quote character (done by using the C-like format operator sprintf on the ASCII value 34, because double-quotes themselves are used to quote other things and can't be used to quote themselves); it uses a Regular Expression to select lines beginning with a P for PUBLIC; and it prints the second field (which contains the FPI). The second time it sets the field separator to the slash character, selects the 'lines' (now just FPIs, because that's all the first use of *awk* let through) beginning with a minus or plus (thus avoiding the ISBNs, IDNs, and ISOs), and printing the third field, which is the Public Owner:

```
awk 'BEGIN {FS=sprintf("%c",34)} /^[Pp]/ {print $2}' catalog |\
awk 'BEGIN {FS="/"} /^[-+]/ {print $3}'
```

Note the use of the vertical bar to 'pipe' the output of the first command into the input of the second one, and the final backslash on the first line used to allow the second command to begin on a new line.

Although this requires the catalog file to follow a convention in respect of line-breaks which is not a requirement of either FPIs or OASIS-format catalogs, this format of file is extremely common. If you've got a lot of catalog entries for multi-file DTDs, or just a lot of entries from the same Public Owner, you'll get a lot of lines the same being output. I leave it to you to use *sort* and *uniq* (see below) to whittle this down to one line for each different Public Owner.

5.1.1.4. tr

This is a very simple command which translates a file by replacing any character you specify with another character. The first argument is the list of characters you want to replace, and the second argument is the list of characters (in the same order) to replace them by. For example,

```
tr '[a-z]' '[A-Z]' <myfile.sgml >myfile.upr
```

will make an entire file uppercase: any occurrences of the first character in the first string will be replaced by the first character from the second string; and so on for the second and remaining characters. The command works as a pipe for both input and output, so you have to give the redirection indicators before both filenames, < specifying the source file and > specifying the destination.

In the next example all TAB characters are replaced by single spaces:

```
tr  '\011'  '\040'  <report.sgml  >report.new
```

You can give characters which might otherwise be misinterpreted in the form of their 3–digit octal (base 8) value preceded by a backslash: a TAB character is 9 in decimal so it's 011 in octal (one 8 plus one 1); a space is 32 decimal or 040 octal (four 8s). This lets you change even unprintable characters which you can't type because they have no keyboard or screen representation.

This command is very useful for changing the shape of a file before piping into another command. In SGML it usually does not matter if you have linebreaks at places within text or even markup where spaces would usually go, nor sometimes even if there are multiple spaces where one would do; in processing command languages, however, the concept of 'lines' of a file is crucial. One common use of *tr* therefore is to translate all linebreaks and TABs to spaces, so the file then appears in effect to be one hugely long continuous line:

```
tr  '\011\012<>'  '\040\040\012\040'  <document.sgml |\
awk '/^[a-zA-Z]/ {print $1}'
```

Here's an example which does that: it changes TABs and Unix newlines (decimal 10=octal 12) into spaces, but then also changes '<' characters to linebreaks and '>' characters to spaces, so that each 'line' now begins with a start-tag or an end-tag, but minus the opening angle bracket. If we follow this command with an *awk* command we can select lines starting with a letter to get a list of all the start-tags used. See below for how to remove duplicates to make a sorted list of the elements used in a file.

5.1.1.5. **sort**

The *sort* command does exactly what it says: it sorts a file into order. By default this is alphabetical order of lines, but options can be used to change the order, or to make it use fields from elsewhere in each line.

```
sort  mylist  >newlist
```

simply sorts the input file and puts the sorted result into the output file. Using *sort* within a pipe (between vertical bars separating other commands) has the effect of sorting the 'lines' output by the preceding program before they are delivered into the input of the next program:

```
grep  -i  smith  addresses  |  sort  |  awk  '{print $3}'
```

A simple demonstration of sorting on a different field can be done with the standard Unix filename-listing program *ls*. Here we list the names and details of all SGML files and sort them into descending order of size:

```
ls  -lg  *.sgml | sort -k 5nr

-rw-r--r--  1 pflynn   staff        4460 Feb 24 11:13 tei.sgml
-rw-r--r--  1 pflynn   staff        2898 Aug 22 16:23 article.sgml
-rw-r--r--  1 pflynn   staff         711 Feb 17 20:23 qrd.sgml
-rw-r--r--  1 pflynn   staff         595 Aug  9 15:04 trial.sgml
-rw-r--r--  1 pflynn   staff         411 Aug 13 10:55 test.sgml
```

The options `-lg` request the long form of file list, with the name of the group owner as well. The `-k` option to *sort* means 'use a specific field to sort on', and is followed by the field number: here the fifth item on each line is the size. The `nr` specifies a numeric field sorted in reverse.

(An earlier version of *sort* used a slightly different syntax for specifying fields: they were counted from zero instead of from one, and were preceded by a plus sign or minus sign to specify which field to start and end sorting on; so the command above would read:

```
ls  -lg  *.sgml | sort +4nr
```

You should check which version you have by reading the manual page for *sort*.)

5.1.1.6. uniq

This command takes a sorted input file (or a series of lines piped from another command) and squeezes out all duplicate lines. It is at its most useful in a pipe, where a preceding sort has arranged a list of names or values in order. Look again at the example of extracting all start-tags from an SGML file:

```
tr  '\011\012<>'  '\040\040\012\040'  <document.sgml |\
awk '/^[a-zA-Z]/ {print $1}'  |  sort  |  uniq
```

This now sorts all the start-tag names, and then extracts only one instance of each, giving us a sorted list of the elements used in the file. A slightly simpler way of doing the same thing would be to turn all newlines and `TAGC` characters (closing angle brackets) into spaces, and reset *awk*'s line-break character to the `STAGO` character (open angle bracket). This now means each 'line' as seen by *awk* by definition begins with the name of an element and has a space after it, becoming field #1, so we can output them, sort them, and *uniq* them into a file for editing into a stylesheet, for example:

```
tr '\012>' '\040\040' document.sgml |\
awk 'BEGIN {RS="<"} {print $1}' | grep -v \! |sort|uniq >document.sty
```

You can also get *uniq* to count how many of each item there were, before it removes the duplicates, by using the -c option. This places the subtotal for each item on the output line, before the name of the item itself, so you can follow it with a second, numeric, sort so that you get a list in descending order of frequency:

```
tr  '\011\012<>'  '\040\040\012\040'  <document.sgml  |\
awk '/^[a-zA-Z]/ {print $1}'  |  sort  |  uniq -c  | sort -k 1nr
```

5.1.2. sgrep (University of Helsinki)

Unix
http://www.cs.helsinki.fi/~jjaakkol/sgrep.html

Despite the implication of the 's' in the name, this is not 'SGML-grep' but 'structured grep', a searching program for structured text of all kinds, not just SGML. It describes itself as a 'tool for searching text files and filtering text streams using structural criteria'. The software is a C command line program for Unix which must be downloaded and compiled: a copy is on the CD-ROM in the Unix folders. It was written at the Department of Computer Science of the University of Helsinki by Jani Jaakkola and Pekka Kilpeläinen.

Instead of using Regular Expressions, it takes a text pattern which matches the boundaries of the 'region' of the file you want to search. For a non-SGML example, the command

```
sgrep '"\nFrom: " .. "\n"' /var/spool/mail/pflynn
```

searches all my incoming mail for lines beginning with From: (using the standard Unix symbol \n for a newline).

To search an element in an SGML file, the command just has to include the start-tag and end-tag in the specification:

```
sgrep -i '("<NAME>".."</NAME>") containing "choc"' recipes/*.xml
```

(The -i has the same effect as regular *grep* in making the search case-insensitive.) The whole search instruction is enclosed in single quotes (apostrophes) and the element names and search string are in double quotes inside it. While that command will find all titles containing 'choc', the following will find any items in the list of ingredients containing 'choc', which may be a better way of finding chocolate in recipes:

```
sgrep -i '("<ITEM>".."</ITEM>") in \
("<INGREDIENTS>".."</INGREDIENTS>") containing "choc"' recipes/*.xml
```

(Note the backslash which is Unix's way of letting you type a command split over several lines but have it interpreted as if it was all on one infinitely long line.) As you can see, doing complex searches can get tedious to type, especially if you have to provide all possible forms of start-tag (with attributes, with the element name followed by a TAB, a newline, or a space,*etc*) — don't forget this is not an SGML system, so it doesn't know all this inherently.

To overcome some of these problems, the authors provided the ability for *sgrep* to read a macro file (written in *m4*, a preprocessor which comes with most Unix systems). A sample file comes with the distribution, which defines a large number of SGML constructions for handling element and attribute syntax. This reduces the above example to:

```
sgrep -i 'NAMED_ELEMS(ITEM) in NAMED_ELEMS(INGREDIENTS) \
     containing "choc"' recipes/*.xml
```

There are additional expressions for extracting (removing) elements and their contents from a file, overlapping and nesting regions, and sequential text ('followed-by'). The current versions do not support Regular Expressions: these are planned for a future version, as is indexing and a built-in macro preprocessor.

5.1.3. Perl (Larry Wall)

Unix, DOS, Windows, Mac
`http://www.perl.com/`

Many dedicated Unix users now avoid using a mixture of the above programs in favor of a single processor language which combines most of their features and adds a lot of new ones. *Perl* is one of these: *Python* (see section 5.1.4) is another. Both are also used for SGML programming and increasingly for XML as well.

Perl is a very powerful language: programs are interpreted rather than compiled like C, meaning they are executed directly from an editable ASCII script file, but it still runs fast enough to handle most day-to-day tasks such as the ones described in the earlier sections of this chapter. The introduction to the book I mention below says it 'provides a more concise and readable way to do many jobs that were formerly accomplished (with difficulty) by programming in the C language or one of the shells'.

Its strength for SGML users is that it is very good at string handling and the use of arrays (tables of values), and it has also become the language of choice among many Unix programmers for utilities, and especially for Web scripts. Its syntax is terse to the point of obscurity, and it has some unusual quirks, but it has the ability to do very significant amounts of processing with a very small amount of code. One important feature is that *Perl* is not just for Unix: there are versions to run on PCs and Macs as well.

Several suites of SGML tools are now available in *Perl*, and these are discussed below. Even though you don't need any knowledge of *Perl* just to run the programs provided in these toolkits, if you are going to use SGML on a Unix system in any way heavily, I would recommend learning even a little *Perl* just to be able to understand more about the tools available.

Perl is far too large to do more than give a small example here. I recommend the O'Reilly book *Programming Perl*[42], by Larry Wall (the original inventor) and Randall Schwartz, if you want to get into learning the language yourself.

The following example is a script to strip SGML markup, written by Robert Seymour. It uses a character-by-character read mode which, though not as fast as a Regular Expression, will strip tags which fall across line or paragraph boundaries. It also preserves white-space so that the line numbers will be the same in the output as the input. This is useful for search engines which don't index markup, but need line numbering to be preserved. [Adapted from the author's comments.]

```
#! /usr/bin/perl

##  Use STDIN if no files are given

$ARGV[0] = "-" unless @ARGV;

##  Strip out anything contained in an SGML markup tag.  This is not
##  very pretty and rather inefficient, but it does take care of tags
##  which cross line or paragraph boundaries.

foreach $file (@ARGV) {
  open(INPUT,$file);
  while($char = getc(INPUT)) {
    if($char eq "<") {
      IGNORE: for(;;) {
        last IGNORE if (getc(INPUT) eq ">");
      }
    } else {
      print $char;
    }
  }
  close(INPUT);
}
```

The trick with `@ARGV` at the start simply sets the input expectation to be the default (symbolized by the minus sign where Unix shell input and output is concerned: in this case, the keyboard) unless the user has given a filename. You can see clearly the nested structure typical of *Perl* (its C heritage): the outermost loop processes each filename the user has typed; the file gets opened, and while there are still characters left to read it gets them one at a time and compares each to the '<' character. If it does not match, the character is printed; if it matches, the loop `IGNORE` is performed, which does nothing except continue getting characters until a '>' is encountered, at which point it resumes printing the characters.

Like most non-parsing, non-validating systems, it is open to failure when unexpected input is encountered, such as entities or attributes containing '<' or '>' signs; `CDATA` Marked Sections; or valid isolated '<' or '>' signs occurring in character data, but for many practical purposes it answers well and processes faster than the *sed* script in section 5.1.1.2 (but that handles character entities as well).

To overcome some of these problems, libraries of code have been developed to use the ESIS output of parsers. The author of *Perl*, Larry Wall, has decided to build James Clark's *expat* parser (see section 4.3.7.3) into *Perl*, so the interface with parsing and validation will be simpler, and its use with XML is likely to be very extensive.

There is an active developer community, and a mailing list hosted at `listmanager@activestate.com` (subscribe by sending the message `SUBSCRIBE Perl-XML`).

5.1.3.1. perlSGML (Earl Hood)

Unix, PC/Win, Mac

This is probably the best known package in *Perl* for handling SGML. It parses both DTDs and instances, and runs anywhere that *Perl* runs. There is a growing body of contributors who are making additional cod and facilities available which work with *perlSGML*.

There are five basic programs:

dtdview Lets you interactively query the DTD and get information about the structure, lists of element names, content models, attribute lists, *etc.* Example: open Elsevier's ART300 DTD and find out what's allowed in paragraphs:

```
% dtdview -catalog ../catalog art300/art300.dtd
Reading catalog(s) ...
Reading art300/art300.dtd ...
(art300) -> content p
Content model for P:
      (((#pcdata | b | it | rm | of | sc | ge | ssf | ty | scp |
         sup | inf | a | ovl | ov | ovr | unl | un | unr | lim |
         fen | box | fr | rad | ar | arrow | hsp | vsp) |
```

```
        (f | fd | fdr | tbl | tblr | fig | figr | l | lir | fn |
         fnr | bibr | secr | appr | qd))*)
(art300) -> quit
%
```

dtdtree Draws a diagrammatic plan of a DTD using plaintext characters. Except for small DTDs (like our example recipe dtd here), you need to provide some element limitation, as many DTDs allow text-containing elements to be infinitely recursive.

```
% dtdtree -dtd recipe.dtd
RECIPE
 |_(name,
 |    |_(#PCDATA)
 |
 |__source,
 |    |_(#PCDATA)
 |
 |__ingredients,
 |    |_(item+)
 |         |_(quantity,
 |         |    |_(#PCDATA)
 |         |
 |         |__substance,
 |         |    |_(#PCDATA)
 |         |
 |         |__comments?)
 |              |_(#PCDATA)
 |
 |...
```

dtddiff Analyses and lists differences between one version of a DTD and another. While this is essential when making or writing updates, it's also useful if you foul up editing a DTD and want to see which bits are now different from the original (assuming you kept a backup, of course...).

```
% dtddiff -catalog ../catalog art300/art300.dtd art400/art400.dtd
                 New Elements/Attributes (art400/art400.dtd)
    --------------------------------------------------------------
        <aff id>                          <anchor>
        <anchor id>                       <art refers-to>
        <atlfn>                           <bottom-border>
        ...many more omitted...
             Old/removed Elements/Attributes (art300/art300.dtd)
    --------------------------------------------------------------
        <appr>                            <appr id>
        <art crt>                         <art crtyr>
        <art dochead>                     <art doctopic>
        ...many more omitted...
    --------------------------------------------------------------
```

```
                          Content Rule Differences
                                 <ABS>
      << old content rule <<
      (p+)
      >> new content rule >>
      ((p|sec)+)
    ...
```

stripsgml Removes all element markup from an instance (but does not read the DTD: this is just a syntactic strip, like the one given earlier). It also attempts to convert character entities to their single-byte (ISO 8859) representation, but does not do anything with attribute values. Careful manual editing of the SGML source to make judicious use of insignificant white-space could result in a very effective SGML-to-ASCII translation.

```
% stripsgml <fudge.sgm >fudge.txt
% cat fudge.txt
  Chocolate Fudge
  A very easy recipe of my mother's

    1  Sugar
    4  Butter
    4  Chocolate
      Only use plain chocolate with a high cocoa
content, never milk or white chocolate or chocolate
substitutes
    4  Evaporated milk

...
```

dtd2html Creates a set of HTML files which document and map the structure of a DTD, allowing you to 'walk' the structure with a browser. Once the files are created, you can of course edit them to add further documentation and explanation.

You can also write your own *Perl* code to add new facilities: there is a DTD parser and an instance parser available, and all the ancillary modules handling catalogs, the command line, and character-set handling.

5.1.3.2. SGMLSpm (David Megginson)

SGMLSpm is an object-oriented *Perl* postprocessor for James Clark's *sgmls* and *nsgmls* parsers. It comprises a *Perl* class library which can be used to build systems to handle ESIS output (see section 4.2.2) on an event-driven basis. *SGMLSpm* requires *perl5* and is not tied to any specific DTD: it's a general-purpose package.

SGMLSpm comes with extensive HTML documentation on the six classes it defines: for the parser, an event handler, elements, attributes,

2 *CHAPTER 1.*

***SGMLSpm* (David Megginson)**

***SGMLSpm* is an object-oriented *Perl* postprocessor for James Clark's *sgmls* and *nsgmls* parsers. It comprises a *Perl* class library which can be used to build systems to handle ESIS output (see section 1.1.1) on an event-driven basis. *SGMLSpm* requires *perl5* and is not tied to any specific DTD: it's a general-purpose package.**

Figure 1.1: LaTeX output of this section generated through *SGMLSpm*.

***SGMLSpm* comes with extensive HTML documentation on the six classes it defines: for the parser, an event handler, elements, attributes, entities, and notations. It assumes an extensive knowledge of *Perl*, as this is a package for the programmer, not the end user.**

The distribution includes a script, `skel.pl`, to write a skeleton conversion script for a document. Running this over the current section produces a file with some *Perl* code like this:

```
# Element: BOOK
sgml('<BOOK>', "");
sgml('</BOOK>', "");

# Element: CHAPTER
sgml('<CHAPTER>', "");
sgml('</CHAPTER>', "");

# Element: TITLE
sgml('<TITLE>', "");
sgml('</TITLE>', "");
```

It's then a matter of editing-in the formatting required for whatever output system you use, and running the system again using the edited script. A few minutes adding LaTeX code to this test produced a file which generated the printed version shown in 1.1.

Figure 93. LaTeX output of this section generated through *SGMLSpm*.

entities, and notations. It assumes an extensive knowledge of *Perl*, as this is a package for the programmer, not the end user.

The distribution includes a script, `skel.pl`, to write a skeleton conversion script for a document. Running this over the current section produces a file with some *Perl* code like this:

```
# Element: BOOK
sgml('<BOOK>', "");
sgml('</BOOK>', "");

# Element: CHAPTER
sgml('<CHAPTER>', "");
sgml('</CHAPTER>', "");

# Element: TITLE
sgml('<TITLE>', "");
sgml('</TITLE>', "");
```

It's then a matter of editing-in the formatting required for whatever output system you use, and running the system again using the edited script. A few minutes adding LaTeX code to this test produced a file which generated the printed version shown in Figure 93.

5.1.4. Python

Unix, DOS, MS-Windows, Mac, Amiga, BeOS, VMS
`http://www.python.org/`

Python was designed to solve the same set of problems as *Perl*, but using features from a different set of languages in a way that would remain familiar to users of those languages (C++, *Simula*, *Smalltalk*, *Scheme*, *Lisp*, and even *Perl* itself), in the same way that *Perl* retains many of the features of *awk*, *sed*, *grep*, and the Unix shells.

It is multiplatform, with versions for almost all operating systems except IBM mainframes, and there's a *python-mode* for editing in *Emacs*. There is a growing body of code for handling SGML with *Python*: an interface to *LT NSL* (see section 7.1.2); an XML parser from Dan Connolly; *PySGML* from Paul Prescod (a library that transforms ESIS into a Python-object grove); and several examples in an article by Seán McGrath[33].

There is a mailing list to discuss *Python*: send an email with the word `subscribe` in either the subject line or the body of the message to `xml-sig-request@python.org`. XML developments are being managed by a SIG (Special Interest Group) at `http://www.python.org/sigs/xml-sig/` , and there are many other SIGs for other languages and applications of *Python* (details on the Web site).

5.2. Programmable conversion engines

The distinction between the tools written in *Perl* or *Python* (or indeed in other general-purpose languages, even C/C++) and the fully-programmable systems in this section is the existence of a separate, well-developed language layer specifically aimed at handling SGML.

These languages vary widely: some have more in common with the language in which they themselves are written (*Balise* and *SGMLC* are based on C/C++, for example); others use their own 4GL (Fourth Generation Language) with a more modern syntax. A similar position has obtained for many years in other fields of processing, where separate languages have been developed for domain-oriented programming languages, which bear little or no relation to the language of the package for which they were developed (for example, the PPL (P-Stat Programming Language) inside the *P-Stat* data management and statistics package has no resemblance to the C in which *P-Stat* is written, or indeed to the Fortran in which it had its early origins).

The choice of system may therefore rest not only on the ability of the system to perform the task required, but on the ease or speed with which specific staff, or clients, or users, will be able to learn the language involved. Programmers from a classical Computer Science background may find the C-like systems preferable; users from a database, stats, or business-programming background may prefer the 4GL systems (this is probably a poor way to pick a system, but it highlights some of the practical difficulties of the choices).

In addition to the systems described here, there is a simple down-translation (SGML to other systems) included in the *LT XML* package (see section 7.1.3).

5.2.1. Omnimark (Omnimark)

Unix, DOS/Windows, OS/2, Mac
`http://www.omnimark.com/`

Omnimark is one of the best-known conversion programming languages for SGML, and one of the longest-established (it was previously called *XGML* when the company was called Exoterica). It is a command line program on most platforms, although the most recent versions are not available for Macs.

There is also a 'lite' version (*Omnimark* 'LE' or *OMLE*) so you can try it before deciding to buy: this version is limited to 200 'actions' (different things the program can do after matching an element or character pattern, apart from just outputting it), which means you can use it very successfully for small-scale processing. This version is on the CD-ROM with this book.

The documentation comes in several volumes, but is also on the company's Web server, so users of *OMLE* also have access to it, and programmers working with a network connection but no paper manuals can refer to it.

The programming language is composed of element-matching and pattern-matching statements for processing a file, with SGML validation when required, and with an output formatting language which includes extensive parameter substitution. This means you can convert in any direction (see below) and reformat the output to suit the application. There is a referential mechanism which lets you hold or bookmark values or their locations and check them off again later, so you can refer to things in the program that you haven't yet encountered in the input file, but which you know will occur (such as `ID`s and `IDREF`s).

Omnimark programs can translate in four 'directions':

non-SGML to non-SGML via an intermediate SGML format ('context-translate');
SGML to non-SGML ('down-translate';
non-SGML to SGML ('up-translate')
non-SGML to non-SGML without parsing ('cross-translate').

The existence of the built-in parser means that input SGML files get validated as they are read, and if you are outputting SGML, your output gets validated as it is written. The non-SGML input methods can be used to pattern-match your way through translating malformed SGML (such as most HTML) into a valid format.

Before installing *Omnimark* you have to install and run the *FlexLM* license manager (supplied) and add a license string from the company. The whole system can be downloaded and set up before purchase of the license which activates it. A dongle is available for systems which do not provide a hostid to generate the license string. The *OMLE* version runs without a license manager.

5.2.1.1. Operation

You write an *Omnimark* program using your favorite plaintext editor (*Emacs* has a very useful *omnimark-mode* which is on the CD-ROM). The language structure is typical of many 4th generation languages and uses a set of English-like instructions.

For translations taking SGML as their *input*, each processing statement in a program is a 'rule', matching an element or other SGML object, optionally with conditions, and providing one or more 'actions' for output or manipulation (see Figure 94). Note the `%c` which specifies the input element content being treated at that point; the `%n` for a newline; and the `%` escape for embedded quotes. The `%v` provides the value of an attribute to the current element. The `%c` element content is reprocessed until all subelements have been matched and their rules performed, and only `PCDATA` is left, which is then output as text.

There is a generic Unix script called `genxom` on the CD-ROM in the `Omnimark` folder, which I use to extract the names of all the elements used in an SGML instance, and write a skeleton *Omnimark* program:

```
% genxom mydoc.sgml
```

It performs no parsing, and only identifies regular element markup, but it is useful for a first pass.

More complex translations can make use of multiple output streams: the content of an element can be sent to a temporary buffer and then reused later at one or more different points in the program. Unmarked element content can also be scanned character by character for patterns,

```
element SECT1 or SECT2 or SECT3
        output "<div>%c</div>"

element TITLE
        output "<h2>%c</h2>%n" when parent is SECT1
        output "<h3>%c</h3>%n" when parent is SECT2
        output "<h4>%c</h4>%n" when parent is SECT3

element EMPHASIS
        output "<em>%c</em>"

element ULINK
        output "<a href=%"%v(url)%">%c</a>"

translate sdata "[aacute ]" output "&aacute;"
```

Figure 94. Omnimark program to translate *DocBook* to HTML (fragment)

so they can be recognized independently from the markup and remarked accordingly.

Translation into SGML uses a very extensive pattern-match language partly modeled on Unix Regular Expressions (see section 5.1.1.1). Any sequence of characters can be matched, tested, and used or discarded: the output syntax is the same as in other translations (see Figure 95). This demonstrates the use of logic switches which can be activated or deactivated, and then detected later to signal the status of the data.

In this example you can see variables being declared at the start, and the `find-start` and `find-end` rules which bound the beginning and end of the program. The remaining `find` rules match some fairly complex patterns which occur in email headers: note the use of the equals sign to record the value of the preceding match into a local variable which is then retrieved via the `%x` operator at the output stage.

To run an *Omnimark* program you use a typed command, with options for specifying input and output files, log file, catalogs, and the passing of values from the environment into the program. For frequent or repeated use, a script or batch file is useful. The program can be run from the shell features of editors like *Emacs* or *PFE*, so it can be made to work with a keystroke or mouseclick. Figure 96 shows my own experimental MS-Windows front-end shell for *Omnimark* which is included on the CD-ROM.

The catalog file does not use OASIS format but it's very close (omit the `PUBLIC` keyword and start the catalog file with a single line saying `LIBRARY`). *Omnimark* takes the System identifier from the instance's DocType Declaration by preference, and if it is there, won't try the catalog. For conversions between different SGML DTDs, the parser

```
cross-translate

   global switch EOH
   global switch quoted

find-start
   output "<message>%n<header>%n"

find "From" white-space+ [any except "@"]+ =local-part
   "@" [any except space]+ =remote-part
   white-space+ [letter]+ =wkday
   white-space+ [letter]+ =month
   white-space+ [digit]+ =day
   white-space+ ([digit]+ ":" [digit]+ ":" [digit]+) =time
   white-space+ [digit]+ =year when not active EOH
   output "<from><user>%x(local-part)</user>"
   output "<host>%x(remote-part)</host></from>%n"
   output "<date>%x(year)-%x(month)-%x(day)</date>%n"
   output "<time>%x(time)</time>"

find ([UC] [lc or UC or "-"]+) =header ":" white-space [any]+ =value
   lookahead ("%n" [letter])
   output "<%x(header)>%x(value)</%x(header)>"

find "%n%n" when not active EOH
   activate EOH
   output "</header>%n<text>%n<par>"

find ("%n" white-space?)+ ">" (white-space? ">")* when active EOH
   do when not active quoted
      activate quoted
      output "</par>%n<quote>"
   done

find "%n" white-space? [any except ">"] =char
         when active EOH and active quoted
   deactivate quoted
   output "</quote>%n<par>%x(char)"

find "<" output "<address>"
find ">" output "</address>"

find "%n%n" when active EOH
   output "</par><par>"

find-end
   output "</message>%n"
```

Figure 95. Omnimark program to translate email headers to a 'message' DTD (fragment)

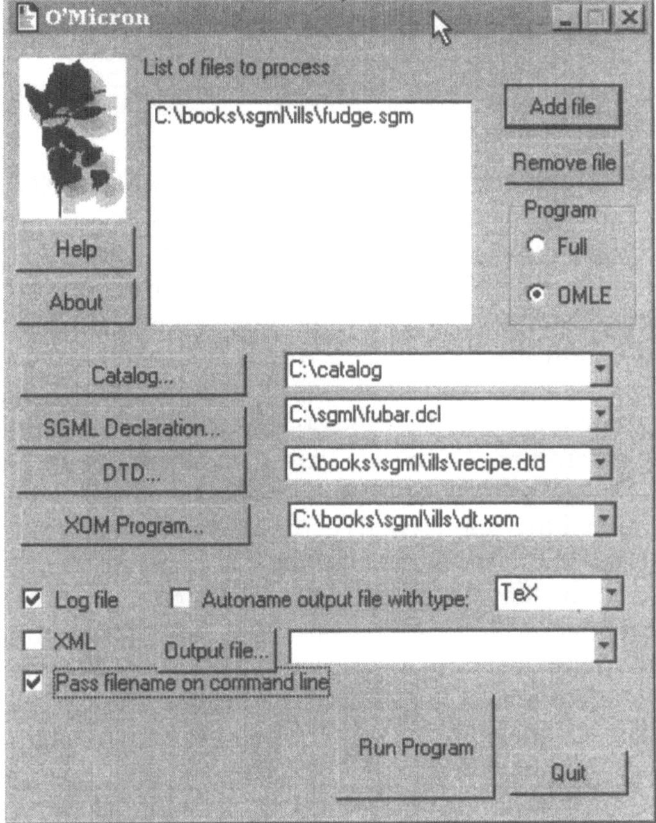

Figure 96. The experimental *O'Micron* windowing shell for *Omnimark*

runs on both the input and the output, providing validation in both directions.

The *OMLE* version on the CD-ROM replaces the *Omnimark* 'Sampler' of previous versions, and provides example conversion fragments for many formats, including Microsoft *Word*, Corel *WordPerfect*, Unix manual pages, RTF, TeX, and others.

For use in a Web environment, Omnimark produce *Konstruktor* (formerly *Banff*), which provides on-the-fly translations in a server mode (*ie* without the overhead of starting the program every time). Using this you can author an entire Web site in a mix of file formats but have everything converted to HTML or some other SGML or XML format at the point of delivery.

5.2.2. SGMLC (SGML Systems Engineering)

MS-Windows
`http://www.dircon.co.uk/sgml/`

SGMLC is a C-based package for developing SGML applications, from SGML Systems Engineering in Somerset, England. It consists of a compiler for MS-Windows (16–bit and 32–bit) with a complete set of functions for creating interactive or batch SGML conversion, browser and publishing applications. The resulting code can be distributed and executed by their run-time processor, which is available free (and is on the CD-ROM).

The compiler comes in two flavors, a converter environment and a publisher environment. The converter environment is for creating SGML file conversion applications only (it can not be used to create viewer or publishing applications); the publisher environment does both conversion and viewing/publishing.

Applications are developed as 'rules' files, composed of functions and event-driven element rules. User-defined and library functions are also available. The output is expressed in their IML (Internal Markup Language), which is interpreted by the runtime processor to produce output for the designated platform. The processing language is a 'major subset' of C with embedded SGML facilities such as

opening an SGML document and reading the SGML Declaration and DTD;
finding the start or end of an element, an entity reference, or a processing instruction;
receiving a DDE command from another application, or user hotspot or menu selection;
SGML parser error or program runtime error handling.

As an example of some code, here is a function to translate the alignment attributes of a table cell to HTML-style `ALIGN` attributes (from their table and equation viewer/converter):

```
function align(x)
{
switch (x) {
case "b": case "l": return "LEFT";
case "r": return "RIGHT";
case "c": return "CENTER";
case "": case "d": case "*": return "LEFT";
default: return "invalid";
}
}
```

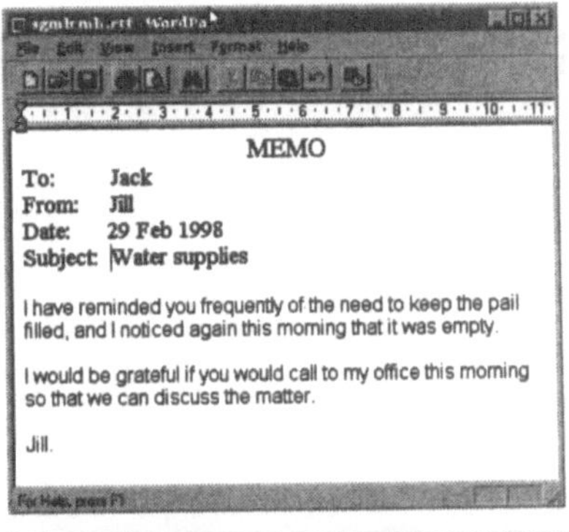

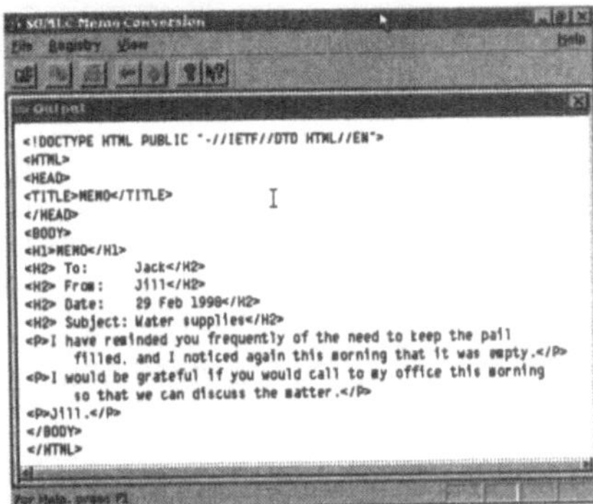

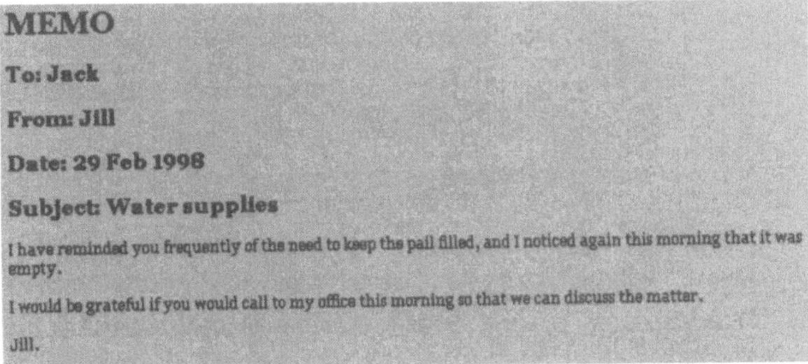

Figure 97. SGMLC Memo sample converted to RTF (top) and to HTML (middle) and displayed in a browser (bottom).

Element rules have a 'start' and 'end' section corresponding to the start-tag and end-tag: this example from the Math sample application translates the <FEN> (fence) element of an equation into the delimiters (brackets) surrounding an expression:

```
element FEN when (inmath)
        start {
            0 << "\\left\\delimiter\"";
```

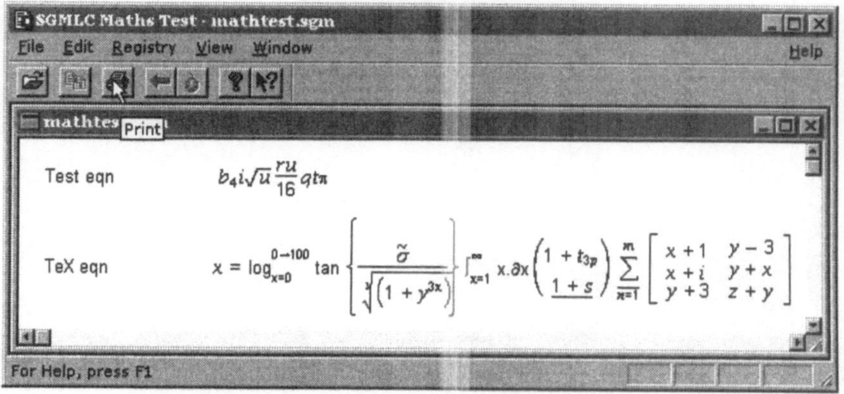

$$x=\log_{x=0}^{0\to 100}\tan\left\{\frac{\tilde{\sigma}}{\sqrt[3]{(1+y^{3x})}}\right\}\int_{x=1}^{\infty}x.\partial x\left(\frac{1+t_{3p}}{\underline{1+s}}\right)\sum_{n=1}^{m}\begin{bmatrix}x+1 & y-3\\ x+i & y+x\\ y+3 & z+y\end{bmatrix}$$

Figure 98. SGMLC math viewer

```
        0 << open_delim(lp);
        0 << " ";
    }
    end {
        0 << "\\right\\delimiter\"";
        if(!exists(0,"rp")) rp=lp;
        0 << close_delim(rp);
        0 << " ";
    }
```

There is an additional unregistered publisher environment available free for personal or in-house use (distribution of the resulting applications is prohibited by the license). This has complete programming functionality, but produces only 16-bit code, and cannot take a command line argument (and support is not available).

SGML Systems Engineering distributes a selection of sample applications, which are on the CD-ROM, so you can judge the suitability of the system for your tasks. Figure 97 shows the memo which we saw in section 2.3.1.3.3, processed with their sample Memo application into HTML and RTF.

The math viewer uses the IML to create math typesetting on-screen: Figure 98 shows our test expression and a more complex equation which it can render both from SGML markup and from TeX primitives

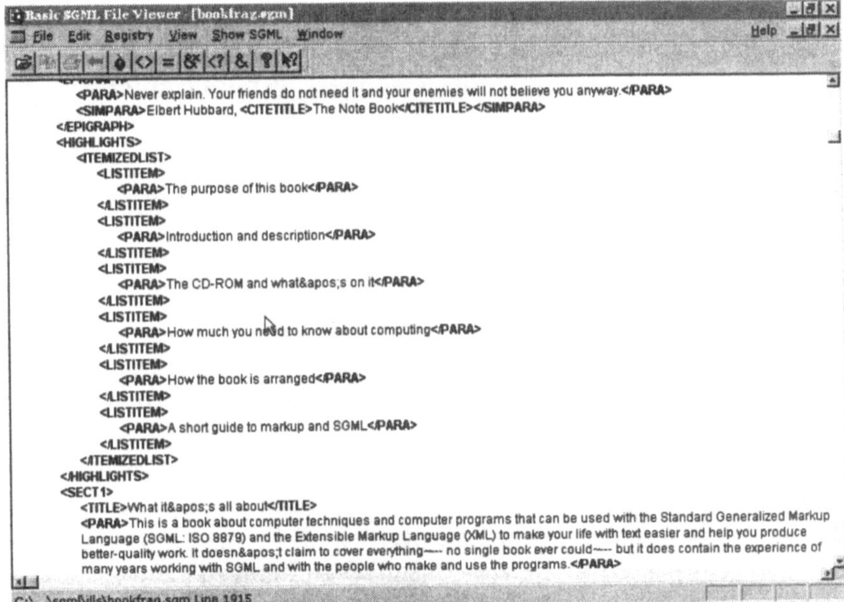

Figure 99. SGMLC viewer for SGML source files

(not from macros). I've added TEX's own rendering underneath for comparison.

Finally, there is a general-purpose SGML file viewer (see Figure 99). This displays any SGML file with the element structure indented (à la *Emacs/psgml*) for elements in element content, and inline where elements occur in mixed content. When opening an instance of a DTD not used before, this application prompts the user for a local filename for any unresolved FPIs or system identifiers, which avoids the user requiring a foreknowledge of the catalog mechanism (although the catalog is in the regular OASIS format in the file `enttable`, so it can easily be edited).

5.2.3. Balise (AIS Berger-Levrault)

Unix, DOS/Windows
`http://www.balise.com/`

Berger-Levrault advertise *Balise* as the 'All-purpose SGML Companion', a kind of Swiss army knife for SGML conversion. AIS have been in the SGML software business for a long time, and this is a mature and well-established product with a strong following in the embedded systems part of the SGML market as well as in conversion systems.

The product is a command line program, installable from disk or CD-ROM with an evaluation version downloadable from the Internet. Separate licenses are available for developers' versions and users' run-time versions. The evaluation copy can be used in two modes: with limited capacity but full features; or with full capacity but with all output PCDATA randomized. This lets you test very large systems exhaustively before making a purchase.

As mentioned earlier, the syntax of a *Balise* program is similar to C/C++, so it is immediately familiar to any programmer. The makers claim that 'any C programmer can read and understand most parts of a Balise program at first sight', which is probably true, but I feel that for non-programmers some preliminary training in C programming principles would be an advantage.

The advantages *Balise* offers are that the system automates (or rather, has preprogrammed) the SGML 'core' tasks such as validation, navigation, identification of elements, attributes, and entity references. Programs get interpreted and byte-compiled (tokenized) into a portable format, so code can be shared between platforms.

The availability of SGML-specific routines means that no time is wasted writing or maintaining your own code to do these tasks. One of the sample programs they provide in the extensive tutorial can be used to illustrate this:

```
// maps element names to use counts
var counters = Map();
var fout = cout;

// create or increment the counter
function registerName(name)
{// associated with name
    // if a name counter already exists
    if counters.knows(name) {
            counters[name]++;// increment it
    } else { // else
            // create and initialize a counter
            counters[name] = 1;
    }
}

default {
    on start { // on each element occurrence
            // record this occurrence
            registerName(GI());
    }
}

// on each content occurrence
```

```
content(CDATA|SDATA|PI) {
    registerName(GI()); // record this occurrence
}

// once the whole document has been processed ...
after {

                // for each element name, sorted by negative
                // (i.e. decreasing) usage counts
    for k in eSort(counters,function(x) { return -counters[x];}) {
                        // display its usage count
            fout >> format("%1 occurences of %2\n",counters[k],k);
    }
}
```

This is a program to gather all the element names used in a document, count how many instances there are of each, and print a list sorted in descending order of occurrence. You can see the array `counters` being declared, and the function `registerName` which tests for element awareness, and creates or increments a counter item accordingly. The processing in this example is set to activate on three events, all defaults as we are not processing specific elements, only counting occurrences:

1. `start`, which processes any start-tag, and here triggers the function `registerName` (there is an end event, not used here, for handling the closing of an element);
2. `content`, which handles the data content of elements (in this example pseudo-elements for stretches of content data between markup, and non-element markup like SDATA or Processing Instructions are treated as a special case of 'elements' for the purposes of counting);
3. `after`, which takes over when processing of the file is completed, and here sorts the array and outputs it in list format.

Running it over an earlier version of this book produced a list starting:

```
12557 occurences of #CDATA
2203 occurences of PARA
910 occurences of PRODUCTNAME
697 occurences of #SDATA
616 occurences of SGMLTAG
504 occurences of TITLE
497 occurences of LISTITEM
484 occurences of INDEXTERM
...
```

Documentation is extensive, and all available on the Web as well as in printed form. There is a tutorial for programmers, with extended examples and instructions in HTML for use with browsers, and a ¼Mb of text to practise on.

Balise uses the *SP* parser internally (see section 4.3.5), so it uses the OASIS catalog format. It also provides access to the whole document tree, so it can perform random access functions as well as regular SGML 'depth-first' event-driven access. Random access to large SGML trees chews up memory, so it works by loading subtrees and combining this with event-driven sequential access. There is a Software Developers' Kit, which provides an API via a C library, so *Balise* can be 'hidden' inside other applications , including database access via ODBC (Open DataBase Connectivity). AIC also distribute an MS-Windows program called the *Balise HTML Package*, which converts an SGML file to HTML, using a stylesheet mapping (see next section).

It is also possible to have *Balise* run and manage multiple child processes, so you could have separate programs working on different parts of the same document. Multiple document access is also supported, and inter-process communication allows one process on one document to pass data to another process on a different document.

5.2.3.1. StyleIt: the Balise HTML Package

MS-Windows, Unix
`http://www.balise.com`

This is a standalone program which creates a mapped transformation between an SGML instance and a HTML representation of it, suitable for the Web. The mapping can then be used with *Balise* in batch mode to perform bulk conversions, specifically of large SGML files into HTML fragments.

The interface has the stylesheet specification panels on the left and the SGML file on the right. You click on a tag in the SGML display (with markup turned on) and then provide its mapping to HTML in the tabs on the left (see Figure 100). The subdivision of a large input file into smaller output files can be controlled by the markup (*ie* on the basis of chapters or sections), and navigation links can be generated automatically for the user.

The transformations are not just to element markup in HTML, but include font size and color, and the generation of 'decoration' before and after the element content (where you can add more HTML markup by hand to achieve the desired effect); regular generated text before and after the element; hypertext linking; page styles like background color, wallpaper, and colored link text; auto-generated table of contents material; and styling data like table bordering.

The stylesheet language is itself in SGML, with expressions in the *Balise* processing language. The styling panels include commonly-used

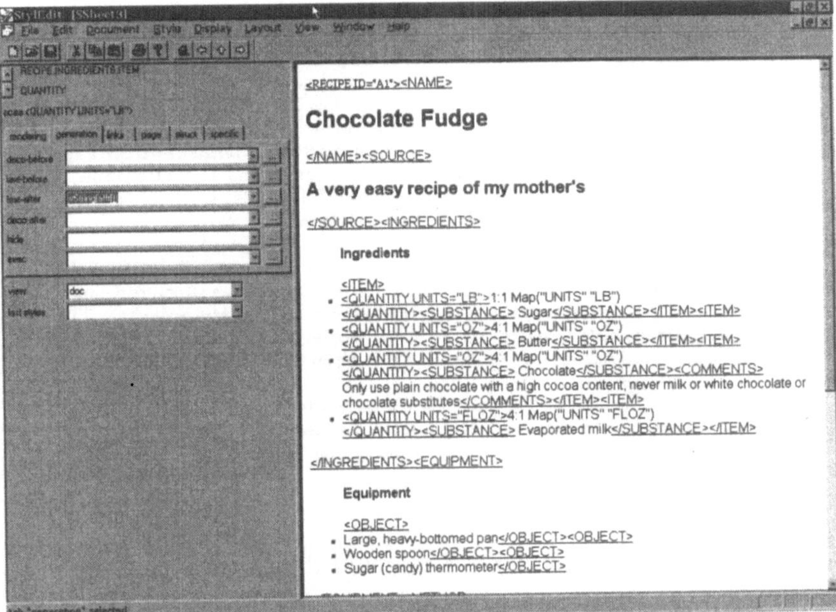
<RECIPE ID="A1"><NAME>
Chocolate Fudge
</NAME><SOURCE>
A very easy recipe of my mother's
</SOURCE><INGREDIENTS>
Ingredients
<ITEM>
<QUANTITY UNITS="LB">1:1 Map("UNITS" "LB")
</QUANTITY><SUBSTANCE> Sugar</SUBSTANCE></ITEM><ITEM>
<QUANTITY UNITS="OZ">4:1 Map("UNITS" "OZ")
</QUANTITY><SUBSTANCE> Butter</SUBSTANCE></ITEM><ITEM>
<QUANTITY UNITS="OZ">4:1 Map("UNITS" "OZ")
</QUANTITY><SUBSTANCE> Chocolate</SUBSTANCE><COMMENTS>
Only use plain chocolate with a high cocoa content, never milk or white chocolate or chocolate substitutes</COMMENTS></ITEM><ITEM>
<QUANTITY UNITS="FLOZ">4:1 Map("UNITS" "FLOZ")
</QUANTITY><SUBSTANCE> Evaporated milk</SUBSTANCE></ITEM>
</INGREDIENTS><EQUIPMENT>
Equipment
<OBJECT>
Large, heavy-bottomed pan</OBJECT><OBJECT>
Wooden spoon</OBJECT><OBJECT>
Sugar (candy) thermometer</OBJECT>

Figure 100. Mapping SGML markup to HTML with *Styledit*

constructions such as the `String(attr["..."])` function for replicating the value of an attribute, and include (uniquely in a windowing interface to a stylesheet) the explicit retrieval and replication of cross-reference numbering from other elements, so a reference of the form `<xref label="Figure" linkend="balise">` can be treated so that it is replaced by the value of the `label` plus the generated value of the element elsewhere in the document whose `ID` value is `balise`. This cross-reference replication, which I referred to on page 210 (this reference is itself one example), is critical in any publishing process, and it is remarkable how few packages implement it in an accessible manner.

5.2.4. Jade (James Clark)

Unix, Windows, OS/2
`http://www.jclark.com/`
`http://clover.slavic.pitt.edu/~djb/sgml/` (for OS/2)

James Clark, author of *sgmls* and *nsgmls*, is also editor of ISO 10179: DSSSL, which provides SGML with standardized formatting, transformation and query languages (see section 2.7.2.3). To implement DSSSL, he wrote *Jade*, which provides an abstract and a concrete interface to

Unix, Windows, OS/2
`http://www.jclark.com/`
`http://clover.slavic.pitt.edu/~djb/sgml/` (for OS/2)

James Clark, author of *sgmls* and *nsgmls*, is also editor of ISO 10179: DSSSL, which provides SGML with standardized formatting, transformation and query languages (see section X.X). To implement DSSSL, he wrote *Jade*, which provides an abstract and a concrete interface to groves via *SP*. As an implementation of this, it takes an SGML document and a DSSSL style file, and can produce RTF or LaTeX output for formatting, or an SGML or XML representation for transformations. *Jade* is available from James Clark for Unix and MS-Windows; David Birnbaum is author of the version for OS/2.

Jade is run as a command with options which determine its action on a file: the default is to look for a DSSSL file and use that to create a transformation to a FOT, a structure defined by DSSSL. The `-t` (type) option is used to specify the type of output (SGML, XML, TeX, RTF, *etc*).

A number of individuals and organizations are developing DSSSL stylesheets for use with Jade, but the most widespread are probably the DocBook ones developed by Norm Walsh at `http://nwalsh.com/docbook/dsssl/`.

Output for LaTeX is handled by the *jadetex* package, written by Sebastian Rahtz. Because of the very wide range of output options available for TeX systems, this means that SGML can be output to almost any device, and to a number of file formats including PDF, used in Adobe's *Acrobat* browser.

Figure 101. *Jade* using RTF output on the current section.

groves via *SP*. As an implementation of this, it takes an SGML document and a DSSSL style file, and can produce RTF or LaTeX output for formatting, or an SGML or XML representation for transformations. *Jade* is available from James Clark for Unix and MS-Windows; David Birnbaum is author of the version for OS/2.

Jade is run as a command with options which determine its action on a file: the default is to look for a DSSSL file and use that to create a transformation to a FOT (Flow Object Tree), a structure defined by DSSSL. The `-t` (type) option is used to specify the type of output (SGML, XML, TeX, RTF, *etc*).

A number of individuals and organizations are developing DSSSL stylesheets for use with *Jade*, but the most widespread are probably the *DocBook* ones developed by Norm Walsh at `http://nwalsh.com/docbook/dsssl/` (see Figure 101).

Output for LaTeX is handled by the *jadetex* package, written by Sebastian Rahtz. Because of the very wide range of output options available for TeX systems, this means that SGML can be output to almost any device, and to a number of file formats including PDF (Portable Document Format), used in Adobe's *Acrobat* browser.

5.3. SGML export and import without programming

In addition to programmable conversion there is a growing market for semi-automated conversions into and out of popular word processing and desktop publishing formats. The demand for this is strong, particularly among users of these systems encountering SGML for the first time, and those handling large backlogs of 'legacy' data.

While there are systems for conversion built into (or closely attached to) many modern WP and DTP formats, older or less heavily used formats will will require a programmed solution. As we saw at the beginning of this chapter, the existence of so many word-processor-to-word-processor conversions at the visual level outside the SGML field has misled many new users to believe that conversion into and out of SGML must somehow be available at the press of a button.

Of course it can be — once it's programmed: it's the setting up which takes the time. I recently completed a conversion program in *Omnimark* for making HTML versions of very heavily marked TEI texts. It took three days' programming to get it consistently working for the range of markup involved, including splitting large single input files into multiple output files for the Web. Now conversion is a mouse-click and takes about 30 seconds for a 1Mb input file on a Pentium 133. It was worth the effort in that project because there is potentially over 500Mb of input data to handle and a regular update frequency.

For a word processing output format you could double that amount of programming time, for an expert in both languages, given the much less tractable binary nature of most WP formats; and to go in the other direction, word processor file into SGML, is even harder, if not impossible. Indeed, it's quite likely for that to be a task of such magnitude that manual conversion would be faster.

The revised and abbreviated SGML FAQ posted regularly on `comp.text.sgml` compares converting visual markup (the traditional word processor) into SGML to asking for a machine which will make a house out of a pile of bricks (with no architect's plans). Others have likened the task to recreating the whole unbroken eggs out of a pan of scrambled eggs (see the box), or making a cow out of hamburger: when the information on what the text represents simply isn't there or has been removed, conversion will always contain some element of approximation.

Making whole eggs out of scrambled egg

To convert meaningfully from word processor formats into SGML is easiest at the two extremes of markup:

- when the document has very light, almost insignificant, markup (*eg* a novel, which probably has just chapters and paragraphs, and perhaps the occasional foreign word or piece of emphasis);
- when the document has markup which has been applied with perfect rigor, so that it is exact and completely unambiguous (*eg* office reports in organizations with a tightly-controlled and carefully thought out document structure, and well-trained staff creating the documents).

In between come most of the world's documents, made up just of paragraphs, nothing else, except some of them are in a different font or have been centered, and some of them are indented or have been prefixed with a number or a bullet. The precious eggs of information ('*why* is this italicized?', 'what's the *meaning* of **CM Bold Extended 8/10pt** ?', 'why are some words centered and others not?'), which are all obvious to a human, have been liquidized, seasoned, and cooked...and now there's a requirement to get the whole eggs back again.

It is just about possible to do it, provided the formatting is 100% accurate, machine-identifiable, and completely consistent. Otherwise if there is at least some trace of markup and consistency, the programs in this chapter can automate part of the process. If there's no reliable way of identifying things at all, it's probably faster to save the file as plaintext (or even scan a printed copy) and put the markup in by hand.

5.3.1. RainbowMaker (Inso)

DOS (Windows), Unix (SunOS and Solaris)
`ftp://ftp.inso.com/pub/TOBEDELETED/nv/dtd/rainbow/`

The Rainbow suite is a collection of command line programs and a DTD which allow word processor files to be converted into SGML with the express goal of serving as an intermediate format for conversion. The DTD has been written so that it models the text structures found in word processing systems. This means that the text, once converted, continues to reflect exactly the features it possessed in the word pro-

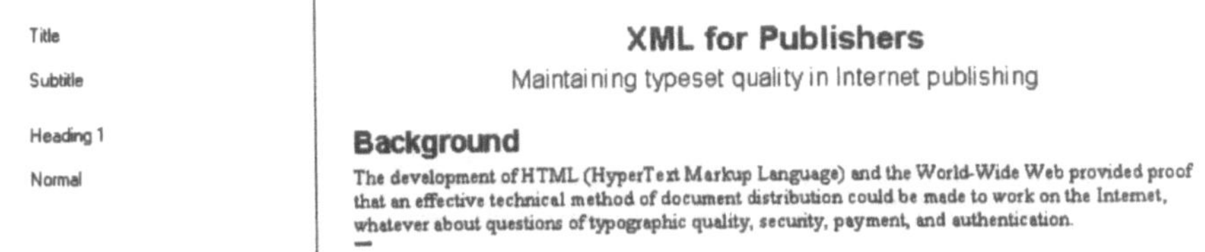
Title
Subtitle
Heading 1
Normal
XML for Publishers
Maintaining typeset quality in Internet publishing
Background
The development of HTML (HyperText Markup Language) and the World-Wide Web provided proof that an effective technical method of document distribution could be made to work on the Internet, whatever about questions of typographic quality, security, payment, and authentication.

Figure 102. Article in MS Word 7 using named styles to do formatting

cessor, but because it is now in an SGML format, it can be manipulated by any regular SGML software, including converters into other DTDs: it is not intended that you would keep data in the Rainbow DTD for any length of time. The technology also underlies Inso's *DynaTag* program (see section 5.3.2), which uses an MS-Windows interface.

The *rbmaker* program is the command-line utility for DOS and Unix. Binaries for *SunOS* and *Solaris* are provided, but source code is available, so versions for other platforms could be generated; the DOS version also runs in MS-Windows. It was originally written by Electronic Book Technologies (EBT, now part of Inso). It is free, and at the time of writing can still be downloaded from the Inso FTP server (a copy is provided on the CD-ROM with this book). It incorporates *RainbowMaker* modules for handling files in Interleaf ASCII, *FrameMaker* MIF, and Microsoft RTF formats: as most word processor files can be converted to one of these three formats, this is the starting point.

The process is best illustrated by looking at a document before and after: Figure 102 shows the start of an article in *Word* 7, using the default stylesheet.

This was saved in RTF (Rich Text Format):

```
{\rtf1\ansi \deff4\deflang1033{\fonttbl{\f4\froman\fcharset0\fprq2
Times New Roman;}{\f5\fswiss\fcharset0\fprq2
Arial;}}{\colortbl;\red0\green0\blue0;\red0\green0\blue255;
\red0\green255\blue255;\red0\green255\blue0;
\red255\green0\blue255;\red255\green0\blue0;\red255\green255\blue0;
\red255\green255\blue255;\red0\green0\blue128;\red0\green128\blue128;
\red0\green128\blue0;\red128\green0\blue128;\red128\green0\blue0;
\red128\green128\blue0;\red128\green128\blue128;
\red192\green192\blue192;}{\stylesheet{\widctlpar \f4\fs20\lang2057
\snext0 Normal;}{\s1\sb240\sa60\keepn\widctlpar
\b\f5\fs28\lang2057\kerning28 \sbasedon0\snext0 heading 1;}{\*\cs10
\additive Default Paragraph Font;}{\s16\qc\sb240\sa60\widctlpar
\b\f5\fs32\lang2057\kerning28 \sbasedon0\snext16
Title;}{\s17\qc\sa60\widctlpar \f5\lang2057 \sbasedon0\snext17
Subtitle;}}{\info{\title XML for Publishers}{\author Peter
Flynn}{\operator Peter Flynn}{\creatim\yr1997\mo9\dy11\hr18\min47}
{\revtim\yr1997\mo9\dy11\hr18\min47}{\version2}{\edmins0}{\nofpages1}
```

```
{\nofwords51}{\nofchars296}{\*\company
UCC}{\vern57443}}\paperw11906\paperh16838
\widowctrl\ftnbj\aenddoc\formshade \fet0\sectd
\linex0\headery709\footery709\colsx709\endnhere
{\*\pnseclvl1\pnucrm\pnstart1\pnindent720\pnhang{\pntxta
.}}{\*\pnseclvl2\pnucltr\pnstart1\pnindent720\pnhang{\pntxta
.}}{\*\pnseclvl3\pndec\pnstart1\pnindent720\pnhang{\pntxta
.}}{\*\pnseclvl4\pnlcltr\pnstart1\pnindent720\pnhang{\pntxta
)}}{\*\pnseclvl5 \pndec\pnstart1\pnindent720\pnhang{\pntxtb
(}{\pntxta
)}}{\*\pnseclvl6\pnlcltr\pnstart1\pnindent720\pnhang{\pntxtb
(}{\pntxta
)}}{\*\pnseclvl7\pnlcrm\pnstart1\pnindent720\pnhang{\pntxtb
(}{\pntxta )}}{\*\pnseclvl8\pnlcltr\pnstart1\pnindent720\pnhang
{\pntxtb (}{\pntxta
)}}{\*\pnseclvl9\pnlcrm\pnstart1\pnindent720\pnhang{\pntxtb
(}{\pntxta )}}}\pard\plain \s16\qc\sb240\sa60\widctlpar
\b\f5\fs32\lang2057\kerning28 XML for Publishers \par \pard\plain
\s17\qc\sa60\widctlpar \f5\lang2057 Maintaining typeset quality in
Internet publishing \par \pard\plain \s1\sb240\sa60\keepn\widctlpar
\b\f5\fs28\lang2057\kerning28 Background \par \pard\plain
\widctlpar \f4\fs20\lang2057 The development of HTML (HyperText
Markup Language) and the World Wide Web provided proof that an
effective technical method of document distribution could be made
to work on the Internet, whatever about questions of typographic
quality, security, payment, and authentication. \par }
```

Not very pretty to look at, but you can see how the preamble is used to describe the styles used by word processor formats. In effect, this is a stylesheet and document in one: if you look carefully you can see the named styles defined in typographic terms.

The conversion command for *rbmaker* is lengthy, and best stored in a script or batch file, or in the DOS task button of an editor like *PFE* (it's broken over two lines to fit here but it's really all one long line):

```
rbmaker -in xmlpub.rtf -out xmlpub.sgm -figdir c:\figs
        -datadir c:\data -tempdir c:\tmp
```

You must specify the options for some directories where it can place figures and data that it encounters, and the one to use for temporary storage: the program will not execute without them. Processing this file gives us the SGML equivalent file in the Rainbow DTD:

```
<!DOCTYPE rainbow PUBLIC "-//EBT//DTD Rainbow 2.5//EN" [
]>
<RAINBOW>
  <FILEINFO ORIGIN="WinWord-RTF1" DTDVER="2.5">
  <STYINFO>
    <PARATYPE FONT-FAMILY="Times New Roman" FONT-SIZE="10"
      LINE-SPACING="12" CHARSET="ISO-8859" JUSTIFICATION="LeftJust"
      FIRST-INDENT="0" LEFT-INDENT="0" RIGHT-INDENT="0"
```

```
      SPACE-BEFORE="0" SPACE-AFTER="0" FONT-WEIGHT="Medium"
      FONT-SLANT="Roman" NAME="Normal">
    <PARATYPE FONT-FAMILY="Arial" FONT-SIZE="14" LINE-SPACING="16"
      CHARSET="ISO-8859" JUSTIFICATION="LeftJust" FIRST-INDENT="0"
      LEFT-INDENT="0" RIGHT-INDENT="0" SPACE-BEFORE="12"
      SPACE-AFTER="3" KEEP-WITH-NEXT=1 FONT-WEIGHT="Bold"
      FONT-SLANT="Roman" NAME="heading 1">
    <CLFTYPE NAME="Default Paragraph Font">
    <PARATYPE FONT-FAMILY="Arial" FONT-SIZE="16" LINE-SPACING="19"
      CHARSET="ISO-8859" JUSTIFICATION="CenterJust" FIRST-INDENT="0"
      LEFT-INDENT="0" RIGHT-INDENT="0" SPACE-BEFORE="12"
      SPACE-AFTER="3" FONT-WEIGHT="Bold" FONT-SLANT="Roman"
      NAME="Title">
    <PARATYPE FONT-FAMILY="Arial" FONT-SIZE="12" LINE-SPACING="14"
      CHARSET="ISO-8859" JUSTIFICATION="CenterJust" FIRST-INDENT="0"
      LEFT-INDENT="0" RIGHT-INDENT="0" SPACE-BEFORE="0"
      SPACE-AFTER="3" FONT-WEIGHT="Medium" FONT-SLANT="Roman"
      NAME="Subtitle">
  </STYINFO>
  <DOC>
    <WPLOC wp-addr="1">
    <PARA JUSTIFICATION="CenterJust" SPACE-BEFORE="12" SPACE-AFTER="3"
      FONT-WEIGHT="Bold" FONT-FAMILY="Arial" FONT-SIZE="16"
      LINE-SPACING="19" PARATYPE="Title">
      <PARACONT>XML for Publishers</PARACONT>
    </PARA>
    <WPLOC wp-addr="2">
    <PARA JUSTIFICATION="CenterJust" SPACE-AFTER="3"
      FONT-FAMILY="Arial" PARATYPE="Subtitle">
      <PARACONT>Maintaining typeset quality in Internet
       publishing</PARACONT></PARA>
    <STRUCLVL>
      <HEAD>
<WPLOC wp-addr="3">
<PARA SPACE-BEFORE="12" SPACE-AFTER="3" KEEP-WITH-NEXT=1
  FONT-WEIGHT="Bold" FONT-FAMILY="Arial" FONT-SIZE="14"
  LINE-SPACING="16" PARATYPE="heading 1">
  <PARACONT>Background</PARACONT>
</PARA>
      </HEAD>
      <WPLOC wp-addr="4">
      <PARA FONT-SIZE="10" LINE-SPACING="12" PARATYPE="Normal">
<PARACONT>The development of HTML (HyperText Markup Language)
         and the World Wide Web provided proof that an effective
         technical method of document distribution could be made to
         work on the Internet, whatever about questions of typographic
         quality, security, payment, and authentication.</PARACONT>
      </PARA>
    </STRUCLVL></DOC></RAINBOW>
```

(It actually gets converted to an unformatted file: I've neatened this up just to make it easier to read.) The documentation is quite explicit that neither the DTD nor the generated SGML is intended for human use, but for subsequent processing. It is clear how *rbmaker* has transferred the named styles into attribute values in the <PARATYPE> elements, and where those names are used in the <PARA> elements to identify the style.

The Rainbow DTD itself is fairly complex, and is explained in more depth in the documentation accompanying the program. Figure 5.3.1 shows the DTD in diagrammatic form: the necessity for it to be able to handle the 'anything anywhere' model of word processor text content means that the same portions of content model in the DTD crop up again and again in many different places.

In source file formats which do not support stylesheet information, text content is simply classed into the 'paragraph level' or 'character level' formatting which we saw in section 3.2, and the content reproduced (with formatting data in attributes) in <PLF> and <CLF> elements respectively.

RainbowMaker provides translations for all the constructions encountered in a source document, and represents those whose intent cannot be determined as generic features. For example, it is not easy to work out why an author used a TAB character at some point in the text (indentation, columns, tables, code alignment...), so TABs get converted to <TAB> and their interpretation needs to be decided by whoever writes the subsequent processing.

For more complex uses, *RainbowMaker* supports index entries, cross-references, equations, graphics, auto-generated numbering, and tables (using a simplified form of CALS), but these features rely on the source document providing adequate markup of its own to enable *rbmaker* to recognize them.

RainbowMaker uses RTF v.1, so if you find an old RTF file won't process, it may be RTF v.0, in which case edit the file and change the `\rtf0` at the start of the first line to `\rtf1` (if you have many files to process, it may be easier to edit the Rainbow configuration file `rbmaker.sts` and change the recognition string at the end of the file instead).

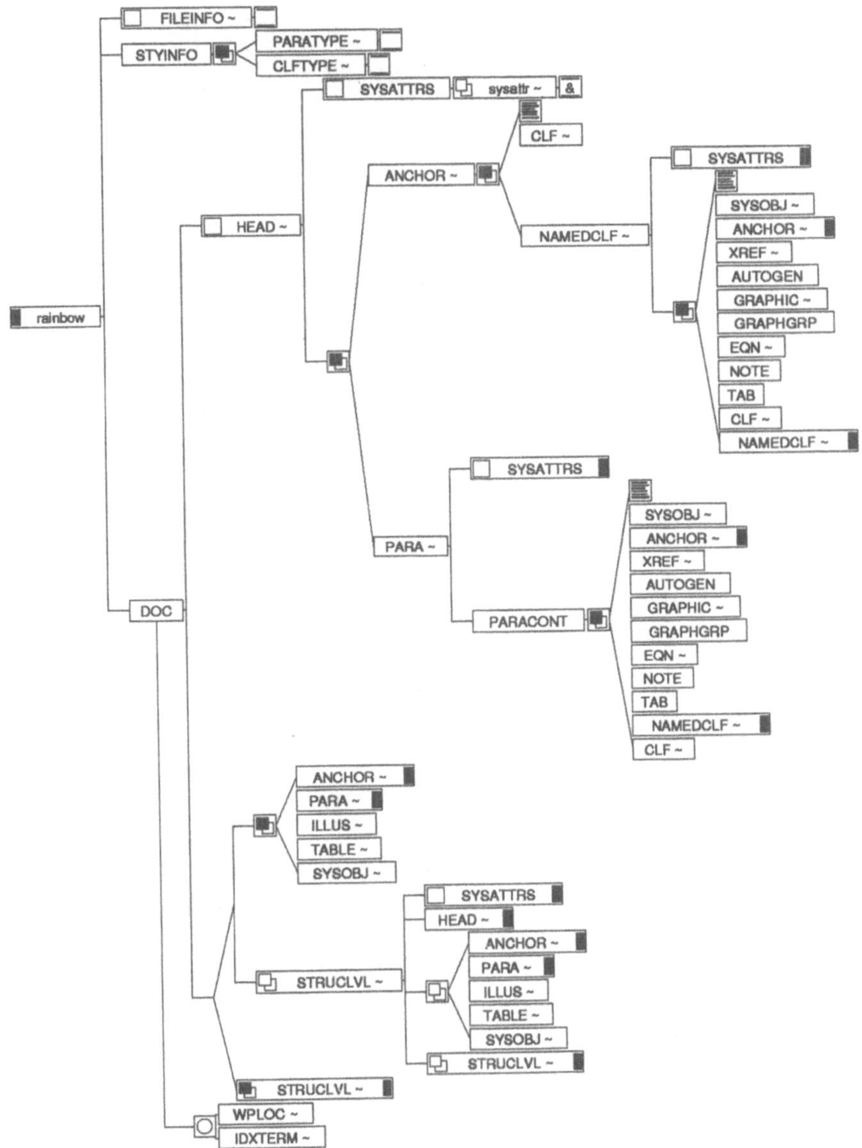

Figure 103. The Rainbow DTD for word processor conversion with *rbmaker*

5.3.2. **Dynatag (Inso)**

MS-Windows 95 and NT, Unix
`http://www.inso.com`

DynaTag is part of the *DynaText* system (see section 6.2.1). It's a one-way converter for word processor documents into SGML or XML. It uses a

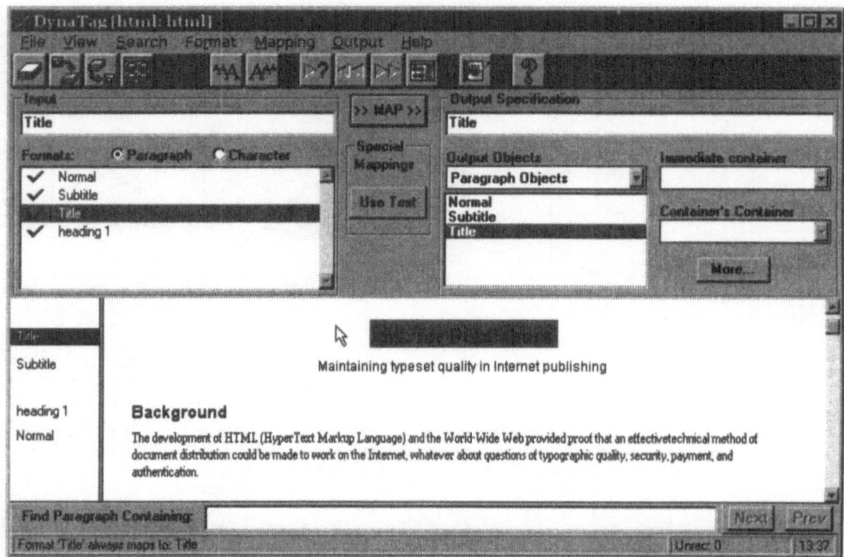

Figure 104. DynaTag converting an RTF file to XML

graphical interface to the *RainbowMaker* technology (see section 5.3.1) which converts RTF or *Word* files to SGML but preserves every aspect of the word processor formatting in attributes in the converted document. Like *rbmaker*, *DynaTag* will also accept *FrameMaker* MIF and Interleaf ASCII files.

If the source document used named styles, these can be converted into elements with the same names. Otherwise, you can map any combination or subset of style attributes to an element, either in a previously defined DTD, or by inventing element names for a DTD-less XML document. The mapping 'language' enables the attribute values to be used to form conditional conversions.

If you have read section 5.3.1, you will have seen that making subsequent use of the *RainbowMaker* format is a non-trivial task. One of the reasons behind *DynaTag* is that it does this for you: it has built-in knowledge about document structures, and about the features which accompany them such as headings, tables and different kinds of list items.

This knowledge lets it handle the flat structure model used by most word processors, where there is no concept of an object called a 'list', nor of the idea of one object 'containing' others. You can see this in most word processor style galleries, where a bulleted list item is merely a special case of a paragraph with a bullet in the indent margin and hanging indentation applied: the idea that it can be a member of a group of such items called a list does not exist. However, some more advanced systems do recognize a very small amount of hierarchy (perhaps 'sequentiality' would be a better word): Microsoft *Word* has named styles for 'continuation items'.

It is on hooks like this that *DynaTag* can hang its markup. You map input styles to output elements, either named or based on combinations of styles represented in the conversion. Style information can be applied to the derived markup, which can then be saved as a separate stylesheet (see Figure 104).

The use of an intermediate format to enable accurate mapping makes this one of the most powerful tagging applications available. The graphical interface only runs under MS-Windows, but the mappings can be saved and used in the Unix batch product, which will perform command-line driven conversions for the same document type pairs (input of a word processor file in that format and output according to the specified DTD).

5.3.3. SGML Author for Word (Microsoft)

Version 1.1 for MS-Windows
`http://www.microsoft.com/`

Despite its name, this is a conversion tool, not an editor or authoring program. It's a plug-in for Microsoft *Word* (6 or 7) which enables *Word* documents to be saved as SGML files or loaded from SGML files, using a mapping between DTD and stylesheet.

The objective is to allow *Word* users to continue using *Word* without knowing anything about SGML (possibly not even that it exists), but enable their files to be used in SGML systems; or to take SGML files and produce *Word* versions which can be re-imported into SGML afterwards.

This will obviously only work if the users can be trained to stick rigidly to a predefined set of styles and never depart from them. Provided this is done, however, it is possible to use the context of the styles to map to a DTD and *vice versa*, and thus to provide translation in both directions.

Once this is established, it would be possible to maintain your corporate or institutional information base in SGML, but have authors create and update the texts using *Word*.

5.3.3.1. Setting up

Setting it up may cause some problems: support is difficult to get, even in the USA, as Microsoft's own HelpDesk staff are largely unaware of the program's existence. It was apparently not intended to be used (or even available) outside the USA, although a number of non-US institutions are now reported to be using it. If you have access to Microsoft's *Select* installation CD-ROMs, especially outside the USA, install it from them in preference to the retail package.

If you have to install from the retail package, make sure that once you have *Word* 7 installed, go to the **Tools|*Options*** menu item, click on the **File Locations** tab and check that both ***|User Templates*** and ***|Workgroup Templates*** have file locations associated with them (I am indebted to Brian Widman for this tip). Then start installing *SGML Author for Word*. If it claims you don't have *Word* installed, you may need to manually edit your Registry to provide the 'right' entries: unfortunately it provides no clues as to what it needs, so you may want to call their HelpDesk at this stage.

Once it's installed, it adds ***|Save as SGML*** to the **File** menu and creates some new directories in your *Word* installation folder. There is no ***|Open as SGML*** because all files opened are native *Word* files. If you have installed (or are going to install) Microstar's *Near&Far Author for Word*, which *is* an editor, you should familiarize yourself with the distinction between the menu items which *SGML Author for Word* adds to the **Save** dialog and those which Microstar's software adds (the 'Save As...' file type ***|SGML - Near&Far Author***).

The manual is reasonably clear, and makes a good effort at explaining what you need to know at each stage, but it aimed at the administrator, not the end user, so it does require a significant level of understanding of text and text-handling, well above the level needed for general office word processing. This is probably acceptable, given that the apparent intention is to shield the end user from the SGML bits. One thing it does make very clear is why this is just a conversion engine: why write a new editor when you have a working one already?

The mechanics of setting up a conversion are fairly intricately explained, although if you already know SGML, and have worked with stylesheets before, a lot of it begins to look familiar after a while:

- You need to have a DTD, of course, and the SGML Declaration if needed;
- There's a catalog file provided, `entm.cat`, in standard format but with the `PATH` keyword on the first line giving the directory paths to search for relative file (System identifier) references. Your DTD file(s) need to be entered in this catalog;
- You create a 'declaration file' with the file type `.dcl` for each DTD you use, in which goes a copy of the SGML Declaration followed by the DocType Declaration — but not the DTD itself.

- You bind the element names from the DTD to stylesheet styles in a .map file, which you create using menus in *SGML Author for Word*.

The .dcl file type is an unfortunate choice, as it is already used by many DTDs for their own SGML Declaration, which will probably *not* contain a DocType Declaration at the end, so some renaming or careful directory selection is needed. If you are using a technical DTD for math, and you want conversion to or from the *Word* equation editor, you need to modify the DTD to include the equation fragment provided (based on the ISO TR 9573 fragment: see section 2.3.8.1.1). You get a warning if this is not done: there's a sample skeleton.dtd supplied which serves as an example of how to use it.

5.3.3.2. Operation

Converting from SGML to *Word* or *vice versa* means assigning a template file to your DTD, which is done from the **File|*New*** menu the first time round by picking a template and a .dcl file. If you don't have any templates of your own (this would apply if you don't use *Word* and are perhaps preparing conversions for people who do), you can pick one of the standard *Word* ones in \MSOffice\Templates*, which is the proper place (unfortunately it's not where the **File|*New*** menu looks for them). Clicking on the .dcl file which you created for your DTD starts the parsing of the DTD and reads the template file. Any parser errors at this stage pop up in an edit window, and have to be corrected before you can proceed.

The catalog file provided unfortunately fails to include the ISO Box and Line Drawing character entity file, the Russian Cyrillic, Non-Russian Cyrillic, and Alternative Greek Symbols ones: you may not use them but some DTDs reference them and won't validate without them unless you disable the references or add the files to your file system and include the relevant lines in the catalog.

By far the most lengthy part is setting up the associations between *Word*'s stylesheet descriptors and the elements of your DTD. The display gives both side-by-side (see Figure 105) so the mechanics of it are fairly simple. However, the DTD elements are displayed in a form which makes available every possible variant of element combinations that is possible, and by default expects you to establish a style for all of them. You just ignore the ones you don't want, but it clutters the panel somewhat.

It is logically not possible to associate a style descriptor with more than one element or descendancy, because to do so would defeat the objective of providing a consistent mapping from stylesheet to DTD. This means that associating <para> with paragraph-style **Normal**, for

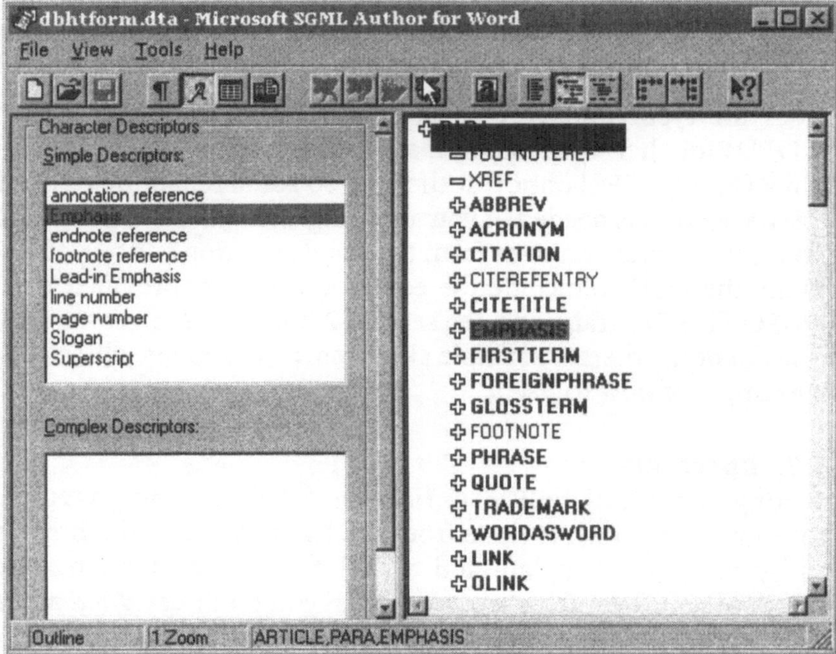

Figure 105. Associating an inline element with a character style descriptor in *SGML Author for Word*

example, makes it impossible to associate any other element with the **Normal** style, and if you try, it will keep trying to tell you that what you're setting up is a paragraph. You can, however, specify a default structural markup conversion (referred to as 'not in Mixed Content', which defaults to paragraph-style **Normal**) and a default inline markup conversion (referred to as 'in Mixed Content', which defaults to character-style **annotation reference**).

You can supply associations for inclusion elements, and for specific attribute values on elements. For *Word* conversion into SGML, you can establish default values for required attributes.

Because of the complexity of the setup, a detailed study of typical documents for the given DTD is essential before you start. It would also be useful to generate a list of the elements actually used, with their frequency of use. This will make it much easier to see where you need to concentrate your association efforts.

Once it's done, you save the association (`.dta`) file. This will take a few minutes, as the files take a frightening amount of disk space: in tests, an association file for the *DocBook* DTD took 8.5Mb even with version 1.1 (which the help documentation claims has been optimized for use with a 32–bit operating system: 'these performance improvements include an increase in speed, and a decrease in the size of the association file').

Finally, you can open a `.sgm` file in *Word*, pick the `.dta` file, and let it convert. It's fairly slow, and needs a lot of disk space: conversion of a 66Kb instance needed around 40Mb of temporary disk. Provided you have taken care in setting up the associations, the results are very good, and for bulk conversion the time and effort spent should be worth it.

The conversion process uses a considerable amount of smarts to achieve what the documentation describes as a 'least-cost' path to the conversion of unspecified or unspecifiable element combinations. This probably accounts for the slow speed by comparison with *Balise*, *Omnimark*, or *SGMLC*. The manual emphasizes that you test any conversion setup by using the standard 'round-trip' methodology. This means converting circularly back into the format the document was originally in, and then studying the results to see what got lost in the process.

5.3.4. **Roustabout** (Apropos)

Mac, PC/Win
`http://www.attd.com/`

Roustabout is a specialist program from Apropos Toy and Tool Development for converting files *QuarkXPress* export files into SGML.

QuarkXPress is one of the most popular and extensible page layout systems for Apple Macs and Windows 95 PCs. Its internal file format is not directly usable for SGML, but there is a plaintext export format called Xpress Tags, and it is this that *Roustabout* translates (despite the name, this is not an SGML 'tagged' file). *Roustabout* is written in *Java* and can read these 'tagged' files produced for both Mac and PC versions of *QuarkXPress*, with or without stylesheet formatting.

Roustabout uses a name mapping file to specify the translation between the *QuarkXPress* stylesheet names and the DTD element names (see Figure 106). Because *QuarkXPress* is restricted to the simple two-level model of paragraph styles containing character styles (see section 3.2), it is not possible to map structures any more deeply unless you use an SGML editor to post-process the output. The mapping specification files are themselves in SGML format, and the system can also produce XML with a suitable DTD.

The *Roustabout* program comes as a zipfile of some 250 classes: there is a demo version on the CD-ROM, limited to the first 5,000 characters of input.

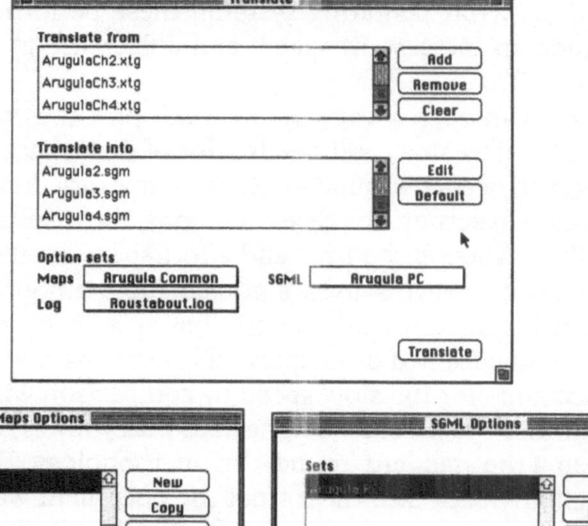

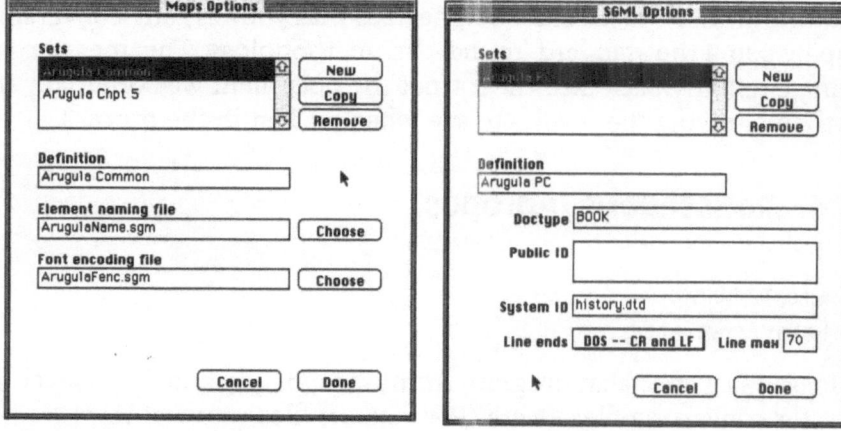

Figure 106. Roustabout setup for *Quark Xpress* conversion

5.3.5. TagPerfect (Delta Computers)

`http://www.jsp.fi/delta/deltatgp.htm`

TagPerfect is a small standalone Windows program to convert RTF (Rich Text Format) files to SGML, originally developed at NICE Technologies by Eric van Herwijnen, author of *Practical SGML*[41]. Unlike the *RainbowMaker* system, which uses its own DTD, *TagPerfect* converts to any DTD: you provide the mapping between identified styles in the RTF file and the elements in the DTD. This has two immediate implications:

- as with *rbmaker*, the input document needs to have been created using a stylesheet in the original word processor, so that the styles have names to map to the DTD elements;

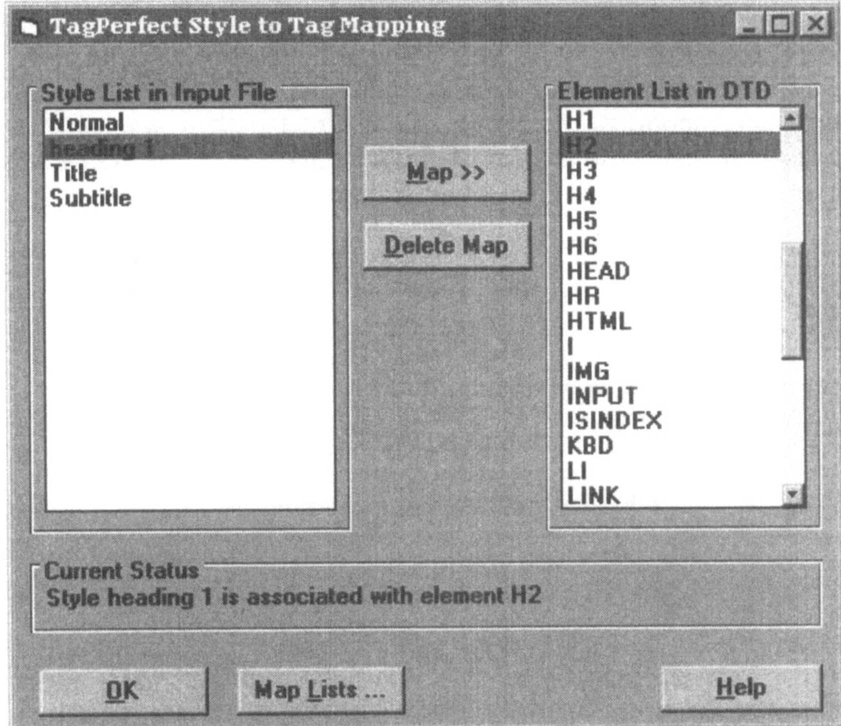

Figure 107. TagPerfect mapping screen

- you can only implement a strict 1:1 mapping from a style to an element or element ancestry: there is no styling language to enable conditional transformation.

(There is a separate program, not covered here, called *Tag Wizard*, which is a Windows plugin for Microsoft *Word* 6 to provide direct translation from *Word* 6 files to SGML.)

The main screen just lets you identify the input and output files, the DTD, and a mapping file (which you can create if this is the first conversion for a DTD). You can also specify an alternate root element for the conversion, which lets you convert a file to be a subsection, or a chapter, or some other subdivision of the DTD, rather than starting with the DTD's default root element.

You can create or modify the mapping file, which brings up another pane (see Figure 107) to let you allocate each style to an element. After processing the document, you can view the output before exiting the program or going back to modify the mapping and reprocessing. The viewer is Windows *Write*, rather than an editor or browser, so you need to ensure that you do not accidentally convert your new SGML file into a non-text format.

TagPerfect is fast and fairly robust, and although it handles only simple one-to-one mappings, it can provide a direct path to a specific DTD without the need for any subsequent conversion. The fragment we converted in section 5.3.1 is shown here converted to HTML.

```
<!DOCTYPE HTML PUBLIC "+//ISBN 82-7640-037::WWW//DTD HTML//EN">
<HTML>
  <HEAD>
  <TITLE></TITLE>
  </HEAD>
  <BODY><ADDRESS><A><H1>XML for Publishers</H1><H3>Maintaining
typeset quality in Internet publishing</H3><H2>Background</H2>
<P>The development of HTML (HyperText Markup Language) and the
World Wide Web provided proof that an effective technical method of
document distribution could be made to work on the Internet, whatever
about questions of typographic quality, security, payment, and
authentication.</P></A></ADDRESS></BODY>
</HTML>
```

The reason for the inclusion of <ADDRESS> and <A> is unknown: they would clearly need to be removed before the file is used, and their presence indicates some further work is needed if the program was to be used on any large scale. Because it uses only the named styles, *TagPerfect* does not retain or record any of the additional information from the RTF file.

5.3.6. ACS (Lockheed-Martin)

ACS was developed from a US Navy R&D program for converting legacy print manuals into Interactive Electronic Technical Manuals (IETMs: see section 2.3.5). It is a Unix system which takes an existing document, either in word processor or SGML form, or page by page from the scanner (separating out graphics from text). Output is to a database where redundancy (duplication of text) is eliminated and hyperlinks established to maintain the integrity of the text.

The process is about as fully automated as a textual analysis and discrimination can currently be, but there are built-in validation points at which the human operator can intervene from the control window to check what has been done and to change it if it's wrong (see Figure 108).

For non-SGML input, document structure is deduced from the physical layout of the original document, but some smarts in an NLP (Natural Language Processing) engine, try to distil semantics from the text, and use this to judge the validity of the redundancy and hyperlinking.

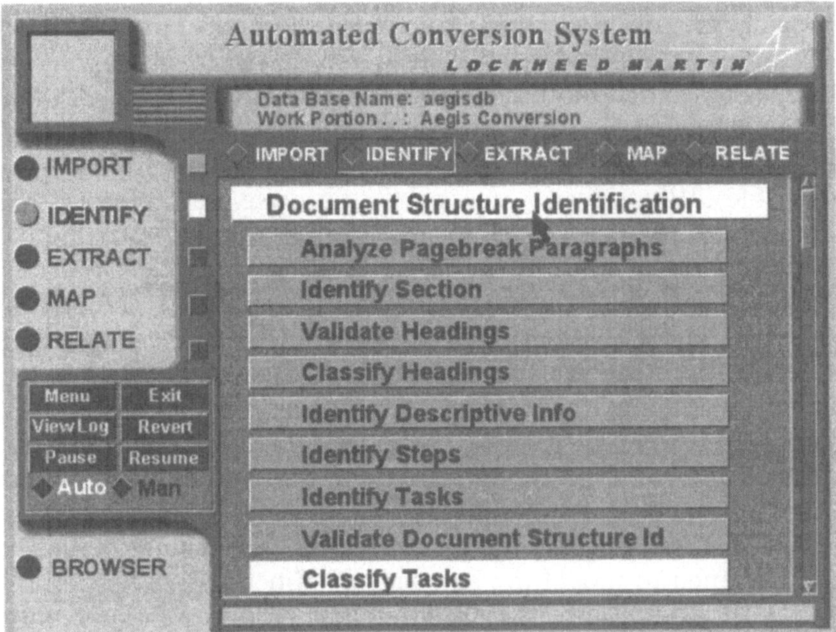

Figure 108. The *ACS* schematic control window

The database approach (see section 6.6.1) means that the hierarchical structure of a manual can be stored in such as way as to remove this duplication, and allow objects to be reused many times in different places. This is important for frequent or repetitive operations such as those encountered in maintenance tasks, where the operation may be a subtask common to several otherwise different routines. The authoring/presentation output of IETM database data supports multiple output formats.

Although expert technical knowledge is still required to judge the validity of *ACS*'s decisions at each stage, this is moving very much towards being a 'black-box' approach to the conversion of older documentation to interactive formats. The success relies on the repetitive and predictable nature of technical manuals, but the application of NLP to these tasks is going to become much more widespread as the processing power to support them becomes available.

5.3.7. SGML-Tools (LinuxDoc)

Linus Torvalds' PC version of Unix has grown rapidly in popularity in the late 1990s, partly because of some major improvements in usability, and partly as a reaction against the perception that Microsoft's dominance of the PC marketplace was leading to a virtual monopoly, which runs counter to the traditional way of working in the Unix community. To some extent it is also seen a reaction against the PC tendency towards 'bloatware' (software requiring massively more resources than is reasonable). When a word processor or a browser requires over 100Mb to install into, perhaps it's time to rethink the design (although Unix itself is notoriously profligate of disk space).

From a relatively early stage, *Linux* documentation was held in two forms: the 'HOWTO' help files in plaintext for anyone to download and read with no special facilities; and the more formal documentation, originally in TEX but now kept in SGML. In fact the ASCII HOWTOs are also now generated from SGML sources. The *LinuxDoc* project, which was started to build a library of documentation, has now been renamed *SGML-Tools*.

The DTD used initially was *QWERTZ*, which is a suite of document types designed to model the standard document types used in LATEX. Users of LATEX (2.09) will be aware that the first line of their files always had to start with `\documentstyle`, followed by the name of a style, and the following standard styles have been around since the early days:

```
report
article
book
letter
```

QWERTZ defined document types for these, following the LATEX markup of chapters, sections, subsections, *etc*, and the LATEX conventions for logical markup of inline features like emphasis. The DTD was modified to become the 'Linuxdoc DTD', and programs were written to parse and convert SGML instances to LATEX or *nroff* for printing, and to HTML and plaintext for documentation online.

Unfortunately, the facilities and restrictions of SGML were not fully documented: as a result, authors in the documentation community, which was more used to LATEX or even *Word*, often found themselves puzzled or frustrated by unexpected program or document behavior or requirements. The development of the system also did not keep pace with either LATEX or SGML, with the result that parsing was still being done using *sgmls* instead of *nsgmls*, instances were still being translated to LATEX 2.09 instead of LATEX2ϵ, and documents were being created with a highly idiosyncratic use of markup which did not contribute to portability.

In 1997–98 the decision was made to move all Linux documentation into DocBook, thereby preparing the way for the benefits of a much richer and more robust DTD, and the support of a very wide range of tools for converting and formatting the instances. Details of the project and its progress are at `http://pobox.com/~cg/sgmltools/`.

6. Finding, viewing, and printing

> If it plese oný man spirituel or temporel to býe ony pýes of two and thre comemoratiōs of salisburi vse enprýntid after the forme of this presēt lettre whiche ben wel and trulý correct, late hým come to westmonester in to the almonesrýe at the reed pale and he shal haue them good chepe : : *Supplico stet cedula*
>
> William Caxton, Advertisement for booklets regulating worship, *c.* 1477

- **Searching SGML**
- **Viewers and browsers**
- **Non-visual representations of SGML**
- **Printing and publishing**
- **Document management systems**

A frequent request from newcomers to SGML is for some way to view what's in an SGML file, usually in order to search or read it. Raw SGML up close is not usually very appealing: it needs to be manipulated by an application in order to be readable more easily. It's interesting to note that Caxton's advertisement, the first known printed advertisement in English, emphasizes that his copies of the Sarum *Ordinale* were 'well and truly correct' and 'printed after the form of this present letter' — attributes which we still use today. We particularly use the latter for displaying or printing SGML 'like this': the use of stylesheets ensures that each document which follows it can be printed to exactly the same layout specification. Correctness of the text, however, remains firmly in human hands.

When the newcomer opens a file in an editor, even an SGML editor, and finds something like the following, it's hardly surprising that the first thing she looks for is a better way to view or print it:

```
<LG N="7"><L N="19"><FRN LANG="iw"><SEG NEXT="acrostic8"
PREV="acrostic6" ID="acrostic7" TYPE="acrostic">G</SEG>ibro</FRN>
```

```
<FRN LANG="iw">praxon agathon</FRN></L><L N="20">deuita <FRN
LANG="iw">athemiton</FRN></L><L N="21">ut sis fretus in <FRN
LANG="iw"><PN TYPE="biblical">Sion</PN></FRN></L></LG><LG N="8"><L
N="22"><FRN LANG="iw"><SEG NEXT="acrostic9" PREV="acrostic7"
ID="acrostic8" TYPE="acrostic">H</SEG>upage</FRN> de auido</L><L
N="23">habit&aunderdot; in <FRN LANG="iw"><DISTINCT
TYPE="latin inflexion/gen">Qurii</DISTINCT> nomo</FRN></L><L
N="24">ut sis heres in <FRN LANG="iw"><PN>Papho</PN></FRN></L></LG>
```

If you are in this position, it's important to bear in mind that an SGML file itself does not normally carry information about formatting. That is kept in a stylesheet, which should accompany an SGML file and its DTD precisely to allow people to see what's in the file in a more readable manner (see Figure 109 for a rendering of the above fragment using a stylesheet).

If you've been given an SGML instance which is intended for reading or display, and you have not been given a stylesheet or some form of display system to use, you may want to contact whoever gave it to you and see if something has been forgotten. Fortunately, even if they have nothing available, it's not hard to set up a viewer to display things readably.

If you don't have or can't get a viewer or browser, then an SGML editor can display the text, and usually print it, at least in draft mode. Many editors now have stylesheets of equivalent sophistication to the browsers mentioned below.

The popularity of the Web made it clear that serving SGML as an information format over wide-area networks was a viable proposition, but to begin with there were few viewers in an accessible form that could simply be downloaded and used in the way that Web browsers can be. Previewers existed, but they were usually tied to editors or formatters for printing.

Now there is more choice, but in all cases, you have to obtain, provide, or create a stylesheet, as there is no easy way for any viewer to guess or predict how you want the information formatted. The principal viewers do come with sample stylesheets for some popular DTDs, but the range is not large, and because of the lag between development of DTDs and the production of software, the versions available may not always be the ones used by the authors of texts.

The increasing use of XML (see section 2.4), for which browser manufacturers have the background experience with HTML to draw upon, means that some XML browsers will work with regular SGML files, and may be able to apply the heuristics derived from HTML. For example, it is reasonable to 'guess' that (in default of any other information) <P>, <PAR>, <PARA>, or <PARAGRAPH> in an English-language

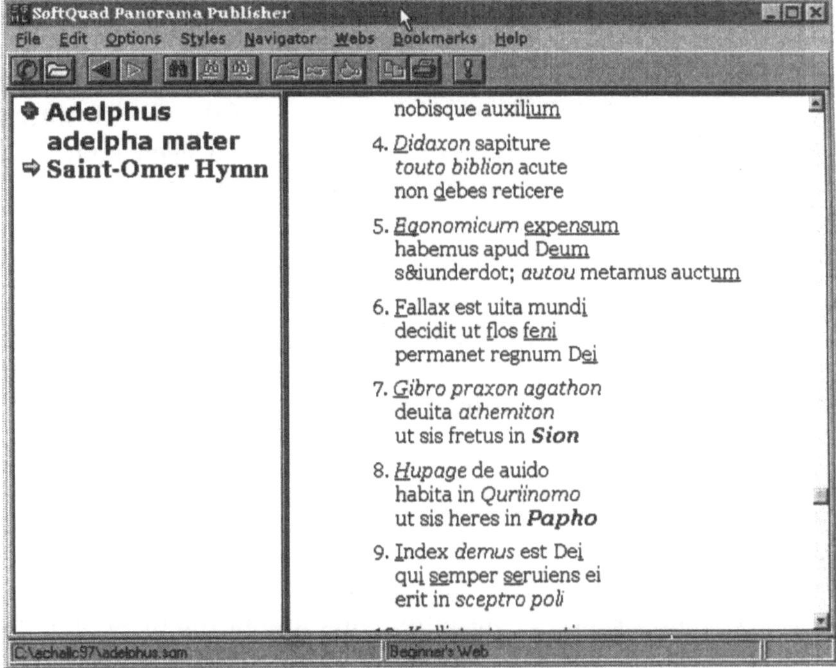

Figure 109. Example of complex markup displayed in a viewer

DTD or well-formed file, is likely to be a paragraph, and it would be reasonable for a browser to format the element as such if it has been given no stylesheet. But you cannot rely on this: a stylesheet is just as important for displaying SGML or XML (or HTML) as it is for displaying a file in *Word*, *WordPerfect*, *FrameMaker*, or any word processor or DTP system.

6.1. Searching

Searching is one of the earliest and most obvious applications of a computer to text. Fr Roberto Busa's famous groundwork in computerized text analysis, which started in 1949, was published in 56 volumes (up to 1980) as the *Index Thomisticus Sancti Thomae Aquinatus Operum Omnium Indices et Concordantiae*[13]St Thomas Aquinus . This work produced two concordances (one lemmatized, the other not), which are one of the basic tools of the textual scholar for locating a specific passage according to key words. 'I want to be able to search it' is still one of the first requests from users who are dealing with a body of text, especially in SGML.

However, while there are dozens of searching systems for general-purpose numeric and alphanumeric data, many of them built into existing corporate databases, statistics packages, and even some word processors, there is a severe shortage of stand-alone systems specifically for SGML.

Yet the very nature of an SGML file — its ability to be rigorous about the description of text data — ought to make it an attractive proposition. Context-sensitive searching is in some ways the ultimate refinement, and something only possible with a system of markup that can be interpreted grammatically by a computer.

I once attended a week-long summer-school on Information Retrieval, hoping to be brought up to date with the latest methods. All of the presentations, however, concentrated on ever more arcane methods of searching unmarked, raw, plaintext data, something I thought had gone out with the Ark when I stopped punching cards to make ends meet as a student. I asked a colleague if he thought the presenters had ever heard of SGML and he advised me never to mention it. I disregarded this advice, and was roundly rebuked for suggesting SGML: the clear implication was that marking up text in order to aid retrieval is regarded by many computer scientists as 'cheating'!

All regular commercial database systems provide searching, but most do not handle SGML as a native structure. Separate SGML search engines are thus something of a rarity: their functionality is usually tied either to a database system or a viewer/browser that *does* support native SGML. Full-scale document management database systems are outside the scope of this book, but I include one as an example at the end of this chapter.

Part of the problem is that for a search engine to be scalable to large files or databases, the text and the markup must be indexed . This process creates a binary file containing pointers to the words, characters, and other objects (elements, attribute names, *etc*), to make searching fast enough to be usable. The key to a good search engine, therefore, depends as much on the robustness of the indexing system as on the interface or the query language.

One excellent standalone search program is (or rather, was) *PAT*, formerly from OpenText in Waterloo, Ontario, but it is no longer available as a separate program, although many sites still use older copies. Its functionality was wrapped up inside a Web server, so to get the search program you would need to buy the entire Web management suite, which is grotesque overkill if all you want to do is search an SGML document.

At the command line end of the spectrum there is the small but very effective non-SGML Unix program *sgrep*, which is in section 5.1.2; and the *mtSgmlQL* program, also for Unix, which implements an SQL-like interface to locating and manipulating elements in an SGML file (see `http://www.lpl.univ-aix.fr/projects/multext/MtSgmlQL/` for further information).

The leading SGML search facility is that built into the *DynaText* suite from Inso (formerly EBT) in Providence, RI. *DynaText* is the oldest and best-known SGML search and viewing application, and is covered in section 6.2.1.

6.2. Viewers and browsers

There are relatively few general-purpose standalone SGML viewers on the market. Some manufacturers of CD-ROM publications using SGML (encyclopedias, product lists, academic text collections, manuals, *etc*) have used browsers with database and search facilities which need preparation, like *DynaText* (see section 6.2.1), or have had special-purpose browsers built for them, and there are some specialist products in restricted areas such as military applications which are not normally purchasable as stand-alone systems.

If you're new to SGML, bear in mind that SGML browsers are not like the general run of HTML-only Web browsers which will accept and display even grossly deformed files without complaint. The programs shown here are conforming SGML systems, and while they have error detection and recovery built in, if you feed them an invalid or non-conformant file they will display error messages, and you will need to fix the errors before you get a file to display.

The first viewer was *DynaText* (see section 6.2.1), part of a system aimed at large documents or collections, and providing extensive search and formatting capabilities: it established some principles about stylesheets and navigation which most subsequent products have followed. In the early 1990s, an experimental SGML Document Archive system (*Darc*) was developed at the Royal Institute of Technology in Sweden. The project was eventually spun off as a company, Synex, and the product was sold for them by SoftQuad as *Explorer*. This became *ViewPort*, from which *Panorama* was developed. Synex is now owned by Inso and *ViewPort* is licensed as the core technology to several SGML browsers in addition to *Panorama*. Because of this common core, I have covered *ViewPort* separately.

Viewers are an important tool for SGML because not all editing systems have the ability to produce near-publishable quality display or print. Indeed even some of the more sophisticated editors make it clear that they are strictly *editors*, and their printing and display is for draft purposes only. While a browser or viewer cannot substitute for a full-scale typesetting and publishing system, it provides a convenient half-way house, with display and print configurations sufficient for office use and superior to most editors, in a package only a fraction of the size of an SGML DTP system.

There is a fundamental difference too, between the browser/viewers designed for use on (or just off) the Web, like the *ViewPort*-based ones, and the bigger and more powerful LAN/CD-ROM/corpus browsers like *DynaText* or *Sara*. The former have to work on the fly, downloading DTDs and entity files from remote sites in real time, and recovering gracefully from errors, misconnections, and the other pleasures of life on the Internet. The latter instead are set up to use data whose DTD is known, tested, and compiled in advance, and for which search indexes have been prepared and a presentation designed. You have to do all this, but it means that the user interface is controllable and there is much less to go wrong or be unaccounted for. The Web-based products *ought* to work for the new user immediately, as all the setting up is the responsibility of the information provider, but as you yourself may be that information provider, and particularly as these products already provide most of what an XML browser may be expected to do, I have included some of the details about how the insides of the Web browser function.

6.2.1. **DynaText** (Inso)

MS-Windows, Unix
`http://www.inso.com` (formerly `http://www.ebt.com`)

DynaText was the first SGML viewer, and its related suite of products has remained among the most powerful, flexible, and robust of SGML applications software. (Then) EBT's Steve DeRose invented the notion of having an expression language in a stylesheet at an early stage in the product's development, and the concept has formed the basis for a large number of other stylesheet languages.

Many large corporations were encouraged to move into SGML by of the existence of the *DynaText* viewer, in the days when SGML rendering software was still a rarity. It is widely used for all kinds of SGML applications, but still has a strong presence in documentation for reliability-critical areas like aircraft and nuclear power plant maintenance, and remains the only system that can render *really* big monolithic SGML documents effectively.

DynaText itself is a suite of programs forming a production and delivery process for creating and publishing large documents or collections on a CD-ROM or LAN (Local Area Network). Although originally employed in the technical documentation market, it is now used in all kinds of industries, and there is a growing educational sector.

DynaBase is a separate product providing content management and publishing system for large dynamic Web sites. The document management modules provide full version control, distributed authoring, and version-aware fulltext indexing and searching. It uses HTML and XML, with some SGML support, and draws on the facilities of *DynaText*, but is not in itself an SGML system.

6.2.1.1. The publishing process

DynaText is not an editor, so any suitable SGML editor can be used for authoring, but for the import of existing documents, the *DynaTag* filter allows the conversion of RTF, *Word*, *FrameMaker*, and *Interleaf* documents. The use and operation of *DynaTag* is covered separately in the chapter on conversion (see section 5.3.2) because of its close relationship with the *RainbowMaker* converter.

The style of the display that you want to user to see in the viewer is governed by a stylesheet: *InStEd* is a graphical editor to manage the creation and testing of the stylesheets (see Figure 110). Element-based styling allows complete control using both the structure and the rendered view. Full mathematical and imaging styling is provided, and the stylesheet language scripting allows generated text and conditional positioning.

As you click on an element in the structure view (upper pane), the corresponding text is highlighted in the text view (lower pane), and if you click on text in the text view, the element name is highlighted in the structure view. Each element is numbered, and style panels for up to three at a time are displayed down the right-hand side of the window. The stylesheet language is itself in SGML syntax, so it is readable and editable outside *InStEd* (which means it can also be generated by other systems, or converted from other formats:

```
<style name="OWNER" group="frontmatter">
<font-family>&frontmatter.font; </>
<font-size>18 </>
<line-spacing>20 </>
```

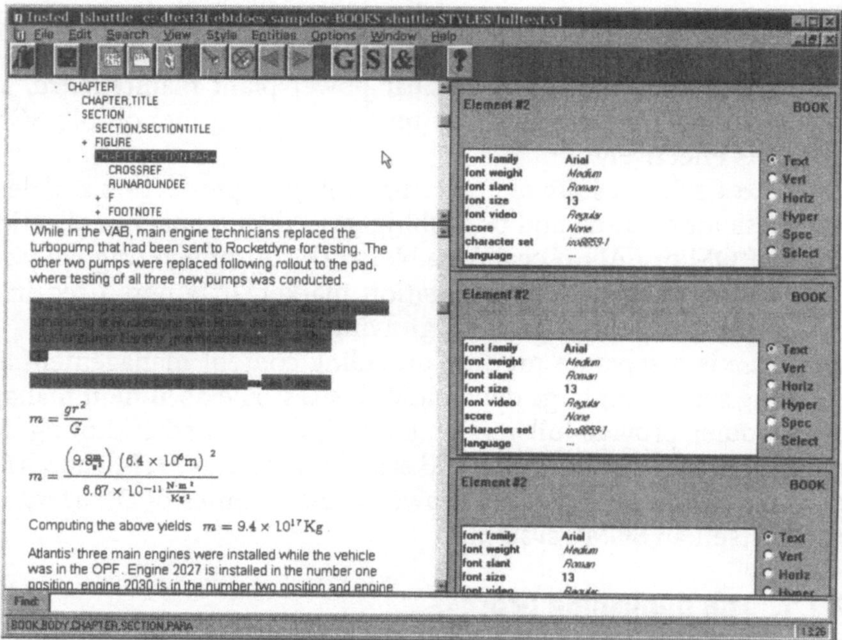

Figure 110. The *InSteEd* stylesheet editor

```
<justification>Left </>
<space-before>18 </>
<break-after>line </>
</style>
```

The core of the viewing system is the *DynaText* browser. This works on LANs as well as CD-ROMs, and provides the reading and searching interface to a document collection (see Figure 111). Texts are represented as *DynaText* 'books', to pursue the paper metaphor, and they use the style file and markup to provide a navigation panel from which you can expand the hierarchical view and click on a subheading to display it.

You can establish alternative navigation views and multiple stylesheets which the user can switch between, and the display can be zoomed for larger or smaller type, and the navigation panel expanded or contracted. Users can add annotations to a document, which are stored separately, and which can be made available to other users on the same network.

The search facilities are customizable by the developer, who can establish search 'forms' based on sections of the document as defined by the markup, or on other search criteria such as proximity. Search results are highlighted, and the total number found in each hierarchical section is displayed next to the section title in the navigator. Whole collections

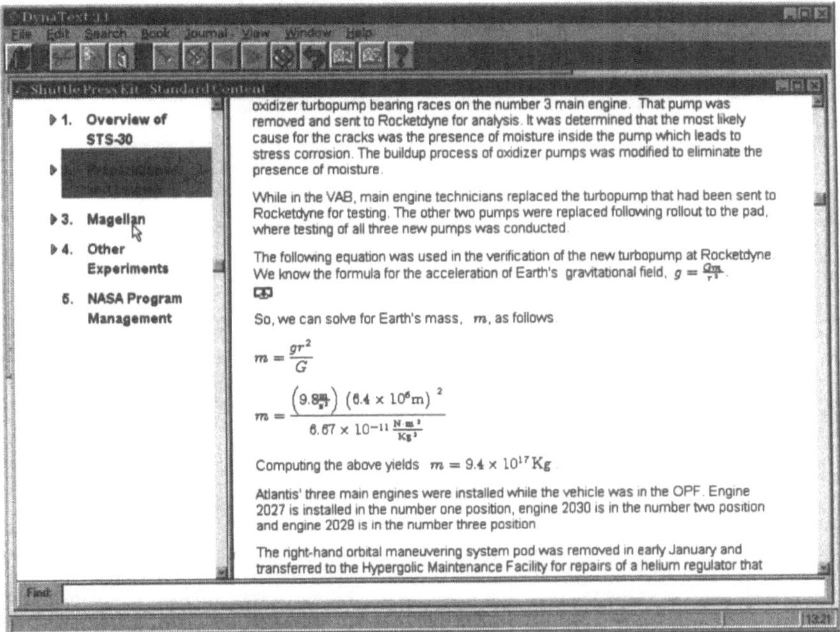

Figure 111. The *DynaText* browser/viewer

of documents can be searched, and the results displayed in summary form.

For delivery outside the organization, the *DynaWeb* HTTP server provides on-the-fly conversion from the SGML of the document or collection into HTML or XML. Search forms are customizable, as with the *DynaText* browser, so a search can return an SGML document fragment expressed in HTML for a regular Web browser (see Figure 112).

Because the server is integrated with the document base, the URLs get interpreted slightly differently from regular Web URLs, giving the server a chance to step in and generate the required document view. This is a similar concept to a regular server running from a shell script but in this case the URL gets 'eaten' at an earlier stage. Because of this, the designer or creator can achieve a much higher level of control over the presentation, as the HTML code sent out is generated on-the-fly from stylesheet specifications held by the server and applied to the SGML data retrieved from the textbase.

If you want to re-write parts of this yourself as separate programs, the *DynaText* Software Developers' Kit is a C++ subroutine library to let the developer embed calls to the *DynaText* system.

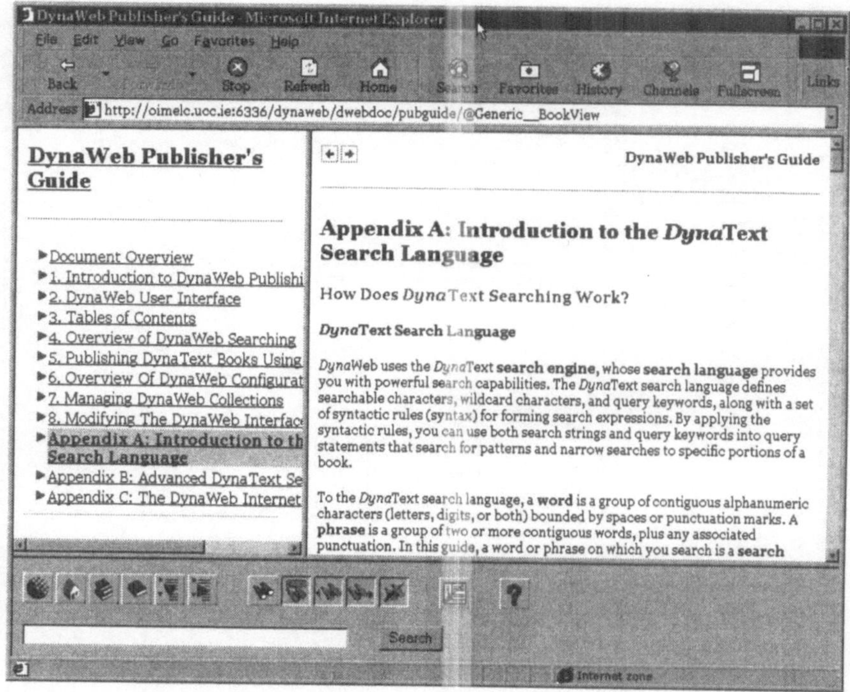

Figure 112. DynaWeb displaying in an Explorer window

6.2.2. ViewPort (Inso)

Windows, Mac, Unix
`http://www.synex.com`

The Synex *ViewPort* is a SGML/HyTime subsystem for adding a browser to any application, using an API written in C++ to handle the SGML functionality. This engine formed the core of the first general-purpose small-scale SGML browser for the Web, *Panorama,* and has also been adopted by *MultiDoc Pro* and others.

There is a stand-alone (non-networked) viewer from Synex themselves which is provided on the CD-ROM for viewing the local documentation and samples of this book. This program is for demonstration only and is not available as a separate product: it is licensed exclusively to you as the purchaser of this book.

These browsers share a substantial amount of common code, so the following points apply to all of them:

Interface For the end user, a *ViewPort*-enabled application provides a scrollable, windowing interface to an SGML file. Markup can be hidden or revealed, appearance can be specified via a stylesheet, and a navigator pane can be established using either markup from the stylesheet or the hierarchical SGML file structure.

The exact nature of network interaction is specific to each implementation: the principle is that you can open an SGML file from your local disk or download one from a network, either directly or via an HTML browser. In the latter case it is the MIME Content-Type `text/sgml` which causes the HTML browser to call the SGML viewer into action. SGML browsers which use HTML browsers to handle retrieval can use that browser's security features.

DTDs and resolution DTDs do not have to be compiled. Because *ViewPort* does not perform a full validation it only needs to parse the DTD and the instance sufficiently to identify the markup and its nesting, and it therefore reads the DTD on-the-fly fast enough not to need precompilation. The assumption is that the each file it downloads must identify the DTD, and that these files are downloadable if not already on the user's local disk (see next item).

The *ViewPort* application reads the file and identifies the Formal Public Identifier (FPI, see section 2.5) in the DocType Declaration. The use of an FPI here is compulsory: System Identifiers are not supported. The browser looks up the FPI in its `catalog` file to see if it is known, in which case the relevant entity file is read from disk. For unknown FPIs, the browser requests a file (also called `catalog`) from the same URL directory as the SGML file came from, and this is required to contain the URLs of all DTDs and entity files needed. Copies of these files are requested, and the instance is parsed (the sequence of files which the browser searches or requests can be configured). Finally the browser checks the local entity resource file, `entityrc`, in a similar way to the `catalog`, this time looking for an entry for the FPI with the names of stylesheet and navigator files; if they're not found, a remote file also called `entityrc` is requested from the same source and searched in turn; and the correct stylesheet and navigator downloaded for display. By this means, the browsers can equip themselves with everything needed for display except additional fonts (Times is used by default). It is the responsibility of the author or provider to ensure that a correct catalog, copies of the DTD and any entity files, a copy of the entity resource file, stylesheets, and navigators, are all available from the relevant URLs.

Stylesheets If a user downloads a file for display, the appearance is fixed by the stylesheet or stylesheets which accompany it. This is cached but its FPI and filename are not added to the local catalog. To edit such an existing stylesheet, the `catalog` and `entityrc` files must be downloaded explicitly, inspected, and the stylesheet and navigator filenames extracted and then downloaded and saved as a separate files in turn, then edited locally to change the styles. You can create new stylesheets and navigators for any file using the interface provided in each application (subject to restrictions: some free versions do not have stylesheet editing enabled). This lets you modify styles graphically on-screen, and it automatically records changes in the stylesheet file, and records the name of the stylesheet in the entity resource file alongside the FPI for the document type you are viewing.

All *ViewPort* applications share the same format for catalog files (OASIS, see section 2.5.4), entity resource files, stylesheet files, and navigator files, so you can provide documents for users of any of them without changes. With a few small differences, the browsers also provide the same styling facilities, although the interface by which you access them differs significantly between applications. The list of facilities follows closely the pattern outlined in section 3.2, but adds some features for online display, like hypertext linking and the iconizing of elements.

The stylesheet and navigator editor lets you attach one or more stylesheets and switch between them. Style editing is via a pop-up dialog box which activates on a right-click on an element tag. This lets you pick the element or its ancestry, and specify its occurrence (its position in a series, for example the first or last `<ITEM>` element in an uninterrupted list of items), and elements can be 'qualified' (restricted) on the basis of attribute values or position in the document (for example, 'first `<PARA>` following a `<LIST>`' could have the indent set to zero). In addition to the 'standard' features of styling, the style menu also lets you hide an element and its content completely, adjust the height or depth of superscripts and subscripts, and provide a number of pop-up widgets for objects like footnotes and links. The 'visibility' setting is useful for elements like index entries, or descriptive material which you don't want viewers to see (although they can always save the file and open it in an editor!).

Searching There are searching facilities at three levels: text in the document content , context-sensitive (elements and entities), and Regular Expressions; and they can be combined to restrict searches for a Regular Expression within a given element, or text in an element with specific attributes.

All 'hits' are highlighted simultaneously, and **Next Hit** and **Previous Hit** buttons let you navigate between them.

Printing You can print the whole or part of a document: partial printing is done by selecting the sections or subsections required in the navigator pane. The navigator itself can be printed, as a Table of Contents, with page numbers referencing the pages of the text body when printed.

Hypertext The hypertext linking facilities of the browsers are extensive, and include the ID/IDREF mechanism built into SGML, HyTime linking (see section 2.7.2.1), and TEI Extended Pointers (see section 2.3.6). Links are instantiated as highlights, optionally with a pointer symbol, and their appearance can be tailored via the stylesheet. Clicking on a link highlight or symbol causes the link to be traversed, and the target element is highlighted in reverse video. If the target is, say, a <CHAPTER>, all of the chapter is highlighted. If the link points at a resource outside the current file, via a URL for example, the file is retrieved and opened. Because HyTime, TEI, and ID/IDREF links are all bidirectional, *ViewPort* can display an inline button beside the *target* of a link, from which one can traverse to the source. Clicking on a target with multiple source links (many links pointing *to* it) causes a panel to be displayed, giving the choice of sources in TEI Extended Pointer notation (see Figure 113 for an example).

Personal 'webs' The linking facilities provided by HyTime are most evident in the feature which they call (rather confusingly) 'personal webs'. These are collections of documents which you can establish, associated by links between them which you can superimpose *without affecting the document markup*. This lets you connect, for example, references to articles in one document with locations in the actual article in another document, not just on your disk but across the Internet, regardless of the DTD or linking facilities provided (or not) in each file.

You can also add personal annotations to documents, and you can bookmark useful locations. All the relevant information is stored in 'web' files on your disk, using HyTime linking to identify the places in each document referred to. Links, annotations, and bookmarks cause an icon to be displayed at each linked location, which you can click on to traverse the link, or pop up the annotation; you can jump to any bookmark from the |*Bookmarks* sub-menu. Because the web file is itself an SGML instance, it can be published, so webs can also be shared between users.

Graphics and special characters The Synex engine does not have its own graphics, so each implementation provides graphical facilities via a third-party package. Both browsers below handle a much wider range of graphics than HTML browsers do, and includes CGM, WMF, and TIFF as well as the more common GIF and JPEG formats. Graphics have to be declared in the DocType Internal Subset (see section 2.1.1) as entities, which means raw HTML graphics references in an `<IMG>` element will not work as inline images unmodified, but implementing them is described in the manuals.

Character entities declared as `SDATA` are handled by a separate file `sdata.map` in the installation directory. While this holds equivalences for all the standard ISO-defined character entities from the ISO Latin 1 and 2, Greek, Cyrillic, Publishing, Technical, and Math character entity sets, many of them are unavailable on some platforms, so this file can be edited to insert your own fonts and definitions.

Synex stylesheets and navigators are SGML documents with their own DTDs, so it is possible to edit them manually if required, and to write conversion programs to exchange style information between their format and (for example) FOSIs (see section 2.3.5).

A feature of Synex's searching is that it not only highlights all 'hits' but indicates in a 'density indicator' where they occur in the entire file: down the right-hand side of the main document pane appears a narrow strip representing the whole document by its height, and showing horizontal lines at each relative location. Thus a search hit one third of the way through the document would be represented by a line one third of the way down this bar. Multiple hits close together make the lines closer (denser), so you can see immediately where they cluster. Clicking on any of the lines jumps you to the location of the hit (see Figure 116).

6.2.3. Panorama (SoftQuad)

Windows, Mac, Unix
`http://www.sq.com/`

This was the first small-scale downloadable SGML viewer for the Web. The *Panorama Free* plugin acted as a 'helper' application for *Mosaic* and some other HTML browsers by using the MIME Content-Type `text/sgml` to deflect the file from the browser into *Panorama* for display, which then requested the relevant DTD and style files via the browser. The

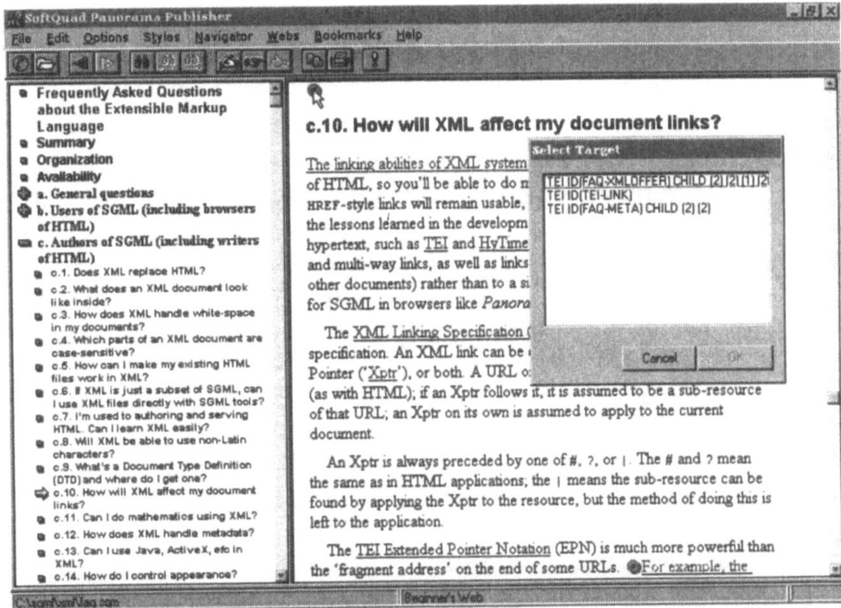

Figure 113. SoftQuad's *Panorama Publisher* showing navigation pane and bidirectional link buttons

commercial version, *Panorama Pro*, could also create style files and open local files from your hard disk, making it suitable for general-purpose SGML viewing.

The current full product is *Panorama Publisher*, and the browser-only version is a plugin called *Panorama Viewer*, which executes inside the browser display pane rather than in its own window. There is a version for CD distribution, *CDWeb Publisher*, which can also update itself and use additional information from the Web. SoftQuad also make the *Author/Editor* SGML editor and the *HoTMetaL* and *Xmetal* editors.

Installation is from CD-ROM or from a downloaded evaluation version of *Panorama Viewer* from their Web site. The fundamental difference between the viewer and the full product is that the viewer is read-only: you can view any SGML or XML file you open locally or download but you cannot create or modify stylesheets or navigators. This makes it ideal for intranet publishing as well as for the wider Internet, in cases where you want a wide audience for published text, but require the layout or formatting to remain under the author's or publisher's control. The *Panorama Publisher* executes in its own window and provides an interactive graphical interface to creating and editing stylesheets.

The split-pane approach of navigator and text can be seen in Figure 113. In this case (the XML FAQ) the navigator specification replicates elements from the document in correct hierarchical order, and a click on any of them listed in the left-hand pane shifts the view in the right-hand pane to display the topic.

This figure also shows the link target button (top of the right-hand pane) and the multiple link source choice dialog box showing (in this case) three locations which point to this section, identified by their TEI Extended Pointer Notation.

Searching in *Panorama* uses a single dialog box: the distinction between plaintext, element-based, or Regular Expression searching is indicated by the syntax of what you type:

Search term	Usage
`weaver`	searches for 'weaver' (this might include the surname)
`<occup>`	searches for all elements <occup>
`wea[rv]er`	searches for 'weaver' or 'wearer' (Regular Expression)
`weaver in <occup>`	searches for 'weaver' only inside <occup> elements

Panorama also implements two features which have been popularized by HTML browsers: frames and forms. A DTD fragment is provided in the documentation which you include in your DTD to enable framing. Frames can each have their own stylesheet and navigator, and can be targeted by hypertext links in other frames. The HTML forms definitions also rely in the inclusion of a DTD fragment supplied, and you can then use a special widget in the stylesheet to display them as fill-in boxes.

The stylesheet implementation in Figure 114 shows a document with styling in progress. Note the unformatted dedication, which will be set to print with a pagebreak (the designer has placed a diamond symbol to represent this as a reminder, and you can see the same reminder at the start of the first `<SEC>` element). You can see the element `<IT>` still displayed in default block-mode and upright type, while it is being made inline and italic via the styling dialog.

6.2.4. MultiDoc Pro (Citec)

MS-Windows
`http://www.citec.fi/`

MultiDoc Pro is a standalone MS-Windows browser for SGML files: it has its own built-in Internet connectivity, so it does not need an HTML browser to handle downloads. It installs from four floppy-disk-size `.zip`

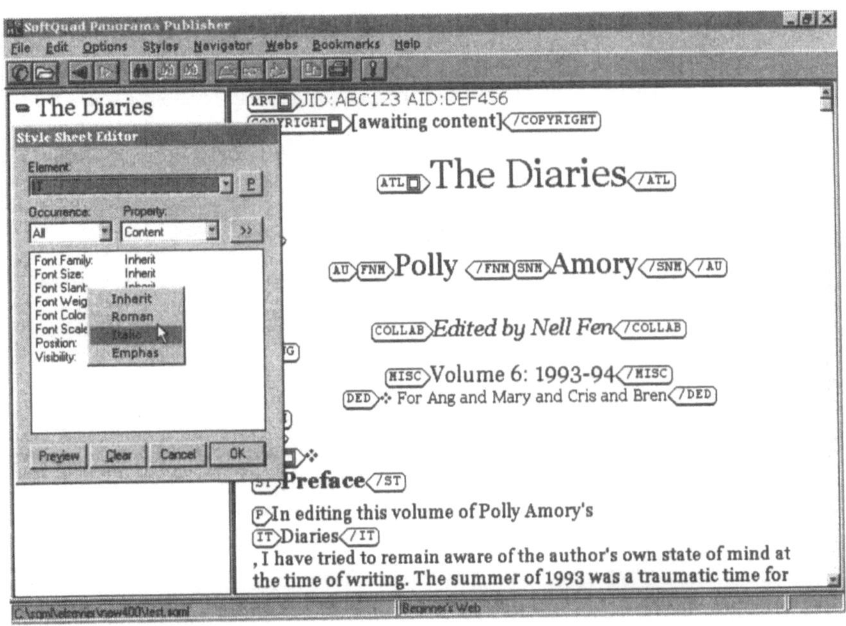

Figure 114. Panorama Publisher styling a document

files (six in the case of the version for Windows 3.1x) and is available with a month's free trial time-expiry, after which you need to buy a license to continue.

There are separate versions available for CD-only use, for database connectivity, and as a plugin to an existing HTML browser rather than a standalone program. A related program is Citec's *Translating Editor*, which uses the same technology to enable the creation of parallel files in other languages (see section 3.4.5).

The installation can detect if another SGML browser has been set to activate on a link from an HTML browser encountering an SGML file, and it offers to replace that browser's function if you wish. There is a separate IETM product (see section 2.3.5) called *MultiDoc LT* with Manual, Spare Part, and CBT (Computer-Based Training) modules.

The browser window contains the standard Synex text and navigator panes, but the *MultiDoc Pro* navigator window can hold multiple navigation views, instantiated with Windows 'tabs' on the navigator. This means you can flip between different views of the document, for example different densities of tables of contents, or lists of figures, or lists of links (see Figure 115).

Stylesheet editing in *MultiDoc Pro* uses a single dialog window with multiple tabs. It separates the autonumbering from the miscellaneous

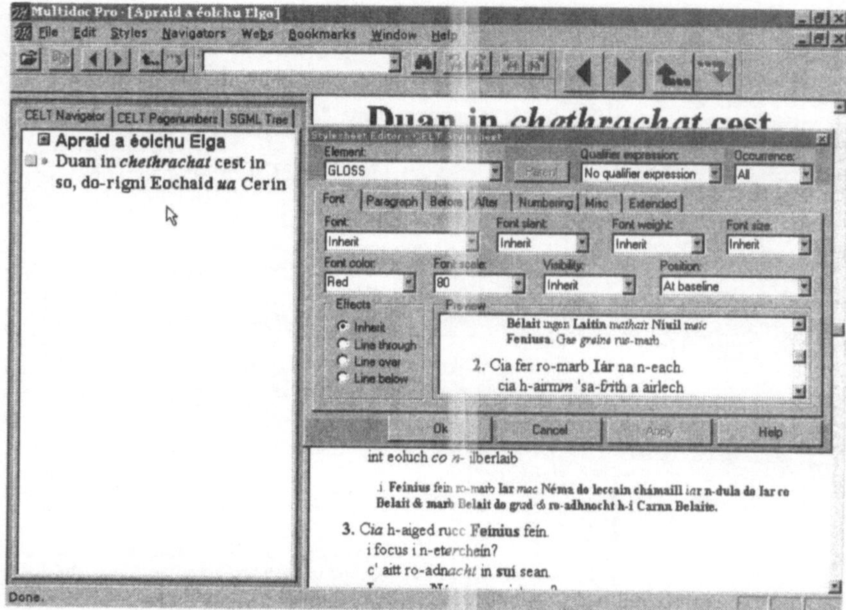

Figure 115. CITEC's *MultiDoc Pro* with multiple navigation panels

group and adds an extra tab giving access to the list of elements with all those which have formatting or positional or attribute qualifications.

The search window also divides out the different modes into separate tabs, one for full text searches, one for context searches, and one for Regular Expressions (REs). The Regular Expression tab provides an excellent point-and-click method of building a REs, useful for the beginner or for those who use them infrequently (see Figure 116).

6.2.5. Babble (University of Virginia)

Windows 95 and NT, Solaris

`http://jefferson.village.virginia.edu/babble/`

Babble is a specialist browser from the Institute for Advanced Technology in the Humanities at the University of Virginia in Charlottesville, VA. It calls itself a 'Synoptic Unicode Browser' — in other words, one that will handle any of the character sets defined in Unicode (equivalent to ISO 10646).

It can be downloaded for use on Solaris, Windows 95, and Windows NT systems, and displays multiple texts in side-by-side windows, such as would be useful for parallel translations. The use of Unicode means it allows both multilingual texts and the use of mixed character sets.

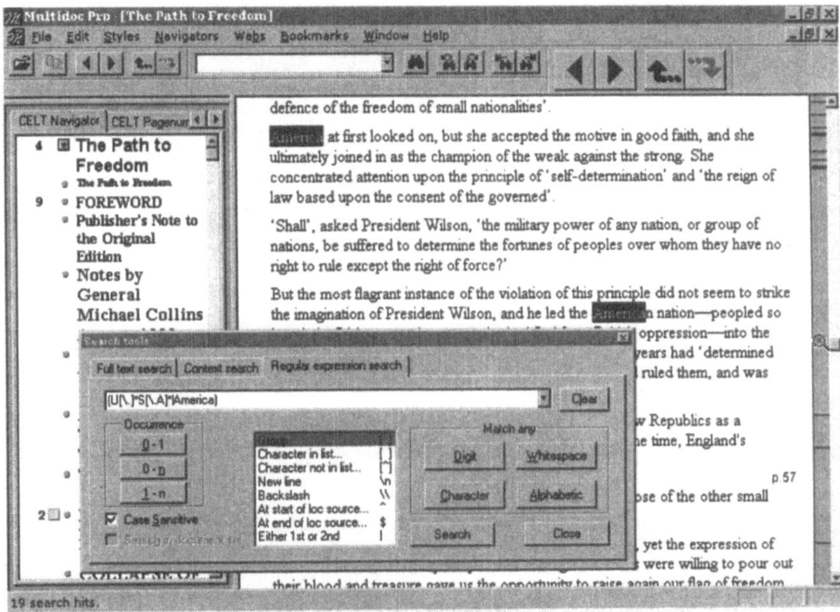

Figure 116. CITEC's *MultiDoc Pro* showing search option tabs and density indicator

It allows users to search within the text content or within the markup, and links can be created between open texts for cross-reference.

Babble requires the *Java* Development Kit (9Mb), Unicode fonts (6.5Mb), and the Babble installation itself (700Kb). It can operate as a plugin to an HTML browser so that downloaded files cause *Babble* to pop up and display the file.

6.2.6. Sara (OTA)

Windows and Unix
`http://info.ox.ac.uk/bnc/sara`

Sara is a search tool from the Oxford Text Archive and Oxford University Computing Services developed for accessing the BNC (British National Corpus), which is a a 100 million word collection of samples of written and spoken language from a wide range of sources, designed to represent a wide cross-section of current British English, both spoken and written.

Both browser and client software is available for several platforms, so you can run the server on your own text collection. Accessing the BNC requires a fee, but there is a 20–day trial period. The search window

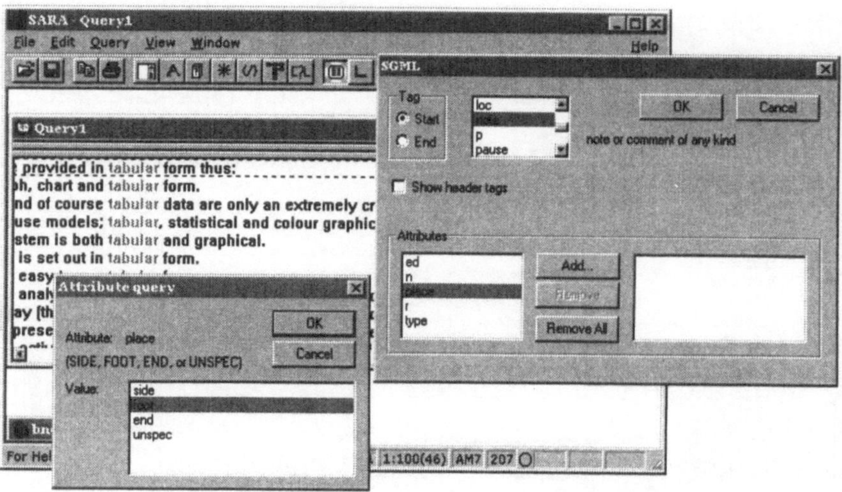

Figure 117. The *Sara* browser searching the BNC

(see Figure 117) provides for several different display formats including the standard concordance format as well as a 'phrase at a time' display. The SGML search panel lets you restrict the search to any element in the DTD, and to any specific attribute values.

General-purpose viewers and browsers are designed specifically to handle as wide a range of SGML usages as possible. When you narrow the field to a particular document type, it becomes possible to introduce additional features related to the content or style of data, because some of the semantics of the topic dealt with are already known (or can be assumed). Thus for a body of literature, even from diverse periods and in different languages, there are many common facilities which a user can be expected to want. Even after 10 years of the Text Encoding Initiative (TEI: see section 2.3.6), there are still only a few large-scale corpora which can benefit from this approach, but the number is growing every year. Many corpora rely on existing HTML browser technology, or supply TEI files for use with one of the browsers mentioned elsewhere, especially (for large-scale work) with *DynaText* (see section 6.2.1), but *Sara* was designed specifically for the TEI as used by the BNC.

6.3. Non-visual representations

`http://www.yuri.org/webable/`

Although few SGML software authors and vendors provide explicit facilities for the disabled, there is a considerable amount of work being done in many countries on making it easier to get Braille or audio output from SGML.

Facilities for making it possible to use browsers for the blind with HTML were introduced in RFC 1866, due in great measure to the persistence of the late Yuri Rubinsky of SoftQuad. This provided SDA `FIXED` attributes for elements which mapped them to elements in the DTD written by ICADD (International Committee on Accessible Document Design), and enabled the use of speaking browsers like *pwWebSpeak*.

It is to the significant discredit of many subsequent HTML DTDs (with the notable exceptions of Spyglass and HTML Pro; there may be others) that they have so badly neglected this important area, which can provide such a significant benefit for so little effort, and the W3C is to be applauded for repairing this deficit in HTML 4.0. The ISO 12083 DTDs also include the SDA attributes (see section 29).

Editing TV Raman has developed a speech output subsystem for *Emacs*, so editing can be enabled for the visually-impaired. This software, *emacspeak*, is on the CD-ROM (Unix only at the time of writing). Dr Raman is well known as the developer of *AsTeR*, an audio system for technical reading (especially of documents containing math) for which he won the ACM Dissertation Award for 1994. His book *Auditory User Interfaces: Toward the Speaking Computer*[36] 'describes a speech-enabling approach that separates computation from the user interface and integrates speech into the human-computer interaction'.

Browsing Productivity Works makes the *pwWebSpeak* browser for MS-Windows, which enables voice output of HTML Web pages and has a large-type display kept in synchrony with the speech. SGML and XML applications are 'under investigation'.

The NASA Johnson Space Center Learning Technologies Project has an information retrieval tool called *ILIAD* which is an off-line email-based retriever which can also be used by the blind to search the Internet. The text version of *ILIAD* is email based and can be used with DOS screen-readers. Details are available by sending a null email to `iliad@algol.jsc.nasa.gov` with the subject set to `start iliad` (no actual email text, just those words in the `Subject` header line) and can also be found at `http://www.jsc.nasa.gov/stb/iliad.html`

In discussions about XML, Harvey Bingham identified a number of simple techniques to improve access to information, which are listed below. While some of these are authoring decisions, and apply mostly to the creation of SGML/XML/HTML for use on the Web, the principles can be applied to all information-creation activities: some recommendations are browser-design topics and need to be studied much more closely by software writers. Attention to these aspects takes a tiny amount of the author's or designer's time, and makes an enormous difference to the usability of the data for those with visual disabilities.

- Give the user the controls to shape the presentation as needed for particular means of understanding;
- Let the information work with speech readers for the blind;
- Give it logical organization and linearized presentation: allow asides [following hypertext links] with easy return;
- Provide large-type options for the low-vision disabled (for example a much larger range of point sizes than browsers currently allow);
- Allow legible font substitution in place of decorative ones;
- Allow reverse video;
- Make it possible to get rid of wallpaper and other chart-junk [a suggestion from Ed Tufte];
- Identify alternate explanatory text for all non-text objects (images, diagrams, tables with complex cells, *etc*);
- Allow color shifting to help the color-blind;
- Make the very accessibility controls themselves accessible.

There is now a W3C Web Accessibility Initiative (`http://www.w3.org/WAI/`), which should help improve matters for HTML and XML. It remains to be seen if vendors can rise to the occasion for the broad spectrum of SGML tools.

6.4. Stylesheet software

Most applications which perform formatting have their own stylesheet interface, and that's the way you use their stylesheets. Some stylesheet languages are expressed in SGML or SGML-like syntax (FOSIs, *DynaText* and Synex stylesheets for example), and XSL is expressed in XML, so it is of course possible to create and edit these stylesheets by hand with any suitable editor, but because they are closely bound to their parent

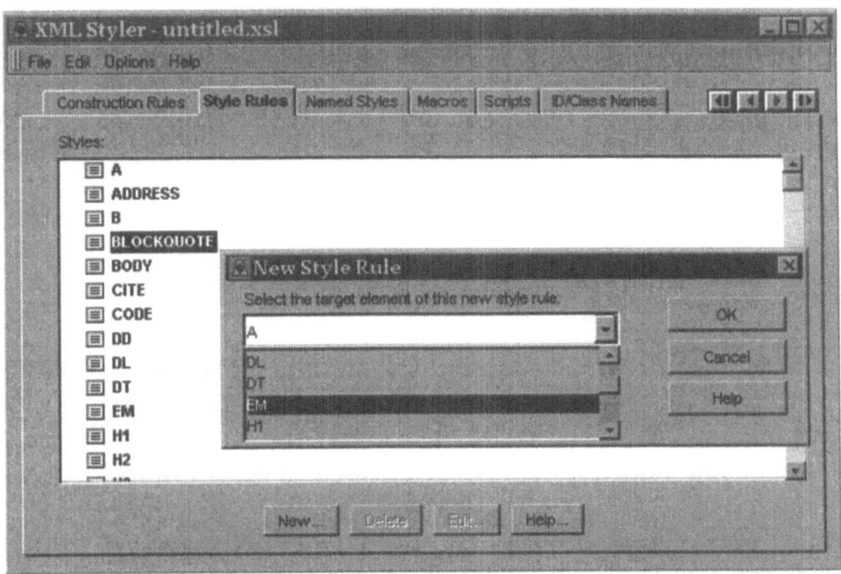

Figure 1.18. ArborText's XML Styler

product (editor, browser, *etc*), they are normally used via the stylesheet interface that comes built in.

More widespread use of XML, however, is likely to be dependent on the widespread availability of editors with styling built in, and of standalone stylesheet editors and converters. The program shown here may represent the advance guard.

6.4.1. The XML Styler (ArborText)

```
http://www.arbortext.com/xmlstyler
```

This is a standalone XSL editor from ArborText, makers of the *ADEPT* editing and publishing series, and of other text-handling software. The editor is free (at the time of writing) and can be downloaded from their Web site. It requires a PC running Windows 95, and an ActiveX-enabled copy of *Internet Explorer* 4 or higher. Their Web site has explicit details on how to activate your copy of *Internet Explorer* for use with ActiveX.

You can either type in element names as you go along, or get the program to read a DTD or instance and extract a list of element names (in which case it also understands their hierarchy and a lot more [the grove]). It also knows about HTML element names, and can add them to the list.

The interface is not entirely intuitive to new users, however, as it presupposes a sound knowledge and understanding of some of the XSL/DSSSL terminology, and because of the separation in XSL between the concepts of 'selection rules' and 'style rules', establishing a style takes more than just a mouseclick on an element name and a font name.

6.5. Printing and publishing

As *printing* was the origin of all this — markup, DTDs, parsers, editors, viewers, formatters — it's not surprising that there is strong demand for printed output. The cry of the person faced with SGML for the first time, 'Yes, it's all very nice, but how do I get it *printed*?', is easily understood.

Whichever route you pick, it is unavoidable that you have to supply a stylesheet to map the elements in your SGML document to specific formats on paper, just as we had to do in the previous chapter when viewing SGML on the screen. In the case of some DTDs, this has already been done for prewritten formats in specific formatting programs, as noted below. If you're using a DTD with no stylesheet, you'll have to write one yourself, either by hand, or using the graphical interface of a viewer, browser, or editor.

6.5.1. Into print fast

If you're in a desperate hurry to print a roughly formatted version of an SGML document, you could always try loading it into a Web browser. Many DTDs use `<P>` as the paragraph element name: if this is the case with your document, you may get a rough-and-ready printout from an HTML browser without the intrusion of any markup, as browsers ignore unknown elements — but you may get some strange results from elements which accidentally have the same names that HTML uses for other purposes. For example, a DTD which uses `<H1>` and `<H2>` for 'highlight–1' and 'highlight–2', normally rendered as bold and italic, is going to get you some pretty odd formatting in a HTML browser where `<H1>` and `<H2>` are heading levels.

The easiest way into respectable print is probably to use the printing capabilities of an SGML viewer like *Panorama* or *MultiDoc Pro* which you can download and run. These have limited abilities on paper compared to fully-fledged desktop publishing or typesetting programs, as they are intended for online use, but provided you don't want complex formatting, this is by far the easiest way, and will produce output approximating to the quality of word processing. Details of both these viewers, and the Synex *ViewPort* engine on which they rely, are in section 6. Prewritten styles exist for the DTDs which come with both systems, so if your document uses one of these, you can just open the document and print it.

Prewritten styles also come with the DTDs shipped with most editors, with the *Jade* DSSSL conversion tool, and with documentation systems like *SGML-Tools* (the former *LinuxDoc*). Specific styles also exist for individual DTDs, such as a DSSSL stylesheet for *DocBook* (see section 2.7.2.3).

6.5.2. Publishing and typesetting systems

A lot of SGML-encoded text is still destined for formal publishing in printed form (like this book) rather than as an electronic edition, or in a database, on CD-ROM, or on the Web. Publishers have traditionally prided themselves on their maintenance of typographic standards, and many still use professional designers, typographers, typesetters, and layout artists to achieve this.

In-house or office-style publishing does not usually warrant this level of investment, as most everyday working documents are simply not worth it. Similar judgment is often used where the document involves a restricted market or where it is likely to have a very short life before revision and reissue.

Professional typesetting for publication is a very different field from desktop publishing, and there are relatively few products on the market capable of working directly from SGML files. More and more of the features demanded by the compositor or typographer are certainly now being found in DTP products, but the precision and fineness of detail to which the typesetter is used to working are not normally included in the general range of DTP systems, as these are specifically aimed at users without typographic training.

Only two systems are included here: *Frame+SGML* and *3B2*. The first is, as its name suggests, an SGML version of *FrameMaker*, the second is a large-scale typesetting package with full SGML support built in. There are many other publishing and document management systems which use external or third-party filters to import or even export SGML, such as Xyvision's *Production Publisher* and Miles 33's *Genera*, as well as full SGML systems like Penta's *DeskTopPro* and Datalogics' *DL Composer*, so these should be regarded as samples of the ones with inbuilt SGML support.

6.5.2.1. Frame+ SGML (Adobe)

Unix/X, MS-Windows, Mac

`http://www.adobe.com/prodindex/framemaker/prodinfosgml.html`

FrameMaker has a long history in the DTP field and is popular for typesetting with both professionals and non-professionals. It had an SGML import filter for many years, but *Frame+SGML* is now marketed as a separate product.

The system comes on floppies or CD-ROM with a large reference manual, quick reference booklet, and 'Getting Started' guide. *Adobe Type Manager* is included as a requirement. Installation is fairly straightforward, although lengthy, and new users should probably have someone with SGML experience on hand to help them decide which bits they need and which they don't, as there are quite a lot of installation options, including sample files and online help, import and export filters, and an abbreviated copy of *DocBook*. It also installs for network use, and can even run direct from the CD-ROM.

Frame+SGML's document management is centered around the EDD (Element Definition Document), which specifies element and attribute names like a DTD does for regular SGML or XML. A file of 'read/write rules' specifies how SGML documents should be imported and exported, and a 'template' file provides the stylesheet facility.

In common with many systems, creation of a new SGML file is based on the assumption is that someone else has prepared the application for you before you start — *Frame+SGML* only comes delivered with a cut-down version of *DocBook* as a sample application, although other 'starter packs' are under development, such as the AECMA one mentioned in section 2.3.2.1. While this concept is understandable, it means that unless you are using one of the starter packs unmodified, the first thing you need to do is create the EDD, read/write rules, and template files. The manual for this procedure is not printed, but available only in electronic form on the CD-ROM, doubtless *pour encourager les autres*.

Establishing the EDD for a new application involves editing the SGML Applications document, which stores details of each new application. This is a structured *Frame+SGML* document, so editing it is fairly straightforward once you turn on the tags (see the right-hand frame in Figure 119). You specify the locations of the DocType Declaration and the other files required, and you can then import the DTD. This creates a new EDD (see the left-hand frame in Figure 119). As usual, the final stage is the longest, assigning read/write rules and styles to each element. The completed application is then added to the list of document types available for users. While this procedure is not much different from adding a new DTD and stylesheet to other SGML

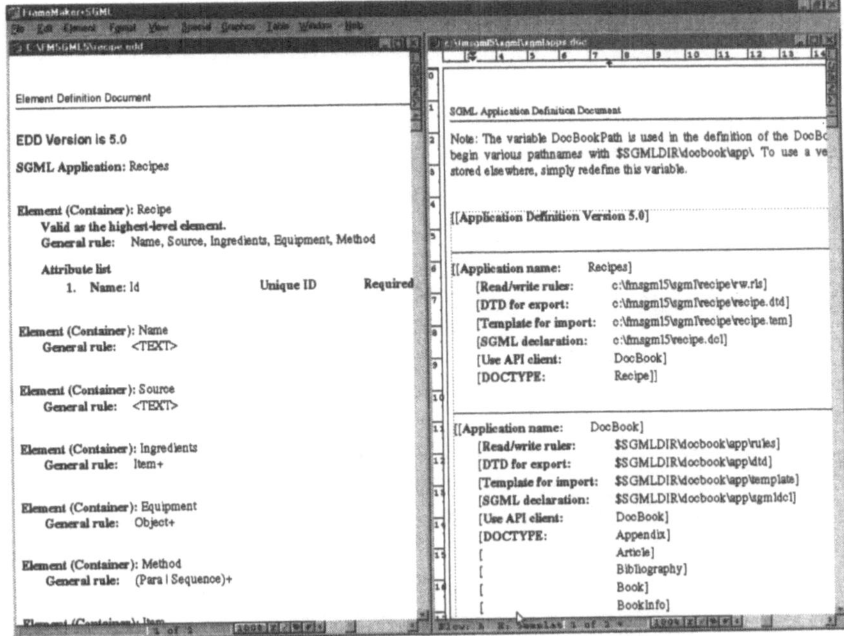

Figure 119. Frame+SGML preparing a new EDD, having parsed the DTD.

systems, it is a little confused by the documentation, which is trying to teach SGML concepts at the same time as explaining the procedure.

Editing documents itself is considerably more obvious. Navigation is helped by a 'Structure View' window, which displays the elements from the DTD in hierarchical form aligned with the first few words of content for each. A marker identifies the cursor position within or between elements, synchronized with the movement of the actual cursor in the document window.

In the document window, tags can be indicated by graphical tags in the form common to other editors, or by square brackets without the element name (*WordPerfect Suite* does this also), which is a conveniently compressed way of indicating the structure if you have it on view in another window. A smaller 'Element Catalog' window lists the elements valid at the current point, and you have the usual 'insert' and 'surround' functions, element join, element split, and markup-sensitive cut and paste. Like *Emacs* with *psgml*, the structure management allows you to insert elements out of place, or proceed without otherwise compulsory elements, creating a temporarily invalid file. You can also apply temporary non-SGML 'touch-up' visual formatting such as font changes, on the basis that it will disappear when the file is validated.

Frame+SGML is a large and robust system, but it is probably slightly more at home as a formatter for text prepared or generated elsewhere than as an editor for file creation, as the richness of its other DTP functions, which are extensive, tends to get in the way of the rigor usually needed for the creation of SGML instances from scratch. Both the non-SGML *FrameMaker* as well as *Frame+SGML* support export into XML.

6.5.2.2. 3B2 (Advent Systems)

Unix/X, DOS, MS-Windows, Mac
`http://www.3b2.com`

3B2 is one of the most powerful multiplatform typesetting and layout systems. It was originally developed in the late 1980s when it became clear that after the move away from dedicated systems and onto general-purpose business computers, especially PCs and Macs, many desktop publishing systems lacked the power, dimensional accuracy, and programmability found in more specialist systems.

The PC version installs either as a DOS or Windows system from the same disks, but in all case (including Unix and the Mac) it uses its own windowing model, with its own menus and conventions, not those of the machine it is installed on, as in Figure 120. In general this is not a problem, although you need to get used to a slight difference in the way it handles mouse editing of string field values like file names.

There is an inherent assumption which distinguishes a typesetting system from word processing or desktop publishing: a typesetter expects the bulk of its input to come in the form of a file, ready-typed, whereas WP and DTP systems spend a lot of time in text-input mode. Although you certainly can type text directly into *3B2*, and it works just fine, most users at this level are dealing with text files that have been authored elsewhere, typically books, chapters, articles, brochures, newspaper or other periodical matter. There is therefore a set of filters available to handle the input of common formats, especially SGML and TEX/LATEX. By the same token, output from high-end systems is usually destined for high-resolution typesetters rather than office laser printers, although the average office printer will obviously do for drafting purposes.

Apart from its own typographic capabilities, and the ability to use installed Windows fonts, *3B2* comes with a selection of Monotype *SmartFonts* on CD-ROM, but these are not usable with any other system (a pity if you want to use your SGML source files in another program with different facilities as well as in *3B2*).

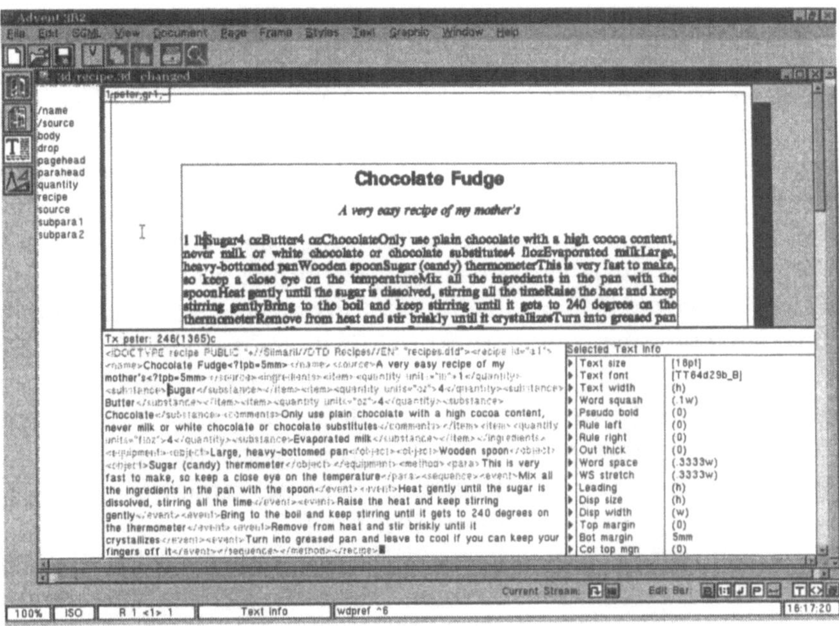

Figure 120. *3B2* part-way through formatting an SGML file

3B2 operates in four major modes: 'document' (page makeup), 'page/-frame' (page layout), 'text' (normal edit mode), and 'graphics', accessible via icons listed vertically beside the main window (see Figure 120). The SGML source display is in a separate resizable panel below or beside the formatted text. This shows exactly what is in the file you are using, in its raw, unprocessed form. This display will be immediately familiar to anyone who has worked on dedicated typesetting equipment, and is essential for making best use of the markup.

There's a good reason for this: from the beginning, *3B2* has used SGML-like markup internally, with the familiar angle brackets and ampersands. This places the system at a clear advantage, as there is almost no conversion from or to SGML required once parsing and validation has been done. There are some significant differences in interpretation, however: once imported, an SGML file is considered a stream of data to be processed, rather than a set of elements conforming to a DTD.

The system takes the purely pragmatic view that a typesetter's job is to get the job typeset, rather than to fret over the niceties of SGML: *3B2*'s primary business is to produce the goods. In *3B2*'s terms, therefore <head> and </head>, for example, are regarded as two entirely separate and unconnected formatting controls. This has disadvantages as well as advantages: you can't assume, as you can with SGML-dependent systems, that the thing which looks like and end-tag will automatically turn off the format you specified for its apparent start-tag. On the other hand, there are many cases when this simplifies processing, as a single end-tag can fulfil multiple functions and reset all kinds of things in one go, which would have been the responsibility of several contiguous end-tags otherwise.

This is a substantial package, with power and facilities above the needs of the average desktop user. For the professional compositor or publisher, however, it is capable of handling all the usual requirements of commercial typesetting, both from SGML and non-SGML sources.

As *3B2* is designed for use in a production environment, the SGML configuration can be held in template files, and the relevant template loaded for each different client, DTD, or *genre* of job. A template holds a default SGML Declaration filename, DTD name, catalog locations, and search paths for public and system identifiers.

There is no attempt to define a resolution algorithm for the public owner or text string values of public identifiers. Instead, the parameter entity name in the DTD which is declared for each public identifier is tried as a filename, both alone and with a variety of filetype suffixes, searching the path defined in the template. Only when this fails does an error occur, but there is no dialog available at that stage to correct the error and continue by pointing at the right file, as with *RulesBuilder* or *SGMLC*. System identifiers are subject to a similar search along the defined system path, and there is provision for an 'alternate' path to be used when both public and system paths fail. This solution relies on the fact that in many cases authors of DTDs and instances do indeed choose filenames for their public texts which map conveniently to the entity names used in the declarations.

Having loaded or defined a template, an SGML file can be imported and parsed. The parser is *nsgmls*, and it reports through the *3B2* interface, so that errors can be viewed and corrected.

Unknown tags (unknown to *3B2*, that is!) are recorded in the order of occurrence in the instance (not sorted or placed in hierarchical order), but only one example of each is listed. Therefore if `<p>` occurs for the first time in the instance in `<chap>`, even though it then also appears in `<sect>`, that portion of the 'unknown tags' list might look like this

```
...
<chap>
<p>
<emph>
</emph>
</p>
```

```
<sect>
...
</sect>
</chap>
```

This list can then be used to generate the style macros which do the formatting. The SGML attributes of elements can be used to implement conditional styles, as can the nesting of one element inside another, in the conventional manner of SGML formatters.

It must be emphasized again that even at this stage, *3B2* itself does not regard the markup as SGML elements, acting as delimiters to the data content, but just as an imported set of undefined *3B2* 'attributes'.

3B2 can also export SGML, by passing a *3B2* file through the parser and saving it to disk. Obviously, for it to pass the validation, all the tags in the file must also be valid start- or end-tags for the DTD in use, and must occur in legal sequence.

6.5.3. Programmable batch systems

Large-scale conversions require a different approach to the visual, on-screen paradigm used by editors, word processors and DTP systems. Anyone who has had to convert a lot of files from one format to another by loading each one in turn, converting it, and then saving it in the new format, will understand the need for automated 'batch' conversion.

For many years this was the standard way of working: edit a file, save it, then run a program which did something with it and created an output file. If it was wrong and needed fixing, repeat the process until correct.

This is still the conventional way of running any standalone program such as a command-line parser, as by definition it has to start at the beginning of the file, run all the way through to the end, and then stop.

6.6. Document management and archiving

Large-scale or mission-critical SGML office systems need a more robust and rigorous level of support than the filename and directory name services supplied by an operating system. The multi-user, multi-access nature of office document work means that these systems leave behind the concept of 'files' and 'folders' for their internal organization, although those terms may be used in the presentation, and users can often be quite unaware of what is going on behind the scenes to make their documents appear when they want them.

A full document management system will handle the filing of documents in whatever way makes most sense for the user, but the storage of the SGML information is done on the basis of the element. In classical relational database terms, one way would be to have each element name being a table, with the tuples being the occurrences of the elements from whatever documents are stored, and the index value of each entry would point into the logical sequential structure the user sees as 'the document'. This way, requesting a document causes the retrieval system to look up a set of keys and locate the elements in order, regardless of whereabouts they are stored in the database.

There are several advantages to this, apart from the speed and the potential for reusing a lot of existing software techniques already developed for similar tasks. Redundancy can be avoided, as identical occurrences can be indexed out of the tree and replaced with multiple pointers, and there are standard techniques for checking the integrity of the structure, which is not possible when the documents are kept in sequential units of storage like files. It is also possible to track the changes made to a document on an element by element basis, providing an audit trail of what has been done.

Document archives are simply the extension of the database technique to the permanent storage of documents which do not usually change. Historical information can therefore be kept inviolate as a matter of record or proof, as distinct from an interactive database where any authorized user can retrieve a document, modify it, and replace it.

6.6.1. Database systems

Because of the rigorous and machine-processable nature of SGML, it is well suited to the formal storage of large quantities of text in databases (whether or not the information contained within it is equally well suited to such storage is a separate question, and beyond the scope of this book). There are relatively few native SGML database systems on the market and they tend to be very large by comparison with editors or viewers, and thus tend to require a more powerful host computer than the average desktop PC; typically a Unix, VMS, or mainframe system.

There is a much larger number of relational database systems and object database systems which have SGML front-ends or back-ends (which can import and export SGML by means of filters), but which do not impose SGML constraints (syntax, parsing, validation) on the components once stored.

The idea of using SGML in conjunction with a database is that the information base is centrally stored, usually on a Unix or NT server, with networked users on Macs, Windows PCs, or X terminals, accessing the information in a tightly-controlled environment, typically a corporate production environment, where arbitrary or *ad hoc* access is not common. Technically it would be possible for the database to be distributed across many machines, but I am not aware of any native SGML system that does this outside the military field.

Among the benefits of having your organization's information base in this form are:

- Rigorous control over the types and natures of the text being stored;
- Reliability and robustness of searching and extraction;
- Very high levels of reusability of the information;
- Homogeneity of the data and the access to it;
- Efficiency of use when done on a large scale.

Such systems are not cheap, however, and new users should be aware that there is also a significant administrative overhead in running a large-scale text database which is typically absorbed only by having an operation large enough to justify it, or where other aspects make it mission-critical.

Among the systems popular with those serving information from databases, including HTML, SGML and XML on the Web, are Poet Software's *Poet* 5, which is a Windows NT and Unix object database with some support for SGML, and Chrystal Software's *Astoria*, a content management system with fine-grained control for multiple file formats including SGML and XML.

6.6.1.1. Information Manager (Texcel)

Information Manager (*IM*) is a native SGML database which uses ArborText's *ADEPT* software for editing and display. Texcel is a Norwegian-based company well known for its long history in the text software business. IM is a client-server system available for Unix servers with clients operating under the X Window system or MS-Windows. There is a Web application of IM under development.

IM treats your information as a series of projects containing documents. The database provides a seamless view of this structure as a repository hierarchy all the way from the top of the project tree down to the most deeply-nested element in a document (see Figure 121): there is no discontinuity between 'projects', 'directories', 'files', and 'markup' as there would be in the traditional desktop operating system use of SGML.

Different levels of security are available, so as with any multi-user system you have to log in with a username and password before gaining access to the database. Two approaches to managing the data are offered: a Repository Browser which gives the hierarchical access already mentioned; and a Workflow Manager, which provides tools for controlling the progress of a project or document from planning to editing to revision to release.

The use and control of projects and documents is separated from the use and control of DTDs: an authenticated user can view, create, and edit documents, but only the database administrator can update the system with new projects, DTDs ('templates' in IM terminology) or database procedures. This avoids the problems inherent in non-database repositories of the conflicting installation of multiple DTDs introduced and modified by different users with no coordination.

IM is a strong contender for the corporate text database, especially for the relatively non-technical end-user, as it goes a long way towards protecting them from the inherent complexities of SGML itself. There is always a case to be made for developing or training users in some of the technicalities in the long run, as people tend to be more productive if they understand what is going on when they click the mouse, but in many circumstances this is not possible, and IM provides a suitable shield for the novice or occasional user, as well as allowing the more sophisticated user full access.

6.6.1.1.1. User facilities The Repository Browser interface lets you double-click on a project, which opens it to show the documents; double-click on a document and it shows the outline structure; double-click on an element and it shows the content. Each stage is color-coded, and the structure is kept typographically distinct from text content. You can view a document on a read-only basis, or edit it, or create a new document by selecting a template, which then opens an *ADEPT*-based edit screen. It is also possible to bulk-load a series of documents prepared elsewhere, assuming they have already been parsed and validated and that the relevant DTD has been installed. You can export documents to external SGML files for use in other systems. If you have the correct level of privilege, you can also delete documents.

Part of the power of using a database approach is that the database management system 'knows' about DTDs and elements across the entire database. It is therefore possible to cut or copy and paste text content from one document to another, assuming they use the same DTD (a limited degree of element mapping is available via the *ADEPT* macro scripting language if the DTDs are similar). An element or entity

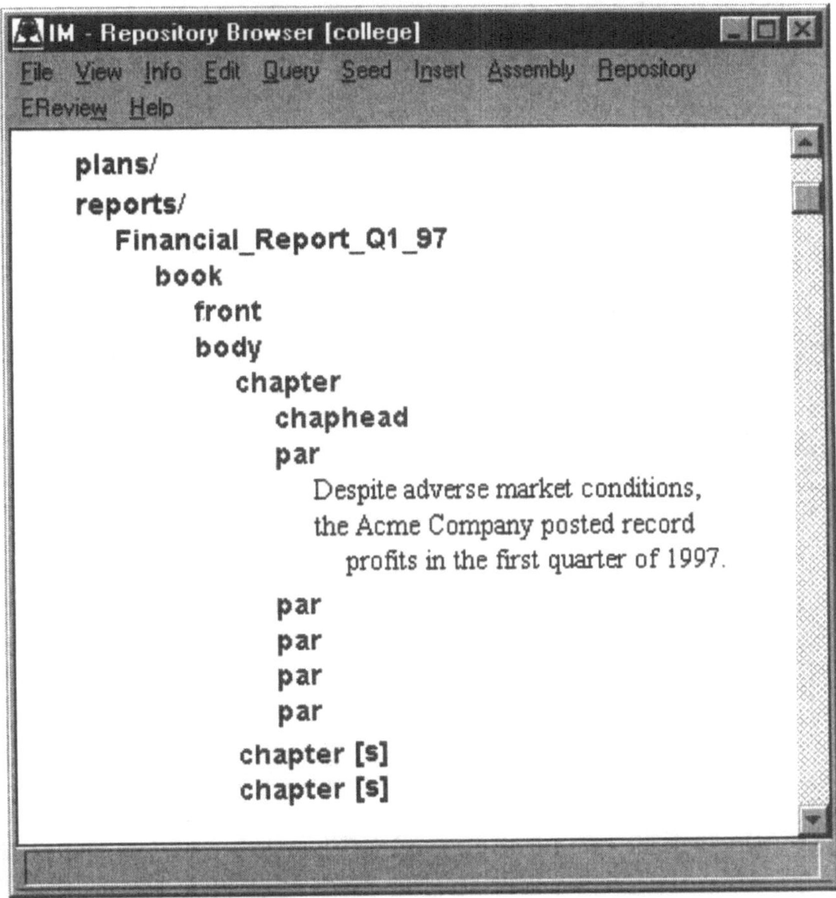

Figure 121. The *Information Manager* Repository Browser showing the hierarchical view of a database

can be reused in many documents, so 'boilerplate' text such as contract clauses or copyright statements can be stored once but referenced in any document. This allows you to assemble documents from templates, gathering text from different sources.

When you edit a document, it is locked against editing by anyone else for the duration of the edit, but it is also possible to edit only a portion of a document, and locking is supported also at element level, so several people can be editing different parts of the same document simultaneously, without conflicting with each other. Bidirectional links are supported from anywhere to anywhere, so related information can be connected together even at the element level, and between documents using different DTDs.

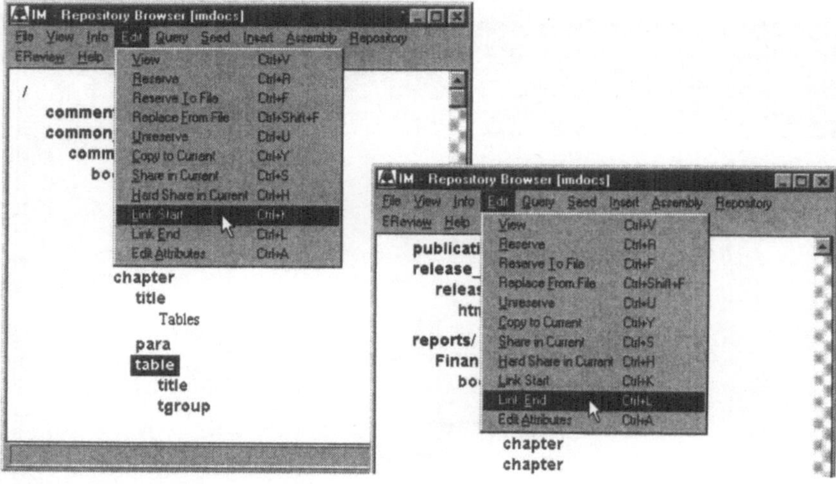

Figure 122. Creating a link between documents in an *Information Manager* database

Comments about document content can be entered without affecting the document itself (that is, the comments are held separately, rather than inside the document, so they are not SGML Comment Declarations). This is used to pass metainformation for review or post-editing, as the comments can be applied to the document by reviewers or other editors. All versions of a document can be maintained, so you can revisit an earlier version to see what was said before a change was made, and versions can be compared automatically to list the differences (even if the DTD has changed). IM provides context-sensitive searching ('seeded' and 'guided' queries) within documents or across projects.

The Workflow Manager provides for 'WorkQueues', in which you specify the stages of a document or a project to completion as a set of tasks. A graphical form of GANTT chart can be displayed to show the stages involved, and the tasks can be grouped into 'folders' so that they can be allocated or attributed to different users.

6.6.1.1.2. Database management and extension At a technical level, there is a complete API with extensive documentation, so it is possible to embed the full functionality of IM within an existing computer system. The API is implemented as a suite of C calls, although the bulk of applications also interface with *rms*, a Tcl-based scripting language.

The database management system is based on *UniSQL/X*, an Object/Relational (O/R) hybrid database from UniSQL, Inc. O/R technology allows *IM* to manage SGML documents at the individual element level even on a very large scale, which pure object database technology less suited to. It still looks like a traditional database (it supports an extended SQL) and allows the database administrator to tailor the user interface to corporate requirements, as well as to manage the creation of the repository, installation of security passwords, and the insertion and removal of projects, DTDs, and documents. Because it decomposes SGML documents down to the smallest element, every element is stored as a row in a table (object in a class), which provides significant processing advantages including the ability to have the extensive SGML query language.

7. Rolling your own

> The computer salesman was presenting his bid to a large electronics company back in the days when such corporations still considered building their own computers rather than buying them.
> 'It's like Noah and the Ark,' he explained, 'he could have gone to a professional ark-builder, or he could have done the job himself.'
> Silence.
> Finally it's broken by a rookie engineer at the back taking the bait.
> 'But Noah *did* build the ark himself!'
> 'Damn right!' roared the salesman, 'and if you've got 40 years experience and God on your side, *you* can build your own computer.'
> The company decided to buy...but from the competition.
>
> Anonymous, possibly apocryphal.

- **Toolkits for the programmer**

In addition to the extensive commercial and non-commercial offerings in the SGML field, there is a strong tradition of homebrewed software. This arose in the earlier days of SGML, before regular manufacturers took an interest, and when the cost of commercially-developed programs was beyond the reach of many researchers.

While there is still an enormous amount of such software around, there are also now some very powerful and high-quality toolkits to let programmers add SGML capability to almost any kind of program. This class of facility is generally termed 'middleware', as it stands between the dedicated SGML engine and the entirely non-SGML product, and is used to bridge the gap.

Typically this consists of subroutine libraries to which the programmer can make calls from C or other code. These may be bound statically at compile time, or more commonly linked dynamically at execute time, using run-time library files.

Having a library of SGML routines available means a programmer can add SGML functionality to almost any system. Spurred by the example, however inconsistent and non-conformant, of HTML and the Web, it is becoming more common to find text-handling applications now offer some level of understanding of SGML.

A similar growth has been in the field of adding Internet functionality to applications software. The development of XML (see section 2.4) would seem to indicate that regular desktop software with built-in SGML capabilities to go with the IP capabilities cannot be far off, but some more experience and education is still needed. One book on the topic of writing SGML software is Seán McGrath's *ParseMe.1st: SGML for Software Developers*[32] which provides a good background in the theory and requirements of SGML systems for programmers.

7.1. Toolkits for the programmer

Programmers' toolkits for SGML started with the release of the early code for the *Mark-It!* parser in 1986, closely followed by the *Amsterdam SGML Parser* (ASP), but the development of specialist, bundled, integrated services for the software developer has been a relatively recent arrival.

It has been led by the practice of systems developers releasing details of the API — at a price — as a means of encouraging others to develop applications conforming to their specification (the MS-Windows API being the most obvious example in recent years).

In the SGML field, new developments are often coded for testing by friends and colleagues on the Internet, so the code is released into the public domain from the very start. The nature of public peer review leads to some very robust and powerful code being available free, but it is in general (although not always) limited to Unix-based versions at the start: other platforms follow later.

7.1.1. YASP

Unix, Mac, DOS/Windows, Windows NT/95, OS/2, MVS/VM
`ftp://ftp.edf.fr/pub/SGML/YASP`

The *Yorktown Advanced SGML Parser* was originally developed in 1991 by Pierre Richard and Geoff Bartlett at IBM Watson Labs in Yorktown Heights, NY, and is maintained by Pierre Richard and Christophe Espert of Electricité de France. It provides a library of SGML functions in C for writing parser applications (see one in section 4.3.6). It compiles on many platforms and is available free from the address above (also on the CD-ROM). Windows NT and Windows 95 versions are available precompiled as DLLs.

YASP is designed with functionality to improve grove building in applications (see section 2.7.2.1 for more on groves). It reports `ELEMENT`, `ATTLIST`, `NOTATION`, and `ENTITY` declarations while it parses them, and gives access to the fully resolved DTD after the document prolog has been parsed so that grove-using applications can use the objects which require access to the prolog. In this way *YASP* gives access not only to the SGML document instance, but also to the document's DTD and SGML declaration: the authors have tried to make it possible for the programmer to get a lot more information about the document being parsed than with other parsers.

It can also handle SGML document fragments (that is, a file entity whose apparent root element is one which would normally occur at some depth into a full document, and whose exact position in a (possibly non-existent) parent document structure may therefore not be easily determinable. The successful handling of document fragments has interesting consequences for the parsing of well-formed XML files, although in the latter case the potential document structure is not known at the start of the parse, because no DTD exists.

7.1.2. LT NSL (Language Technology Group)

Unix
`http://www.ltg.ed.ac.uk/software/nsl/index.html`

LT NSL is designed for use in developing corpus-based document processing systems. It uses *SP* as its parser, but provides support for multiple versions and multiple levels of annotation. It consists of a C-based API for accessing and manipulating SGML documents and an integrated set of SGML tools for subsequent processing. The Language Technology Group also make the *LT XML* package (see section 7.1.3).

Because of the complexity of corpora, the process is treated as two steps: first, produce an optimized representation of the DTD, and second, use this to produce a fully normalized version of the instance, which can then be post-processed by an application.

It provides access both to the sequential stream of markup and text, and to the hierarchical structure of the document, and allows both to be queried for a portion of the document structure to be returned.

7.1.3. LT XML (Language Technology Group)

`http://www.ltg.ed.ac.uk/software/xml/`

LT XML was the first publicly available XML toolset written in C and comes from the Language Technology Group in the Human Communication Research Centre (University of Edinburgh, Scotland), who also produce the *LT NSL* package for regular SGML (see section 7.1.2) of which this is a subset.

It includes stand-alone programs for processing well-formed XML documents, including searching and extracting, tokenizing and sorting, and 'down-translation' (*ie* transforming XML into a non-SGML format, such as report generation or output for a formatting system). The tools use a plain command line interface and the authors' claim a speed of three seconds per megabyte on a Pentium 133, fast enough to handle big XML files such as whole books, or large sets of data.

The first part of the package is the collection of integrated tools. The output from programs can be a well-formed XML file (not a valid file) so that it can be piped as input to other tools. The following is not a complete list, as some of the tools are component parts of or complementary to the ones listed here.

sggrep Similar to regular Unix *grep*, except that it finds and extracts pieces of an XML document using Regular Expressions, but these are preceded by a string describing the element path from the root, specifying which element name to search, for example:

```
sggrep ".*/SECT3/.*/LISTITEM" "money"
```

This would search any element `<LISTITEM>` occurring only in and below `<SECT3>` elements, but at any depth within them. The *sggrep-mark* variant of this program does the same, but encloses the 'found' elements inside new markup, so they can be identified in subsequent processes.

textonly Strips all XML markup from a file and emits text only. A `-t` option can restrict its operation to a specific element name.

sgcount Counts the number of occurrences of elements within a file. This can be a useful tool for comparing or checking documents after updates, or for providing volume information for bibliographic purposes.

knit 'Knits together' files which contain hyperlinks (as in the XML linking specification, see section 2.4.2), in such a way as to perform an `#include` of the linked file inside the master file. This in effect 'flattens' a series of hyperlinked files into a single instance.

sgmltrans A simple element-based down-translation tool which takes a file of rules specifying what to do for each start-tag and end-tag. This is a similar process to other element-based translators (*eg Omnimark*) but without an associated programming language, although it can use the same element-search specifications as *sggrep* to identify which elements to apply the rules to.

The package includes executable programs for a range of platforms, including Windows 95 and Windows NT, FreeBSD, Linux and Solaris (an Apple Mac version is under development). DTDs referenced in documents are parsed and used, but the system does not perform validation. In standard Unix (and some DOS) practise, the programs can be chained together (pipelined) together to achieve complex results by passing the output of one program into the input of another.

The second part of the package is the C-based API for developing your own programs or adding functionality to those supplied. It provides both event-oriented and tree-fragment-oriented access to the input document stream (*ie* a linear stream or a hierarchy) and provides data structures and access functions to support both these methods.

7.1.4. S4-Desktop (I4I)

MS-Windows, Mac
`http://www.i4i.org`

S4-Desktop is a collection of libraries implemented as compiled code library files. It lets the programmer add SGML functionality to a program by providing subroutine calls for handling parsing, searching, element and attribute retrieval and specification, and all the ancillary functions needed to make a product 'SGML-aware'.

7.1.4.1. Installation

The software installs from CD-ROM in the normal way with a setup program into a default directory called `c:\i4is4`. A minimal installation takes about 2Mb for the libraries and include files; a full installation takes about 30Mb and includes the manuals, technical notes, examples, sample DTDs and programs.

The paper documentation with the disk is minimal, as everything is in the PDF files (a copy of Adobe's *Acrobat* reader is provided). Emphasis is laid on reading the documentation before trying to write a program using the routines provided, and I4I clearly recognizes the existence of a discontinuity in the learning curve for those whose first approach to SGML is having to write a program to use it.

7.1.4.2. Facilities

The manual has plenty of examples, starting with simple file reads and progressing to more complex ones, and these are all analyzed in some depth. There is a brief introduction to basic SGML concepts, with references to the SGML Web pages, the SGML University pages, and books by Charles Goldfarb and others.

The technical notes cover some more specialist aspects, with detailed documentation on specific aspects of how some of the calls are expected to be used, and where they can or cannot perform their tasks.

The core of the system is the API calls, grouped into eight services. *S4-Desktop* works with the concept of a 'session', which generally entails opening a catalog and importing an instance. Instances are passed to a parser as they are opened, and any parse error causes failure of the read, with an error code returned. Once an instance is successfully parsed, it is represented as an S4 internal structure and is available for work with the service calls provided:

DTD Services (mostly element, entity, and attribute calls)
Data Initialization (file opens and closes, retrieval of the DTD and FPIs)
Navigation (finding by name and value)
Content model (element and attribute by type and depth)
Data Extraction (retrieval by offset)
Data insertion (adding, changing, and removing objects)
Metacode (mappings)
Annotation (detection, loading and removing)

I4I also provide two sample DTDs of their own, for practice and testing. These illustrate

1. a simple document sectional structure, with sections and subsections containing title, paragraphs and conclusion (`decomp.dtd`)
2. an ingenious hierarchical representation of the structure of a house in SGML, with the building containing walls and a roof; walls containing windows and doors, *etc* (`house.dtd`).

There is also a copy of the HTML 3.2 DTD.

Extras include the catalog management program *CatEdit* for editing an OASIS catalog file (see section 2.5.4.2).

A. The CD-ROM

> 'All complete!' said the Toad triumphantly, pulling open a locker. 'You see...everything you can possibly want...you'll find that nothing whatever has been forgotten...'
>
> Kenneth Grahame, *The Wind in the Willows*

The disk that accompanies this book contains software and documentation for systems designed for use with SGML, and also for some which are more general-purpose but have some specific SGML applications. Although I have tried to make the documentation as obvious as possible, I have avoided starting on the bottom rung of trying to teach the use of the keyboard, the mouse, and the operating system (see the assumptions alluded to earlier, which are in section 1.3).

Not all the programs described in the book are on the disk, as many of them are regular commercial products for which no free or demo version exists. By the same token, not all the programs on the disk are necessarily described in the book, as I have tried to make the disk as up to date as possible, and the lead-time for printing is longer than that for making the disk.

If you don't have access to MS-Windows to use the Synex *ViewPort* browser provided (see next section), you can read the same information by using your regular Web browser to open the `INDEX.HTM` file on the CD-ROM. The disk is written in ISO 9660 format, so that it is usable on Macs, PCs, and Unix systems.

A.1. Browsing the CD-ROM: using Synex/Inso ViewPort

Synex, makers of the *ViewPort* SGML browser engine for MS-Windows, have kindly provided a copy of their demonstration browser for you to use with this CD-ROM. It's not marketed as a separate product, because they license it to people who want to embed the browser technology in their own products, but this is the latest version and it provides a useful way of seeing what's what and using SGML to do so.

If you're not running MS-Windows, you can use any regular (HTML) Web browser to view the same information in HTML files.

MS-Windows users can run the browser directly off the CD-ROM using the `browse.bat` file. If you wish, you can copy the browser installation (the `SYNEX` folder) to your hard disk (for example to `c:\Program Files\Synex`), but you will need to update the configuration file SV.INI in the `c:\windows` directory to reflect the correct hard disk letter.

A.2. Words of warning about the software

Two small warnings are needed:

1. The conditions in which you use the software, the nature of your data, and the configuration of your computer are outside my control, so please ask the manufacturer or the software author if you need further details about a product or the way it works, not me or my publisher.
2. All the programs on the disk have been obtained from reliable sources, either from the manufacturers themselves (in the case of commercial software), or from a trusted archive or the original author (in the case of public domain software). Where facilities exist the executables have been virus-checked, but as neither I nor my publisher wrote the programs, we cannot be held responsible for their contents, nor their effect on your system or data.

A.3. How does it work?

The CD-ROM is written in plain ISO 9660 format, so you can use it on Apple Macs, PCs (MS-DOS and MS-Windows), and Unix workstations which support the CD File System, but on older computers you may need to update your CD-ROM driver software (consult your supplier for details).

CD-ROM format and filenames

The ISO 9660 CD-ROM format (sometimes called a 'multisession' CD-ROM) can be used on multiple platforms because it restricts two aspects of the file system:

- the file names and folder names are all UPPER CASE;
- no folders can nest more than eight deep.

For this reason, all software is kept in the following archive or compressed formats which contain the applications with preserved mixed-case filenames within them:

- ZIP files (DOS/Windows and VMS): unwrap with UNZIP;
- HQX files (Macs): unwrap with UnStuffIt;
- TAZ files (Unix): unwrap with gunzip then tar;

In most cases there is a self-installing `SETUP` or `make` program which you run to install the application. In a few cases the setup is manual, and the software author has provided instructions in a `README` or `INSTALL` file. Unzipping and other public decompression tools are in the `UTILS` folder in each platform directory.

I have not modified any of the software in any way, so if there are installation problems, inquiries should be directed to the software author, please, not to me.

Apart from the software, some of which is specific to certain platforms, there are DTDs, stylesheets, and SGML documentation which can be used on all systems (see section A.5 below). Most of the examples and illustrations have been taken from MS-Windows versions of the software because that was the closest to hand at the time of writing, but the principles apply equally to all platforms.

The top-level (root) directory of the CD-ROM has folders for the various platforms and one for the *ViewPort* browser (an application for MS-Windows to let you browse the SGML documentation on the disk):

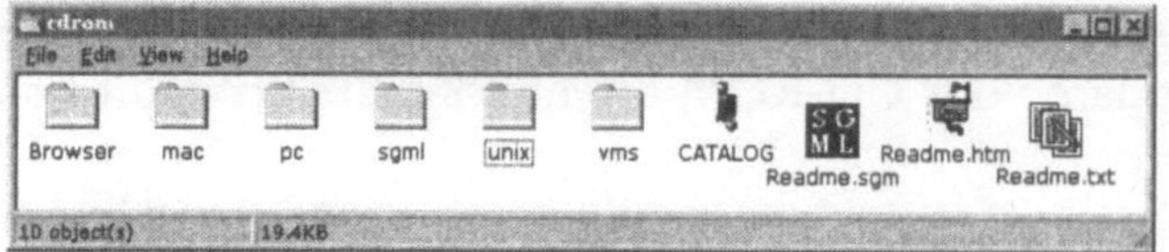

The SGML folder contains DTDs and reference documentation and has a different structure to the platform-specific folders. The PC folder is subdivided into DOS and Windows (I am not aware of any SGML software exclusively for Windows NT alone yet: 32–bit software for Windows is typically written to execute on Windows 95 as well as NT). Within the platform folders, the structure follows (where possible) the life-cycle approach of the chapters of the book:

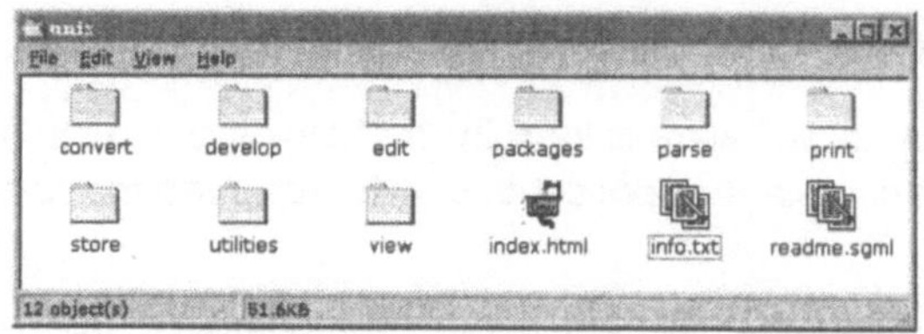

Each of the upper-level folders has a plaintext `INFO` file containing information in unmarked text, so you can read it in any simple editor or word processor even if you haven't started using SGML yet. The same information is in two other files, an SGML `README` which you can use with the *ViewPort* demonstration browser supplied on the disk, and a HTML `INDEX` file which you can read with any standard Web browser such as *Opera*, Netscape *Navigator*, or Microsoft *Internet Explorer*.

In the SGML folder, the `DTDS` subfolder contains zipped copies of all the Document Type Descriptions covered in section 1.5.1.5, and the `ENTITIES` folder contains zipped copies of the standard ISO character entity files which are referred to by DTDs to specify symbols and accented characters. These are all plaintext files, so they are usable on all systems. There is a master `CATALOG` file in standard OASIS (SGML Open) format at the top level of the CD-ROM directory structure, which gives the equivalences between the file names for all the DTDs (and the character entity files) and their Formal Public Identifiers (explained in sections page 145 and page 153). You can install all these files on your hard disk by using the `setup` program if you use a PC, or by copying them manually on other systems. The following folder names are recommended for installation, with '`dtds`' and '`entities`' subdirectories within them:

Platform	Disk prefix	Directory name
PC	`c:`	`\sgml`
Mac	`Hard Disk`	`:sgml`
Unix	[none]	`/usr/local/lib/sgml`
VMS	`SYS$LOGIN:`	`[.sgml]`

On shared system such as VMS and Unix, you may not have access to the root directory or the system disk, so you may have to install the folders by hand elsewhere withing your personal directory structure and make the relevant changes to the catalog file.

In the other folders, the software is supplied either as self-extracting installation programs (`.SEA` files for Macs; `.EXE` files for PCs) or as plain compressed files (`.ZIP`, `.GZ`, or `.SIT` archives). The Unix software is in `.TAR.GZ` format. The dearchiving and uncompressing programs needed to handle these are in the `UTILS` folders for Macs and PCs (Unix systems come with copies themselves already). If a program has installation instructions supplied by the author, these are included in each program subdirectory *without change*; sometimes in a file with a name such as `INSTALL`. If there were no separate instructions, I have provided some in a file of that name. Most of the self-installing software must be copied to your hard disk before trying to run the self-installer, because it needs to create temporary files, and this is not possible on a CD-ROM.

I am told that there is a small amount of SGML software for the Atari and Amiga, which are still popular and useful machines, but I have been unable to track it down, even after many requests. Regrettably, there is still very little SGML-specific software available for VMS or Macs by comparison with the PC or Unix world. Despite two decades of proving its worth, the Mac is still regarded by many software developers as a niche machine for artists.

In addition to the SGML software, there is a complete base-level TEX installation for all three main platforms, because several public-domain SGML systems use TEX as the formatter. Please note that this is the base installation only: there is a large amount of additional free software for TEX for use in more advanced formatting. You can download any of it from any server of the CTAN (Comprehensive TEX Archive Network) on the Internet (see `http://www.tug.org` or `http://www.ucc.ie/cgi-bin/ctan` for details.

A.4. What am I allowed to do with it?

The software falls into three categories:

1. Some of the programs are copies of regular commercial packages, provided by the manufacturer for you to test with your own data, before you decide to buy. In these cases the programs are usually demonstration copies or limited versions which let you run them for a fixed length of time or for a fixed number of occasions, after which you need to buy the package to continue using it.
2. Some other programs and packages have been written by members of the SGML or computing community themselves, and generously made available at no charge to everyone else: this software is entirely free, and you can continue using it forever. A large amount of it is protected by the 'copyleft' terms of the GNU General Public License, which means you can use it and redistribute it freely, but you may not prevent anyone else from doing the same. A copy of this license text is on the CD-ROM in the files `gnugpl.sgml` and `gnugpl.txt`.
3. Lastly, some of the software is shareware: you can try it for nothing, and you are encouraged give away copies to others to try for themselves, but if you decide to use it, you are required to buy a license, usually at a relatively low price, which gives you access to the manuals and future updates. Some of these programs you can continue using free of charge for personal use, but you have to pay if you use it commercially or on a multi-user local network.

Please do not misuse or breach the terms of these licenses. Whatever your views on the rightness or wrongness of copyright and charging for software, the law as it stands requires that you observe it. Details of alternative approaches which are under constant discussion are referenced from the GNU General Public License mentioned above.

A.5. Documentation

Some of the key online documentation of SGML and program facilities is included on the disk in the SGML folder to save you the trouble of downloading it.

- Where SGML versions of these files exist, they have been used, and can be viewed with the copy of the *ViewPort* demo browser for PC/Windows in the root directory.

- If the documentation was in HTML, that is supplied unmodified. Be aware that some of these files may be non-conformant (do not match any DTD) so they are best viewed with your regular Web browser.
- Some is in PostScript form, and is intended to be printed. If you don't have a PostScript printer, you can install the *GhostScript* interpreter and its associated viewer, which let you display and print PostScript files on most common systems and printers.
- Some documentation is just plaintext, and can be viewed or printed with any editor or word processor.

Where new or experimental public software is developing rapidly, however, it is always best to go back to the Internet source for an updated copy.

A.6. GNU software

A large amount of the free software has been contributed to the GNU project by individuals and institutions everywhere. GNU stands for 'GNU's Not Unix', and is a project to create an independent, free computer operating system, with programs being written by contributors all over the world.

The project solicits sponsorship and contributions in cash, code, or 'quipment, 501(c)3 tax-deductible in the USA (similar terms may apply in other places). Further details are at `http://www.gnu.org/`.

All GNU software is freely distributable under the 'copyleft' terms of the GNU General Public License (see the copy of the license text on the CD-ROM: it can also be downloaded from the Web at `http://www.gnu.ai.mit.edu/copyleft/copyleft.html`). This license applies to all GNU software on the CD-ROM accompanying this book. Put simply, it licenses you to use the software, and to give it to others: it explicitly probihits you from preventing other people from doing the same. Copies of GNU software may not be distributed without a copy of the license, and without a similar condition, including this condition, being imposed upon the subsequent user.

B. SGML resources

B.1. On the Web

The principal resource is Robin Cover's SGML Web pages at `http://www.sil.org/sgml/` (there's XML-specific information at `http://www.sil.org/sgml/xml.html`). These pages are updated almost daily and contain comprehensive pointers to just about everything that is going on in SGML.

Many other people, especially the leaders in the field, have made topic-specific pages about areas they are involved in. These are all linked from the SGML Web pages, and you can usually find information about the topic you want by using the front page (URL above) to select the topic first: the list of topics doubles as the index. There is a search engine attached to the pages if you can't find what you're looking for in the categorizations.

There are numerous SGML and XML FAQs, but the most up-to-date (and shortest) SGML FAQ is maintained by David Megginson and can be found at `http://www.infosys.utas.edu.au/info/sgmlfaq.txt`, and the XML FAQ is maintained by me at `http://www.ucc.ie/xml/`.

B.2. Usenet news

News is a bulletin board service which runs across many networks including the Internet. Your ISP (Internet Service Provider) or computer center can tell you how to access it. News posts look like email, but whereas email is aimed specifically at a single recipient (or a restricted list of recipients via a mailing list), news is pinned up in public for anyone and everyone to see. You can't therefore delete news posts, but newsreading software automatically keeps track of the posts you have read, and won't show them to you again unless you specifically request it. News is organized into a hierarchy, with each topic and subtopic named by separating the elements of the hierarchy with a period.

The SGML newsgroup is `comp.text.sgml`. There is no specific XML newsgroup (yet) but there is an active hierarchy of HTML groups under `comp.infosystems.www`. Most technical newsgroups are intended for serious discussion, and it is expected that you read the FAQ first and phrase your queries and comments accordingly: most of the inhabitants have plenty of other work to do. Products annoucements and the occasional job advert are tolerated: spam and plain advertising is not. All posts to `comp.txt.sgml` are archived at `ftp://ftp.ifi.uio.no/pub/SGML/comp.text.sgml/`.

B.3. Mailing lists

Mailing lists are run at various locations around the networks and provide a means for users to join in discussions by email only: direct interactive Internet access is not required. All mailing lists have two addresses: one (the 'list server' address) is for administrivia like subscribing and unsubscribing; the other (the actual 'list address') is for sending your discussion messages to.

It is a major breach of protocol to send subscription or unsubscription requests to the list address instead of the server address, as all that does is broadcast your request to hundred of people instead of having it acted upon.

You should normally only send plaintext messages to mailing lists, as not everyone will have the same formatting or graphical capabilities as you do. In particular you should *turn off* anything like HTML formatting, word processor style files, style attachments, and other non-text appendages. Never send attachments to mailing lists unless by agreement with the other subscribers: some people have to pay to receive email by the byte, and don't like having unwanted extras forced down their line. If you use a signature file, it is courteous to restrict it to 3–4 lines.

Davenport (DocBook) To subscribe to the Davenport mailing list, send a 1–line email message to `davenport-request@berkshire.net` saying

```
subscribe davenport
```

in the body of your message.

DSSSList The DSSSList is provided by Mulberry Technologies as a service to the DSSSL user community: to subscribe, send a 1–line email message to `majordomo@mulberrytech.com` saying

```
subscribe dssslist
```

in the body of your message. The DSSSList archive is at `http://www.mulberrytech.com/dsssl/dssslist/archive`, and the archive search page is at `http://www.mulberrytech.com/dsssl/dssslist/search.html`.

OMUG-L The *Omnimark* User Group Mailing List is hosted by Omnimark: to subscribe, send a 1–line email message to `listproc@omnimark.com` saying

```
subscribe omug-l forename surname
```

in the body of your message, substituting your own forename and surname.

SGML-L There is an SGML mailing list at the Heidelberg *LISTSERV*: to subscribe, send a 1–line email message to `listserv@urz.uni-heidelberg.de` saying

```
subscribe sgml-l
```

in the body of your message. Archived messages can be got by sending the command

```
get sgml-l logyymm
```

to the server address, substituting the 2–digit year and month.

TEI-L The TEI mailing list is hosted on the Chicago *LISTSERV*: to subscribe, send a 1–line email message to `listserv@uicvm.uic.edu` saying

```
subscribe tei-l
```

in the body of your message. Archived messages can be got by sending the command

```
get tei-l logyymm
```

to the server address, substituting the 2–digit year and month.

XML-L The XML mailing list is hosted on the Dublin *LISTSERV*: to subscribe, send a 1–line email message to `listserv@listserv.heanet.ie` saying

```
subscribe xml-l
```

in the body of your message. Archived messages can be got by sending the command

```
get xml-l logyymm
```

to the server address, substituting the 2–digit year and month.

xml-dev The XML Developers' list is hosted at Imperial College: to subscribe, send a 1–line email message tomajordomo@ic.ac.uk saying

```
subscribe xml-dev \textit{yourname}@\textit{yoursite}
```

in the body of your message, substituting your own name and site as in your email address. The list traffic is publicly archived (via hypermail) and WAIS-searchable at: http://www.lists.ic.ac.uk/hypermail/xml-dev/.

XSL List The XSL List is hosted by Mulberry Technologies as a service to the XSL user community: to subscribe, send a 1–line email message to majordomo@mulberrytech.com saying

```
subscribe xsl-list
```

in the body of your message. The XSL List archive is at http://www.mulberrytech.com/xsl/xsl-list/archive/.

There are other lists for associated software, companies, services, and standards: see the page at http://www.sil.org/sgml/lists.html.

B.4. SGML User Groups

The International SGML Users' Group (ISUG) is made up of national, regional, and sectoral user groups world wide. The principal site for information is at http://www.isgmlug.org/. The objectives of the SGML Users' Group are to promote the use of the Standard Generalized Markup Language and to provide a forum for exchange of information about SGML.

The current primary contact (editorial address) for the ISUG is: Pamela Gennusa, SGML Users' Group, PO Box 361, Swindon SN5 7BF, Wiltshire, United Kingdom. Phone: +44 1793 512515, Fax: +44 1793 512516, Email: plg@dpsl.co.uk.

ISUG was founded in 1984 by Joan M Smith and has just over 150 corporate and just under 300 individual members. It has liaison representatives to ISO/IEJ JTC1/WG4, the ISO entity responsible for SGML (see section 2.7.1.1). The Annual General Meeting of the Users' Group is normally held in conjunction with the International Markup Conference sponsored by the Graphic Communications Association. For an address list of elected members, national chapters, SIGs and pending chapters see the current online listing at http://www.sil.org/sgml/sugExec1998.html.

In addition, there are many specialist SGML and XML user groups for specific industry, project or technology applications (details on the User Groups page at http://www.sil.org/sgml/groups.html).

References

1. Abensour, L.: 1927, *Le problème feministe: un cas d'aspiration collective vers l'égalité*. Paris: Radot.
2. Ahonen, H., H. Mannila, and E. Nikunen: 1994, 'Generating Grammars for SGML Tagged Texts Lacking DTD'. In: *Workshop on Principles of Document Processing*. Darmstadt.
3. Alschuler, L.: 1995, *ABCD...SGML*, 1–850–32197–3. Boston MA: ITCP.
4. Anon: 1987, 'Automated Interchange of Technical Information'. Technical Report MIL-STD-1840A, US DoD, Washington DC.
5. Anon: 1988a, 'Computer-Aided Acquisition and Logistic Support (CALS) Program Implementation Guide'. Technical Report MIL-HDBK-59A, US DoD, Washington DC.
6. Anon: 1988b, 'Markup Requirements and Generic Style Specification for Electronic Printed Output and Exchange of Text'. Technical Report MIL-M-28001A, US DoD, Washington DC.
7. Anon: 1989, 'Technical Manuals: General Style and Format Requirements'. Technical Report MIL-M-38784, US DoD, Washington DC.
8. Anon: 1995, 'Understanding the SGML Declaration'. Technical report, Omnimark Corporation, Nepean ON. `http://www.omnimark.com/resources/white/dec/`.
9. Anon: 1997a, 'General Content, Style, Format, and User Interaction Requirements for Interactive Electronic Technical Manuals'. Technical Report MIL-PRF-87268A, US DoD, Washington DC.
10. Anon: 1997b, 'Revisable Data Base for the support of Interactive Electronic Technical Manuals'. Technical Report MIL-PRF-87269A, US DoD, Washington DC.
11. Bartholomew, D. J.: 1973, *Stochastic Models for Social Processes*, 0–471–05451–8. Chichester, England: John Wiley & Sons.
12. Brown, F.: 1942, 'ETAOIN SHRDLU'. In: *Unknown Worlds*. New York NY: Street & Smith Publications.
13. Busa, R.: 1980, *Index Thomisticus Sancti Thomae Aquinatus Operum Omnium Indices et Concordantiae*. Stuttgart–Bad Connstatt: Fromann-Holzboog.
14. Cournane, M.: 1997, 'The Application of SGML/TEI to the Processing of Complex Multilingual Historical Texts'. Ph.D. thesis, University College Cork, Cork, Ireland.
15. Dern, D.: 1994, *The Internet Guide for New Users*, 0–07–016511–4. Boston MA: McGraw-Hill.

16. DeRose, S.: 1997, *The SGML FAQ Book: Understanding the Foundation of HTML and XML*, 0–7923–9943–9. Boston MA: Kluwer Academic Publishers.
17. DeRose, S. and D. Durand: 1996, *Making Hypermedia Work: A User's Guide to HyTime*, 0–7923–9432–1. Boston MA: Kluwer Academic Publishers.
18. Ensign, C.: 1996, *SGML: The Billion Dollar Secret*, 0–13–226705–5. Upper Saddle River NJ: PTR Prentice Hall.
19. Flynn, P.: 1995, *The World Wide Web Handbook*, 1–85032–205–8. London: International Thomson Computer Press.
20. Goldfarb, C. F.: 1990, *The SGML Handbook*, 0–19–853737–9. New York NY: Oxford University Press.
21. Goldfarb, C. F.: 1996, 'SGML: Grove and Grove Plan'. *comp.text.sgml*. `http://www.sil.org/sgml/grove-CFG.html`.
22. Goldfarb, C. F., S. Pepper, and C. Ensign: 1997, *The SGML Buyers' Guide*, 0–13–681511–1. Upper Saddle River NJ: Prentice Hall.
23. Ide, N. and J. Véronis: 1996, *The Text Encoding Initiative: Background and Context*, 0–7923–3704–2. Dordrecht, Netherlands: Kluwer.
24. Kimber, E.: 1996, 'SGML: Groves'. *comp.text.sgml*. `http://www.sil.org/sgml/groveKimber.html`.
25. Kimber, E.: 1997, *Practical Hypermedia: An Introduction to HyTime*, 0–13–309899–0. New York NY: Prentice-Hall.
26. Knuth, D. E.: 1984, *The TeXbook*, 0–201–13447–0. Reading MA: Addison-Wesley.
27. Krol, E.: 1997, *The Whole Internet User's Guide and Catalog*, 1–56592–025–2. Sebastopol CA: O'Reilly.
28. Lamport, L.: 1988, 'Document production: visual or logical?'. *TUGboat* **9**(1), 8–10.
29. Lesk, M.: 1976, 'Bell Laboratories Computing Science Technical Report'. Technical Report 49, Bell Laboratories.
30. Maler, E. and J. el Andaloussi: 1996, *Developing SGML DTDs: From Text to Model to Markup*, 0–13–309881–8. Upper Saddle River NJ: Prentice Hall.
31. McEvilly, C.: 1997, *How to make great Web pages*. Los Alamos NM: Carlos McEvilly. `http://www.c3.lanl.gov/~cim/webgreat/`.
32. McGrath, S.: 1997, *ParseMe.1st: SGML for Software Developers*, 0–13–488967–3. Upper Saddle River NJ: Prentice Hall.
33. McGrath, S.: 1998, 'XML Programming in Python'. *Dr Dobbs Journal*.
34. Pepper, S.: 1997, 'The Whirlwind Guide to SGML Tools and Vendors'. Technical report, Steve Pepper, Oslo, Norway. `http://www.infotek.no/sgmltool/`.
35. Ramalho, J. C., J. G. Rocha, J. J. Almeida, and P. R. Henriques: 1997, 'SGML Documents: Where does Quality go?'. In: *Proceedings of the SGML/XML'97 Conference*. Alexandria VA, pp. 171–177.
36. Raman, T.: 1997, *Auditory User Interfaces: Toward the Speaking Computer*, 0–7923–9984–6. Boston MA: Kluwer.
37. Smith, C. M.: 1857, *The Working Man's Way in the World*. London: WF & G Cash. Reprinted 1967 by the Printing Historical Society, Bride Lane, London EC4.
38. Smith, N.: 1996, *Practical Guide to SGML/XML Filters*, 1–55622–607–1. Plano TX: Wordware.
39. Sperberg-McQueen, M. and L. Burnard: 1994, 'Guidelines for Electronic Text Encoding and Interchange'. Technical report, Oxford and Chicago.
40. Steinberg, S. H.: 1974, *Five Hundred Years of Printing*, 0–14–020243–5. London: Penguin/Pelican.

41. van Herwijnen, E.: 1994, *Practical SGML*, 0–7923–9434–8. Dordrecht, Netherlands: Kluwer.
42. Wall, L. and R. Schwartz: 1992, *Programming Perl*, 0–937175–64–1. Sebastopol CA: O'Reilly.

Glossary

abstract syntax The theoretical instantiation of a grammar, designed to allow explanation of the ideas behind it without having to use any one particular syntax. In ISO 8879, the abstract syntax allows us to discuss the concepts of markup without tying us to a specific system.

ASCII The American Standard Code for Information Interchange, equivalent to ISO 646 International Reference Version, which defines the 7–bit coded character set used on most computers, made up of the 52 letters of the Latin alphabet (26 capitals and 26 lowercase), the digits 0–9, and some punctuation. Sometimes called 'plain-text' to distinguish it from 'binary' data, which is unprintable. It is an error to refer to accented letters and other symbols as being 'ASCII'.

attribute Additional item of information about an element, contained within a start-tag, in the form of a name and value separated by an equals sign. Minimization, if permitted in a DTD, may allow the name and equals sign to be omitted where it is unambiguous to do so, and the quotation marks around the value may be omitted if the value uses only name characters. In XML no minimization is allowed and all values must be quoted.

attribute list declaration In a DTD, form of markup declaration that defines the attributes of an element, listing their types and values.

binary Composed all or partly of non-printable characters ('control characters'). The opposite of a 'plaintext' or ASCII file. Binary files cannot normally be read or used directly by humans: they need a program to do something with them.

capacities Measures of program storage requirements calculated from quantities specified in an SGML Declaration.

catalog File listing Formal Public Identifiers and their System Identifier equivalents for the user's local file system (or network file repository, such as the Web).

CERN Originally the *Conseil Européen pour la Recherche Nucléaire*, now the European Laboratory for Particle Physics. The birthplace of the World Wide Web and its development centre until responsibility passed to the W3C in 1996.

compilation The process of creating a binary representation of a DTD in computer-readable form, so that documents can be processed without the DTD having to be re-read from scratch (and thus re-parsed and re-validated) every time.

concrete syntax An actual real-life syntax instantiating a grammar. In the case of ISO 8879, the default concrete syntax involves angled brackets, ampersands, semicolons, slashes, and percent signs as delimiters for various purposes: this is provided in ISO 8879 for reference purposes and is called the Reference Concrete Syntax. A different concrete syntax could use entirely other characters.

connector In DTDs, the sequence of elements in a content model is symbolized by the characters '&' (and: the elements must all occur, but may be in any order), '|' (or: only one element of those listed may occur), and ',' (seq: all the elements listed must occur in the order given).

content markup Markup occurring within mixed content, typically in running text such as paragraphs and paragraph-level elements. The opposite of structural markup.

content model In a DTD, the specification of what mix of further [sub]elements or text data an element may contain.

crossed boundaries An error in SGML markup when an element end-tag occurs outside the bounds of the containing element in which its start-tag occurred.

descriptive markup A form of content markup used to describe identity or intent rather than function. Also used to mean optional markup, added for informational purposes.

document type The principal identity of an SGML document, declared by its Document Type Declaration, defined in the DTD, and named as its root element.

document type declaration The declaration at the top of an SGML instance which specifies the name of the root element and the identity of the DTD.

document type definition See DTD.

DTD Document Type Definition. The formal definition of the elements, entities, and notations which go to make up a specific document type in SGML.

element A named component part of the text or structure of an SGML document entity, identified in the markup hierarchy, containing other elements, or text data, or both, or nothing. The names given to elements and their potential location in the markup hierarchy are declared in the DTD.

element content The state pertaining within an element when the only content allowed is more element markup, not text. Typical of the outer structure of DTDs, where sectional elements can contain a variety of structures (paragraphs, tables, figures, notes, headings, *etc*).

element declaration In a DTD, form of markup declaration that defines an element, giving its name, minimization parameters (omitted in XML), and content model.

end-tag See tag.

entity An abstract term for a variety of parts of a whole SGML document, which must all resolve to a concrete instantiation when the document is parsed. A parameter entity is a component of a DTD whose value requires interpretation and action; a character entity is a named representation of a glyph; a general entity is a fragment of text or data named for multiple reuse or external reference; a file entity is a file containing a part of the document or its DTD; the document entity itself is the root element and all it contains.

entity resolution The process of identifying, retrieving, and inserting files specified by Formal Public Identifiers or System Identifiers during parsing, so as to construct a whole SGML document.

exclusion The attachment of an element or list of elements to a content model to specify that they may not occur in that content in any instance, despite being included in another part of the content model. Often used to remove a definition of a structural element like a displayed formula or table or figure from being included within itself.

FPI Formal Public Identifier. A label for a resource referred to in an SGML context, constructed according to the syntax defined in ISO 8879, as a way of avoiding the need to hard-code an author's or user's local file or directory names into a document.

glyph A printable symbol, possibly compounded from other symbols.

grove The in-memory result of parsing an SGML document: a complete collection of tree-like maps of every object (markup as well as text content) and every relationship between them. Groves are defined as part of the HyTime and DSSSL standards. These do not specify how a parser should implement groves (that is left to the implementors): instead, they provide an abstract vocabulary and syntax for communicating information about the parsed document between parser and application.

HTML HyperText Markup Language (an application of SGML). Formally defined as HTML 2.0 in RFC 1866 but existing in a multitude of previous and subsequent versions of greater and lesser utility.

HyTime Hypertext and Time-based (SGML multimedia standard), ISO 10744.

IETF Internet Engineering Task Force. The body responsible for the technical specification of the Internet. The IETF traditionally achieved rapid advance in technology via RFCs on the basis of 'rough consensus and running code' (*ie* get some agreement that it's a good idea, and a program that shows it working).

inclusion The attachment of an element or list of elements to a content model to specify that they may occur anywhere in that content in any instance. Often used to add a definition of a globally-occurring element like a footnote.

instance An instance of a DTD: more commonly called 'an SGML file'. Usually composed of the author's text, enclosed in the start- and end-tags of the root element. It *excludes* the DTD, Document Type Declaration, and SGML Declaration.

INRIA *Institut National de Recherche en Informatique et en Automatique.* French National Computing Research Institute at Sophia-Antipolis near Cannes, and other sites in France. With MIT, one of the original sponsoring members of the W3C.

ISO International Organization for Standardization (Geneva). Despite the apparent misacronym, the letters refer to the Greek ισος ('equal') as in 'isobar', 'isotherm', *etc*, and were adopted as an synthesis of all the ISO/OIS/IOS acronyms of the organization in various languages.

LaTeX See TeX.

logical markup The use of markup systems to represent the structure, intent, or function of a document's components, leaving their appearance to be determined by a stylesheet.

markup Symbols or characters used with text to indicate significance or action. SGML uses inline markup (markup inserted within the text at the points of significance); some systems use out-of-line markup, where the markup is stored separately from the text it applies to.

markup declaration In a DTD or a Document Type Declaration, the actual specification of markup being defined, rather than the markup itself being used. Usually indicated by an exclamation mark following the open-angle-bracket.

MIME Multipurpose Internet Mail Extensions. The Internet standard (actually a collection of many standards) for the description of the content format of attachments and extensions to email messages, also used in Web servers to stamp the type of document on outgoing files. Each different type is recognized by its MIME Content-Type, for example `text/sgml` for SGML files.

minimization Techniques in SGML for allowing markup to be represented with a smaller number of characters or keystrokes than normal.

minimization parameters In an element declaration, the combination of hyphen or letter-O which signal whether or not the start-tag or end-tag (or both) may be omitted.

MIT Massachusetts Institute of Technology, Cambridge, MA. The Laboratory for Computer Science was a founding organization of the W3C.

mixed content The state within an element where both text data and more element markup are valid. Typical of all paragraph-type elements (paragraphs themselves, list items, notes, captions, labels, titles, *etc*).

names In SGML, the names of elements and attributes and some attribute values, restricted in the set of characters they can use. By default these must start with a letter, and continue with letters, digits, periods, or hyphens for up to eight characters, or as specified in an SGML Declaration. In XML the underscore and colon are added to the valid characters, and the length limit removed.

normalization The technique of expanding all minimization during parsing and validation so that the output instance contains all the markup fully expressed.

occurrence In DTDs, the way in which elements may occur is symbolized in content models by the characters '?' (optional: the element may occur once or not at all), '+' (repeatable: the element must occur once but may occur more times), and '*' (optional-repeatable: the element may be absent or may occur once or many times).

omission In standard SGML, the practise or ability of a DTD to allow the start-tag or end-tag (or both) of an element to be omitted when it is unambiguous to do so.

parameters Values or sets of values which one part of a processing system passes to another in order to enable, control, or restrict its actions.

parsing The process of identifying and distinguishing between text and markup in a document, and between this and markup declarations in a DTD, and using this information to determine the document's structure.

plaintext `Computer text (or file) using only the 96 printable characters of the ASCII character set (ISO 646irv); that is: A-Z, a-z, 0-9, and punctuation, plus the space, TAB, and linebreak characters. No fonts, no accents, no symbols, no hidden characters or encoding. This format is one of the lowest common denominators: it is public property so it can be used without license, and is portable to every computer system in the world.`

prescriptive markup Markup which is designed so that the user or author must follow a (usually rigid) document structure, to ensure conformity with some external standard. Prescriptive markup usually has many compulsory elements.

property set The SGML property set is the complete repertoire of objects and their properties that may occur in SGML, categorized into a number of classes. For any given document, a document property set therefore defines the set of possible classes and properties that each component can be allocated as it is parsed.

prolog The SGML Declaration, DTD, and Document Type Declaration which must precede an instance, either implicitly or explicitly.

quantities Measures (in terms of length or occurrence) of the items specified in an SGML Declaration used in calculating capacities.

reference concrete syntax The syntax provided in the ISO 8879 standard as a concrete example of how the abstract syntax of SGML could be instantiated, and used as a reference point for the construction of other concrete syntaxes. The Reference Concrete Syntax forms part of the default SGML Declaration.

Regular Expressions In Unix and Unix-like systems, a syntax for expressing patterns of characters, typically used in search programs like *grep* to allow complex matching.

RFC Request For Comment. The class of document in which technical suggestions are made relating to the conventions and standards used on the Internet. RFCs are subdivided into two tracks by the IETF, 'informational' and 'standards', depending on their content and potential effects.

root element The element named as the document type in the Document Type Declaration. The start- and end-tags bearing this name must enclose all the user's text and markup, forming an SGML Instance.

RTF Rich Text Format. A language devised by Microsoft for describing the appearance of text, so that it can be passed between different makes and models of word processor. Internally, RTF looks like a cross between TEX and PostScript, and can be generated by SGML systems such as *Jade* and *InContext* to provide printed output.

schema A formal statement describing the features of objects in a database and how they are related to each other.

script Interpreted program or list of actions grouped together in a file for use as a single command or action.

selection rule In DSSSL and XSL, a specification governing which element[s] or element-attribute combinations are to be used in applying subsequent style or other rules.

SGML Standard Generalized Markup Language (ISO 8879:1986). The international standard for defining and describing markup languages.

SGML Declaration The specification of coded character set, special characters, names, quantities, capacities, and other restrictions which a document type designer may with to place on or lift from a DTD. Many small DTDs use the default SGML Declaration specified in the SGML standard.

start-tag See tag.

style rule In DSSSL and XSL, a specification governing which element[s] or element-attribute combinations are to be formatted in accordance with the given style.

stylesheet File containing a specification of how a document or its components are to appear when displayed, printed, spoken, or otherwise represented. Stylesheets for SGML are written in a language designed for the task, for example a public standard like DSSSL, CSS, or XSL; or a language designed to go with a specific product like *DynaText*, *Synex*, or other browser or formatter.

subset A portion (or all) of a DTD stored in a separate file (an external subset) or between square brackets at the end of a Document Type Declaration (an internal subset).

system identifier A filename, directory path and filename, or a URI (URN or URL), giving the exact location of a file entity within a retrievable file system.

tag A markup object which signals the start or end of an element (in the case of empty elements a single tag signifies the existence). A tag is made up of the element name, enclosed in angled brackets (by convention: the actual characters can be changed in an SGML Declaration). Start-tags may contain additional information (attributes) between the name and the closing bracket; end-tags identify themselves with a slash (again by convention) between the opening bracket and the name.

TEX Typesetting language and program designed by Donald Knuth and made available in the public domain for almost any make or model of computer (commercial versions also exist). Used extensively in research and academic work as well as commercial typesetting, and common as a formatting tool with SGML systems because of its programmability. LATEX is a set of macros for TEX to improve the consistency of document preparation by dissociating visual formatting from the structure of the document.

validation The process of analytically applying the result of parsing to ascertain if a document structure matches that declared in the DTD.

visual markup The use of markup systems to represent the appearance of a document on screen or on paper without distinguishing between the functions of different components of the document.

W3C World Wide Web Consortium. An association jointly hosted by MIT (USA), INRIA (France), and Keio University (Japan) which took over responsibility for Web development from CERN in 1995. Membership is open to corporations only.

Index

Index of people and organizations

Index of markup elements and parameters

Index of acronyms and abbreviations